CELTIC STUDIES IN EUROPE

and other essays

SEÁN Ó LÚING

GEOGRAPHY PUBLICATIONS

Published in Ireland by
Geography Publications,
Kennington Road,
Templeogue, Dublin 6W

ISBN 0-906602-76-9

Design and typesetting by Phototype-Set, Lee Road, Dublin Industrial Estate, Dublin 11.
Printed by Leinster Leader

Latin, Russian and Irish are the 3 great glories of the human race, achievements, splendours, stars; orchards; symphonies.

Stephen MacKenna

To two dear friends
Karl-Ludwig Wimberger, President,
and John Marin, President Emeritus
of the German-Irish Society, Bonn

Contents

Acknowledgements

Two essays in the following collection, those on Douglas Hyde and the Gaelic League and on Robin Flower, appeared originally in the quarterly *Studies*, to the Editor of which my thanks are due. 'Seán Óg MacMurrough Kavanagh' was first published in a New York publication entitled *Kerrymen 1881-1981*, edited by Denis P. Kelleher. The essay on Carl Marstrander appeared in the *Journal* of the Cork Historical and Archaeological Society 1984. That on George Thomson was published in *Classics Ireland* vol. 3 (1996). Irish language variants of it appeared in the *Journal* of the Kerry Archaeological and Historical Society and in *Saoir Theangan* (Masons of Language) published by Coiscéim (1989). The essay 'Donn Sigerson Piatt agus an Oidhreacht Úgónach', first delivered as a talk in the Tailors' Hall, Dublin, as a modest tribute to a colleague of shining integrity, is reprinted from *Féile Zozimus* vol. 3, published by Gael Linn, Baile Átha Cliath 1994. 'An Leabharlann Náisiúnta' was written as foreword to Dr. Pádraig Ó hInnse's account of his fruitful years of service as Director of the National Library of Ireland.

My thanks are due to Friedrich Krollmann for his kind permission to reprint from *Lebende Sprachen* Heft 1, 1995, my essay on the present position of the Irish language.

For his driving skills I owe a special word of gratitude to John Marin who was my companion and guide to many destinations in Germany in my quest for knowledge of Celtic scholars. In the course of these journeys my interest became his, a fact which I deeply appreciate.

The essay 'In the footsteps of Kuno Meyer' was published in the series *Hibernia jenseits des Meeres* by the German-Irish Society of Bonn to which it was originally delivered as a talk.

For encouragement from my friends in the German-Irish Society I am deeply grateful. To them I owe the honour of being appointed an Honorary Member of the Society, a distinction which I cherish.

For a useful collection of letters from Kuno Meyer to his Liverpool colleague John Sampson, I am indebted to the kindness of Anthony Sampson whose biography of his celebrated grandfather *The Scholar Gypsy* has been published by John Murray (1997).

The Royal Irish Academy supplied a selection of the photographs used in this book. For this my gratitude is due, in sincere measure, to Siobhán Uí Raifeartaigh, the Librarian, and to Íde Ní Thuama, the Assistant Librarian, to both of whom I remain deeply indebted for their interest and courtesy.

I should like to record my obligation to the Council of Trustees of the National Library of Ireland for their kind permission to quote extracts from materials in the Library. To the staff of the National Library of Ireland I owe more than I can say. I have been for many decades an *habitué* of that intellectual treasury, which offers the research student a pleasant and sympathetic ambience and the assistance of a staff whose courtesy and willingness to help are beyond praise.

My debt to Dr. Hans Hablitzel is considerable. Being the foremost authority on the life and work of Johann Kaspar Zeuss, the father of Celtic philology, I have found his advice and suggestions invaluable.

To the ever-constant support and encouragement of William Nolan of Geography Publications, I can again gratefully testify. My thanks go also to Phototype-Set Ltd. and all those involved in the production of this book.

Both author and publisher gratefully acknowledge financial subventions towards publication costs from the National University of Ireland and Bord na Gaeilge. For valued support and encouragement I should like to express my thanks to:

Acadamh Ríoga na hÉireann
Kit Ahern, Ballybunion, Co. Kerry
Anders Ahlquist
Diarmuid Breathnach
Breandán Ó Buachalla
The Rt. Rev. Dr. Donald Caird
Verena Multhaupt
Tomás Ó Canann
An tOllamh Seán Ó Coileáin
Doncha Ó Conchúir, M.A., A.T.O.
Uaitéar Mac Craith
Risteard agus Máire Anna Dáibhis, An Tasmáin
Deirdre Davitt
Máirín Ní Dhomhnalláin
Seán Ó Dubhda
An Canónach Pádraig Ó Fiannachta, Tigh na Sagart, An Daingean
Rolf Ködderitzsch
The Library, School of Celtic Studies, D. I. A. S., Dublin
Mgr Domhnall Ó Lúing, P. E., An Neidín (*nach maireann*)
Pádraig Ó Héalaí
Ríonach Uí Ógáin
John and Mairead Pierse, Listowel
Máire Ní Mhurchú

William and Teresa Nolan
Pádraig Ó Riain, Roinn na Sean- agus na Meán-Ghaeilge, Ollscoil Náisiúnta na hÉireann, Corcaigh
Fr. Kieran O'Shea
Dick Spring, T. D.
An tAthair Pádraig Ó Siochrú, Cillín Tiarna, Co. Chiarraí
Andrea Nic Thaidhg
Íde Ní Thuama
An tAthair Tomás Ó hUalacháin, Ard-Fhearta, Co. Chiarraí
Kees Veelenturf, Zoeterwoude-Dorp, An Isiltír

Ba mhaith liom focal speisialta buíochais a ghabháil le John Robb.

In some cases, more specific acknowledgements are made in their due place in the book. For faults and errors the responsibility is wholly mine.

Táim buíoch do mo mhac Gearóid as a chabhair dhícheallach chun an Clár Saothair agus an tInnéacs sa leabhar seo a chur le chéile agus as a chúnamh in go leor bealaí eile.

Seán Ó Lúing
Blackrock
County Dublin

Note:

The *Zeitschrift für celtische Philologie* is abbreviated to *ZCP* in the references.

Some surnames (e.g. Ó Crithin, Ó Súileabháin) appear in more than one form in the following essays, these forms deriving from the context in which they appear.

Whilst every reasonable effort has been made, it has not been possible to trace some copyright holders. Apologies are offered to anyone who may have inadvertently been omitted, and any such omissions will be rectified in future editions.

Seán Ó Lúing died on 10th February, 2000. We spent many happy hours together working on this book. He had corrected the proofs, and I very much regret that he did not see it in print. I would like to thank Professor Bo Almqvist for bringing my father alive in his wonderfully insightful introductory essay.

Gearóid Ó Lúing

List of illustrations

Seán Ó Lúing

Seán Ó Lúing – An appreciation

Seán Ó Lúing was known to me for about two decades before I ever set eyes on him. For all that time I was acquainted with him through his writings. I read his first major book, *Art Ó Gríofa*, the biography of the national philosopher Arthur Griffith, in 1967 or 1968. What I read impressed me so much that I acquired the author's other books in Irish on leading nineteenth- and early twentieth-century patriots: *John Devoy* and – as soon as they were published – the two volumes of *Ó Donnabháin Rosa*. I also added to my collection two of Seán Ó Lúing's books in English on historical topics: *I die in a good cause,* a moving study of the short heroic life of the Corca Dhuibhne martyr Thomas Ashe and *Fremantle Mission,* the astonishing story of the daring rescue of Irishmen imprisoned in a jail in southern Australia, carried out from the whaling ship *Catalpa.* All of these books became so important to me that I acquired two copies, in order to have easy access to them not only in Dublin, but also in my summer house in Dunquin in Kerry. These books by Seán Ó Lúing are in fact the only non–fiction books I have ever honoured by this extravagance!

My interest in history has never been more than amateurish, and my reading in that field tends to be limited to works about ancient times. Therefore my enthusiasm and admiration for Seán Ó Lúing's works on modern history puzzled not only those to whom I tried to convey it but, for a while, even myself.

Part of the explanation for my delight was obvious, however. Ó Lúing's style was eminently attractive. In the Corca Dhuibhne Gaeltacht where he was born and bred conversation was a fine art. A combination of this early training in the art of communication with his native gifts, his academic education and his long and dedicated work as translator developed in Seán Ó Lúing a directness, preciseness and clarity of style. Everything he wrote, whether in Irish or English, no matter what it was about, was a pleasure to read. Whether Seán Ó Lúing would be better referred to as a 'near native speaker of Irish' (as Máirtín Ó Cadhain jokingly called him) or 'a near native speaker of English' (a phrase by which he, also in jest, referred to himself) may be a moot point. But absolute mastery of the two languages is not in doubt. For those who like me have enjoyed the privilege of hearing the beautiful Corca Dhuibhne variant of Irish as spoken by the best native speakers, it was also a special pleasure to see it put to such good use in scholarly writing.

But equally gripping was the insight the books gave into the mind of their author. The delight Seán Ó Lúing took in unearthing fresh and unexpected facts in rare books, newspapers, letters, diaries and other manuscript material in libraries and archives glowed from almost every page, and gave his books freshness, vividness and immediacy. In addition to all of this, Seán Ó Lúing was able to energize his narrative with information from living oral tradition, through interviews with people who had direct knowledge of the persons and events described. He was one of the first oral historians, although he never used that term himself to my knowledge. The recent past is often more distant and obscure than the distant past, but Seán Ó Lúing had the ability to make readers feel that they had personally seen and known the people he describes. They engage us because they are of such obvious interest to him. In other words, Seán Ó Lúing's love for his heritage and for scholarship was highly contagious.

The same qualities are the hallmark of the other main category of Seán Ó Lúing's scholarly productions, his works on the history of learning. These were of a more direct interest and importance to me, since they touched my own profession. These writings deal in particular with Celtic studies. In many cases they centre on scholars who visited and worked on the Great Blasket, such as Marstrander, Flower, George Thomson and Marie–Louise Sjoestedt. In conjunction with these articles can also be taken those on the lexicographer and author Seán Óg MacMurrough Kavanagh ('Seán an Chóta') and his brother 'Kruger', a great personal friend of Seán Ó Lúing's. But Seán Ó Lúing also dealt with other Celtic scholars, both Irish and foreign, e.g. in the collection *Saoir Theangan*, in the attractive survey on Celtic Studies in Europe in chapter 2 of this book, and in his last major work, *Kuno Meyer*. The local perspective is still strongly present, but the Irish culture is viewed in a wide international perspective. Seán took an obvious delight in demonstrating that Irish culture was as much a concern of the whole of Europe as of Ireland. Like George Thomson, whom he so greatly admired, he was a born educator, with an ambition to convey this message. Just like Thomson, he considered it essential that the Gaeltacht people, the speakers of the Irish language and the possessors of a unique part of Europe's cultural heritage, should themselves be aware of their importance in both an Irish and international context.

It was in relation to work on the storytelling tradition on the Great Blasket that I had special reason to pay close attention to Seán's work in the field of the history of learning. It was also, appropriately enough, in connection with an *éigse* in Dunquin on a Blasket topic that I first met him. I am not absolutely sure of the year though it is likely to have been 1985 or 1986, but I have a vivid memory of our first conversation.

It took place in Kruger's pub, and revolved around Robin Flower. The flow of knowledge conveyed in Seán's calm and precise voice came as no surprise to me, but I was highly impressed by the great generosity with which he let everybody willing to listen partake of his latest unpublished findings. Seán was not a monopolizer or hoarder. He delighted in sharing with others and encouraging them to write about topics that many a lesser man might have considered his private territory. The help and encouragement Seán gave in connection with my own work on Robin Flower and on Kruger was invaluable, and it would surprise me if any person or institution who turned to Seán ever went away empty–handed. In this connection I can speak for the Department of Irish Folklore, to which he rendered many services, and I also know that he had special ties with the National Library. One might imagine that a man whose daily task, in the translation section of Dáil Éireann, had been to translate and supervise translation of official documents into Irish should have had more than enough of that task. But it would seem that Seán, whether still officially employed or retired, never considered it beneath him to turn down a request to check and correct any Irish text, be it an application form for readers' tickets or a signpost. We might sometimes despair at the sheer volume of execrable Irish we see all around us, on public signs and every kind of official document, but how much worse might it have been were it not for Seán Ó Lúing!

All this he did because he was a good man and because he loved his native language. He ceaselessly and untiringly worked to uphold its dignity and to proclaim its rights nationally and internationally. It was obvious that he took particular pride in having played a part introducing Irish to the European Community, an experience he vividly described in his book *In Ardchathair na hEorpa.*

Apart from being a nationalist, Seán was also a European and internationalist in the best sense. His life-long fondness for classical studies, which was yet an additional reason for his admiration for George Thomson, underlies much of his writings. He had a great love for Latin poetry. His favourite poet was Catullus, many of whose poems he translated into Irish. Seán also took special pleasure in French poetry. Among his favourite poets in this language were Baudelaire, Mallarmé, Verlaine, de Nerval, Valéry and Éluard, and he rendered some of their poems into Irish. Having learnt German late in life in order to research his biography of Kuno Meyer, he also came to like Hermann Hesse and translated one of his poems. As I found out already during our first conversation in Kruger's, some of those poets Seán translated and knew by heart were the same as I knew and treasured. Because of the memories that were attached to them, *Il pleure dans mon cœur ...*, *Seltsam, im Nebel zu wandern! Leben ist Einsamsein*, and other such lines had a common meaning for us. Because of this I knew that Seán's translations were not chosen haphazardly, but were deeply personal documents. In a similar manner, it is possible to read his translation of Franceso Petrarca's 'Ad Italiam' – beginning *Sé do bheatha, a chrich ró-naofa is annsa le Dia, sé do bheatha* – as a greeting to his native Dún Urlann and what is Fréderic Mistral's vigorous exhortation to his Provençal countrymen 'Cant a la raço latino' in Seán's translation 'Rosc an Laidin–chine' but a glorification of the Irish language, *Largant l'ámour, largant lou lume – Ag tiomnú grá agus lasrach anma*?

In spite of the equality of English and Irish on the intellectual level in Seán's personality, there is no doubt that it was in Irish that he expressed his deepest feelings. A moving example of this is offered by the description he himself gives in the article 'In the footsteps of Kuno Meyer' of the prayers he offered up at Kuno Meyer's grave. Like the verse translations, Seán's original poetry in his three slim but surprisingly varied collections, *Bánta Dhún Urlann, Déithe Teaghlaigh* and *Dúnmharú Chat Alexandreia,* express a variety of emotions in finely chiselled stanzas. A note of sadness is heard in several of these poems, which vary the *ubi sunt* theme, lamenting the passing away of the great men of yore. The poems on Thomas Ashe and Robin Flower fall within this group. It is typical of Seán, however, that his heroic gallery also includes such characters as his ancestor Tomás Mhicil Ach Muircheartaigh, a small farmer from Ballyferriter, who in 1851 sold a cow in order to buy the nine volumes of *The Annals of the Kingdom of Ireland,* and the blacksmith Seán Búlaeir from the same parish, whose smithy served as a convention or parliament, like the Dáil we find described in the Blasket books. Seán's strong sense of social justice is also to the fore in some poems in which the hard work conditions of servants and farmworkers are realistically depicted. Indignation aroused by injustice towards the Irish language is also forcefully expressed in Seán's poetry, as well as biting satire on those 'great writers of our time' who have nothing to say that is not common knowledge. The verse books also contain several examples of Seán's impish sense of humour. Though it is but seldom met with in his historical writings, this is often displayed in his works on Irish scholars, for instance in highly amusing comments on their monumental quarrels. Sometimes, as in the poem 'Traein an Daingin', on the Dingle train, tender humour is combined with the love for the places and people of his home area, which is so prominent everywhere in his writings. Far from appealing exclusively to the people of Corca Dhuibhne at home or in exile, such poems speak to all those who seek fully to understand and to be what they really are.

All scholars are vain to some extent, but Seán was unusually free from vanity. He seldom, if ever, made use of the doctoral title that was conferred upon him in Galway in 1995 by the National University of Ireland, though he no doubt was grateful for this well–deserved honour. He was always pleased to see the fruits of his scholarship in print though, as the book–lover he was, he more often commented upon their outward appearance than on their contents. For this reason it is especially touching to read what he says in this book in the previously unpublished essay on the making of *Art Ó Gríofa:* 'Bibliographically it was a splendid production, of stout and firm binding, finely printed by Fleet Printing Works in Times new–roman on antique Drimnagh paper, presented with pride in a format worthy of its great subject by a great publisher'. This, *mutatis mutandi,* holds true about *Celtic Studies in Europe and other essays* which gives the essence of so much that was uppermost in his mind. What a great pity that it was not granted to Seán to live to see it! But he was actively following its progress to the last day he lived, and thanks to the filial devotion of Gearóid Ó Lúing, to whom the task of the final editing fell, it now stands as a worthy monument in his memory.

When my wife and I visited Seán in hospital only a few days before his death he was much fatigued, but nevertheless had a good deal to say about Robin Flower and about Corca Dhuibhne, where I was going the following day. Then he talked about the book that was in preparation and said with a smile 'I have told Gearóid to see to it that you will get two copies!' Had somebody told him what I had never let him know, namely that I had duplicate copies of his books, or was it that he had been endowed by the supernatural power of special insight, attributed both by the ancient Greeks and the people of Corca Dhuibhne to those about to pass away from this world?

Seán Ó Lúing was an honest, straightforward and independent man. Pretence and snobbishness were completely foreign to him. Towards those who wanted to dictate and tyrannize he adopted the Catullan attitude of *nil nimium studeo, Cæsar, tibi velle placere...* He had a clear idea of what a good cause was, and the fact that it might seem difficult or even hopeless to follow never deterred him.

He was also a man of special personal qualities. He had the rare gift of being able to make people feel better about themselves as soon as they talked to him; he was able to engage with them totally. This, I think, was due to the fact that he was deeply self–assured in the best possible way, independent in his opinions, and possessed of rich inner resources. In spite of the touch of sadness, the unavoidable concomitant of anyone with intelligence and sensitivity who has observed the parting of the old ways and ideals in the Gaeltachts of

Ireland, he always gave me the impression of being essentially a happy man, conscious of his own reliable sources of joy – his deep roots in his native ground, his firm anchorage in French and German culture, his wide reading and his beloved scholarship. Thanks to all this he had the rare ability not to feel the need to push himself forward; he was able to concentrate fully on whoever he was talking to. He was a kind man with perfect manners, courteous, considerate, engaged. Not prudish, judgemental, or in any way negative about life's sensual pleasures, he seemed to me the closest thing to a secular saint that I have come across.

I can think of no epitaph worthier of Seán Ó Lúing of Dún Urlann than the two last lines of his own poem 'Cuimhne ar Bhláithín': *... chleachtais fírinne an léinn / Gura séanmhar do luí.*

Bo Almqvist
Ceathrú an Fhirtéaraigh 10. VII. 2000

Chapter 1

Retrospective

In the year 1838 Lady Henrietta Chatterton wrote an account of her travels entitled *Rambles in the South of Ireland* which was published in two volumes the following year in London. She was a lady of inquiring and sympathetic mind and the details of her adventures in the far western end of the Dingle Peninsula have a special interest. When there she was fortunate to make the acquaintance of Father John Casey, the parish priest of Dunurlin, a noted scholar and antiquarian who became her guide to the various antiquities of the district. The following is an extract from her book (Vol. 1, pages 187-89):

> On the shores of Ferriter's Cove, we found our car awaiting us. Father Casey was at a little distance along the road, taking shelter in a cottage from the shower that had suddenly and not the less violently fallen.
>
> The old Father had borrowed a horse, that he might accompany us on this afternoon's expedition. We had written to give him notice of our intention of revisiting his neighbourhood, and he came to this spot to meet us. After our greetings were over, he led us off in the direction of a group of houses, at the foot of Bally Ferriter's hill.
>
> Before the miserable little shop of a blacksmith, whose whole property consisted of one old hat, a coat, an anvil and a hammer, Father Casey stopped to hook up his horse, and beckoned us to follow him to a neighbouring cottage, not much better-looking than the blacksmith's; into this we entered, to take shelter from the rain, which was still falling.
>
> The room was certainly cleaner than most Irish rooms, in peasants' cabins; it opened into another, by a thin door, tottering upon rusty broken hinges, in a thin partition warped by heat and cold, and darkened by smoke.
>
> Beyond this, there was a 'parlour' remarkably well furnished, with a square leaf table, on three legs whole, and the fourth broken; a bookcase much out of the perpendicular, two chairs and a turn-up bed, for use by night and ornament by day.

The inhabitant of this humble chamber was a poor man; one who appeared to spend his slender income more in relieving the wants of others, than his own. He was a pale-faced individual, with an intellectual and pleasing countenance, dressed in a coat originally black, bearing testimony to its long duration by a sadly threadbare state – evident more particularly on the folds. We were introduced to him as a Mr. – no, a 'Reverend Mr.' something! He was a poor Roman Catholic curate!

In this little cabin we waited till the rain was nearly over, and then started for Bally Ferriter's Hill, with the addition of the interesting-looking curate to our party.

I was born in that house in 1917. Only the outlines of its walls remain. In my neighbour John Moriarty's house as a boy I heard it being discussed that a priest used to live there, giving it a reverential tradition. It was built of local sandstone with thick walls of which the broad window-sills gave ample room for the traditional Christmas candle. The rains of a century had discoloured and softened the outer texture of the stone and it would crumble under the pressure of one's hand.

There were no professional thatchers in the district in my time who might have given the house a durable cover of thatch, so my father, with his helpers, put on a thatch every autumn of freshly scented rushes, cut on our own rough meadowland. As boys we loved to roll on heaps of this and fashion from it peaked *caipíní cogaidh*, or war caps, while our elders worked at setting the thatch, securing it with parallel lines of súgán rope and a row of stones along the lower borders to keep it in place. No matter how well done, it was not proof against the heavy rains of winter which resulted in the dreaded *braon anuas* or drop-down.

The last occupant of the house was my grandfather Daniel Manning. He lived in it until 1931. We had a new dwelling built for us in that year by three stonemasons of the district, again of the attractive local red sandstone, only it was regrettably plastered over. I believe that the building of it was helped by the Gaeltacht Housing Acts which transformed dwellings in the Gaeltacht from the thatched cottage to the slate-roofed habitation, with incalculable benefit to health and amenity. The building was also helped by the generous assistance of my uncle Father James Manning. When in the summer of 1931 I returned from boarding school in Killarney it was to find that my grandfather persisted in remaining all by himself in the old house. It took much persuasion to make him change. His reluctance was understandable in bidding farewell to the house where he had lived his life in all the vicissitudes of happiness with a large admixture of tragedy.

My native parish of Ferriter, formerly Dunurlin, is reached by a fuchsia-lined road leading west from Tralee through the Dingle Peninsula, twisting and coiling its way for some forty kilometres through upland and glen to the old maritime port of Dingle. From there you have a choice of roads, my favourite one for cycling going by way of Milltown village through the high gap of Baile na nÁth to open on a dramatic vista of Smerwick Harbour and Sybil Head and a panorama of sand dunes, small fields and bogland, a landscape totally bare of trees.

The fuchsia shrub is everywhere. Botanically a stranger to the land, it has taken possession of the entire country, growing along the fences, much favoured by the farmers who plant it as shelter for their animals from the summer heat, richly colouring the August landscape with crimson flowers which hang like fairy dancing girls, exude honey and hum with the music of bees.

The landscape in which I grew up was dotted with little villages, each a compact community, consisting of some five to sixteen houses nestling together for company and convenience. In my native village there were six houses, five occupied by the Mannings and Moriartys and one, my own, by the Longs or Ó Lúing family. Nearly all the families of my village were related in one degree or another, being part of a fabric of wider texture, for the whole district was interconnected by marriages contracted over the generations.

Enclosed by the surrounding sea and the lofty barrier of Brandon Mountain, Shrovetide marriages were bargained out within the physical confines of the district, on the commerce of land or cattle. The bride and groom might have known each other before marriage or might not. Personal affection had no place. Their consent to each other was secondary to the importance of the property transaction between families. Parental authority was respected by the couple, whose own views were hardly consulted. Such was the tradition for generations. I would listen to the speculation of my elders about who would make a match with whom. Bottles of whiskey had a talismanic virtue in opening negotiations.

The national school where I received my early education stood opposite the parish church. Any day in Shrovetide we schoolboys might be diverted by the animated scenes as wedding groups, emerging from the church, made the place lively with rejoicings. There was much traffic of sidecars which were used for transport. There might be several weddings in the course of a day. It was human theatre, a folk celebration, good for the fortunes and character of the parish, no less than for the economics of the presbytery. Wedding parties moved from the church to the local taverns, of which there were four in the nearby village of Buailtín, and the rhythms of set-dancing and music of the melodeon blended with the notes, not always harmonious, of 'sean-amhráin na Mumhan', stimulated by frothy quaffings of Guinness or Murphy. Irish was the normal language of the environment. English was used in the shops of Buailtín for business purposes, usually in transactions with commercial travellers, but I noted that the shopkeepers, who were all natives of the district, preferred Irish in their own social life.

The dowry and property exchanges given in marriage were naturally modest, being related to the extent and character of land comprised in the local farms. In my schooldays the dowries would vary from £200 to the substantial sum of £600, which would apply when the bride married into a well-maintained farm of good land. Farms consisted of part arable, part bog, very important for fuel, and part rough grazing such as hillside or very rough pasture. The grass of six, or ten, or any number of cows, was the yardstick of land values. I do not know precisely what the extent of our own family holding was except that the figure of fifty acres remains in my memory since reading the census details, filled in for my father by an obliging and talented young lady from a neighbouring cottage and accepted by him. That would be the average size of holdings in the district. Every so often, an official windowed letter would arrive seeking payment of land annuities due on the farm on foot of a national land settlement of earlier times. The farms were divided into widely scattered fields, in the manner known as rundale, and this, I believe, came from subdividing complete or compact farm areas at an earlier time between two or more members of a family. This led to much energy being wasted going distances between fields, but the habitations of people remained close together in tight little villages, good for company, security and bright social life.

Hemmed in though it was by sea and mountain, the district was far from isolated from the outside world. Almost every family was linked with America or Australia through the emigration of one or more members of the family. Many households had priests serving in the foreign missions. Of the six households in my native village, every single one had an American or Australian connection. My uncle Father James Manning was ordained in Baltimore, Maryland by Cardinal Gibbons and ministered in Des Moines, Iowa. My aunt Julia Manning, emigrating in 1906, with a good knowledge of English, lived first in New England, later in Brooklyn and from there she moved to Eighth Avenue, New York City. There were four emigrants from Séamas Moriarty's house next door to ours, two priests, John and Michael, Paddy who settled in a Minnesota ranch and James who spent a period in Chicago and returned to work the family farm. From John Moriarty's house there were at least four in the United States – Father Pat, a college friend of the Leinster football star Martin O'Neill, ministered in Nebraska while his brothers Mike, Tommy and Dan settled in New York. And so with practically every family in the district.

The American papers arrived regularly, complete with 'Funnies', coloured cartoon pages which were very popular, like *Little Orphan Annie, The Gumps, Winnie Winkle the Breadwinner* and others, mainly comic in character. Politics and everyday events in the United States were followed with the keenest interest. The tabloid *New York Daily News* circulated in the district, also the weekly *Kerryman*, but only rarely the Dublin daily papers. I remember the interest created by the major boxing contests. Jack Dempsey and Gene Tunney were household names and the details of their famous bout which featured the 'long count' were followed round by round with intense interest. They were the heavyweights but other weights were equally familiar, Jack Sharkey the Lithuanian, Jack Delaney who was thought to be Irish, Jimmy McLarnin the speediest of lightweights, Paolo Uzcudun the Basque, a formidable fighter, Paul Berlinbach and the boxing promoter Tex Rickard, described by John Moriarty as the greatest man in America. These and their careers and prospects were the stuff of conversation. Stories of Luis Firpo, Jack Johnson and Battling Siki circulated. At times the title of greatest man in America would fall to Babe Ruth of baseball fame, and the rivalry of Yankees and Brooklyn Dodgers would be followed with as much interest as Kerry and Kildare.

The postman was kept busy delivering letters from many parts of the United States, likewise from Australia where my Manning cousin Sister Constantia served in Leichhardt, Sydney, or Fathers Jerry and John Flaherty of Teerivane, the latter one of Australia's great classical scholars, ministered, or others of the O'Connor and Moriarty families, for the ties with Australia were numerous. The *Daily News* of New York was a lively tabloid, much sought after during the celebrated Presidential Election of 1928, when Al Smith, the 'Happy Warrior' for the Democrats challenged Herbert Hoover who promised a chicken in every pot on behalf of the Republicans and won thanks to a California landslide, only to beget Prohibition, bootlegging, the speakeasy, gangsterdom and Al Capone. The culture of my boyhood environment had a strong American flavour. New York and Brooklyn, Springfield and Holyoke were names more familiar than Dublin. The 'cost' would be sent home by a member of a family to enable another cross the Atlantic to prospects that promised a better life.

The changing situation in the United States was reflected in correspondence in the Tralee-printed *Kerryman* and I read an absorbing controversy lasting many weeks between two young ladies who initiated it under the title 'The truth about America', advising would-be Irish emigrants to expect no Utopia. They were contradicted by a young naval officer who counter-advised that they gave a misleading impression. The two young emigrants rejoined 'Ahoy there! Lieutenant, you're all wet' and so the contest proceeded and may be read in the files of the *Kerryman* of the latter 20s or so. The Wall Street Crash of 1929 impoverished many an exile while the breadlines lengthened. The concern for this spread to my native parish.

My national school years were not happy and I do not dwell on them. It was with no regret that I boarded the Dingle train in the fall of 1929 bound for the diocesan Seminary of St. Brendan's in Killarney to settle in to a four or five year term of study that was designed as a preparation for the priesthood. It was, in effect, an act of separation from my native place which I was to revisit only for holidays and at intervals in later years. St. Brendan's Seminary had been established perhaps about the middle of the 19th century and laid a strong emphasis on Latin and classical Greek as appropriate subjects for Church learning. My friend and fellow-student Tom Woulfe told me that the school game was rugby in the years before the national resurgence influenced the character of education and games. Hurling and Gaelic football supplanted rugby and the Irish language was given a place of honour, but the classical languages remained firmly at the core of study. French was introduced in the senior classes.

As a result of my Killarney years I acquired a love for Latin and Greek which opened up for me a striking world of history and literature. My Latin teacher in Killarney was brilliant but totally eccentric and unpredictable. One year you would be his 'god' and the next he would have a 'set' on you. These phases of his were inexplicable and part of his odd personality. Yet I learned from him and for that I am grateful.

At University College Dublin I failed my First Arts examination in the uncongenial subject of Mathematics. In my second year I chose Logic instead and attended the lectures of dear old Father Shine who spoke away in a low key monotone and set an end of year test nobody was ever known to fail. Along with my major subjects of Latin and Modern Irish I had taken the delightful course of Celtic Archaeology as subsidiary and in the autumn of 1938, following two years of serious concentration, I graduated with a success that surprised myself. I was faced at once with the necessity of getting a job. A practical man, not of the University, whose way of life was politics and whose help I sought pointedly asked me 'what in the hell ever possessed you to do a degree like that?' I was desperately seeking a post as secondary teacher, the only kind of work I could see on the horizon for which my degree qualified me. In those arid years there were few teaching jobs to be had and in my efforts to keep a foothold in Dublin where the only jobs of any kind might be had, I applied for some teaching hours in the Technical Schools where literary subjects such as Irish were taught as a sideline, fully realising that it was a venture of last resort and a final aspiration. To obtain the few hours that might be available you had to sign your name to a panel and await your luck. 'Don't tell them you know Latin' warned the administrator of a technical school. The Philistine is a tough weed. Even my application for teaching Irish hours met with rejection. I was only one of many. These were called the years of the Emergency. Many of my friends emigrated.

My Professor of Modern Irish, Cormac Ó Cadhlaigh, wrote me a brilliant reference which, if things had been as well-ordered as our degree courses were designed to prepare us for, would have opened the door for me to a teaching post in any college in the land. But I only received one rebuff after another. He advised me, for the sake of getting a foothold in employment, to take up an Irish or Latin post plus a subject I had no skill in. I am grateful to him for the interest he took in me, as I am for the broad educational character of his Irish lectures in which he introduced us to the achievements of the great European Celtic scholars. He would give us notes on these from a bulky typescript which he called *Bolg an tSoláthair*, into which he had copied numerous articles and essays from learned journals and other expensive or out of the way sources. He went far outside the confines of the printed syllabus. He obviously worked hard to make his lectures as interesting and informative as possible. Cormac was afflicted with severe rheumatism which caused him to walk with a limp and as he suffered much discomfort from this you might expect a learned discussion in which he partook to be suddenly interrupted by a cry of pain, *'Ó Chríost na dathacha!'*

With a view to qualifying for secondary teaching I completed my lectures for the degree of Higher Diploma in Education. Our Professor of Education was Timothy Corcoran, S.J. who regulated his day's work with clockwork precision, arriving punctually at 4.30 p.m. every afternoon for his lecture and completing it at 5.30 to the second. He forbade the taking of notes in class. The theme of his lectures was the Theory and Practice of Education and a central feature of his teaching was the educational value of the Jesuit text the *Ratio Studiorum*, or System of Education. I have seen it stated that it was his purpose to diminish the influence of Cardinal Newman on university education, which caused me astonishment, since I received the clear impression from his lectures that he held Newman, if not this side of idolatry, at least pretty near to it. His advice on details I considered excellent. He advised that learners of a language should be taught to proceed from grammar to literature as early as possible. He decried the emphasis on Caesar as an introductory textbook on Latin. The Commentaries were only a military manual. He had produced a Latin textbook for beginners with an Irish context. We learned much from him of the great philosophers who had an influence on education, of whom I can remember William James, Pestalozzi the Swiss educator whose class, he told us, disappeared through the window, Herbert Spencer and others. His greatest praise was reserved for Aristotle, progenitor of so much that was excellent in Christian philosophy. Never once were we told how to control a class or keep its attention, unless his proposition that a teaching method was essentially personal covered the situation. When we went into the city schools to fulfil the degree condition of teaching one hundred hours we found such a divergence between the pleasant hours of lecture instruction and the far from easy practice of teaching boys from a variety of city backgrounds. You usually taught under the disadvantage that a second class was in progress in charge of another teacher in the same classroom. There was a world of difference between academic theory and the rugged realities of the urban schoolrooms.

Portarlington, in Co. Laois, where I spent the school year of 1940-41, teaching Irish and Mathematics in St. Joseph's Christian Brothers, was a Huguenot settlement with many fine period houses, some lived in and others falling into decay. In those years of World War Two, there was little or no town improvement and in any case Ireland had not yet awakened to the meritorious idea of enhancing its civic or environmental culture. Against all my inclinations, I found myself burdened with the teaching of mathematics, a task I did not relish, though I had only the very junior class to teach. The advice my Irish professor had given me, even if well meant, was the reverse of good and I would never recommend it. I have no doubt that my pupils noted my deficiency in the subject. What I dreaded was the coming of the inspector, as come he did and sat by while I explained a blackboard problem, with no feeling of easiness. But the dear man, Mr. McKeown, perhaps noting my predicament, was kind and sympathetic. He asked me how long I had been teaching and told me that as time went on I would doubtless find ways of making things easier for myself.

In Portarlington I joined the Local Defence Volunteers and went on route marches. One Sunday two sergeants arrived from the Curragh to put us through drill instruction. One of these was a common martinet whose orders were sharp and vicious. I was not in his company, happily, but a teacher colleague was, who in one of the formations was found a yard out of line and was reproved in fiercely vituperative terms by the martinet, in front not only of his fellow-volunteers but of a large crowd of townspeople who, out of curiosity, had followed us to the parade ground which was the local G.A.A. pitch. Drill over, we sympathised with our companion's ordeal and the comment was made that officers of that type were the authors of mutiny. He was no advertisement for recruitment and indeed nobody of his stamp was ever sent again. Our own commandant was Paddy Cobbe, who though civilian as to authority, could truly be called an officer and a gentleman.

Portarlington was the centre of great cycling country. A leading cyclist, Alo Donegan, had a business in the Main Street. While there I bought a new Royal Enfield bicycle for some seven pounds seven shillings, one of the most useful purchases of my life and cycled with companions the whole surrounding territory between Kildare and Slieve Bloom, skirting the Seven Hills of Laois which profile the skyline. Laois was a land of champion ploughmen, whose tracts of mathematically straight furrows we would admire. It was a time of intensive tillage, when the farmer was King and the ploughmen took pride in their skills. The land was of prime quality.

In Portarlington there was no sea, nor beaches, nor mountain peaks to admire. There was the sky, in all its colour changes and moods and this we would gaze at and wonder as we walked the trafficless roads around the town, sometimes out to Killenard, a pleasant wooded place alive with squirrels and other wildlife, where Mr. Stack taught school and whist drives were held in the schoolroom. It was a delightful location where one might live forever without pining for the city. We would visit it Sunday after Sunday, sometimes to Mass, always for the recreation its peaceful environment guaranteed.

My teaching duties in Portarlington lasted one year, after which I gravitated to Dublin. There followed two and a quarter years of teaching in a commercial college which I describe elsewhere. Following an open competition, I was appointed a translator in the Translation Section of the Houses of the Oireachtas. The year was 1943 and the Second World War was raging across Europe, North Africa and the Pacific. Ireland was isolated and facing the challenges of relying on itself, not unlike the position of the Netherlands in the First World War.

St. Jerome is the patron of translators and we return to him as the great exemplar for the classic definition of the art – *hanc esse regulam boni interpretis, ut idiómata linguae alterius suae linguae exprimat proprietate* – this being the principle of the good translator, that he should render the idioms of another language suitably in his own. My own choice of work, had I the choosing of it, even were it available, would have been the teaching of Latin, my favourite study, in a well-regulated school. This remained a dream. At no time had I envisaged that I might become a translator. There was a constitutional obligation to provide a translation of the Acts of the Oireachtas and of the secondary legislation known as Statutory Instruments, from English into Irish or, in the rare cases where the text as passed by the Dáil and Seanad had been in Irish, to produce an English version.

Our Translation Office had been set up as one of the services attached to the first Dáil Éireann. Because of the association of the Irish language with the national resurgence this was a natural detail. The celebrated correspondence that led up to the Treaty negotiations of 1921 was bilingual on the Irish side and addressed to Dáithí Onórach Leód Seóirse, 10 Sráid Downing, i Lonndain. The English text, which was the actual primary text, is described symbolically as the 'Official Translation' and is signed by Éamon de Valera and dated August 10th, 1921. I cannot say who the translator was but it might well have been Seán Ua Ceallaigh who used the *nom-de-plume* Sceilg. I have reason to believe that the actual debates of the First Dáil were translated into Irish, although not published, and that drafts of these may be in the State archives. With the establishment of Saorstát Éireann the Translation Office was set up and staffed on a regular basis with the duty of translating the primary and secondary legislation, Standing Orders and various official documents and correspondence.

There were translation offices attached to the Canadian and South African Parliaments. The translation staff of the Belgian Parliament caters for the Flemish and French languages and the parliamentary debates appear in both languages. Flemish had a long battle for recognition. Three major languages, German, French and Italian are catered for by the Swiss translation staff which is probably the oldest established in Europe.

There was nothing literary about our translation work. The text consisted of legal phraseology and as such had to be translated with precision. I have seen treatises entitled 'The Art of Translation' but they usually related to works of prose or poetry. Eric Dodds has appreciative things to say about translation in the domain of literature. I would not describe our translation work as an art. Rather was it a craft. It was certainly good for the discipline of writing. Translation goes to the heart of a meaning. A knowledge of other European languages gave a decided advantage in that they supplied useful terms, not always found in English, which would fit naturally into an Irish dress. A knowledge of law is an advantage. To our certain knowledge there was at least one man who read every one of our translations. That was Earnán de Blaghd.

Our workplace was on the top back floor of Leinster House where we had a view of Leinster Lawn and Merrion Square and the tall graceful Peppercanister Church at the far end of Mount Street. We could go into the typists' room on the opposite side which gave us a view of the front courtyard, the National Museum and National Library and Molesworth Street. From these vantage points we saw the removal of the Queen Victoria Statue, the arrival of Dwight and Mamie Eisenhower, of Pandit Nehru and, most memorable of all, arriving from the Merrion Square side, John Fitzgerald Kennedy whose helicopter landed on Leinster Lawn. Appealingly youthful in looks, he was welcomed as no one ever before, with the country feeling almost a proprietorial claim on him as the first Irish man, though American by birth, of the Catholic faith to become President of the United States and achieving the zenith of Irish ambition after many generations of exile. He put an end forever to the pishogue-like belief that there was in the American constitution a clause forbidding the Presidency to a Catholic, a notion reinforced by the experience of the 'Happy Warrior' Al Smith in 1928.

The great rejoicing of his visit lived in the public mind long after he bade farewell from Shannon Airport, hard by 'old Shannon's face', until the world was shocked by his assassination in Dallas late in 1963 and joy was dissipated. A pall of gloom settled over the land as the loss seemed personal to each individual. In the emotional aftermath it was the wish of all that his memory should be perpetuated by a worthy memorial in Dublin City. Many sites were proposed for this and finally a place was selected, well away from the heart of the city, on the southern side of the Beggar's Bush district if I am not mistaken, and a monument of impressive shape planned and its design published.

Alas for plans, so soon does public feeling evaporate. The design is in the archives, gathering dust, discarded and forgotten. Kennedy is remembered by the lovely arboretum in his ancestral district of New Ross, where visitors can walk in the shade of the finest trees provided by nature, a memorial far more attractive. His tenure of Presidency marks a high point in the interest in the United States of the Irish people. Thereafter their westward attention waned and began to be drawn increasingly towards an opposite horizon, the European Economic Community, popularly called the Common Market, capital Brussels.

Kennedy died in 1963. Ireland joined the European Community in 1972, marking a decisive and significant change of direction in the country's interests. It affected us in the translation staff in that it became our pressing duty to go to Brussels to translate into Irish the treaties on the basis of which the Community was formed. Chief of these was the

Treaty of Rome. It was not difficult to realise that it was a momentous time. I decided to make notes on the day-to-day happenings of the event in so far as they related to our work. It is not easy to keep a diary when each day is so full of other duties that one lacks the time.

Our translation staff worked first in the Rue Ravenstein, later in the Bâtiment Charlemagne. I do not easily forget my introduction to my first translation session, at which a chairman presided and the translators, grouped around a table, read each his own version of the primary text which was in French. The torrent of French which greeted my ears was intimidating and outside my comprehension. With other members of our staff I was in due course obliged to attain a working knowledge of French, taught us by a highly efficient group of teachers in Lansdowne House and other centres. Because French was the primary language of the translation process, the first text supplied by the drafting committee for translation was in French, and was invariably accompanied by an instruction to which we came to have a particular aversion – *Priorité absolue*. Everything was urgent. The translation was expected to be provided at the shortest notice. I cannot explain why French was arrived at as the primary tongue, except that being located in mainly, but not wholly, French-speaking Brussels, it was thought most natural. We were not long in Brussels when we came to notice tensions and antipathies between French and Flemish speakers. Italian or German were used but rarely in these early years. A person is not acknowledged to be a translator in the European requirement unless proficient in French, German and English, apart from his mother-tongue, if he were none of these nationalities. I later saw a situation in Luxembourg when Italian was given the status of a secondary or minor tongue, little to the pleasure of the brilliant officials who spoke it.

I have described our experiences in the translation of the basic European Treaties in a little book *In Ardchathair na hEorpa* (In the Capital of Europe) based on notes which I took at the time. On later visits to Brussels and Luxembourg on translation assignments we noted that the influence of English had made marked headway. In Brussels many people considered it fashionable to display their knowledge of English.

I shall never regret having had to learn French as part of the task our European assignment made necessary. A new and fascinating literature came into the ambit of our study. We learn a language not for its grammar or idiom but to discover what its literature has to say to us. The 19th century French poets were a revelation. I cannot easily forget, on my first reading of him, the impact on my consciousness of Baudelaire, Jansenist and Catholic, whose tortured mind ranged on the borders of hell, from which he called himself back, and who indeed might very well have been a saint, as John Broderick surmised. A reading of the introductory poem of *Les Fleurs du Mal* gives one the feeling of having been present on the first night of an old-style Redemptorist mission. He translates well into Irish.

In 1982 I retired from the Oireachtas Translation Office where I had served since 1943. I should like to praise my colleagues in that office, which a voice from the higher academic echelons of Dublin in a radio interview, described, not incorrectly perhaps, as an obscure office in the civil service. The definition of anonymity is classically described in Irish as: 'I gan fhios don saol is fearr a bheith ann', 'unknown to the world it is best to be'. That is how we functioned. We laboured quietly and in agreement, with the Irish language the bond between a company of individuals who held strongly divergent views on many other things. We never clashed on extraneous matters. Our staff was totally dedicated to the Irish language. In the material sense they might have done better had they applied their talents to more promising avenues. Their impact on the Irish language in bringing it into congruence with the modern world has been significant.

A tradition of writing has become attached to the office, beginning in the person of Liam Ó Rinn, survivor of 1916, versatile essayist, student of Russian literature and biographer of the Hellenist Stephen MacKenna. No doubt it will continue to be a nursery of Irish language writers. Among the distinguished persons who have praised its work were Eoin MacNeill and Earnán de Blaghd and, of a later generation, John Kelly and Professor John A. Murphy.

GRAMMATICA CELTICA

E MONUMENTIS VETUSTIS

TAM HIBERNICAE LINGUAE

QUAM BRITANNICARUM DIALECTORUM

CAMBRICAE CORNICAE AREMORICAE

COMPARATIS GALLICAE PRISCAE RELIQUIIS

CONSTRUXIT

I. C. ZEUSS
PHIL. DR. HIST. PROF.

EDITIO ALTERA

CURAVIT

H. EBEL
PH. DR. ACAD. REG. HIB. SOC. HON., ACAD. REG. BORUSS. ADI. COMM. EPIST.

BEROLINI
APUD WEIDMANNOS
MDCCCLXXI

PARIS
MAISONNEUVE & CO

The title-page of *Grammatica Celtica* (second edition) by Johann Kaspar Zeuss.

Chapter 2

Celtic Studies in Europe: a brief sketch

> Sweet is the Irish tongue
> Speech to foreign aid unbound
> Rich and limpid its address
> Crystal clear its pleasant sound.
>
> Though Hebrew tongue be old in grace
> Though Latin first in learning
> We owe to them nor word nor phrase
> Our Gaelic speech augmenting.

The voice is Geoffrey Keating's (ca. 1570-1650). His philology is faulty. His Irish, prose or verse, is a joy to read. Suppressed for centuries by hostile policies, his writings lay hidden in manuscript. When, at the end of the 18th and beginning of the 19th centuries, investigators came to be inquisitive about the relations between the languages of Europe, the origins and character of the Irish tongue baffled them. Theory and fancy flourished. Writers put forward the most fantastic notions about the identity of the language. These might be divided into two classes, those who wished to degrade the language and those who wished to elevate it. Chief of those who wished to degrade everything Irish was a Scottish writer named Pinkerton. He had his disciples. It passes belief what they thought. Some held that the Irish language had its true affinities with the Ostyak and Tungus dialects of Northern Siberia, or with the tongue of the Jaloffs or Hottentots of Africa, or with the dialect of a tribe of North American Indians who inhabited the Susquehannah region. The realms of Irish were truly described by the French Celtist Henri Gaidoz to be dark and trackless as the storied forest of Brocéliande.

On the other hand there were those, almost equally ignorant, who wished to exalt the language. They said it was related to the Hebrew, or to the Phoenician tongue of ancient Karthage. One of the earliest efforts in this category was Charles Vallancey's *Essay on the antiquity of the Irish language, being a collation of the Irish with the Punic Language*, published in Dublin in 1772. He was a well-meaning man. Joaquin Villaneuva was the author of a treatise called *Phoenician Ireland* (translated by the Kerry-born scholar Henry O'Brien), a work full of curious and outlandish etymologies. A Lieutenant-Colonel Vans Kennedy, of the Bombay Military Establishment, in an elaborate study of the languages of Asia and Europe, concluded that Celtic, by which he meant Irish, was a peculiar language that had no relationship whatever with Greek, Latin, the Teutonic languages, Arabic, Persian or Sanskrit.

It was the period of Celtomania, the term applied to it by later and enlightened scholars, a time of absolute lingual darkness, in which there was no acknowledgement that Irish might be classified with the Indo-European family of languages which, originating from Sanskrit in India, spread westward into the Middle East and Europe to form Latin, Greek, German, French and the other prestige languages of Europe – no, claimed the bogus philologists, utterly impossible that the Irish language could be related to this premier family of tongues.

There were genuine scholars whose researches led them to different conclusions. James Cowles Prichard was an ethnologist. In a study called *The Eastern Origin of the Celtic Nations* he decided, on the basis of language comparisons, that the Celtic people were of Eastern origin, a kindred tribe with the nations who settled on the banks of the Indus and on the shores of the Mediterranean and the Baltic. A Franco-Swiss philologist, Adolphe Pictet, came very close to the truth in his study *De l'affinité des langues celtiques avec le sanscrit* published in Paris in 1837. He said there was no doubt that Old Irish possessed many particulars which derived directly from Sanskrit or from the Indo-European family in general. Pictet was an excellent scholar but he, like others, was handicapped by the limited sources available. He also considered that the necessary investigations could only be carried out with success in Ireland. Such, however, did not turn out to be the case. At this point we might skip a century and a half to draw attention to the work of Myles Dillon, whose comparative investigations in Irish and Sanskrit patterns are printed in his absorbing study, *Celts and Aryans*, published in Simla in 1975.

Turning to the situation in Ireland, we find, in the mid-nineteenth century, a group of scholars who made immense contributions to Irish literature and history. Two in particular are pre-eminent, John O'Donovan and Eugene O'Curry. They died within a year of each other, O'Donovan in 1861, O'Curry the following year. They had the native knowledge of the Irish language which was a priceless asset to them in their work. They never had access, however, to the earliest sources of the Irish language, which were to be found in Europe where Irish missionaries had trodden one thousand years before their time. They had no training in comparative philology, which enabled linguists to dissect and examine the structure and vocabulary of language from a strictly scientific viewpoint. Comparative philology was a new study which began to flourish in Europe in the early 19th century. It opened up fresh avenues in the comparison and relation of languages with each other. It provided a key to history and to the movements and associations of peoples and races.

The solution to the ancestry of Europe's languages lay deep in India. As early as the 5th century B.C., India's own grammarians had been giving attention to the structure of their language and had arrived at its grammatical outline. It was not, however, until the 17th and 18th centuries that European pioneers, mainly German Jesuit missionaries, came to study Sanskrit with the result that grammars of the language reached the stage of print. Thereafter the examination of India's languages progressed.

> The East (wrote Russell Martineau) in a larger sense had preserved languages only beginning to be known … The Ganges had on its banks cities of fabulous antiquity, and a people that inherited a language, venerable no less by its traditional age than by its sanctity, which was not a thing of yesterday. Sanskrit was the tongue which would throw more light than any other on the formative process of language generally, and on the unity in variety observable in the Western languages.[1]

The English conquest of India at the end of the 18th century helped to disclose the vast literary riches of Sanskrit to European scholarship. Sanskrit, though unspoken itself for ages, was the cradle tongue of the important group of languages which came to be spoken throughout Europe and the western parts of Asia. They are called Aryan, Indo-Aryan, Indo-Germanic or, more generally nowadays, Indo-European. The discovery of Sanskrit led to the science of comparative philology. An excellent linguist named William Jones gave an address to the Royal Asiatic Society of Bengal in 1786, in which he called attention to similarities between Sanskrit on the one hand and Greek and Latin on the other, which pointed to an affinity between them. This was the beginning of a process which developed into the science of Comparative Philology and which came to its full fruition in Germany in the 19th century. Two scholars in particular became the main agents in its advance. The first of these was Jacob Ludwig Grimm (1785-1863), one of the celebrated Grimm brothers (the other was Wilhelm Karl,

1786-1859) who delighted us as children with their fairy and folk tales. Not alone were they folklorists, they were also distinguished philologists. Jacob Grimm was the author of a German grammar (4 vols) built on scientific principles, which he finished in 1837.

The second was Franz Bopp (1791-1867), author of the *Vergleichende Grammatik des Sanskrit, Zend, Griechischen, Lateinischen, Litthauischen, Gottischen und Deutschen* (1833-1852) who is acknowledged to be the founder of the science of Comparative Philology, without whose labours, writes Russell Martineau, the Science of Language might not have been. In the troubled years of 1848 and 1849 he lectured on Sanskrit in Berlin to an audience of two students, one of whom was Rudolf Thomas Siegfried, a native of Dessau, a small city 30 miles north of Leipzig. Siegfried is a shadowy but important figure in the development of Celtic studies. Pictet, mentioned earlier, noted in 1837 that Bopp did not include the Celtic languages in his comparative philology survey. In the following year Bopp made up for this, in a paper entitled 'The Celtic Languages in their relations to Sanskrit, Zend, Greek, Latin, German, Lithuanian and Slavic', read to the Akademie der Wissenschaften on 13 December 1838 and published in Berlin in 1839.

Before 1853, the best scholars could only produce probability, inference, tentative efforts in the direction of truth, approaching without achieving it. The origins and lineage of Irish remained in darkness until an unknown Bavarian scholar named Johann Kaspar Zeuss took to examining the earliest written records of the language. These were miniscule glosses written in between the lines of Latin scriptural or devotional tracts, by way of comment or explanation. They were to be found in the libraries and archives of Central Europe, where Irish missionaries had settled in early mediaeval times to establish and promote Christian teaching. They remained unknown to the world until they attracted the attention of Zeuss, an unregarded schoolteacher and historian, who was barely able to make his living and was never in robust health. In the great saga of Celtic scholarship, this man calls for special appreciation.

He was born in 1806 in the little village of Vogtendorf, some miles outside the city of Kronach in Bavaria. His mother hoped he would enter the priesthood, but he had made up his mind to follow a secular career. A studious and thoughtful young man, a gifted linguist who learned Latin from his parish priest, he graduated from the University of Munich in 1830 with a sound knowledge of Oriental and Classical languages. Early in his career he was discouraged from continuing his Germanic studies and transferred his attention to the unexplored field of Celtic, which he had already touched on in his Germanic researches.

The political outlines of Germany in Zeuss's time were different to the shape they took later in the 19th century under Bismarck. Bavaria, in the south, was a separate kingdom. Elsewhere there were many territorial divisions. It is useful to have before one a map of the Central Europe of his time for reference to Zeuss's travel to the various libraries and archives. Despite his fine qualifications he could secure only modest teaching jobs. While teaching in the city of Speyer, on the left bank of the Rhine, not far from Heidelberg, he travelled at weekends to the libraries of Heidelberg, Darmstadt and Karlsruhe, and during holidays to places further afield, Würzburg, Munich, Milan, St. Gall in Switzerland, Turin, the British Museum in London, the Bodleian Library in Oxford. He copied the early Irish writings in these centres, and in his spare time, in his study in Speyer, he examined and translated them, mastering the grammar and idiom in which they were written, working in isolation, without guide or help. He never met an Irish speaker, nor did he have a speaking knowledge of any Celtic tongue. The Irish glosses which he copied were explanations or interpretations of scriptural texts, written on the margins or in between the lines of the Latin. To take one example: The Würzburg Glosses, probably eighth century, first housed in the Cathedral Library there, consisted of annotations to the Letters of Saint Paul. For all of ten years Zeuss studied and wrote, until in 1853, without advance notice, he published in Leipzig the *Grammatica Celtica* in two volumes, amounting to twelve hundred pages, written in Latin, an ordered and scientific survey based on Jacob Grimm's *Deutsche Grammatik*, in which pride of place was given to Irish. It took the learned world some time to realise its significance. His friend Rudolf Thomas Siegfried wrote about the event.

> Zeuss's case is a rare one. He solves the great Celtic problem, which for centuries had baffled the scholars of England, France and Germany – he gives us a sudden and complete light, where we had made up our minds to sit forever in darkness – he creates a critical method where dreams and licence had become a chronic disease – and when he has achieved all this, there was hardly a voice to say 'well done!' … the man of paramount merit and genius dies without so much as a word of praise having reached his ear.

In the very first sentence of the book, in the most celebrated statement in the history of comparative philology, the place of Irish as the most westerly of the group of tongues deriving from the ancient language of India is affirmed. Why did he write in Latin? For two reasons, one thinks. He wrote for the learned world in the language that scholars understood. He was also following the tradition of the great Latin grammarians, like Donatus, Servius and Priscian. In the Abbey of St. Gall he found a manuscript of Priscian's Grammar which had been used and annotated by Irish missionaries.

Zeuss lived only three years after the publication of the *Grammatica Celtica*. He was busy in these years preparing a second edition but was handicapped by ill-health. His way of life was ascetic. He neither smoked nor drank beer nor wine. He filled his pocket with sweets and drank milk. He had a speech impediment which would have handicapped him in lecturing but not in library work. His health was never robust. The scourge of tuberculosis invaded his family, four members of it dying at an early age. He returned home to die in his native Vogtendorf, sadly unable to avail of the invitation from James Henthorn Todd of Trinity College Dublin to take up an appointment. He is buried in the family grave in Kronach. Some years ago when the municipal boundaries of Kronach were extended to include his native village, the city authorities found that they had another distinguished son to celebrate. Kronach's most famous citizen until then had been Lucas Cranach the painter. Zeuss has now been adopted with pride and a bronze statue of him was set up a few years ago in a central park of the city and unveiled by the mayor. A fine modern school, the Kaspar-Zeuss Gymnasium, perpetuates his memory. One of the city avenues is named after him and it is proposed presently to name one of the important thoroughfares in his memory.

Important works about Zeuss have appeared in Germany in recent years.[2] In his native Kronach they are building up a a repository of materials about him, such as essays and studies. In the Kaspar-Zeuss Gymnasium a student of the Art class has made a fine copy in oils of his portrait.

A brief, but significant, postscript to this sketch of Zeuss is the striking tribute to his memory by John Fleming, Editor of the *Gaelic Journal*, in a letter to Kuno Meyer:

> I had seen boys flogged in school for speaking their own language. Later on, when I was learning to read Irish, my teacher often set my school-fellows laughing 'with counterfeited glee' by sneering at my Irish 'thrash'. And who has changed all this? Caspar Zeuss.

This was written in 1905. The following year marked the centenary of Zeuss's birth. His memory was celebrated with speeches and music in Bamberg and wreaths were placed on his grave in Kronach cemetery. In the most emotional moment of the whole celebration

Joseph O'Neill stood at his graveside and in the name of the Gaelic League spoke his praise in Irish and laid on the grave a wreath with the inscription:

'Ó Chlannaibh Gaedheal i ndilchuimhne an té do chéad-chuir cruinneolas na Sean-ghaedhilge ar bun' – From the Irish people in loving memory of the man who first established the scientific canon of Old Irish.[3]

The best essays in English about Zeuss have been written by Fr. Francis Shaw, S.J. and I quote one sentence which puts his achievement and his importance to Ireland in perspective. It says: 'It must be rare for a nation to owe as much to one man as the Irish people owes to Johann Kaspar Zeuss'. (*Studies*, Summer 1954, p.194). His is the premier name in Celtic studies. All roads lead back to him. With the publication in 1853 of *Grammatica Celtica* the study of the Celtic languages became international. The investigation of Irish became firmly established in Germany and spread to France, Italy, Poland, Scandinavia, the Low Countries, Denmark, Great Britain and North America and, in the person of Whitley Stokes, to India. Scholars dedicated to the Irish language in these countries have become household names in the republic of learning.

In Germany, where the new methods of scientific philology developed, following the work of Grimm and Bopp, the most striking advances were made in the study of early Irish. Zeuss had established the canon of Irish grammar. Following him, scholars directed their attention to the literature of which it was the framework. The main thrust in the progress of Celtic studies was provided by Ernst Windisch of Saxony (1844-1918), a major figure in the development of Middle-Irish literature. It is of interest to note that nearly all the European scholars who worked at Irish were not professors in that study, but rather in allied fields like Sanskrit, Classics, Germanic studies and Comparative Philology. While they were aware of the historical forms and structure of Irish they were generally unable to pronounce it correctly. Daniel Binchy has told us of how painful it was to listen to Rudolf Thurneysen's pronunciation. Windisch laid all students of early Irish under an obligation by ploughing through the *Grammatica Celtica* and providing a digest of it in the shape of a college grammar and reader, which was in turn translated into English, twice, by different scholars. Windisch stated in the Preface that his purpose was 'to facilitate and spread the study of the highly interesting language and literature of ancient Ireland'. Windisch's great achievement was to reveal some of the riches of mediaeval Irish literature in two massive volumes. The first was a miscellany of Irish texts with accompanying dictionary, making up a volume of some 900 pages, in the *Irische Texte* series, published in 1880. The second was his imperial edition of the ancient epic tale, *Táin Bó Cualgne*, containing over 1200 pages, with a translation and a preface which includes his comment that Ireland might well be proud of its epic tale. This appeared in 1905. The text was taken from the *Book of Leinster* and the edition, after more than nine decades, still commands authority. Windisch has a special importance in that he was the teacher of two very dissimilar but distinguished students, Kuno Meyer and Heinrich Zimmer. He was a highly respected teacher, gentle in character, methodical in his work, man of industry rather than genius.

Before considering the career and achievement of Heinrich Zimmer we might first ask ourselves what was the perception of the Celts, and consequently the Irish, in Germany and other parts of Europe. To answer this it is necessary to take a look at what were the views on the subject of one of Germany's greatest historians, Theodor Mommsen (1817-1903), the first German to receive the Nobel Prize for Literature (in 1902). His influence in Germany and Italy was vast, and though we do not know to what degree he coloured public opinion, it is certain that his views had an influence in many academic quarters. His celebrated *History of Rome*, which brought him international fame and was translated into many languages, was published in three volumes between 1854-6, when he was teaching Roman Law in Zürich and Breslau. This is what he has to say of the Celts and Irish:

> With reason the Celts of the Continent suffered the same fate at the hands of the Romans, as their kinsmen in Ireland suffer down to our own day at the hands of the Saxons – the fate of becoming merged as a leaven of future development in a politically superior nationality ... in the accounts of the ancients as to the Celts on the Loire and the Seine we find almost every one of the characteristic traits which we are accustomed to characterise as marking the Irish. Every feature reappears: the laziness in the culture of the fields; the delight in tippling and brawling ... the hearty delight in singing and reciting the deeds of past ages, and the most decided talent for rhetoric and poetry; the curiosity ... the childlike piety, which sees in the priest a father and asks him for his advice in all things; the unsurpassed fervour of national feeling ... the inclination to rise in revolt under the first chance leader that presents himself and to form bands, but at the same time the utter incapacity to preserve a self-reliant courage equally remote from presumption and pusillanimity ... It is, and remains, at all times

and places the same indolent and poetical, irresolute and fervid, inquisitive, credulous, amiable, clever, but – in a political point of view – thoroughly useless nation; and therefore its fate has been always and everywhere the same.[4]

Some indictment! Although stated in such blunt and uncompromising language, Mommsen's views probably would not have sounded strange to the Italian statesman Cavour who, although he admired O'Connell, thought O'Connell's Repeal policy mistaken and irrelevant. The Young Ireland movement got little encouragement from France. John Devoy was surprised when, in 1877, he approached the Russian ambassador in Washington, at a time of crisis, for prospective help. But, replied the ambassador, all we understand Ireland is looking for are some improvements in education and land tenure. We might well ask what kind of profile, if any at all, the notion of an autonomous Ireland had on the European mainland. The fact that there was little or no knowledge of her literary heritage only helped to make the incomprehension more profound.

It is well to remember that the *Grammatica Celtica* appeared in 1853, a short time prior to Mommsen's pontifications, and that its influence kept spreading steadily throughout the ensuing decades. He could not help but notice the rise of Celtic studies in Germany and elsewhere in the last quarter of the 19th century and there is evidence that he read the *Grammatica Celtica*. Perhaps he was influenced through his acquaintance with the versatile Irish scholar George Sigerson, who would have been in a position to brief him well.[5] It was at his suggestion that a Chair of Celtic Philology was founded in 1900 in the University of Berlin which, at his instance, was occupied by Heinrich Zimmer who up till then was Professor of Sanskrit and Philology in the University of Greifswald, a small city on the Baltic coast of North Germany. Let us pardon Theodor Mommsen while we pay special attention to Heinrich Zimmer.

Long before his appointment as the first Professor of Celtic Philology in Germany, Zimmer had made his mark as a combative scholar in Celtic learning. A target for names, he was called the Tiger of Greifswald, the Ismael of Celtic studies whose hand was against all men, and in whose writings the personal attacks surged from every page, in the words of a French Celtist. Of his learning and achievements there is no dispute. He spent periods in Wales to learn Welsh and preach in Chapel, and on the Aran Islands to learn Irish. The son of a peasant, as described in contemporary references, he supported the Land League of Ireland and had an unfriendly confrontation with a landlord's agent on Aran. A historian by inclination, with a cosmic view of world events, he envisaged the dissolution of the British Empire since Gladstone's yielding to the Celt by agreeing to Home Rule.

Kuno Meyer wrote of him that he loved the Celt and believed in the Celtic imagination but thought the influence a disruptive one in politics. He was a begetter of ideas. His lively and robust intelligence transformed every subject which he touched, bringing to light new aspects and unperceived horizons. He was an iconoclast in that he attacked received notions of history. He stated that the great upsurge of learning in Ireland in the sixth and following centuries did not come about through the influence of St. Patrick and the advent of Christianity, but from the settlement in Ireland, prior to St. Patrick, of learned rhetoricians who had crossed from Europe in flight from the Vandals and demon-begotten Huns. He supported his contentions with an impressive array of learning and his views led to vigorous controversies.

In an important essay in the *Prussian Yearbook* of 1887 he spoke of the great influence the Celts had exercised upon the peoples of Europe, how in the first centuries B.C. they transmitted to the Teutonic race the Mediterranean culture, how during the Middle Ages they were the only nation which preserved the treasures of classical civilisation and handed them over to the Teutonic and Romance nations.

Zimmer glorified the Celt. He supported Douglas Hyde in his battle for the inclusion of Irish in the Intermediate Education programme and laid stress on the educational value of the language. A disastrous fire in 1903 destroyed his valuable Celtic library, but it was all but completely restored through the munificence of institutions of learning throughout the world and of friends who admired his work.[6] But it damaged his health which was already weakened by a serious nervous malady, which he fought against but eventually without success. His end was tragic. He thought his malady incurable, and bade farewell to life by drowning himself. In his last great essay dealing with the fortunes of the Irish language in the 19th century and the forces which militated against it he uttered a grim warning:

> ... if it be not found even possible to induce the still Irish-speaking counties of Western and Southern Ireland to lay aside the feeling of being ashamed of their Irish speech, and also to stem the tide of emigration which year by year tends to depopulate more and more these counties especially, then all the attempts made in Eastern Ireland to galvanise it will not be able to hinder the Keltic idiom of Ireland from, in the course of the present century, vanishing from the number of living languages.[7]

It is sad and strange that in Ireland, which he served so well, his reputation is muted and he has never received the recognition which he deserves. At the instance of Kuno Meyer, Frau Zimmer kept his great library intact until an offer to purchase it came from the recently founded University College of Dublin. Eoin MacNeill went to Berlin to finalise the purchase and for the modest sum of £750 the entire collection became the property of the University, where it was housed in the Zimmer Library. We might well say that it was an important purchase. Many distinguished Celtic graduates pursued their degree studies in that library. Zimmer left two sons, one of whom planned a career in philology, but his mother forbade him to touch Celtic. It is hard to blame her. The intense controversies in which her husband continually engaged, the industry which would keep him working into the small hours, denying himself a fair chance of health, the attendant anxieties, these were things which must have caused her no little suffering.

At the beginning of the 20th century Kuno Meyer was able to say that:

> ... at no time have Celtic studies been in a more flourishing condition than they are at the present moment. The number of students, both native and foreign, has for several years been rapidly and constantly increasing. ... Students of Aryan philology are finding out that a knowledge of the Celtic languages is to them as important as that of the other great branches of the Indo-European family. The public at large is at last beginning to realise that ... there is here a vast field of research waiting for workers, that for the history of mediaeval literature, for the history of these islands, for the history of early western Christianity – that literature is of the utmost value and importance, that indeed such histories cannot be written until all the materials that this literature furnishes, are before them in critical editions.[8]

As these words were being written by Meyer, German scholars active in the domain of Celtic studies included, besides Meyer himself, Rudolf Thurneysen, Heinrich Zimmer, Ernst Windisch, Ludwig Christian Stern in the Royal Library of Berlin, whose edition of the *Midnight Court* is the best known of a significant body of work from his hand, and Alfred Holder, also a librarian, who spent his holidays and midnight oil working at his immense corpus *Altkeltischer Sprachschatz*, old Celtic expressions and placenames garnered throughout Europe and culled from the classical languages.

Since Celtic civilisation is part of the early historical experience of

France, it might be said that France was favourable and fruitful ground for Celtic studies. There the chieftain Vercingétorix, who rallied the Celtic nation to challenge the might of Julius Caesar at Alesia in 52 B.C., is regarded as a national hero and has merited a major biography by Camille Jullian and, more recently, a study by the distinguished Celtist Jean Markale. Vercingétorix was the Hugh O'Neill of his time. In our time he was a hero of Charles de Gaulle.

France provided the first important journal devoted entirely to Celtic studies, the *Revue Celtique*, founded in 1870 by Henri Gaidoz, which may be described as one of the learned branches that grew out of the *Grammatica Celtica*. It continued in existence until 1934 and its contributors included all the great scholars of Celtic learning from different countries of Europe. After 1934 it was continued as *Études Celtiques* which still flourishes.

Two Celtic scholars of France, in particular, are associated with *Revue Celtique*, namely Marie-Henri d'Arbois de Jubainville and Joseph Loth. These two scholars were the authors of the impressive *Cours de Littérature Celtique*, a twelve volume survey of all aspects of Celtic civilisation, mythology, literature, metrics and law, one volume of which has been translated by Richard Irvine Best and published in 1903 under the title *The Irish Mythological Cycle* and had a wide influence. I have seen a copy of it bearing the owner-signature of AE, George Russell, from whose work it is fair to suppose that he studied it well.

D'Arbois, born in Nancy in 1827, in the beginning studied law, but was drawn by preference towards historical research. Preoccupied with the origins of the French nation, he soon became convinced that early French history could only be clarified through a knowledge of the Celtic tongues. He devoted himself especially to Irish and in the course of assembling the pioneer bibliography of Irish literature, the impressive *Essai d'un Catalogue de la Littérature Épique de l'Irlande* (Paris 1883, reprint Nieuwkoop 1969) he visited Dublin where he made the acquaintance of William Maunsell Hennessy whose help he gratefully acknowledges. Historian rather than linguist, language for him was never more than the auxiliary of history. His forthright support for the Irish language movement has been chronicled by M. Barry O'Delany in *Bean na hÉireann*.

Joseph Loth (1847-1934) in the course of a long and fruitful life devoted himself to the better connaissance of the origins and development of Breton, of which he was a native speaker, and of the Breton people. Because of the affinity of Brittany and Wales he devoted himself also to Cornish but most of all to Welsh. His translation of the Mabinogion tales forms a milestone in Welsh scholarship and his three volume study of Welsh metrics is indispensable.

Joseph Vendryes compiled an etymological lexicon of Old Irish which has been published under the imprint of the Dublin School of Celtic Studies, while his student and protégée, the brilliant and tragic Marie-Louise Sjoestedt, has produced the only scientific survey of the language of Dunquin and the Blaskets. She has written a striking and lyrical description of life in the Blasket Island where she lived for some time in the twenties. Her name is legendary in West Kerry, where she made for herself a home from home and formed a romantic companionship with the no less legendary dictionary-maker Seán Óg Kavanagh. Celtic studies in France are now concentrated in the University of Rennes, while the learned periodical *Études Celtiques* continues to print valuable material as well as supplying a biographical record of Celtic scholars, on the example of its predecessor *Revue Celtique*.

In the scholarship, lexicography and literature of the Breton language the name of Roparz Hemon of Brest (1900-1978) stands out for enterprise, volume and quality. When official ostracism forced him out of Brittany he found refuge in Ireland where much of his learned work was performed under the banner of the Dublin School of Celtic Studies. A youthful name in Irish-Breton scholarship is Éamon Ó Ciosáin, who taught Irish in Rennes University, published collections of modern Irish poetry with Breton and French translations and corrected and completed and saw through the press the Irish-Breton Dictionary, published 1987, of the scholarly sea-captain Loeiz Andouard (1904-1985).

The achievement of Italian Celtic scholars is impressive. Foremost place goes to Graziadio Isaia Ascoli (1829-1907) for his editions of the Irish codices held in the Ambrosian Library of Milan.

Ascoli was 'The greatest philologist of Italy and perhaps of the world' as claimed in his necrology in *Marzocco* 7 February 1907, in patriotically Italian terms, and not unjustifiably, because his profile in scholarship is immense. His scientific career falls into two periods, his early attention being occupied by such diverse fields as Indo-European, Semitic, Turkish, Chinese and Dravidian, in which he was the author of many Oriental studies. From the end of 1870 he turned his attention to Neo-Latin and Celtic and may be numbered amongst the linguists who received their inspiration from Zeuss. His studies in Celtic are published in the *Archivio glottologico italiano*, volumes V and VI, under the title of *Il Codice irlandese dell' Ambrosiana*, the second volume of which (published Rome, Turin and Florence 1891, and containing the *Glossarium Palaeo-hibernicum* with meanings in Latin), is dedicated to Whitley Stokes *come tardo tributa di una gratitudine antica*.

Almost coaeval with Ascoli was Constantino Nigra (1828-1907), diplomat, associate of Cavour, philologist, personal friend of Napoleon III and of the Castlegregory-born scholar William Maunsell Hennessy. Under Ascoli's influence he became interested in Celtic studies to which he contributed *Reliquie Celtiche* and other researches.

Kuno Meyer, born into a learned family in Hamburg in 1858, came into contact with Scottish Gaelic on the Isle of Arran, off the coast of Scotland and wondered at the strange tongue, about which he made further enquiries. He had come to Scotland as a schoolboy of 15 to help a blind German scholar in Edinburgh and remained two years in the course of which he gained a perfect command of English. On returning to Germany he completed his secondary education in Hamburg. His elder brother Eduard was employed in Leipzig University as lecturer, and Kuno joined him there, taking the opportunity to study Celtic under Ernst Windisch. His other studies included German philology and comparative grammar but Celtic Studies called for his special zeal and he took out his doctorate with an edition of an Irish text of the Alexander legend published in 1884. Just then a vacancy for a Reader in German occurred in Liverpool and for this he applied with success, being appointed in 1884.

Liverpool was a good vantage point from which to observe how matters stood with regard to Celtic, especially Irish. He saw that the situation was far from satisfactory. He had many opportunities of crossing over to Ireland, where he took a critical view of the state of affairs regarding the language.

A controversy about Irish gave him the opportunity of making his views public. He pointed out that, apart from the *Gaelic Journal*, founded 1882, there were no prints or periodicals to cater for the modern spoken tongue. Handbooks and grammars were few and scarce. There was no satisfactory dictionary to serve the spoken language, nor was there any to represent the earlier phases of the language. 'Now' asked Meyer, 'who is called on to do this work? Surely, those who alone can do it, and from whom for many decades it has been expected', namely Irish scholars themselves. It was likewise the duty of Irishmen to accomplish the editing and translating of their great and unique mediaeval literature, a task which they had long ago completely handed over to foreigners. Surely, he argued, if Irish nationality has any vitality at all, it cannot be indifferent to its own undisputed heritage.

Rudolf Thomas Siegfried had put forward the same view thirty years earlier, when he said: 'We hope they do not mean to leave all to be done by the Germans.' Whitley Stokes once taunted the native Irish scholars by saying that two German professors had, within the last thirty-five years, done more for the knowledge of Irish than all the native scholars that had ever lived. He referred scathingly to 'Celtic with its forged words, inaccurate texts, deceptive facsimiles, unfaithful translations, and (at least in the case of Irish), ignorant and reckless native scholars'.

The School of Irish Learning was Meyer's outstanding contribution to Ireland. Its objects were, in the first place, to train students in the scientific study of the Irish language, and in reading and interpreting Irish manuscripts. Its final aim was, with the help of students so trained, to investigate the history of the Irish language from the earliest times to the present day, and to open up, by means of texts and translations, the rich treasures of Irish literature, which were gathering dust in various libraries. He took advantage of the groundswell support for the Gaelic League as the milieu for his project. He set out the programme of instruction.

> The subjects taught should embrace in the first place Old and Middle and Modern Irish, both language and literature, grammar as well as reading and critical interpretation of texts, palaeographical studies, i.e., learning to read and classify MSS., then classes for the study of history and archaeology.

A well-furnished working library was essential, which should have all handbooks, editions and periodicals bearing on the studies. Teaching was to be mainly in the form of practical classes. Meyer had no use for examinations. Master and pupil were to work together from the raw materials, that is to say, the manuscripts. The true bond between teacher and student was to advance together in the cultivation of knowledge. He designed the motto of the School as: increase of scholarship, advance of knowledge and learning, for the benefit of mankind, for the Glory of God.

With his colleague teacher John Strachan he founded *Ériu*, a periodical in connection with the School devoted to Irish learning and research. This was the first journal in Ireland devoted to the scientific investigation of the Irish language.

Meyer's method in organising the School is worthy of attention. In it he introduced to Ireland and Irish studies the concept of *Altertumswissenschaft*, 'The Science of Antiquity', that is to say the study of everything connected with ancient Ireland, language, poetry, law, metrics, religion, manuscript study, palaeography, archaeology and history, in order to form a unified and full perspective of the past. Without this all-embracing investigation, he argued, the true history of Ireland could not be written. It was a distinctly German concept, and one which took centuries to develop. It made for thoroughness. Its application to Irish studies may be seen in the plan which Meyer elaborated for the School of Irish Learning. It may also be seen in the design which he proposed for the department of Celtic Studies in the new National University.

The National University, he said, should have on its staff men capable of teaching all the Celtic tongues, Irish, Welsh, Breton and Scottish Gaelic and all kindred subjects; there should be a Professor of Comparative Philology and Professors of the chief branches of the Indo-European family of languages. A thorough phonetic training was indispensable. Palaeography should be catered for; to determine the exact period of the origin of letters in Ireland, and with it the introduction of learning into Ireland, to determine the age and home of our oldest and, indeed, various schools of writing MSS – these are tasks that can only be undertaken by a skilled palaeographer.

The School was a phenomenal success, from its inception in 1903 until the outbreak of the first Great War in 1914. As its secretary recorded: 'Just as in the seventh century students flocked to Ireland from all parts in pursuit of knowledge, so they came from England, Scotland, Wales, the Continent, and America, year after year to obtain in the School that instruction which was not to be held elsewhere.'

Meyer was an evangelist for the Irish language. He was an inspired teacher. He proclaimed the importance of Irish, its language and literature; he claimed for it equality in status to the classical languages; it was the avenue of knowledge to much of the civilization of Western Europe; it was the repository of some of the finest things in literature. He used himself unsparingly in its promotion: A witness to his commitment has described his 'in and out of trams in the dripping tempests' on his devoted way to lectures and classes, his patience and fortitude, how he was alone in believing a Dublin School could be formed, how he rode down all doubts and criticism and carried through his work triumphantly.

The work of compiling an Irish dictionary was envisaged by Siegfried in a memorandum as a 'full interpretation, critical and historical, of every word of the language in which the past of the country speaks to us, in which the annals, the laws, the poetry, the records of religion and family life are present, and the echo of which will sound for ages to come in the names of places and persons'. This memorandum dates from about 1859. After many disappointments, the work of producing such a dictionary was laid on Kuno Meyer in 1907, to be performed under the auspices of the Royal Irish Academy. Too busy himself to take a personal hand in it, the task of producing the first fascicule fell on Carl Marstrander of Norway, but unfortunately a time limit was imposed on him in order to qualify for a bequest of £1000, the gift of Rev. Maxwell Henry Close.

This first fascicule which appeared in 1913 was severely criticised by Meyer, who considered it too elaborate and detailed for the needs of the day. Marstrander's vision of an Irish dictionary differed from Meyer's. Meyer would have the entries and examples on a more modest scale on the example of his own *Contributions*. He did not think Irish scholarship had yet reached a standard to merit such exhaustive detail. Marstrander considered that it should be all-embracing and comprehensive, with numerous sources, examples and citations, something on the model of Du Cange's *Glossarium mediae et infimae Latinitatis* or Forcellini's *Totius Latinitatis lexicon*. In the unfortunate exchanges which followed, Marstrander's promising services were lost to Ireland as he went back to Norway.

Rudolf Thurneysen (1857-1940) was a native of Switzerland who easily integrated into the German university system, sharing a common language. He is best known to students for his very detailed *Grammar of Old Irish* which incorporates all the revisions made since the time of Zeuss, and is a standard university textbook. He was an authority on Early Irish Law. His major work on the Irish Hero Tales and King-Legends is acknowledged to be the best in the field, and we can say 'well done' to find it recorded on the title page: *Foillsigheadh an Leabhar so de bharr cabhrach ó Aireacht na Gaedhilge fé Shaorstát Éireann.* When the news of his death in July 1940 reached Ireland while the Second World War was raging, a leading national daily devoted its editorial essay to him under the single word 'Thurneysen', so respected had his name become. Part of it reads:

> Through such scholars as Thurneysen Irish has been given its place on the Continent as one of the great formative languages of European civilisation. His death robs international scholarship of an outstanding figure, but he had reached the fullness of years, and it is a comforting thing to know that to the last his genius was active, and death found him engaged in his work. The National University of Ireland honoured him fifteen years ago, but his books setting forth the importance of our language – the still living language of our people – and the dignity of our nation will be the permanent memorial to his greatness and our gratitude.[9]

In what were the worst of times, few were spared distress, the great scholar's wife being no exception, as a letter from Julius Pokorny to a correspondent shows:

> It may interest you to hear, that Mrs. Thurneysen has, after

unbelievable hardships, succeeded in coming to Switzerland, where she is being well cared for by her Swiss relatives. She had walked on foot the whole long way from Bavaria to Bonn, where she arrived almost as a skeleton, and had partly been mentally disturbed. But I am told, she has quite recovered in the meantime.

Anton Gerard Van Hamel (1886-1945) made a significant contribution to Celtic learning in the Netherlands, as author of many important studies and teacher-trainer of some outstanding students. His was evidently a sunny and sympathetic nature, who enjoyed music and became in his own words 'a famous fiddler'. Besides Celtic he was a scholar in Icelandic, and his learned productions are numerous. A letter to his friend Richard Best speaks for itself:

My dear Best – I have not forgotten you, but an unimportant cause was indispensable to induce me to resume a correspondence, which had been dropped for such a long time. What brought back to me, like a flash of lightning, the memory of those dear old days spent either at Dublin or Ballyferriter, was the reading of George Moore's preface to his 'Spring Days', which has just appeared in the Tauchnitz edition. There I found back, like a treasure lost for a long time, whose splendour strikes us even more than when we beheld it almost every day, your name and your wife's name. The thing you said to the novelist was so very much like you, and the respect Moore shows to your wife is so well-deserved, that I can no longer refrain from telling you something about myself, expecting to hear from you, too, ere long. I am really very sorry I have not been able to come over to Ireland for all these years; I am longing for the *seanbhean bhocht*, who will turn a beautiful young girl in the nearest future. I think there will not pass an equal amount of time as there has already passed since my last visit, before you see me back. I am returning to my smouldering Celtic sympathies. I am going to spend on them, for five months, all my time and, in fact, all my money. I got a post at Rotterdam, where I must be in September, and I leave my present situation at Middelburg in April; in the interval I shall be quite resourceless and forced to live on my poor savings, but the great advantage is that I am going to spend all that time at Berlin in an edition of *Leabhar Gabála*, of which text Kuno possesses enough to send me, and which, accordingly, I have been copying these last months. At Berlin I shall be able to speak with him about the difficulties, to compare other recensions, to make a theory of the relation between the MSS, and, perhaps, to suggest a hypothesis on the origin of the occupation-tales. All this is highly attractive and I am sure I shall have a grand time, when Celtic, once more, will be everything to me. I never hate my practical daily work, but it necessarily bars in a certain degree the purer domains of knowledge and research. You will easily understand how glad I am to make a short trip to them, and the more because it will involve a trip to that other earthly paradise: Ireland. Now you know the most important things about me. Another thing that may be of some interest to your wife is that I am ever making progressions – *ag dul a bhfeabhas* – on the fiddle. I practise daily, and so my technical faculties have greatly improved. How delighted shall I be to play at Percy Place once more! When I think over the many good things I had and have still in the world, life sometimes even seems beautiful to me: science, art and a few good friends – even far away in the Western World – is all a man may want, at least a sworn bachelor, as I am growing more and more. With my best greetings to you and to Mrs. Best, your as always A.G. Van Hamel.

One of Van Hamel's more distinguished students was Maartje Draak (1907-1995). Her numerous Celtic writings include *De reis van Sinte Brandaan*, a scholarly edition of the Middle Dutch version of the *Voyage of St. Brendan* and, jointly with her fellow Celtic scholar Frida de Jong, translations into Dutch of the earliest Irish stories, *Van helden, elfen en dichters*. The interest in Celtic studies in the Netherlands is on the increase. In 1988 Maartje Draak was honoured in a symposion in the Royal Netherlands Academy of Arts and Sciences to mark her 80th birthday while in 1991 the A.G. Van Hamel Foundation for Celtic Studies was established in Utrecht for the promotion of Celtic studies in the Netherlands. *Celtic Studies in the Netherlands: a bibliography* assembled by Marc Schneiders and Kees Veelenturf (1992) is a revelation as to the extent and importance of the labours in this field of Netherlands scholars.

Students may remember Osborn Bergin's lovely poem, *Wanderlust*, which begins:

Mhuise caithimís i dtráth uainn
Pokárny 'gus Brúgmann

and introduces us to one of the great individualists of Celtic learning. Julius Pokorny, whose life span was 1887-1970, was a native of Prague in Bohemia, which until the end of the First World War was part of the Austro-Hungarian Empire. In Vienna he studied law, philosophy and comparative philology, receiving a Doctorate in Philosophy for his thesis on an early Irish text. By 1914 he had been made lecturer in Celtic philology. Prior to that he learned spoken Irish in Dunquin, Ring and Tourmakeady and had for one of his mentors the lexicographer Seán Óg Kavanagh, whose society he must have enjoyed, sharing as they did a Bohemian approach to life, while at the same time profiting from Seán Óg's incomparable stock of phrase and idiom. As a young man the free and easy atmosphere of Vienna suited his artistic and romantic cast of mind. He committed himself absolutely to Irish nationality. Students of the Irish language will appreciate him for his vigorous support for the campaign for essential Irish in the National University. 'Pokorny is on the warpath again' remarked Richard Best. The reference was to his celebrated appeal, written from Vienna, printed in *An Claidheamh Soluis*, entitled: 'Open letter to every patriotic Irishman, and especially to the priesthood of Ireland'. (See Appendix 1)

It was designed especially to counter the argument that the Irish language requirement would discourage foreign students from attending the National University. It is tempting to quote from it. Here is one paragraph to indicate its spirit:

> People of Ireland!
> The twentieth century is the century of the nations, the century of artistic and national individuality. The Hungarian people, the Slavonic nations, peoples that have no great past, no great literature, peoples that are much inferior in culture to the Teutonic or Celtic races have attained national independence as to their language and education. ... And you, with your great past, with your fascinating literature, should allow your nationality to be killed? Arise at last from your long sleep, and remember that 'the people that cannot fight will die'.

He gave the Irish cause valuable publicity and support in Europe. In his *History of Ireland*, first published in Germany in 1916 under the simple title *Irland*, he takes the stand from which the Irish people traditionally view their history. In the Introduction he states that 'he has seen the traces of Ireland's vanished splendour and greatness, and lived with her people in their present wretchedness, and he is full of sympathy for this noble but unhappy nation'. An English language edition of this History was published in Dublin in 1933. He promoted Ireland's cause in bringing to the knowledge of European readers the poems and stories of Patrick Pearse and his colleagues in *Die Seele Irlands* (1922) and made a striking translation of early Irish lyrics – *Die älteste Lyrik der grünen Insel* (1923).

In the impressive volume of essays dedicated to him for his 80th birthday in June 1967, the editor Wolfgang Meid calls him one of the greatest names in Celtology, the last survivor in the proud succession of German celtologists reaching from Zeuss, through Windisch, Zimmer, Meyer and Thurneysen up to Pokorny himself. The volume, published in Innsbruck, was made up of contributions from colleagues, friends and students of his own. Appreciation of his work, and his scholarly repute, stand high in Europe. One hopes his name will be established in Irish classrooms every time Osborn Bergin's lovely poem is read.

Danish scholars have made important contributions. Christoph Sarauw's *Irske Studier* (1900) was a pioneer work. Holger Pedersen's *Vergleichende Grammatik der keltischen Sprachen*, a magisterial opus in two immense volumes (1908-1911) was reviewed in terms of high praise by Joseph Vendryes in *Revue Celtique* Nos 30, 31 and 32. For wealth of detail this work was so formidable that an abridgement of it in English (by Lewis and Pedersen, 1937) was found necessary 'to serve as a sort of preparation for it, giving in condensed form as much of the material in the greater work as seems to suffice for university courses in the Celtic countries'.

Pedersen's versatility was phenomenal. Along with being a master in the field of Celtic philology, he was the author of valuable studies in the Slavic, Albanian and Armenian languages. But his fame rests on the Comparative Grammar of the Celtic Languages, an achievement of the first order, dedicated to the two great names of Zimmer and Stokes. Pedersen was preceded in the linguistic field by his eminent countryman Rasmus Rask (1787-1832).

A place of honour amongst European scholars who contributed to Irish studies must readily be accorded to Ludwig Bieler of Vienna. Although not a Celtic scholar his interests were not unrelated to the Celtic milieu. In his special field of Mediaeval Latin he is a worthy successor to Ludwig Traube with whose work he was familiar. Although he made the life and labours of St. Patrick a special interest his wide learning took in many prospects. As a classical scholar his *History of Roman Literature* (1966) is a fresh and stimulating approach, bringing clarity and judgement to a subject which time and time again has been worked over by scholars of too serious vein. It is a translation, with improvements, from the German original (1961). Widely appreciated, a modern Greek version was published in Athens (1965) with the author's German and Greek foreword signed at Dublin 10 August 1965.

Bieler came to live in Dublin, bringing distinction to the city's scholarly milieu with his unique breadth of culture and learning.

His *Codices Patriciani Latini* (Dublin 1942) subtitled *A descriptive catalogue of Latin manuscripts relating to St. Patrick*, though dealing with the state of research anterior to the historic date of 1 September 1939, is an invaluable working index for Patrician students. To the *Scriptores Latini Hiberniae* series he contributed editions of *Four Latin Lives* of St. Patrick (1971) and *The Patrician Texts in the Book of Armagh* (1979). *The life and legend of St. Patrick* (1949), rich in learning, and written in English, a language not his own as he explains, is an intellectual pleasure, while *Ireland, a Harbinger of the Middle Ages* (1963), translated by the author from the German, is a classic and finely illustrated survey of mediaeval Irish Christianity and its seminal influence on Europe. Ludwig Bieler's contributions to knowledge are printed in many learned journals throughout the world.[10]

The vision of Kuno Meyer, that the scholarly study of Irish literature should be centred in Ireland, was confirmed by the Irish government in giving effect to the Institute of Advanced Studies Act in 1940, which included provision for a School of Celtic Studies with functions and duties corresponding to those of the original School. It was an enlightened piece of legislation, totally in harmony with Irish tradition.

In the course of its 52 years the School has done invaluable work. To take just one example, it has published the full corpus of early Irish law, comprising over 2000 pages, edited by Dr. D.A. Binchy. It is with a sense of unbelief that we read, in its 50th anniversary report, that its abolition was being considered in 1987 by the government. That an Irish government should even dream of abolishing a School, the genesis of which goes back to 1903 and which was founded to establish for Ireland its autonomy and self-reliance in its native literature, is surely incomprehensible. Let us fervently hope that this execrable notion is despatched forever to oblivion.

After the 1914-18 war the interest of continental Europe in Celtic studies was contracting. The Celtic Chair in Berlin continued in existence but with the escape of Pokorny into Switzerland it lapsed and is now extinct. Interest in Celtic studies in Germany centres in Bonn, where Dr. Karl Horst Schmidt edits the *Zeitschrift*, which is now up to Vol. 50, with the cooperation of Rolf Ködderitzsch, Patrizia de Bernardo Stempel and Herbert Pilch.[11] In Bonn there is the very important and active German-Irish Society which provides a platform for a wide variety of Irish-interest studies. Elsewhere in Germany there is a lively interest in Celtic studies in Würzburg.

In France, Rennes, the capital of Brittany, is the centre of Celtic studies. There are many important periodicals catering for Celtic learning. When George Thomson went to Cambridge with the intention of taking up Irish studies, he found he might do Swahili, which was important for Empire administration, but not Irish, which was not.

Things change. For the last ten years Cambridge has been publishing the *Cambridge Mediaeval Celtic Studies*, which caters to a high standard for all the Celtic countries. It continues under the title *Cambrian Mediaeval Celtic Studies*.[12]

In recent years, one of the most prolific writers on Celtic themes has been Jean Markale. Born in Paris in 1928, the son of Breton émigrés, 'at once a Breton and of Irish descent', he proudly avows his character as a Celt, claiming that it has its origins deep in his conscience. All his life he has spent interpreting the Celtic presence and psyche in the fabric of European history. A long list of writings carries his name. The range of his work includes practically every facet of Celtic interest. Among his studies are *Les Celtes et la civilisation celtique, mythe et histoire* (Paris 1969 and 1975), *La Femme celte, L'Épopée celtique d'Irlande* and *Histoire secrète de la Bretagne*. The first two of these have been translated into English. In his autobiographical *Mémoires d'un Celte* (Paris 1992) he discusses the convictions, influences and interior experiences that shaped his celticism. His portrait on the cover is a delineation of character and vision, denoting a mind of deep and reposeful strength.

With the accession of Ireland to the European Union in 1972, the Irish language, in its translation of the European Treaties, became integrated into the society of the other great languages of the European Community. The team of Irish translators, who laboured early and late at the Irish version, took justifiable pride in the capacity of their tongue to render into comparable style and accuracy the protocols and framework of the emerging Europe.

At an important Conference on Irish-German Connections held in the University of Limerick on 4-6 September 1997 an extensive series of lectures included one on 'The Present State of Celtic Studies in the German-speaking Countries'. The lecturer was Dr. Hildegard L. C. Tristram of Freiburg and Potsdam. A wide-ranging project is envisaged to monitor and promote Celtic Studies in the German-speaking countries, which include Austria and Switzerland. A Centre for the Study of the Celtic Languages and Cultures was founded on 4 April 1997 with headquarters in an imposing 18th century house, 'Im Rebstock', Haupstrasse 449, Königswinter, near Bonn. The main purpose of the Centre is 'to supply information on and documentation of the Celtic languages and cultures, accessible on the Continent' and Dr. Tristram's paper went into extensive detail on what it is planned to include in the field of Celtic Studies. In the light of this, the prospect is promising for the future of Celtic Studies in Germany.

References
1.   *Transactions of the Philosophical Society 1867,* 305.

2. Amongst these may be mentioned Gerhard Schlesinger: *Johann Kaspar Zeuss, ein blick auf Leben, Werk und Nachlass des Gelehrten*, Kronach 1964. The author gained his Abitur in 1966 from the Kaspar-Zeuss-Oberrealschule in Kronach. Dr. Hans Hablitzel; *Prof. Dr Johann Kaspar Zeuss 1806-1856.* Kronach 1987, a valuable source book on Zeuss. *Erlanger Gedenkfeier für Johann Kaspar Zeuss*, herausgegeben von Bernhard Forssman. Erlangen 1989. Contains a number of valuable studies of Zeuss and his work.

3. *Zeitschrift für celtische Philologie* Vol. VI (1907-8), 225.

4. *The history of Rome*, Vol. IV (Everyman ed. 1921) 268-9.

5. C.P. Curran: *Under the receding wave* (Dublin 1970) gives an interesting account of Sigerson, whom he states (p.88) to have been a friend of Mommsen.

6. The Council of the Irish Texts Society agreed to send him a complete set of its publications. *Irish Texts Society. The first hundred years.* Ed. Pádraig Ó Riain. 1998. p. 80.

7. ... gelingt es aber nicht in kurzer Zeit, der noch Irisch redenden Bevölkerung in den westlichen und südlichen Küstengrafschaften die Scham vor der irischen Sprache zu nehmen und den Strom des Auswanderung, der besonders jene Grafschaften von Jahr zu Jahr weiter entvölkert, zum Stehen zu bringen, dann werden alle Galvanisierungsversuche im Osten von Irland nicht verhindern können, dass noch im Laufe dieses Jahrhunderts das keltische Idiom Irlands aus der Reihe der lebenden Sprachen schwindet. – Heinrich Zimmer: Sprache und Literatur der Kelten im Allgemeinen p.23 in *Die Kultur der Gegenwart* herausgegeben von Paul Hinneberg, Teil I Abteilung XI, I Berlin und Leipzig 1909. Translation in *Freeman's Journal* (Dublin) 10 April 1909.

8. *The Gael* (New York) October 1902. Lecture given at the Celtic Congress in Dublin.

9. *The Irish Press* (Dublin) 15 August 1940.

10. Cf. John J. O'Meara and Bernd Naumann eds: *Latin script and letters A.D. 400-900. Festschrift presented to Ludwig Bieler on the occasion of his 70th birthday.* Leiden 1976. The bibliography, pp 1-18, indicates the wide range of his learning.

9a. The most recent issue of the *ZCP* (Tübingen 1997) is the massive double volume 49-50 in celebration of its 100th year of publication, an event which, taken with other developments, appears to presage a renaissance in European Celtic Studies.

10. *Cambridge Mediaeval Celtic Studies* was first published in 1981. From Winter 1993 (No 26) it appears under the title *Cambrian Mediaeval Celtic Studies* and is published by the University of Wales, Aberystwyth. Edited by Patrick Sims-Williams.

The above is the substance of a lecture given in Dingle to the Kerry Archaeological and Historical Society on 11 March 1993.

Chapter 3

William Maunsell Hennessy

I

The most accomplished Irish scholar

One of the treasures of the National Library of Ireland is an interleaved first edition, two volumes, of Zeuss's celebrated *Grammatica Celtica*, published by Weidmann of Leipzig in 1853, in the front end page of which are inscribed details of its succession of ownership as follows:

> C. Lottner
> post Rudolphi Siegfriedi
> mortem acquisivit anno 1863

> This copy of Zeuss's *Grammatica Celtica* belonged to the late Rudolph Siegfried, of Trinity College, Dublin, and after him to the late Carl Lottner, his successor, after whose death it came into my possession.
> W.M. Hennessy

> The notes are all, or nearly all, in Siegfried's handwriting.
> W.M.H.
> Succession in proprietorship.
> Rudolph Siegfried, Professor, T.C.D.
> Carl Lottner, Professor T.C.D.
> William Maunsell Hennessy.
> William Reeves, D.D. Bishop of Down, President of the Roy.
> Ir. Academy,
> Who purchased the book at poor Hennessy's sale, 1890.
> Hennessy was the most accomplished Irish scholar of his day.

What an interesting lineage of scholarship. Rudolf Thomas Siegfried, a native of Dessau in Germany, is an important, if shadowy, figure in the history of Celtic studies, and a personal link with Zeuss whom he visited in 1856. Invited over from Wales to Trinity College Dublin by James Henthorn Todd he worked in TCD Library before becoming

Professor of Sanskrit. Whitley Stokes studied philology under his guidance and both are stated by Kuno Meyer to have been the only two people in Ireland to master the *Grammatica Celtica*. While this may be true, it must be qualified in our present study by the knowledge that Hennessy shows familiarity with it, for which one may cite his essays on the Ossianic controversy printed in the *Academy*. Siegfried's death in his early thirties cut short a life that offered much promise for the future of Celtic studies. He was succeeded by Carl Friedrich Lottner, philologist and friend of Hennessy's with whom he shared common interests. William Reeves is best known, perhaps, for his impressive edition of the *Life of Saint Columba* by Adamnan but there is so much more excellent work to his credit that his name is deservedly held in respect. That is why his estimate of William Maunsell Hennessy as the most accomplished Irish scholar of his day must be taken seriously.

William Maunsell Hennessy was born in Castlegregory in 1829, this being the date normally assigned to his birth, although two sources at least give it as 1828. He was educated at private schools and passed his early youth with his uncle Dr. Finn. That his education was an excellent one is borne out by the achievements of his later career. It was probably largely classical in content, as education in those times tended to be, but the familiarity with German and French which his later scholarly pursuits indicate suggests that instruction in these also formed part of his early education. His schooling completed, he emigrated to America where he lived for some years. On his return he became a journalist and was one of the writers of the revived *Nation* from 1853 to 1856. In 1856 he obtained a position in the Lunatic Asylums office by public competition. His favourite pursuit from an early age was Irish literature. The language was his mother tongue and he improved his knowledge of it by assiduous study of the manuscripts in which it was written. He often wrote his transcripts from Irish manuscripts in the Roman character, but his handwriting in the characteristic Irish script was beautifully clear, and has been said to resemble that of the famous Irish genealogist Dubhaltach Mac Firbhisigh.

Hennessy was well known and esteemed in his native county,[1] in the topography and antiquities of which he was deeply interested and versed. His correspondent Mary Agnes Hickson, author of *Old Kerry Records*, quotes Hennessy's suggestion regarding the Irish name of Dingle, this being given usually as Daingean Uí Chúis with the inference that Uí Chúis represented a personal name. Hennessy thought it was wholly a place-name, and Miss Hickson gives the versions *Daingean na Cuas* or *Daingean Cuas*, that is, the fortress of the cove, as being his.[2] So exact an Irish scholar as Hennessy, a native

Irish speaker of the district, would be unlikely to propose either of the foregoing versions, but he might very well have suggested *Daingean a' Chuais*, which would be plausible. In her interesting discussion on the names of Smerwick and Ard na Caithne, she imagines that Hennessy, who confirmed Ard na Caithne as correct, 'must have constantly heard the Irish speaking people of Smerwick repeat its old Irish name long before Dr. Joyce wrote his valuable works'.[3]

At a time when a visit of the Society of Antiquaries to Kerry was being envisaged Hennessy wrote to her

> ... You should suggest to the antiquaries to visit Killagh, near Milltown, and Kilmacidae, beyond Ballyheigue. If Colonel Crosbie were at home he might be able to show them the caved raths there, especially the one I visited near Kerry Head five years ago. They astonished me, and I wish some competent person would examine them fully.[4]

Hennessy's interest in Irish topography and antiquities is attested by his library which included all the authoritative studies in the subject, and his mind was richly stocked in consequence of his wide reading and personal investigations. In an assessment of Hennessy, one writer has stated that he was specially familiar with the early history and geography of Ireland. 'His knowledge was, unfortunately, not worked up permanently into a connected whole, such as would adequately represent his learning; Celtic scholars would have been grateful indeed for the heritage of an Irish Encyclopaedia of archaeology and geography, such as perhaps he alone could have written. But though no monumental work remains, enough is left to show clearly the range and accuracy of his scholarship.'[5] James F. Kenney calls Hennessy 'a not unworthy follower of O'Donovan in history and topography'.[6]

A significant example of his topographical learning is his essay on the history and antiquities of the Curragh of Kildare which was printed in the Royal Irish Academy *Proceedings*.[7] That he obtained his knowledge of topography and antiquities largely out of his intimate familiarity with Irish manuscript sources is a conclusion we may reasonably come to from his review of James Ferguson's *Rude-Stone monuments in all countries; their age and uses* in the course of which he writes:

> Any one acquainted with the still unpublished materials of Irish history must know that the monuments hitherto discovered do not amount to a tithe of those mentioned in the Irish MSS., under various names, and referred to various ages and persons; and of those hitherto brought under notice, not one-fourth has attracted

his attention ... The author's personal investigation of the Irish monuments, though fruitful and instructive, was really very limited ... He has certainly been industrious in consulting published authorities on the subject of his work; but it is not his fault that the most accurate sources of information are as yet unavailable to all but the few acquainted with the tongue in which they are written. Until these are published, all attempts at deciding the vexed question of the age of these structures must prove futile.[8]

Otherwise he praises Ferguson's book as valuable, interesting, well-written and beautifully illustrated.

II

The Warring World of Celtic Scholarship

'You know', said Ernst Windisch, 'that I take a very great interest in the old Irish language and literature, though my first enthusiasm is cooled down a little by the feuds and personal attacks among the Celtic scholars.'[9]

So well might the quiet and industrious Windisch say so, having suffered a fierce attack from his own pupil Zimmer. The world of scholarship in which Hennessy laboured could be polemical and acerbic when argument was taken up by scholars like Whitley Stokes and Heinrich Zimmer from either of whom kind words came seldom. Stokes, one of the Olympians of Celtic studies in the later decades of the nineteenth century, received his training in Sanskrit and comparative philology from Rudolph Siegfried, a teacher he designated as *anamchara* and to whose memory he dedicated three of his important studies. Choosing the law as a profession Stokes took his degree in London and presently went to India where as President of the Indian Law Commission he carried out the massive task of codifying the Anglo-Indian laws.

In addition to this official work he continued his intense interest in Celtic studies, publishing the results at his own expense, whence it comes about that texts which are vital to the study of the Irish language bear imprints of Calcutta and Simla. But Stokes brought to his studies something besides learning. This was an asperity which became his greatest weakness and was to cost him friendships. He proclaimed his approach to learning by a quotation from Aristophanes, 'yet progress means contention, to my mind,'[10] and the further observation that 'why, the healthy progress of science depends on antagonism: it is by flails of disputation that the truth is threshed out',[11] asseverations which he pursued to the letter, with consequent war of words. In 1875 he published at Calcutta his *Remarks on the Celtic additions to Curtius' Greek Etymology and on the Celtic comparisions in Bopp's Comparative Grammar, with notes on some recent Irish publications*. One might be forgiven for supposing, on a look at the title, that here was a sophisticated excursus on some classical arcana, in the politest tradition of the humanities. Not so. It was, amongst other things, a resounding denunciation of '… Celtic, with its forged words, inaccurate texts, deceptive facsimiles, unfaithful translations, and (at least in the case of Irish) ignorant and reckless native scholars'.[12] These are hard words, commented Stokes. 'I do not of course refer to the dead O'Donovan or the living Hennessy, O'Grady or O'Mahony. Of these I can truly say 'Nolo esse laudator, ne videar adulator' (I do not wish to praise, lest I might appear to flatter).[13] His verdict on Edward O'Reilly was devastating: 'On behalf of sound philology, I must protest against the use of O'Reilly's Dictionary for scientific purposes. The book is quite untrustworthy; it swarms with forgeries and blunders; and its only value lies in the extracts which it contains from O'Clery and other old glossarists, whose explanations O'Reilly often misunderstands'.[14] Elsewhere he calls O'Reilly a 'wretched lexicographer'.

Such was the spirit in which he formed his canon of criticism and examples of its application are not wanting. In an exchange with Dr. Bartholomew MacCarthy on the subject of *Celtic Latinity and the Tripartite Life* he concludes by calling his opponent one 'who as an Irish linguist and palaeographer might at present say of himself: "Ce que je sais, je sais mal, ce que j'ignore, j'ignore parfaitement".'[15] Norman Moore tells us that the severity of Stokes's studies sometimes broke down his health, and produced conditions of extreme irritability or depression, which explain the violence of his language.

During the greater part of the nineteenth century the study of the Irish language was being approached from two quarters, on the continent by linguists following the scientific principles of Franz Bopp and Johann Kaspar Zeuss who, excellent though they were, had no knowledge of the modern spoken tongue and whose interest was wholly philological, while in Ireland the language was being studied by native scholars like O'Donovan and O'Curry and following them by W. M. Hennessy, acknowledged by many as their worthy successor in talent and knowledge, Standish Hayes O'Grady, Dr. B. MacCarthy, J. O'Beirne Crowe, all of whom had the advantage of being native speakers of or well versed in modern Irish. The work being done on the continent presented a challenge to Irish scholars and had the beneficial result of promoting critical accuracy. The folklorist Alfred Nutt, hailing the appearance of Zimmer's *Celtische Studien* as marking a new era in Irish philology, hoped that henceforth the 'uncritical slovenliness which has been the curse of Celtic studies' would vanish.[16] In philological controversies one senses that lines of allegiance were being drawn, as it were, between those who approached the study of early and middle Irish through the scientific methods of the continent and those on the other hand who used their native knowledge for the study and interpretation of the older tongue. Whitley Stokes was the advocate of the scientific, continental, method, and considered the contributions of European scholars to be superior, while Standish Hayes O'Grady championed the native scholar.[17] Stokes was a great controversionalist, O'Grady less so but more than anyone's match if it came to argument. Hennessy did not engage in controversy but was hit by ricochets.

Not all continental scholars reciprocated Stokes's goodwill towards them. Heinrich Zimmer, 'the tiger of Greifswald', whose ethic it was to make life miserable for his fellow-celtologues and wrote as was said with one eye on his paper and the other on a rival, whose faculties of scholarship only improved with battle, attacked Stokes and others without ceremony, not sparing his own teacher Windisch. To counter him, R. I. Best once proposed an anti-Zimmer league. In the realms of Celtic learning, perfection was beyond reach. W. M. Lindsay said nothing copied by Zimmer was to be trusted and Meyer, checking through the work of Stokes himself after his death, discovered surprising errors.

A thoughtless reference by Stokes to 'the corrupt dialects of modern Irish',[18] brought a rejoinder from the editor of the *Gaelic Journal*, John Fleming, who delivered his views on scholars of early Irish who despised the modern spoken tongue, and fell into egregious errors through ignorance of it, of whom one of the most pertinent examples was Mr. Stokes himself, whose errors John Fleming proceeded to demonstrate in detail.[19] Stokes declined combat, wisely, for Fleming could be formidable.[20]

His less than just obituarist in the *Athenaeum*[21] remarks that Stokes never learned how to pronounce the Irish language, nor could he read aloud a single sentence with correct accent, nor did he ever show any affection for the great names of Irish literature. Norman Moore tells us he pronounced Irish as a schoolboy would pronounce Latin. He could write Old Irish with facility. Critical though he was of the scholarship of his fellow-countrymen, he was proud of his nationality. Hibernus sum, non Anglus, he reminded Hermann Ebel.

In later years he confessed to Bergin that he deeply regretted not availing of the opportunity to learn modern Irish.

Standish O'Grady, friend of his youth, became estranged from Stokes because of the latter's harsh criticism of Joseph O'Longan. Facsimiles of Irish codices had been made from O'Longan's transcripts which Stokes denounced as untrustworthy. Facsimiles of actual codicès made later proved Stokes to be wrong and O'Longan, who had in the meantime died, to be all but absolutely correct. Standish O'Grady was a native Irish speaker of Castleconnell, Co. Limerick, intimate like O'Longan with Irish tradition, utterly devoted to it and forever its champion as against the unsympathetic face of scientific philology. He was an incomparable translator of the Irish language, prose or verse, and the first 672 pages of the *Catalogue of Irish Manuscripts in the British Museum,* from his hand, are a virtual treasury of Irish literature. In the Preface to his *Silva Gadelica* he defends 'the able and inoffensive man (last of a line of scribes) ...' who 'had his last years embittered, if not his end hastened by outrageous onslaughts of incompetent critics. I knew Joseph O'Longan well'.[22] The sentiment, in no affable spirit, was aimed at Stokes.

Stokes, in a linguistic duel with O'Grady, proffered the comment that two German professors had, in the previous thirty five years, done more for the knowledge of Irish 'than all the native scholars that have ever lived' and took O'Grady, 'the best living Irish scholar', to task for alleged errors that were 'not Irish', ending a lengthy disquisition by saying a certain disputed phrase would never be explained 'until it is taken in hand by Prof. Windisch, Prof. Ascoli, or Prof. Thurneysen'.[23]

O'Grady replied: 'As to the phrase ... which my critic says "is not Irish", I deny his jurisdiction. He and all the continental scholars together are incompetent to judge the point. In such a collocation as mine (not in his) the words *are* good Irish. Good they were for centuries before Eg.91 or the Book of Lismore were written, and good they will be as long as the language lasts'.[24] O'Grady showed no deference to continental scholars.[25] His review of Kuno Meyer's *Cath Finntrága* in the Philological Society's *Transactions,*[26] done at the urgent request of Stokes himself according to Norman Moore,[27] although less a review than a calculated onslaught, may have been prompted by the wish to demonstrate that continental scholarship was not impeccable. It was quite unfair, and Meyer, then a beginner, felt hurt and complained to Stokes.[28] In due course, aided by Stokes, he struck back with effect[29] and their respective contributions stand as a classic instance of *certamen celticum* in the disputatious field of Irish studies.

Stokes's approach to the language was clinical and scientific without emotional attachment. With Hennessy and O'Grady it was different. For them it was not only a matter for scholarship but an affair of the heart. 'Bhí sé ar lasadh le grádh do'n Ghaedhilg, teanga do labhair sé ó n-a óige' says Douglas Hyde in the course of a remarkable tribute to O'Grady's patriotism and scholarship.[30]

A brief greeting of Hennessy's given in his own hand to an unknown correspondent will convey his dedication to the language:

> go g-cuiridh Dia rath ort, agus ar gach aon aile ghrádhaighean agus lessaighean an sen teanga agus do chuiren an sean aimsir a gcuimne.
>> Do chara rodhuthrachtach
>> Uilliam Ua hAonghusa
> a mBaile Atha Cliath
>> an tsechtmad lá fichet
>> don ched mis don gheimriud, 1871[31]

William Maunsell Hennessy, taking his knowledge from European studies and from his own deep acquaintance with native tradition, represented the highest standards of Irish scholarship for most of the interval between the deaths of O'Donovan and O'Curry and the closing years of the nineteenth century.

The dichotomy of continental versus native approach to Celtic scholarship was eventually resolved with the founding in Dublin in 1903 of the School of Irish Learning by Kuno Meyer and John Strachan for the scientific training in Ireland of Irish students. The School was supported by Whitley Stokes and by continental savants like Thurneysen, Pedersen, Loth and others. Its tradition is continued, now state-funded, by its present day successor the School of Celtic Studies which is a constituent part of the Dublin Institute for Advanced Studies.

III

The Chronicum Scotorum

In 1866, two years before his appointment to the Public Record Office, Hennessy published a text of considerable importance, the title page of which reads:

> Chronicum scotorum. /a/
> CHRONICLE OF IRISH AFFAIRS,/ From the earliest times to A.D. 1135; / with / a supplement, / containing the events from 1141 to 1150; / edited, with a translation, / by / William M. Hennessy, M.R.I.A. / published by the authority of the Lords Commissioners of Her Majesty's / Treasury, under the direction of the Master of the Rolls. / LONDON: / Longmans, Green, Reader, and Dyer. / 1866.

That he had been chosen to edit a volume of the Rolls Series points to the reputation Hennessy had already attained. In the course of a forty-eight page Introduction, Hennessy explains that the text had been taken from a TCD Library manuscript, collated with a good copy in the RIA collection, the TCD text being 'in the fine, bold Irish handwriting of the celebrated Irish scholar and antiquary, Duald Mac Firbis', or Dubhaltach Mac Firbhisigh, whose biography he outlines, as well as the vicissitudes of the TCD manuscript, once the property of the learned Roderick O'Flaherty, author of *Ogygia*, later of John O'Brien, bishop of Cloyne and Ross and author of an important Irish-English dictionary published in Paris 1769. Acknowledging that his translation was strictly literal and might appear rugged, Hennessy explained that such a kind would best serve the objects of the historian and the philologist. Two special friends had contributed to the work, William Reeves by reading the proof sheets, and James Henthorn Todd with his 'friendly aid and counsel'. It is a substantial volume of text, including supplement 1-349, Glossary 351-6, Index 357-419.

Its appearance was greeted by an enthusiastic if not critical notice in the *Dublin University Magazine*[32] under the heading 'One of our old chronicles' which reads in part:

> The care, and research, and ability, employed in the editing of this national work reflect much credit on Mr. Hennessy. The well arranged introduction gives evidence of great industry, and of an intimate acquaintance with our manuscript literature, and the memories of the patient and earnest men who from early times have supported the character of our country in its love of letters. The accurate translation and the number of valuable notes exhibit the intimate knowledge of ancient and modern Gaelic possessed by the editor. This is further evidenced by the skill and judgement shown in the emendation of corrupt passages, the supplying of deficiencies, and the correction of dates ... We are happy to hail in the editor of this book, a worthy successor to the lamented scholars lately removed from us, and exhort him and the other zealous students of the old tongue, which must in time cease to exist as a spoken language, to make themselves every day more proficient in the language of their ancestors.

It appears that Hennessy's knowledge of Irish manuscripts attracted the attention of Lord Mayo, 'who was a keen observer of the qualities which fit men for the public service'.[33] Richard Southwell Bourke, sixth earl of Mayo, fated to fall by an assassin's hand in India, was Chief Secretary of Ireland 1852-69 and well-disposed towards the Irish language. It may well be that it was the edition of the *Chronicum Scotorum* which influenced him to consider Hennessy for appointment to the Public Record Office which was shortly afterwards set up.

Hennessy was a contributor to the earliest numbers of the *Revue Celtique*, volume 1 of which is dated Paris 1870-72 and had for editor Henri Gaidoz. His essay on 'The Ancient Irish Goddess of War',[34] the substance of which had been read as a paper before the Royal Irish Academy on 25 January 1869, took its origin from the discovery by Adolphe Pictet of a Gallo-Roman inscription republished in the *Revue Archéologique* of July 1868. Hennessy hailed Pictet as 'the veteran philologist for which the students of Celtic languages and archaeology cannot be sufficiently thankful'[35]. Pictet in his essay *Sur une Déesse Gauloise de la Guerre*, suggests that C was the letter missing from the incomplete inscription ATHBODUAE, thus making CATHBODUAE, i.e. the *Badbcatha* of Irish mythology. Hennessy's essay considers at length the ancient tracts, romances and battle-pieces which, preserved in Irish manuscripts, teem with details respecting this Badbcatha and her so-called sisters, *Neman, Macha* and *Morrigan,* or *Morrigu,* who were generally depicted as furies, witches, or sorceresses, able to confound whole armies, even in the assumed form of a bird. In a commentary[36] on Hennessy's paper Carl Lottner describes it as 'a valuable contribution to the comparative mythology of the Germans (chiefly Scandinavians) and Celts'. Another scholar who took notice of Hennessy's paper was Whitley Stokes, who comments: 'To Mr Hennessy in particular, every student of the early Irish literature, language and mythology, is deeply indebted. He has so much of the spirit of a true scholar, that I am sure I cannot lighten my obligations more agreeably to himself than by correcting a few slips in his paper on the Ancient Irish Goddess of War,' and having supplied a short list of corrections in a reasonable vein he adds 'so much for corrigenda to this valuable and most interesting paper'.[37] Another contribution to *Revue Celtique* was the text of *The Battle of Cnucha* with brief introduction, translation and notes.[38] In the introduction Hennessy recalls his visit of the previous autumn along with the premier Scottish folklorist John Francis Campbell of Islay to the Hill of Allen where they were shown the thicket out of which Fionn's hounds Bran and Sceolán were fabled to start nightly, to the alarm of late wayfarers, but could find no trace of such a dún as was referred to in the text.

John Francis Campbell's association with Hennessy appears from many references. Some of these will be found in Campbell's great work, *Leabhar na Féinne, heroic Gaelic ballads collected in Scotland chiefly from 1512 to 1871,* published London 1872. Campbell was actually in Kilmakillogue in the parish of Tuosist, County Kerry, when the printing of this book was completed by August 1872.[39] When working on it he consulted Hennessy, whose familiarity with the content of Irish manuscripts was well known, on the subject of Fenian literature, and records their meetings, held in Dublin, under dates of 4, 9 and 17 December 1871.[40] Campbell toured Ireland in 1872, was disappointed with the amount of traditional lore which he found in the country, but this was probably due to his being a stranger who did not know from whom to seek information. Hennessy, writing to him from 11 Gardiner's Place, Dublin,[41] regretted the difficulty he experienced and blamed the English colonisation of 1608 for the sparsity of materials. He felt sure, however, that many stories were still to be found in certain districts. In a letter of 28 December 1872,[42] he asked Campbell to help him persuade Lord Romilly, Master of the Rolls, to put the *Annals of Ulster* on his list of records to be published by the Public Record Office. This text was the most important historical source for early mediaeval Irish and Scottish history and its publication was undertaken by the PRO in 1887, volume 1 being edited by Hennessy. In the same letter Hennessy commented on details of *Leabhar na Féinne*, a copy of which he had evidently received from Campbell, as it appears in the sale catalogue of his books, item 85, 'with autograph letter from the Editor'.

Writing to Campbell from Tralee[43] Hennessy discussed the reliability of John O'Mahony's translation of Keating's *Foras Feasa* and contrasted Keating's use of 'a large mass of poems, ballads, stories, pedigrees', etc., with their treatment by Macpherson, author of the spurious *Fingal* and *Temora*, who had abstracted material from Keating. Discussing Archibald Clerk's edition of *The poems of Ossian* (1870)[44] in a two part notice which he wrote for the *Academy*[45] Hennessy made what was acknowledged by Sir Norman Moore and Standish Hayes O'Grady to be an important contribution to the Ossianic controversy, in the course of which he said:

> As regards the Gaelic text itself, it would be difficult to conceive anything more deplorably corrupt. It is nothing short of an offence against common sense, excluding other higher considerations, to publish it as the language of an almost forgotten age, even after making due allowance for modernisation. But the Gael of Scotland will have it so; and on this subject it is hardly an exaggeration to say that the Ossianic mist still encircles the Scottish mind in folds as thick as shrouded the spirits of the Gaelic dead long ago, in their damp and inhospitable elysium. It is to no purpose, so far as Ossianists are concerned, that scholars like Zeuss, Ebel, Stokes and Nigra have demonstrated, on scientific

data, that the Gaelic of these poems had no separate existence five hundred years ago, and was but a modern and mutilated dialect of the tongue common to Ireland and Scotland at that time.[46]

It was a work creditable to the industry of the editor but not to his scholarship.[47]

IV

The Public Record Office

The Public Record Office was set up under the Public Records (Ireland) Act, 1867. It was located in the Four Courts, Inns Quay, beside the Liffey, and the *First Report of the Deputy Keeper of the Public Records in Ireland* stated (page 5) that 'a large and commodious Building' had been erected there for the purpose. The staff, senior and junior, was constituted on 1 January 1868. It included William M. Hennessy, M.R.I.A., of the Office of Inspectors of Lunatic Asylums, who was appointed to the senior staff as First Class Clerk. Amongst his colleagues were the Assistant Deputy Keeper John James Digges La Touche, M.R.I.A., Secretary John T. Gilbert, M.R.I.A., Librarian of the Royal Irish Academy, best known as the historian of Dublin, Robert Godfrey Day of the late Landed Estates Record Office and, in charge as Deputy Keeper of the Public Records, Samuel Ferguson who needs no advertisement.

Hennessy assisted La Touche in the Search Department. The general nature of his duties is outlined in a paragraph of the *First Report* which says:

> The Senior and Junior first Clerks will assist the Deputy and Assistant Deputy Keeper in examining copies of Records; and will, to applicants for searches and inspection of Records, give all convenient information and assistance; and such one of them as shall from time to time be appointed to that duty by the Deputy Keeper, will, in an Attendance Book, keep the accounts of the daily attendance and employments of the officers and servants, receive all cash for fees, and make all disbursements for wages of workmen, and other outgoings.[48]

That he laboured conscientiously and hard at his daily tasks we cannot doubt. We are told by Standish O'Grady that the pressure of his official duties was one of the reasons why his scholarly output was less than his talents commanded. It is the fate of many scholars to be kept shackled to administrative or official duties when they might be engaged, with greater profit to learning, in more congenial pursuits. The later case of Robin Flower comes to mind. We know from his biography that John T. Gilbert suffered his share of frustrations. Official duties tend to be unremarkable and unrecorded. Of Hennessy's life and experiences in the Public Record Office we know little or nothing. Nor is there anything of interest concerning him in the PRO records.[48a]

About one matter, however, we may have little doubt. It was through his advice that an elementary knowledge of the Irish language was made a requirement for admission to the Public Record Office. Following an examination made by Hennessy and La Touche of the Index to the Calendar of James I, it turned out that

> ... on a careful comparison of an average folio (73) with the original, twelve names of places were, in an early examination conducted by Mr. La Touche and Mr. Hennessy, found in a greater or less degree erroneously transcribed, without counting mere misprints ... It appearing that the errors in question had arisen mainly from ignorance of the meanings of the words, as local designations, in the Irish language, it was thought advisable by the Right Hon. The late Master of the Rolls, that, in qualifying for admission to this office, some knowledge of the Irish language ... should be secured in the officers of this department whose duty it is to make and give certified copies of instruments containing such matter. On his Honor's recommendation an elementary knowledge of Irish ... was required as one of the conditions of examination for this office.[49]

Was this the earliest instance of a knowledge of Irish being made a condition for entry to an official post?

V

The Annals of Loch Cé and Other Works

Hennessy translated the tripartite Life of St. Patrick specially for the Nun of Kenmare, Mary Frances Cusack, in whose *Life of St. Patrick* published London and Dublin 1870, it is printed on pages 369-502, and given appreciative acknowledgement by the author who says:

For the kindness of Mr. Hennessy in undertaking such a work, the writer can never be sufficiently grateful. The readers of this volume are under deep obligations to him also. There are not, perhaps, more than three or four other philologists in this country capable of such a task; for the language in which the original is written differs so completely from the Irish spoken at present as to be unintelligible to those who have not made Celtic philology their special study.[50]

Probably Hennessy's best known scholarly work was his fine two volume edition of *The Annals of Loch Cé*, a chronicle of Irish affairs from 1014 to 1590, prepared for the Rolls series of *Chronicles and Memorials of Great Britain and Ireland during the Middle Ages*, to which he supplied a useful preface of over fifty pages, giving such history as was available of the manuscript, with interesting commentary and notes on the text. His acknowledgements indicate some scholars of the day of whom he was friend and associate and who might indeed be regarded as part of his familiar circle. He laments the death of his revered friend Rev. James Henthorn Todd, by which he was deprived 'of the generous assistance and friendly counsel, so freely accorded to me on all occasions (and they were many) when I found it necessary to avail myself of his mature judgement, and intimate acquaintance with the materials of Irish History'. Todd was editor of the important historical text *Cogadh Gaedhel re Gallaibh*, which relates the invasions of Ireland by the Danes and other Norsemen, along with graphic details of the Battle of Clontarf, and Hennessy had collaborated with him in reading the proofs and supplying the very ample index.[51] Hennessy further thanks Rev. Eugene Murphy, C.C., of Dromod, near Waterville, Co. Kerry, 'an accomplished Celtic scholar', for much valuable assistance, and Carl Lottner, for supplying a translation from the Norse. Another friend who helped him with the topography of Connacht was Denis Henry Kelly, of Castle Kelly, an associate of Hennessy's on some other projects. He records his special obligations to Samuel Ferguson for many useful suggestions in the translation of obscure passages and for the preparation of the Preface. Another to whom he acknowledges his debt for his careful reading of the proof sheets was 'my generous friend, the Rev. Dr. Reeves .. for his great kindness in this, as well as for many other like favours, I owe him an amount of gratitude ...'

The *Annals of Loch Cé* has its Irish text printed in the Gaelic font, so visually attractive though not much beloved of scientific philologists, and the two finely produced volumes have an overall content of more than 1300 pages.[52]

The final section of the annals, covering the period 1577-90 is, the Four Masters apart, the only native source for the history of these eventful years, being especially detailed, and dealing with the period when Gaelic Connacht was finally disrupted.[53] Because of its importance to students of history the Irish Manuscripts Commission decided to have it reprinted in 1939 by the Stationery Office.[54] This reissue has in its turn gone out of print.

The Vision of Mac Conglinne

In *Fraser's Magazine* for September 1873 there is printed a translation with notes by Hennessy of *Aislinge Meic Conglinne*, from the original Irish in the *Leabhar Brec Mhic Aedhagáin*, a manuscript in the Royal Irish Academy which he dates to between 1400 and 1411. The translation is entitled *Mac Conglinny's Vision* and described as a humorous satire. The theme, as Hennessy points out in his introduction, was one common to the lore of many ancient nations, namely, the presence in the human body of a diabolic creature, in this instance the *lón-craes*, which, lodging in the stomach of Cathal Mac Finghuine, King of Munster, caused him to devour prodigious quantities of food. Finally the demon was lured from the king's body through the astuteness of Anier Mac Conglinne, a scholar of wit and personality. Hennessy points out that, although the Irish tale antedates by centuries Rabelais' creation of Gargantua, there are certain affinities between the two tales.

The *Vision* was written in a very obscure dialect of Irish. 'The translation is close, and much of the literary effect of the story is therefore lost.' The brief introduction is signed by Hennessy as at the Public Record Office, Dublin. Three years after Hennessy's death the Irish text of the *Vision* was published, with a translation based on Hennessy's, to which were added notes and glossary, by Kuno Meyer, who has this to say:

> As regards the translation, my first intention was simply to republish the late W. M. Hennessy's spirited rendering of the *Leabhar Breac* version in *Fraser's Magazine* of September 1873. However, on carefully comparing it with the original, I soon became convinced that this was not feasible. Mistakes, inaccuracies, and omissions were too frequent. I should have had to alter and to add so much that the character of Hennessy's work would have been completely changed. Nor did I feel that Hennessy had been happy in his style. Like many of his countrymen, he seems to have been over-fond of Romance words, and to have preferred these where the simpler Saxon

equivalents were at least as effective. For these reasons I decided to make a translation of my own, basing it on Hennessy's and adopting his rendering wherever it seemed accurate and forcible. I thought it right, however, in the notes to indicate where my rendering differs most from his, as also to give a list of the more serious mistakes into which he has fallen. I hope no one will think this was done in a fault-finding spirit. I honour the memory of W. M. Hennessy as one of the few native scholars who did not shut their eyes to the progress of Celtic research on the Continent, and as one who was generous enough to place his intimate knowledge of his mother-tongue at the disposal of any students wise enough to consult him. It is always instructive to see how and where a man of Hennessy's learning went astray. One of the snares into which he often fell was his habit of reading older Irish with modern pronunciation, as I have repeatedly heard him do: a source of error, against which native students cannot too carefully guard themselves.[55]

While wondering how early Irish was or should be pronounced and in what way the application to it of modern Irish sounds could be a source of error, one feels that Meyer was courteous in his comment and trying to be fair, which cannot be said of Whitley Stokes whose view will be considered shortly. The unusual character of *Aislinge Meic Conglinne*, which was first given prominence by Hennessy, has drawn the attention of other writers. It was given a modern Irish dress by an tAthair Peadar Ua Laoghaire in *An Craos-Deamhan*, and is the theme of *The Son of Learning* by Austin Clarke.

The review of *Aislinge Meic Conglinne* in *The Athenaeum* (29 April 1893, p.530), unsigned but probably from the hand of Standish H. O'Grady, begins with the interesting comment:

The late Mr. William Allingham, though unacquainted with the Irish language, was deeply interested in its literature, and in every way in his power encouraged its study. As a native of Ballyshannon he felt a local as well as a national pride in the 'Annals of the Four Masters', the chief compilers of which were born within a few miles of his home, and whenever he met an Irish scholar he was ready to talk with him on Irish writers and their works. It was this taste for Celtic literature and desire to have it appreciated which led him to induce the late Mr. Hennessy to send to *Fraser's Magazine* a translation of the 'Vision of Mac Conglinne'.

Todd Professor

After James Henthorn Todd died in 1869, some of his friends decided to honour him by founding in his memory a lectureship in the Celtic languages. They collected some £1300 for its endowment and placed it under the aegis of the Royal Irish Academy, of which Todd had been president. Leading scholars in the Irish language were elected to give the Todd lectures. They included Robert Atkinson, Dr. B. MacCarthy, Edmund Hogan, S.J., and Kuno Meyer. William Maunsell Hennessy was elected Todd Professor for 1882-4. In that capacity he prepared a text of the tale *Mesca Ulad* which, although ready for press in 1884, was not published until 1889, immediately after his death.[56]

It was 'reviewed' in his characteristic style by Whitley Stokes. He was not enthusiastic about the tale. 'As to its merits as a work of art, like all the Irish sagas, like almost all mediaeval literature, the whole exists for the sake of the parts, not the parts for the sake of the whole.' Although the Irish type was employed, the Irish text was tolerably correct, 'but the translation is full of that guesswork which deforms the publications of most native Irish scholars', Having given a list of his corrigenda, he comments: 'These mistakes are, indeed, lamentable; no continental celtologue would have made them; but they will surprise no one who has examined the lengthy list of blunders in Mr. Hennessy's translation of the *Vision of Mac Conglinne*, which Dr. Meyer has pointed out and corrected in his edition of that singular specimen of medieval literature.'[57]

Not Stokes in the best of humour. Not normally unkind to Hennessy, he may have been smarting under animadversions of Standish O'Grady's such as printed in the preface to *Silva Gadelica*.[58] Examining the same text, D'Arbois de Jubainville, in a keen and percipient scrutiny,[59] drew attention to its faults but in doing so presents us with an estimate of Hennessy which, critical though it be, does proper justice to his standing as a scholar.

'One would be wrong to conclude from these criticisms', writes D'Arbois, 'that I do not have the highest possible regard for Hennessy's work. The actual translation of an Irish text presents more difficulty than is commonly thought. Hennessy possessed a better knowledge of Irish vocabulary than do most of the scholars who study Old Irish on the Continent, but like many of his countrymen, he had not made a sufficient study of grammar, he sometimes neglected grammatical analysis, he did not always fully appreciate the utility of a word for word rendering; and lastly, he did not clearly grasp in what respects a word for word rendering and a translation should resemble each other, and should at the same time differ one from the other. There is no scholar whose learning is free of imperfection, and despite his shortcomings, Hennessy was a man of great talent, a Celtic scholar of the first rank. I was for some weeks a pupil of Hennessy's and would that I had better profited from the lessons of that master, so scholarly, so unassuming, so kindly, whom an early death has just taken from us!'[60]

A worthy tribute, from France's finest Celtic scholar.

Alfred Nutt, recognised as a leading authority on Celtic folklore,[61] introduces an extended consideration of *Mesca Ulad* with the following comments:

> A melancholy interest attaches to this posthumous publication of the thorough and accomplished scholar whose name appears on the title-page. As is the case with too many other native scholars, the amount of printed work which Hennessy has left behind him represents most inadequately his knowledge of the history and literature of early Ireland. He was one of the few remaining depositories of the traditions handed down through O'Donovan and O'Curry, those last of an unbroken line of great antiquaries reaching up to the early Middle Ages. Modern philological and historical criticism has done and can do much for the elucidation of the oldest records of the Irish races but it cannot dispense with the native tradition. Every gift from the hand of a pupil of O'Curry's is therefore most welcome, and it is with lively satisfaction that I note the promise of the Royal Irish Academy to revise and publish Hennessy's remaining Todd Lectures, with as little delay as possible. If, however, this feeling of satisfaction is to be justified, the future lectures must be 'revised and published' in a very different way from the present one. I do not hesitate to say that this publication reflects the utmost discredit upon the Royal Irish Academy and is most unfair to Hennessy's memory. The Lectures were delivered in 1882; the preface is signed 1884. The long delay in publishing may reasonably be attributed to the lecturer's feeling that the text translated by him demanded far more comment, both critical and exegetical, than is here given it. The present introduction is quite insufficient, restricted as it is to three or four points of comparatively minor importance; and those historical and topographical notes which the editor was so well qualified to supply are almost entirely missing. At the very least, the historical conditions of the tale, and its relations to other texts of the same saga-cycle, should have been clearly set forth.[62]

From this it would appear that editorial restrictions placed on the work inhibited the full scholarly apparatus which Hennessy was capable of supplying.

Another text in the Todd Lectures series which Hennessy had in hand was the *Bruiden Da Derga* but delays likewise attended it and caused queries. Standish O'Grady speculated about what its fate would be[63] although at some stage its publication seems to have been expected. James Graves could not understand the situation of 'W.M. Hennessy holding back the "Bruden". It seems inexplicable. He says he has it all ready, and that five weeks would see it done, but why it is not done is the mystery'.[64]

The mystery is all that remains. The text reached proof stage but was never published, and the type was eventually broken up, why we do not know.

VII

The Book of Fenagh

In 1875 appeared *The Book of Fenagh*, originally compiled, according to the title-page, by the abbot and founder of Fenagh, St. Caillin who flourished *tempore St. Patricii.* However there is little, if any, of the published text that can be ascribed to the saint. We are told further that the original text had been as far as possible restored, the whole being carefully revised, indexed and copiously annotated by W. M. Hennessy, done into English by D. H. Kelly,[65] whose work it may be surmised the title page was, and printed in Dublin by Thom.

It was an interesting production, setting forth the dues and privileges of the ancient monastery of Fenagh in County Leitrim, compiled by a noted Irish scholar in 1516 from earlier materials. Hennessy and Kelly worked from a transcript, not faultless, of John O'Donovan's in the library of the Royal Irish Academy. The volume, privately printed, has a dedicatory address from the editor D. H. Kelly to Lady Louisa Tennisson, 'that rare being, a fashionable English woman who … has made herself acquainted with our old Celtic tongue' explaining that its publication was most desirable 'whilst still the spoken tongue remains to correct the speculations of those who only study it as a dead language'.[66]

D. H. Kelly likewise wrote an Introduction from which it appears (p.x) that the major contribution to the book was Hennessy's, whose cordial assistance he acknowledges, 'who accompanied him to Fenagh to personally inspect the locality; who kindly went over to London and searched the Irish MSS in the British Museum, and then went to Oxford and examined the Irish collections there'. He goes on to express his great obligations to Hennessy for revising his manuscript and correcting its errors, for his valuable annotations and his inestimable aid in putting the volume through the press, so that if any credit be given to it, it is due to him more than to the Editor, 'a mere country gentleman, who for love of the literature of his native land, has for nearly thirty years applied himself to its production', throughout which prologue shine the courtesies of an older world.

Only fifty copies were printed,[67] so that it became a rarity, and as the text was of some importance, the Irish Manuscripts Commission reprinted it by reflex facsimile process in 1939. It was found necessary to issue at the same time a supplementary volume based on the autograph text and other materials not available at the time to Hennessy and Kelly.[68] This companion volume was edited by the archaeologist R. A. Stewart Macalister and is the subject of critical scrutiny by Rev. Paul Walsh.[69] Macalister held Hennessy in the highest regard as 'a scholar in attainments worthy to stand along with the elder pioneers O'Curry and O'Donovan – their inferior in the actual amount of work to his credit, but on the whole their superior in accuracy and general scholarship'.[70]

VIII

The Society for the Preservation of the Irish Language

As a native speaker it was natural that Hennessy should have a strong interest in the position of the modern Irish language. He was amongst those who took the initial steps in 1876 towards the founding of the Society for the Preservation of the Irish Language, a precursor of the Gaelic League and noted by Douglas Hyde as 'without any doubt the first effort made to attract the ordinary people to the cause of Irish'.[71] Hennessy, seen by Hyde as 'an sgoláire mór Liam M. Ó hAonghusa',[72] was on the Provisional Committee, and his name, along with David Comyn, John O'Daly, Rev. John O'Hanlon, Joseph O'Longan, T. O'Neill Russell, George Sigerson, Brian O'Looney and others, with Secretaries J. J. MacSweeney and Rev. John Nolan, appears on the first appeal issued by that body which reads in part:

> Dear Sir,
> Good Irishmen at home and abroad, and Scholars in every land, have long regarded as a national reproach the absence of any adequate endeavour on the part of the Irish people for the preservation, as a spoken language, of their ancient, interesting, and beautiful Gaelic, one of the oldest and most expressive forms of speech in the world... In the opinion, however, of many

persons... the decay of the Irish language can be arrested, and a knowledge of it greatly extended among our people... Several facts within our own knowledge indicate the existence of a very general desire among the young men of Ireland to keep the olden speech of their race alive in the land...

Impressed with these views and feelings, a number of gentlemen in Dublin have resolved to make a beginning with the good work. They have formed themselves provisionally into a Society for the preservation and cultivation of the Irish language, and they now appeal to the public to aid them in carrying on their patriotic undertaking...

Hennessy was elected to the Council, on which he served for many years, his name appearing on its list of members up to 1887, within two years of his death.[73] The Society had considerable success in promoting a knowledge of the language, due in no small part to the generosity of Hennessy's colleague, Rev. Maxwell Close, 'our Maecenas, who aided the Society out of his own pocket many a time', witness to the fact being Douglas Hyde, himself a member.[74]

Hennessy's name was well-known to Celtic scholars outside Ireland. Amongst his friends was the Cavaliere Nigra, himself an accomplished celticist,[75] whose guest Hennessy was at the Italian Embassy in Paris. His work was highly thought of by the great French celticist Henri D'Arbois de Jubainville. D'Arbois visited Dublin in 1881 to collect material in the city's libraries for the important pioneer survey *Essai d'un Catalogue de la Littérature Épique de l'Irlande* (Paris 1883) in the Introduction to which he expressed his appreciation of Hennessy's learned counsel by which he was enabled to solve many difficulties.[76] Hennessy introduced him to C. P. Meehan, well known as Mangan's friend, of the quayside Church of SS Michael and John, who in turn introduced him to the Franciscan Library on Merchants Quay which housed Irish manuscripts.[77]

It may be noted that the third edition of the *Poets and Poetry of Munster*, with Mangan's poetical translations, which is claimed to be the best edition of this popular anthology,[78] was edited by Father Meehan and had its Irish text revised by Hennessy.

IX

The Annals of Ulster

The *Annals of Ulster*, volume 1, was Hennessy's last major published work, details on the title page of which read:

Annala Uladh. / Annals of Ulster./ otherwise, Annala Senait, / Annals of Senat: / A chronicle of Irish Affairs / from A.D. 431 to A.D. 1540./ Edited, with a translation and notes, by / William M. Hennessy, M.R.I.A., / the Assistant Deputy Keeper of the Records. / Vol. 1./A.D. 431-1056... Dublin: ... 1887.

In a prefatory note signed and dated June 1887 Hennessy explained that the Introduction must appear in the last volume. The chronicle, so named by James Ussher because of the prominence given in it to the affairs of Ulster, was the work of Cathal MacManus, recorded obit 1498, and had been used by the Four Masters as a source book. Its importance to students of history was long recognised by Hennessy who wished it to be brought to the attention of the Master of the Rolls for publication. It was reviewed by Whitley Stokes after Hennessy's death in two issues of the *Academy* (28 September 1889, pp. 207-8 and 5 October, pp. 223-5) in the course of which he says (page 207) that

> The Council [of the Royal Irish Academy] employed the best native Irish scholar then living, and the result is the volume under notice.
> The text now published is certainly a great, indeed an immense, improvement on O'Conor's [published in 1826, with Latin translation by Dr O'Conor, in the fourth volume of the *Rerum Hibernicarum Scriptores,* 'most inaccurate']... Facing the text is an English translation; and the footnotes not only point out many of O'Conor's blunders, but supply a mass of information relating to the persons and the places mentioned in the text.

Stokes supplies a list of printing errors and corrigenda.

D'Arbois de Jubainville in his review of it, part critical, but on the whole appreciative, in *Revue Celtique* IX (1888) 402-6, wondered why Hennessy, in the interests of history, had not preferred to undertake an edition of the Annals of Tigernach which dated from the eleventh century. Hennessy continued his work on the remaining portion of the text up to a short period before his death. He must have found the going difficult, between the distress of domestic tragedies and the declining health which beset him in his last years. Finally he had to give up. Writing in *Revue Celtique* X (1889) p. 142, D'Arbois de Jubainville said his readers would hear with keen disappointment that Hennessy was obliged for health reasons to retire from editing the *Annals of Ulster,* the first volume of which he had published with the same profound scholarship that his previous works had accustomed one to expect. In the very same issue his death was announced.

The remainder of the *Annals of Ulster* was taken in hand by Dr. B. McCarthy, whose editions of Volumes II and III, completing the text, were published in 1893 and 1895 respectively and scanned by the eagle eye of Whitley Stokes in *Revue Celtique* XVIII (1897) pp 74-86, in which scrutiny they did not fare too well.

Varia

Amongst other works of Hennessy's which may be noted is his revision, dated 1856, of *The Pedigree of the White Knight* (from the Russell and Colter MSS) by James Graves. For his interesting paper 'On the forms of ordeal anciently practised in Ireland' which he read on 28 January 1867 before the Royal Irish Academy, he drew his material from the *Book of Ballymote*, folio 143 et seq.[79]

Volume I (published 1872) of George Petrie's *Christian inscriptions in the Irish language*[80] contains two poems copied and edited with translations by Hennessy, one of which is the celebrated 'Cathir Chíaráin Cluain mic Nóis' by Enog Ó Gilláin, from the Bodleian manuscript Rawlinson B. 486, F29, the other a composition of Conaing Buidhe Ó Maoilconaire from the TCD manuscript H.I.17.

The *Calendar of State Papers relating to Ireland, of the reign of James I 1606-1608* (London 1874) contains in pp 586-8 the text and translation by Hennessy of the Confession of Ineen Duv, mother of the Earl of Tyrconnell , made to George Montgomery, bishop of Derry, in 1608, the original of which is in the Carte Papers vol 61, p.251.

Hennessy corrected for press that portion of the text of Volume IV of the *Ancient laws of Ireland* (Dublin 1879) left unrevised by Rev. Dr. T. O'Mahony who had been forced by illness to relinquish the task. An essay of his on *Irish Missals* is printed in the *Academy* of 31 January 1880.

Included amongst a series of Notes on the Life of St. Brendan printed in the *Irish Ecclesiastical Record* there appears the complete text, 69 quatrains, of the *Rule of St. Ailbhe*, as preserved in TCD and the Royal Irish Academy except for some verses supplied from the O'Curry Manuscripts through the kindness of Mr. O'Looney, the entire translated by 'our distinguished Celtic scholar, W.M. Hennessy'.[81]

An eminent historian to avail of Hennessy's help was William Forbes Skene, author amongst many other studies of the three volume work *Celtic Scotland, a history of Ancient Alban*, volume II of which, relating to Church and Culture, includes a contribution from Hennessy described by the author as a valuable aid by which he was enabled 'to enrich his work with a translation of the Old Irish Life of St. Columba, by that eminent scholar'.[82]

Comerford's *Collections relating to the dioceses of Kildare and*

Leighlin, second series, Dublin (1886) contains Hennessy's edition of the *Cáin Emine* (Emine's Tribute), pp 209-13.

It has been remarked by those who knew him that Hennessy was liberal in his aid to others, and in support of this it may be appropriate to instance the review by Whitley Stokes of Robert Atkinson's booklet *Old Irish Metric* (Dublin 1884) by which that scholar's claim to be an authority on Irish metrics is dismissed with crushing finality in an ambit of eleven pages of *Revue Celtique*[83] in all of which he pays Atkinson the single compliment of saying he was sorry to write thus of a scholar whose 'Contents' of the Book of Leinster[84] was a piece of thorough work '(if he was not largely helped by Mr. Hennessy)' for which all Celtic scholars should be grateful to him, from which it is fair to conclude that Atkinson must share the credit with Hennessy for the merit of the 'Contents'.

Hennessy's obituary in the *Irish Times*, 14 January 1889, says that he also contributed to the *Revue Critique*, Kuhn's *Zeitschrift* and the *Beiträge für vergleichende Sprachforschung*. The writer regrets he had not the leisure to check these journals.

X

Tragedy and closing years

'Your Excellency was further pleased to appoint Mr. William Maunsell Hennessy, the eminent Celtic Scholar, and Senior First Class Clerk in this Department, to be Assistant Deputy Keeper ...' So runs the extract from the *19th Report of the Deputy Keeper of the Public Records*.[85] It is dated 29 April 1887.

Material advancement, perhaps, but coming at a time when it was of little moment. By then Hennessy's life was overshadowed by the tragedy related in the words of Standish O'Grady: 'In 1885 he was visited by a family bereavement almost tragic in its sadness; and this, again, was before long followed by a second blow, the effect upon his sensitive and affectionate nature being such that he never fairly rallied.'[86] Sir Norman Moore tells us that he lost his wife and a married daughter and that these afflictions induced a condition of nervous depression from which he never rallied.[87]

His name had been mentioned early in 1888 in connection with a project for editing old Irish texts envisaged by the Royal Irish Academy about which Sir John Gilbert wrote for advice and comment to Whitley Stokes.[88] Stokes, busy on the Anglo-Indian Codes, was unable to take part himself and commented that 'As there is now no one in Ireland, except Mr. Hennessy, competent to edit a Middle-Irish manuscript, it is obvious that the Academy ... must resort to such scholars as Mr. Standish Hayes O'Grady, Dr. Kuno Meyer, Prof. Thurneysen, Dr. Schirmer and ... Prof. Windisch.'[89] Gilbert regretted to say that from what he heard of Hennessy's state of health there was not very much prospect of his doing work for some time. His 'Annals of Ulster' was still unpublished.[90] Amongst those to whom Gilbert had written about the project was Rudolf Thurneysen, who agreed to participate and expected that his fellow workers would include Hennessy and Atkinson.[90] The project however did not come to fruition.

For the last decade or so of his life Hennessy lived at 71 Pembroke Road, Ballsbridge, and there on Sunday 13 January 1889 he died at the age of 60. Not old surely, despite the report in the *Times*[92] that it was 'ripe' and one thinks that he had only come to an age when he might be expected to add much more to the records of Irish studies. All sources are agreed on his eminence. Amongst those affected by his loss was D'Arbois de Jubainville, who had known him personally from his visit to Dublin in 1881 and wrote from Paris 'J'ai appris avec un grand regret, le mort de ce pauvre Hennessy, qui est une très grande perte',[93] the note of sympathy in his words being patent. D'Arbois had been finishing his report on matters of Celtic interest for the *Revue Celtique* when the tragic news arrived 'like a thunderbolt'.[94] His obituarist in the Dublin *Daily Express* describes Hennessy as one of the most eminent students of ancient Irish History, one whose learning and literary accomplishments made him well and widely known, his reputation being more highly esteemed on the Continent even than in his own country.[95]

His generosity in sharing his knowledge, time and the contents of his library with others is stressed by his memorialist in the Royal Irish Academy *Proceedings* who wrote that 'the liberality with which he responded to requests for aid of any kind: loans of MSS., verifications of text, explanations of words and phrases, identifications of persons or localities, everything was granted with instant readiness', concluding with the view that 'His name in the future will form no unworthy pendant to those of O'Curry and O'Donovan'.[96]

D'Arbois de Jubainville was very positive in his view of Hennessy's merits.

> Mr. Hennessy, he wrote, continued, with a pronounced superiority over his predecessors, the tradition of O'Donovan and O'Curry. I have never met a scholar more liberal than he with the treasures of his learning. He was always ready to offer help to anyone who asked for it and more than one person has written and signed a transaction unaware and therefore unable to say that the major

part of it had its origin in Mr. Hennessy's dictation. This he would do, as a matter of course, during the brief intervals of recreation he would allow himself every day in the library of the Royal Irish Academy on leaving the Record Office following the performance of his daily task and before returning to his home where other duties awaited him.[97]

In forming our estimate of Hennessy we must defer particularly to the witness of three men of his time who knew him personally and were in a position to make a fair assessment. Sir Norman Moore[98] says his chief works were editions of Irish texts with introductions and translations which invariably display a wide knowledge of the Irish language and its literature. He left no greater Irish scholar behind him in Ireland. His conversation was full of learning, and he was liberal in his communication of knowledge. The estimate of Dr. William Reeves as written in his copy of *Grammatica Celtica* has been already noted.

The tribute of Standish Hayes O'Grady is worthy of special attention, as a man who shared with Hennessy a native knowledge and love of the Irish language and the sympathy of fellowship in their first hand experience of Gaelic milieu and tradition. It is a striking appreciation. Hennessy's name, he tells us,

> has for years been familiar as their own to all who, professionally or otherwise, were drawn to those studies in which he was at once an enthusiast and, in his own line (from which he never deviated), a master. Furthermore, such contingent of his survivors in the field as, being competent to form an opinion, may also be blest with candour sufficient to give it words, will find no difficulty in admitting that by his removal an important and difficult branch of Celtic research has suffered loss which it is not too much to call irreparable... Changed times forbid the hope that he, any more than Eugene O'Curry and John O'Donovan, can be replaced by a compatriot. As for the foreigner, his orbit is well-defined; in that let him be content to revolve and, as sometimes he does brilliantly, to shine; accepting the inevitable, and recognising that with the subject of this notice vanishes a mass of special knowledge forbidden to outsiders, the lack of which makes itself felt in their every page. But in proportion to his erudition was the hearty liberality which ever placed it unreservedly at the service of all comers; the genial welcome and the hospitality which in his house awaited the 'angehender Keltolog' from foreign parts. To his friends, his books and transcripts were as accessible as to himself, and freely lent to take away.

Having listed Hennessy's chief works, O'Grady, answering his own question as to why the purely Irish work of such a man should not have been more abundant, explained that 'his official duties in the Public Record Office necessarily took up much of his time; and, for the rest, that in some most important matters he was, to their great detriment and the public loss, purposely set aside, and the rich store of his knowledge left unutilised'.[99] What these matters were, and why Hennessy was purposely set aside in their regard, we do not know, but we may consider it a cause for regret.

Douglas Hyde, in his essay 'A plea for the Irish Language', calling for its preservation, put forward the argument that

> All our scholars, nearly all those who have done anything for the elucidation of our MSS, O'Conor of Ballingar, O'Donovan, O'Curry, Petrie, Hennessy, all these spoke the language naturally from their cradle, and had it not been so would never have been able to accomplish the work they did, a work which first made it possible for a Jubainville or a Windisch to prosecute their Celtic studies with any success.[100]

James F. Kenney numbers Hennessy amongst the last representatives of native Gaelic scholarship, along with Owen Connellan, John O'Donovan, Eugene O'Curry, Standish O'Grady and others,[101] they being the inheritors of 'the traditional learning which scribe and bard and shanachie and hedge-schoolmaster succeeded in preserving until the middle of the nineteenth century'.[102]

Hennessy's death is recorded by a brief announcement in the *Freeman's Journal* and *Irish Times* of Monday 14 January 1889, followed next day with the news that the funeral would leave his residence, 71 Pembroke Road, 'this, Tuesday, morning for Glasnevin Cemetery'. The chief mourners were W.C. Hennessy, Casimir O'Meagher, John Maunsell and S. McNamara.[103] There was a large attendance of friends and of members of the legal profession. Those present included Lord Justice Barry, Rev. Canon Lee, P.P., Rev. Alfred Murphy, S.J., Rev. Maxwell H. Close, Treasurer Royal Irish Academy, Dr. E.P. Wright, Secretary RIA, John Macsheehy, solr., President Incorporated Law Society, J.J. Digges La Touche, Assistant Keeper of Records, R.F. Maunsell, C.E. Maunsell, R.I. French and S.E. Bramwell, The Library TCD, R.M. Hennessy, B.L., James Mills, P.W. Joyce LL.D., John H. Maunsell, R.W.S. Maybury, Valentine J. Coppinger, B.L. and many more. The newspaper reports are spare and undiscursive and little can be gleaned from them.[104]

Hennessy's son, William Charles, was a member of the Irish Bar.

Casimir O'Meagher may be identified with Joseph Casimir O'Meagher, M.R.I.A., author of *Some historical notices of the O'Meaghers of Ikerrin* (1886), of which there was a copy in Hennessy's library, Hennessy being included in the author's list of acknowledgements which took the form of a decorative round robin device. O'Meagher was a colleague of Hennessy's in the Society for the Preservation of the Irish Language.

Hennessy's grave in Glasnevin Cemetery is number UB 98 South. It is unmarked by any memorial. The other burials in the grave are: Kate O'Callaghan, Beggar's Bush, died 7 September 1855, aged 25 years, Helen Hennessy, Vavasour Square, died 16 November 1855, aged 11 months, Anne Hennessy, Silver Acres, Killester, died 4 November 1859, aged 32 years, in giving birth to David Hennessy, died same date, who is buried with her, William Maunsell Hennessy, 71 Pembroke Road, died 13 January 1889, aged 60 years, and William Hennessy, National Club, Rutland Square, died 11 June 1898, aged 38 years. As may be inferred, the family was visited by sadness enough, but it is strange that Hennessy's wife, who, we are to understand, died in tragic circumstances in 1885, is not buried in the same grave. A feature about Hennessy's life is its anonymity. Knowledge which at the time was commonplace has been lost to us through not being placed on record. There may have been personal and family correspondence and it is possible that records of some kind have survived to document the career of the eminent scholar whose name is often mentioned in context with O'Curry and O'Donovan. Sir Norman Moore mentions letters. This essay is being written in the hope that further materials may come to light and tell us more about the man who deserves recognition as 'the most accomplished Irish scholar of his day'.

XI

A Celtic Scholar's Library
Hennessy's library was sold by auction on 26 and 27 June 1890 by John W. Sullivan at his literary, art and general salerooms, 8 D'Olier Street, Dublin. It contained 490 lots in all, but some of these were multiple volumes, such as for example seventy four numbers of the Kilkenny Archaeological Society's *Transactions* 1852-1888.

A man's library says much about him. Hennessy's library included the important classical authors like Cicero, Plato, Thucydides, Livy (the latter a three volume printing, dated Amsterdam, 1665, of the celebrated Elzevier firm), works in German and French on linguistics, mythology, early European history, Jacob Grimm's *Deutsche Mythologie*, Wilhelm Grimm's *Deutsche Heldensage*, a substantial content of English literature and history, volumes on archaeology and topography, works on Sanskrit grammar; works on humanism, many of them early printings, works on Scottish Gaelic like *Leabhar na Féinne*, edited by John F. Campbell, with autograph letter from the editor, John F. Campbell's *Popular tales of the West Highlands,* four volumes, a presentation copy from the author; Armstrong's Gaelic Dictionary 'with considerable marginal Notes, Alterations and Additions, by W.M. Hennessy', Carl Lottner's copy of the Edda, 'with a considerable amount of Manuscript additions, in his handwriting'; nine volumes of the English Historical Society's Publications, thirty three titles of The Master of the Rolls Publications, including Hennessy's own two volume *Annals of Loch Cé*, 'with Copious Manuscript Notes &c by the Editor'.

The section headed Irish history, antiquities, language, topography, biography, etc., is of special interest. No. 159 comprises the second edition of Zeuss's *Grammatica Celtica*, edited by Hermann Ebel (Berlin 1871) which 'Contains a large amount of manuscript marginal notes, corrections, and additions, by the late W.M. Hennessy', and with it Guterboch et Thurneysen, *Indices Glossarum et Vocabulorum Hibernicorum quae in editione altera explanantur.* This latter, published 1881, was a presentation copy from the authors to the 'Senior of Irish Philology', a respectful and significant compliment. Under the same number came Molloy's *Index* to Zeuss, No. 1, and a manuscript critique on Ebel's edition of Zeuss, which seems to have been by Hennessy. There were two copies in the library of the first edition of 1853, two volumes, one being Siegfried's copy as noted earlier and the other with manuscript notes by Hennessy. Many Irish grammars are included, about ten of Whitley Stokes's Celtic publications, some with manuscript notes by Hennessy, Zimmer's *Keltische Studien* and *Glossae Hibernicae*, the latter with manuscript notes by Hennessy, works of Windisch, Henri d'Arbois de Jubainville, Diefenbach's *Celtica Sprachliche Documente,* Molloy's *Lucerna Fidelium* (Rome 1676) and a number of the Todd Lecture Series, including the *Destruction of Bruiden Da Derga*, the Irish text with English translation and notes by Hennessy, proof sheets of pages 1-65, all printed. This was the work which James Graves could not understand being delayed and about the fate of which Standish O'Grady was concerned but the sad story of its end is stated here to be that 'The printing of this unpublished tract proceeded no further than the proof sheets, and the type was distributed without even one revised copy of it being struck off'.

Irish Manuscripts, etc.

Items 200 to 276 come under the above heading. A small number of these are copies made by anastatic process from transcripts of O'Donovan and O'Curry. Item 207 is Hennessy's own handwritten copy of the *Annals of Ulster* 1014 to 1475 (only printed to 1056). Of special interest are items 208 and 209, the first being 'Keating's History of Ireland (in Irish) in the beautiful handwriting of Ferfesa MacConor Reagh O'Duignan, having date on fly leaf, and at page 168, of 23rd November 1666,' the second being 'Táin Bó Cualgne, or the Cow Plunder, a beautiful copy of Irish in current Roman hand with all the contractions in extenso, marginal annotations and English translation to page 10, intended for publication, folio, 232 pp hf. Bd'. It is not said whether this was Hennessy's own transcript but the strong probability is that it was. The statement that it was intended for publication is interesting, and it seems to have been among the many projects which Hennessy did not have the opportunity to pursue.

Item 230 is intriguing: 'An English-Irish Dictionary, 12mo, pp 718, hf. Cf. 'In a Note on last page Pat Glynn announces that he will shortly Publish an English-Irish Dictionary with upwards of 100,000 words which have never been published in any Dictionary of our Vernacular. "To Subscribers 10s. only".' Amongst the texts copied by Hennessy from manuscripts, and intended either for his own study or for publication, were *Beatha Patraic*, the Tripartite Life, copied from a manuscript in the Bodleian Library and collated with a manuscript in the Egerton collection in the British Museum, folio pp 162, the *Féilire Aengusa*, copied from MS Laud 610 in the Bodleian Library, folio pp 117, *Rules for the different measures of Irish versification*, copied in current hand by W.M.H. from the Book of Ballymote, *The Race of Conaire Mór*, copied in current hand from MacFirbis' Genealogies (R.I.A. copy), *Alphabetical Book*, a large folio, with several Irish entries under 'Rare words, as groundwork of a Dictionary of Archaic Irish words', by W.M.H., the *Senchas Naomh Erend and other Extracts*, from the Book of Lecan, made by W.M.H., quarto, *Agallamh na Senorach*, transcribed by W.M.H., folio, *The Book of Occupations of Ireland,* from the Book of Leinster, transcribed by W.M.H., quarto, *The Tract of the Boroma, and the Battle of Dunbolg*, copied from the Book of Leinster, and translated by W.M.H., folio, 2 fascicles, *The Voyage of Maildun*, translated into English from the Leabhar na h-Uidhri, by W.M.H., (described as 'Valuable'); *Irish text of the Life of St. Brendan Mac Finnloga,* copied in current hand by W.M.H from the Book of Lismore; *Transcript of historical tales*, from the Books of Ballymote and Lecan, in current hand by W.M.H., quarto, and very many others. Reading through the list of transcripts, the words of Standish Hayes O'Grady about Hennessy are borne in mind.

Hennessy was a man of talent, and certain it is that after him other men of talent will arise and wish to follow in his steps; but, for want of similar qualifications to start with, never again will any to such purpose spend the better part of forty years in close familiarity with the great tomes (to speak of Dublin only) known as 'The Book of the Dun Cow'; the Books of Leinster, of Ballymote, of Lecan; the *Lebhar Breac* and the Yellow Book of Lecan; and, in the same degree as did Hennessy, know them from end to end.[105]

His copy of O'Curry's *Lectures* carried 'copious MS. marginal notes, and detached memoranda' and of the same author's *Manners and Customs* carried manuscript marginal notes and detached memoranda. There were presentation copies of Shearman's *Loca Patriciana,* Comerford's *Collections relating to the Diocese of Kildare and Leighlin,* numerous histories of Ireland, many Irish local and county histories including Smith's *Kerry* and Hickson's *Old Kerry Records,* first and second series. Norman Moore, in his entry in the DNB about Hennessy, says he had made numerous additions to Edward O'Reilly's *Dictionary.* Hennessy had two interleaved copies of O'Reilly, numbered 369 and 370 in the catalogue, the first, wanting the Grammar, with Supplement by O'Donovan, two volumes, Dublin 1817-64, 'containing a very large amount of manuscript notes, annotations and additions by W.M. Hennessy', the second, with the Irish Grammar, Dublin 1817, 'containing a considerable amount of manuscript notes, etc., by W.M. Hennessy'.

It is interesting to note that his copies of Whitley Stokes' publications are annotated by him, e.g. *Irish Glosses* has 'numerous manuscript marginal notes by W.M.H.', *Cormac's Glossary,* translated by O'Donovan and edited by Stokes, has 'manuscript marginal notes by W.M.H.' An item of particular interest is O'Conor's *Rerum Hibernicarum Scriptores Veteres,* volume 1, Dr. John O'Donovan's copy with numerous manuscript notes, and pedigree of the O'Donovan family, 'Presented to Mr Hennessy as a slight token of her gratitude for his kindness – by Mrs. O'Donovan'. This links him with John O'Donovan, who died in 1861. Did they know each other? There seems no reason why not. O'Flaherty's *Ogygia* (1785) 'the gift of my dear friend, Father Shearman', Sir Samuel Ferguson's *Poems* (Dublin 1880) 'with kind regards from the author', presentation copies from Aubrey de Vere of his various works, are amongst the numerous other items which made this library one of exceptional character, of which but a small section of its content is represented in the foregoing description. It was the library of a man dedicated to the study of the

Irish language in all its aspects, whose life was devoted to the interests of scholarship and literature and who numbered amongst his friends many of his time whose distinction was manifest in the realms of scholarship, literature and history.

XII

William Charles Hennessy

Hennessy's talent was inherited by his son, William Charles, although his interests lay in a different direction. There is a brief account of his career in D. J. O'Donoghue's *Poets of Ireland*, 2nd edition (Dublin 1912), as follows:

> HENNESSY, WILLIAM CHARLES. -Ye Kingstown Ballade by Ye Kingstown Barde, 1870(?), 16mo (probably by Hennessy); VARSITY VERSICLES (published over initials of 'W.H.'), Dublin, 1879; IRELAND'S BOTCH AND SCOTCH RULERS, a satire (published over the signature of 'Mr. Ellem'), in imitation of 'Byron's English Bards and Scotch Reviewers,' Dublin, 1886 (?); THE SECEDERS, a series of squibs (printed at Naas), Dublin, 1894, 8vo.
>
> A Kerry man, and son of the late William M. Hennessy, M.R.I.A., the eminent Irish scholar. Born in or about 1860, and educated by the Jesuits at Belvedere College. Called to the Irish Bar, and wrote for *Nation* over signature of 'Seehaitch', to *United Ireland* over those of 'Truthful James', and to a Dublin journal called *Froth*, over those of 'Charles Herbert', 'Charles Hennessy', etc. Wrote two pantomimes for Gaiety Theatre, Dublin – 'Robinson Crusoe' and 'Cinderella' (1888-9) – and has produced a comedy in one act, entitled 'Dora's Dowry', which was played by the 'Caste' Company in the provinces. Wrote much for Dublin *Evening Herald*, and about 1892 was preparing a new volume of his 'Varsity Versicles'. He died at Whitworth Hospital, Dublin, in June, 1898. One of his best-known pieces was 'On an Outside Car.'

With regard to the probable authorship of *Ye Kingstown Ballade* mentioned above it may be noted that William Maunsell Hennessy lived for many years in Kingstown (now Dún Laoghaire) at 8 Islington Avenue, and that the *Ballade* may reflect some impressions his son garnered there. The present writer has seen only one of the above writings, entitled *The Seceders, a series of 'Squibs'* (Dublin 1894) of which there is a copy in the National Library. It is a fragile pamphlet of

19 pages, reprinted from the Dublin *Evening Herald*, and autographed on the title page 'With the author's Compts/W.C. Hennessy'.

The *Dedication* reads:
　　I dedicate these verses/to two/latent entities/whom I never met/and never hope to meet,/namely,/prosperity/and/happiness,/and as regards whose existence/I am more or less/a/sceptic.

William Charles was obviously an ardent Parnellite, an inference it is fair to take from the Preface, in which he says:

My opinions regarding Messrs. Dillon, O'Brien, *et hoc genus omne...* are freely expressed in the following squibs. The reader may find them bad workmanship, but he will find them disgustingly *true*. And truth is such a scarce commodity just now in Irish politics that he ought not to grumble when he finds it. The author's new work, 'The Curse of Erin', will be ready in a fortnight. It will, perhaps, do his writing capabilities more credit, but the same cannot be said of the 'melancholy humbugs', 'gifted members', and 'Spenccrian bootblacks', of which it will deal. With those observations the author subscribes himself the readers' very humble servant.

The pamphlet contains some vigorous invective against the leading anti-Parnellites.

Acknowledgement

I should like to record my thanks to Mrs. Bridget Dolan, Librarian, Royal Irish Academy, for her kindness in supplying from the Academy archives the photograph of William Maunsell Hennessy, which accompanies this essay, to Mr. David Thomson, of Glasnevin Cemetery Office, for details of burials in the Hennessy grave, to the young man from the same office who kindly directed me to where Hennessy is buried, to Rev. Kieran O'Shea who sent me extracts from Kerry newspapers, and not least to the staff of the National Library where most of the research for this essay was done.

References
1. *Kerry Evening Post* 16 Jan 1889.
2. *Royal Soc. Of Antiq. Ire. Jn.* (1891) 688.
3. *Ibid.,* 689.
4. Letter dated 7 May 1874 quoted in *RSAI Journal* (1891) 409.
5. *Proc. Royal Ir. Academy*, third series, vol. 1 appendix, 31. Dublin 1888-91.
6. J.F. Kenney: *The sources for the early history of Ireland: Ecclesiastical* (New York 1929) 68.
7. 'The Curragh of Kildare' in *Royal Ir. Academy Proc.,* vol. 9 (1864-6) 343-55.

8. *The Academy* 1 July 1872, 242.
9. Windisch to John T. Gilbert 3 Feb 1888, printed in R.M. Gilbert: *Life of Sir John T. Gilbert* (London 1905) 343.
10. Quoted on title page of his *Remarks on the facsimiles published by the Royal Irish Academy* (Simla 1875).
11. From *The Ibis* July 1874, 276. Quoted on title page of *Remarks on the Celtic additions to Curtius' Greek Etymology etc.*
12. *Op. cit.,* 5.
13. *Ibid.,* 64-5.
14. *Ibid.,* 2.
15. *The Academy* 1 Dec 1888.
16. *The Academy* 20 Aug 1881. Nutt comments that 'Henceforth, we may hope to be rid of the uncritical slovenliness which has been the curse of Celtic Studies. And I trust that Irish scholars will be roused to the scandal and shame of allowing Germans to annex the whole of their rich and precious literature while they stand idly by, and content themselves with publishing at rare intervals garbled scraps'.
17. There was no doubt about which side would have the support of Canon Peter O'Leary who, in a controversy of later times, poured scorn on the notion of approaching the study of Irish through its oldest forms. 'In order to climb a tree you must begin at the top!' The respective values of the two approaches are considered by Dr. D.A. Binchy in his lecture *Osborn Bergin* (University College Dublin 1970) 10-12.
18. *The Academy* 1 Dec 1888.
19. *The Academy* 24 Aug and 14 Sept 1889.
20. Cf. Canon Patrick Power: 'The Gaelic Union', *Studies* Dec 1949, 417. Cf. also 'The Revival of the Irish Language' in *The Irish Fireside* Vol. VI, 2 Jan 1886.
21. 24 April 1909. Alfred Nutt in the following issue, 1 May 1909, wrote to redress the balance: 'He was the ablest of the successors of Zeuss in the task of establishing *Celtische Philologie* (which means so much more than Celtic philology) upon a rigidly scientific basis. In addition he did more than any other man to make Irish mediaeval *literature* accessible to the world at large by providing texts, edited with the utmost accuracy, and translations equally admirable for their faithfulness and their literary quality'.
22. *Silva Gadelica* 2 vols (London 1892); Preface xxvi-xxvii.
23. *The Academy* 6 April 1889.
24. *The Academy* 13 April 1889.
25. But praises Windisch as 'one of the few distinguished continental scholars' who performed his own task without injury to his fellow. *Silva Gadelica* Preface xxvi, footnote 1.
26. 'Remarks on the Oxford edition of the Battle of Ventry', *Philological Society Transactions* (1884) 619-647.
27. *Times Literary Supplement* 28 Oct 1915, in the course of a long and interesting biographical letter about O'Grady.
28.

University College
Liverpool
Jan 17, '86

Dear Dr. Stokes,

... I cannot help being greatly annoyed at the tone which he has used, but much more by the unfairness of his criticism... whatever is just in his remarks I am the first to acknowledge and be thankful for, but why he, with his great knowledge of Modern Irish and of Irish literature, should thus try to do serious harm to a beginner who has had the bad luck to get at a text of such difficulty, without one word of acknowledgement or of encouragement, I do not comprehend. I consider it a very unfortunate thing that he should have broken his long silence in this manner.

I wonder whether I ought to answer him. He has made many mistakes himself... Yours very sincerely, Kuno Meyer (TCD MS 7970, 182)

29. *Revue Celtique* XIV, 321-337; XV, 108-122, 371-382. Meyer writes, RC XIV, 322: 'In textual accuracy and critical insight Dr. O'Grady's work falls below that of O'Donovan, O'Curry and Hennessy ...'

30   *Mise agus an Connradh* (Baile Átha Cliath 1937) 15.

31. National Library of Ireland Ms 11002 (67). Original in Gaelic script.

32. *Dublin University Magazine.* Vol. LXX (Sept 1867) 352-60.

33. *Daily Express* (Dublin). Obituary notice reprinted in *Kerry Evening Post* 16 Jan 1889.

34. *Revue Celtique* 1, 32-55.

35. *Ibid.,* 32.

36. *Ibid.,* 55-7.

37. *Remarks on the Celtic additions to Curtius' Greek Etymology,* 65-6.

38. *Revue Celtique* II (1873-75) 86-93.

39. *Leabhar na Féinne,* 224.

40. *Ibid.,* pp 53, col. 1, 57, col. 2, 58, col. 1, 62, col. 1, 63, col. 2, 67, col. 2, 74, col. 2, 92, col. 1, 94, col. 1, 96, col. 1, 105, col. 1, 131, col. 1.

41. *Celtica,* catalogue of exhibition of MSS and books of Celtic interest. National Library of Scotland (Edinburgh 1967) 36. Hennessy's letter dated 17 Oct. 1872.

42. *Ibid.,* 36.

43. *Ibid.,* 37. Date of letter given as 1872.

44. *The Poems of Ossian,* in the original Gaelic, with a literal translation into English, and a Dissertation on the Authenticity of the Poems, by the Rev. Archibald Clerk. Together with the English Translation by Macpherson. In two volumes. Edinburgh and London: William Blackwood & Sons, 1870.

45. *The Academy* 1 Aug 1871, 365-67, 15 Aug 1871, 390-94.

46. *The Academy* 15 Aug 1871, 393.

47. *Ibid.,* 394.

48. *First Report of the Deputy Keeper of the Public Records in Ireland* (Dublin 1869) Appendix No. 7, 40-41.

48a. In a letter of 15 Oct 1986 to the present writer David V. Craig, Senior Archivist, Public Record Office of Ireland, says that nothing of any interest about Hennessy can be traced in the records nor does there seem to be anything extant in the way of personnel records for the nineteenth century.

49. *Third Report of the Deputy Keeper of the Public Records in Ireland* (Dublin 1871) 12.

50. M.F. Cusack, *Life of St. Patrick* Preface 6-7.

51. James Henthorn Todd: *Cogadh Gaedhel re Gallaibh* (London 1867), Introduction, ccv.

52. *Annals of Loch Cé* (London 1871).
     Vol. I Text and translation 1-653 pp + Catalogue 31 pp + map
     Vol II Text and translation 1-519 pp + Index 523-689 + Catalogue of Record Office publications.

53. P. Walsh, *Irish Ecclesiastical Record,* August 1940.

54. Cf. Irish Manuscripts Commission. *Catalogue of Publications 1928-1966* (Dublin) 35.

55. Kuno Meyer, *Aislinge Meic Conglinne: the vision of MacConglinne, a Middle-Irish Wonder Tale* edited with a translation (based on W.M. Hennessy's), notes, and a glossary (London 1892), Preface viii-ix.

56. *Mesca Ulad: or the Intoxication of the Ultonians.* With translation and introductory notes, 16 + 58 pp. Dublin 1889.

57. *The Academy* 8 July 1893.

58. *Silva Gadelica* II Preface xxvi-xxvii.

59. *Revue Celtique* X (1889) 244-7.

60. *Ibid.,* 247.

   De ces critiques on aurait tort de conclure que je n'aie pas la plus haute estime pour le travail de Hennessy. Seulement la traduction d'un texte irlandais présente plus de difficulté que le vulgaire ne le croit. Hennessy connaissait le vocabulaire irlandais mieux que ne le savent la plupart des érudits qui étudient le vieil irlandais sur le continent, mais, comme un grand nombre de ses compatriotes, il n'avait pas fait d'études grammaticales suffisantes, il négligeait quelquefois l'analyse grammaticale, ne sentait pas toujours assez l'utilité d'un mot à mot rigoureux; enfin il ne comprenait pas bien en quoi un mot à mot et une traduction doivent se ressembler, doivent en même temps différer l'un de l'autre. Il n'y a pas de savant dont l'érudition n'ait ses lacunes, et malgré ses côtés faibles, Hennessy était un homme d'un grand talent, un celtiste de premier ordre. J'ai été pendant quelques semaines l'élève d'Hennessy, que n'ai-je mieux profité des leçons de ce maître si instruit, si modeste, si bienveillant, que vient de nous enlever une mort prématurée! H. d'A. de J.

61. Alfred Nutt. Career outlined in Richard Dorson, *The British Folklorists* (London 1968) 229-39.

62. 'Hennessy's Todd Lectures', *Archaeological Review* (1889) 206 et seq.

63. *The Academy* 26 Jan 1889.

64. Rev. James Graves, Stoneyford, to John T. Gilbert, 27 June 1883, printed in R.M. Gilbert: *Life of Sir John T. Gilbert* (London 1905) 305.

65. Denis Henry Kelly (1798-1877) of Castle Kelly, Co. Roscommon. Kelly, described by R.A.S. Macalister as 'an enthusiastic member of the Royal Irish Academy in the middle years of the nineteenth century, whose varied interests and accomplishments are attested by his contributions to the publications of that body'. (*The Book of Fenagh: Supplementary Volume, 3*). There is a brief but critical appraisal of him, and an outline of his interests and activities, in the 1982 publication of the Killian-Killeroran Historical Society, Ballygar, Co. Galway, pp 31-38. For this reference I am grateful to Dr. Patrick Melvin, Oireachtas Library, Leinster House.

66. *The Book of Fenagh,* iii.

67. S.H. O'Grady, *The Academy* 26 Jan 1889, 56.

68. Irish Manuscripts Commission. *Catalogue of Publications 1928-1966* (Dublin) 34.

69. P. Walsh, *Irish men of learning* (Dublin 1947) 49-73, more particularly pp 55-73.

70. *The Book of Fenagh: Supplementary Volume* (Dublin 1939) 3-4.

71. *Mise agus an Connradh,* 20.

72. *Ibid.,* 21.

73. The origins and progress of the Society are documented in its *Reports,* and in miscellaneous pamphlets and newscuttings, in the National Library, Call Nos. Ir 49162 s 5 and s 24.

74. *Mise agus an Connradh,* 21.

75. Constantino Nigra: Italian diplomat and Celticist, author of *Reliquie Celtiche, Il Manoscritto Irlandese di S. Gallo*, Firenze-Torino-Roma 1872 and other studies.

76. *Essai*, Introduction, xvi.

77. *Ibid.*, lxxix.

78. The/Poets and Poetry/of/Munster: A Selection of Irish Songs/by the poets of the last century./With poetical translations/by the late/James Clarence Mangan,/and the original music;/Biographical sketches of the authors;/and Irish text revised by/W. M. Hennessy,/M.R.I.A./Edited by C. P. Meehan, C.C../Third Edition./Dublin;/James Duffy and sons, 15 Wellington quay,/And 1 Paternoster Row, London. Dated 1883 by O'Grady, 1884 by O'Donoghue Preface xix to Mangan's *Poems*, Dublin 1922. Cf. Hodges Figgis Catalogue 21 (1966) New Series *Books relating to Ireland: History and Modern Literature*. Item 839, p.70 'The third and best edition edited by C.P. Meehan'.

79. *R.I.A. Proceedings* x, part 1 (Dublin 1867) 34-43.

80. In two vols, ed. Margaret Stokes (Dublin 1872-78). The poems with translation appear in Vol I, 5-7 (Ó Gilláin) and 79-82 (Ó Maoilconaire).

81. *Irish Ecclesiastical Record* VIII (1871) 178-90.

82. Vol. II (Edinburgh 1877) Preface ix. Hennessy's contribution, Appendix 467-510, is introduced as 'The Old Irish Life of St. Columba,/being/A discourse on his life and character/delivered to the brethren on his festival./Translated from the original Irish text by W. Maunsell Hennessy, Esq., M.R.I.A., and a brief preface goes on to say that 'the following is a literal translation of the Irish Life of St. Colum Cille, as contained in the *Leabhar Breac* (Royal Irish Academy Library, indicated by the letters L.B. in the foot-notes), collated with another copy preserved in the *Book of Lismore* in the same library (distinguished in the notes by the letter L.) and with the text of a Gaelic MS. in the Advocates' Library, Edinburgh (indicated in the notes by the letters A.L.)'.

There are many explanatory footnotes.

Other contributions by Hennessy to Skene's work are acknowledged in Vol. III (Edinburgh 1880) Preface vii, one in relation to 'the curious poem' *Baile Suthain Sith Eamhna* printed in Appendix II, 410-427, 'An Irish poem relating to the Kingdom of the Isles, copied from a fragment (paper) of an Irish MS written circa A.D. 1600, in the possession of W.M. Hennessy, Esq., collated with a copy contained in the Book of Fermoy (R.I. Academy), transcribed about A.D. 1457', as well as a tract *Na Trí Colla*, p.462 et seq., taken from Ms TCD, H.3, 18 and translated by Hennessy.

83. Tome VI (1883-5) 298-308.

84. *The Book of Leinster*, a lithographic reproduction of Joseph O'Longan's transcript, with Introduction, Analysis of Contents and Index by Robert Atkinson (Dublin 1880).

85. *Report*, p.3.

86. *The Academy* 26 Jan 1889, 56.

87. Entry on Hennessy in *Dictionary of National Biography*.

88. Gilbert to Stokes 24 Jan 1888. *Life of Gilbert* by Rosa M. Gilbert, 336-7.

89. Stokes to Gilbert, 25 Jan 1888 *Life of Gilbert*, 337.

90. Gilbert to Stokes 26 Jan 1888, *ibid*, 339.

91. Thurneysen to Gilbert 5 Feb 1888, *ibid*, 342.

92. *The Times* 14 Jan 1889, p.9, col. e.

93. H. d'Arbois de Jubainville to Gilbert, 26 January 1889. *Life of Gilbert* 348.

94. *Revue Celtique* X (1889) 151.

95. Reprint in *Kerry Evening Post* 16 Jan 1889.

96. *RIA Proceedings* Third Series Vol. I, Appendix, 32.

97. *Revue Celtique* X (1889) 151-2. M. Hennessy continuait avec une grande supériorité sur ses devanciers la tradition des O'Donovan et des O'Curry. Je n'ai jamais recontré un savant plus libéral des trésors de son érudition. Il était toujours prêt à donner aide à qui de lui demandait, et plus d'une personne qui a écrit et signé un mémoire n'a pas compris et n'a pu donc penser à dire, que la plus grande partie avait été dictée par M. Hennessy. Il l'avait fait, comme en se jouant, pendant les courts instants de récréation qu'il se donnait tous les jours dans la bibliothèque de l'Académie Royale d'Irlande en sortant des Archives après l'accomplissement de sa tâche officielle, et avant de rentrer chez lui où d'autres labeurs l'attendaient.

Paris, le 16 Janvier 1889. H. d'Arbois de J.

98. Sir Norman Moore (1847-1922). Medical doctor, author and scholar, born Manchester of Irish parentage. For details of his career see Pádraig de Brún and Máire Herbert, *Catalogue of Irish Manuscripts in Cambridge Libraries* (CUP 1986) Introduction xiv, footnote 23, and sources there cited. See also *The Countryman* (Oxfordshire) Spring 1971, 82-91. Possessed an excellent Irish library (O'Grady *Silva Gadelica* II, Preface xxvi). Wrote a history of St. Bartholomew's Hospital while engaged on which he confided to Kuno Meyer (from whom he became estranged in time of war) that he would rather be engaged on Irish. Contributed 459 entries to *Dictionary of National Biography* in which, curiously, he has so far not been given an entry for himself.

99. *The Academy* 26 Jan 1889, 56.

100. Quoted in Dominic Daly: *The young Douglas Hyde* (IUP 1974) 64. Petrie is included in error. He was not a native speaker of Irish.

101. J.F. Kenney, *The sources for the early history of Ireland: Ecclesiastical,* 68.

102. *Ibid.,* 66.

103. *Freeman's Journal* 16 Jan 1889.

104. *Irish Times* 16 Jan 1889.

105. *The Academy* 26 Jan 1889, 56.

Chapter 4

Douglas Hyde and the Gaelic League

'He was an old imperialist!' That statement, which one has heard drop from the lips of different people, conjures up a picture something like what occupants of the Kildare Street Club were in popular imagination. It was an opinion held formerly, if not now, by many people who considered Douglas Hyde a congenial citizen of regions where dukes walked and vice-regal *soirées* were held, a sort of crown-colony figure but not authentically native, and far from republican. It is a view of Douglas Hyde which must be judged in the light of his work and achievement.

On the last page of his *Literary History of Ireland* Hyde describes himself as 'of the stock of the Anglo-Irish in Ireland'. His Irish ancestor Arthur Hyde was an Elizabethan planter from Denchworth, Berkshire, who received a grant of land in County Cork, on the north side of the Blackwater at Carraig an Éide, where his successors built the fine family mansion of Castle Hyde. In Denchworth parish church there is a brass memorial to Olyver and Agnes Hyde, whom some ten generations separate from their descendant, the first President of Ireland. Douglas Hyde tells us that his first Irish ancestor 'was a friend of the Queen's favourite, that rascal Dudley',[1] otherwise the Earl of Leicester, whose place in Elizabethan history is celebrated enough.

First steps in Irish
Douglas Hyde was born on 17 January 1860 in Castlerea, Co. Roscommon, spent the first seven years of his life at Kilmactranny, Co. Sligo, and came to Frenchpark, Co. Roscommon, in 1867, when his father, Rev. Arthur Hyde, took up duty there as Church of Ireland Rector. The environment of Douglas Hyde's boyhood, embracing central and northern Connacht, played an important part in the development of his consciousness, superlatively rich as it was in bardic culture, legend and folklore. Readers of Father Paul Walsh's scholarly studies will have noted the wealth of the area in Gaelic tradition.

Hyde received all his early education at home, apart from three weeks at what he calls 'a wretched school' in Dublin. He was expected by his father to enter the Church, following family tradition, and for that purpose a knowledge of Latin and Greek was desirable. His father gave him a start in these and he continued to study them on his own. His aunt, Cecily Hyde, introduced him to German, a language combining the dual prestige of fashion and scholarship, and before 1877 was out he read his first French book, learning everything with great method and perseverance. From all this it seems obvious that he had a talent for languages. The most interesting to him by far of these he found on his own doorstep, as he relates himself:

> But as to my Irish, I began to learn a little of it *viva voce* from Séamus Ó Hart, keeper of the bogs, and before he died I knew a good lot, except that I wasn't able to understand a great deal when I heard it spoken, although I was able to say practically every word I wanted myself. But on the death of poor Séamus, the most estimable and honest of men, and a man whom I held in greater respect and affection than anyone I ever knew or ever shall know, in 1875 in the month of December, I thought my Irish would have left my memory, but then I began to converse with Mrs. William Connelly when she came to milk the cows in the evening. I wasn't long talking to her when I found my Irish much improved for she was more useful to me than Séamus, he being too contrary and proud so that I feared to trouble him a great deal. Similarly at times I got vocabulary and knowledge from Seán Ó Láimhín and his wife, and from people I would meet while out fowling. It wasn't long until I was able to understand and speak it…[2]

His reading of Irish he learned out of a New Testament 'written in English [i.e. Roman] characters' which had been left in the house by a clergyman who did not want it. He explains what attracted him to the study of the language:

> When I began to learn Irish I had not expected that it would ever be the object of interest, or that it would be of any use to myself, except just that I thought it was a fine and worthy tongue.[3]

Early Patriotism

Although the young Douglas Hyde does not seem to have been particularly robust, having had pleurisy, eye-trouble and an injury to his left thigh, all in his early years, yet he was usually to be found leading an active life out-of-doors. His favourite recreation was fowling and he carefully recorded his shooting successes in his diary. He was fond of tennis and cricket (in later life of golf) and liked long country walks and adventures. He studied on his own from five to six hours a day.

He learned methodically, with considerable will-power and application. He learned his Irish out-of-doors too, recording his progress and experiences in learning it in his diary. His sincere and pleasing personality helped him to make friends, and he had an impish sense of humour. The mature man, who set new standards in the study of Irish folklore, had a fondness for the little animals, as a good folklorist should, so much so that he did not keep a cat (which might have prevented the mice from raiding his papers and devouring every bit of one important document).[4]

Douglas Hyde learned more than language from the local people. Some of them were Fenian and anti-British, and he took their political views from them with great willingness, composing in Irish rebel poems in praise of O'Donovan Rossa,[5] and in English the splendid lament for the Fenian chief John O'Mahony,[6] to whom he warmed in sympathy because of their common love of the Irish language. All the feeling of his youthful years was with Parnell, Davitt, Dillon and Rossa and his favour towards them would hardly have pleased his neighbour Lord de Freyne, nor would it have been well received in most of the social circles in which Hyde moved. There are times when one is inclined to marvel at the way in which the sagacity and conservatism of the grown man contrast with the fiery sentiments of the youth. Were they then really no more than a convention, these rebel thoughts, taken from the Gaelic poets who breathed fire and at every sunrise expected Stuart ships on the horizon? One cannot think so. Their sincerity is indisputable. They were part of his growing-up, no doubt, but more than that they were a deeply felt identification with his Gaelic environment, its tears and tragedy. O'Donovan Rossa commended him with warmth, and was proud of his friendship.

His diaries, which began when he was sixteen, are a remarkable production. Except for some early entries, they are written entirely in Irish, but the milieu, *familiares*, background, society and functions he describes are separated widely from the Gaelic world. They are a revealing commentary on the social preferences of the man who became first President of the Gaelic League and in time first President of Ireland. They are a record of a world of which an tAthair Peadar Ó Laoghaire or Pádraic Ó Conaire knew nothing and would have no sympathy with, being as separate and distant from theirs as the South Pole from the North, and having in common only the bond of the Irish language. There were later times when Douglas Hyde would come up from the country surroundings of the Connacht squire, or emerge from the tranquillity of his study, to preside at a Gaelic League meeting in the restless area of the Dublin labour troubles and feel an uncomfortable sense of difference between himself and what he considered to be the Larkinite elements of the Gaelic League – to such an extent that he would wear his oldest coat to these meetings lest he appear affluent (which he was not).

One of the most important events of his early years was his purchase at a Dublin auction of books and manuscripts from the library of John O'Daly, the Anglesea Street bookseller. His father gave him six pounds for the occasion and in three days of keen business the eighteen-year-old youth bought the considerable collection of books and manuscripts that were to form the basis of his Irish learning. Out of their study grew in later years his great *Literary History of Ireland*.

Trinity College Years

At the age of twenty Hyde took the entrance examination for Trinity College, Dublin, but continued to study at home, not attending lectures until nearly two years later, in the Trinity Term of 1882, and then only because to attend would be easier on his eyes. He took up residence in the College in November 1883. His father kept urging him to enter the Church, but Douglas Hyde had no taste for the Church, and profound disagreements with his father on religious and biblical interpretation led to a deep rift between them. In deference to his father's wishes, however, he followed a course in Divinity, in which he graduated with great distinction. His poor eyesight may have deterred him from studying medicine, towards which he thought he had an inclination. Despite his all-round brilliance, he seems to have been undecided about what career to follow. Perhaps at the back of his mind there was already the undefined thought of devoting his life's energies to the promotion of Irish. The death of his mother, to whom he was deeply attached, and the tension between himself and his father, made home a less attractive place and he must have been glad to get away to Dublin. In October 1886 he returned to Trinity College to pursue the more mundane study of the law, taking out his LL.D. degree in 1888.

Hyde's university career was particularly brilliant, abounding in prizes and medals, but his most important experiences took place outside the lecture hall. In Roscommon life had been quiet, in Dublin it was lively and stimulating. He took to it with great spirit and enjoyed the society of eager friends and companions. He attended the discussions of the Contemporary Club, which was what its name implies, a place where all questions of the day were debated with great vigour and frankness. Participants in these discussions included Maud Gonne, John F. Taylor, W. B. Yeats, John O'Leary, T. W. Rolleston, C. Litton Falkiner, Michael Davitt and George Sigerson. The experience he gained in debate was not without future value. His girl companion of these years was Frances Crofton. Some discussion of the Irish language in the newly launched *Dublin University Review* prompted Douglas Hyde to contribute a thoughtful essay to the August 1886 issue entitled 'A plea for the Irish Language'. He stated that while social and commercial relations made it a necessity for everyone on this island to learn English, tradition and national honour made it imperative 'to establish for all time a bi-lingual population in those parts of Ireland where Irish is now spoken'.[7] Putting it simply, English was a necessity for all, but national honour called for the preservation of Irish where it was spoken.

Reviving Spoken Irish

It is worth noting that Hyde had not departed from these views in 1894, a year after the Gaelic League was founded. In an address to the Irish Literary Society of London in that year he said:

> Let us sympathise with and let us aid the Gaelic League in its new born efforts to keep alive this great speech as a spoken language along our west coast and in our islands, side by side with the vulgar English tongue.[8]

He gave as his reason, that the western Irish-speaking districts would provide the vernacular knowledge which would assist scholars in perfecting their studies.

In a speech in New York in 1891 he laid emphasis on the need for speaking Irish if the language was to be kept alive, and asked what stronger or more lasting bond might be found to weld together the Irish nation.[9] In stressing the importance of speaking it he was saying something new and anticipating what became the main object of the Gaelic League. The thought which he had been giving for many years to the language and kindred subjects was concentrated in an address to the Irish Literary Society on 25 November 1892, which became famous for its importance and results.

The content of this address, later printed, is best given in a summary which is taken from Hyde's own notes:

> The whole gist of that address was to point out how indefensible and illogical it is for people who profess to abhor England and the English to be nevertheless actually going out of their way to imitate that country.
>
> I noticed four things especially in which self-respecting Irishmen should leave off attempting to imitate the English, four lines upon which we must proceed to de-Anglicise ourselves if Ireland is ever to become anything but another Britain.

I pointed to the suicidal policy we are pursuing in allowing our language with the great literature behind it to become extinct.

I showed the abysmal infamy, cowardice, snobbery and stupidity of dropping O and Mac and changing their honourable Milesian names into any villainous and ugly appellation so long as we were only English sounding.

I showed the rapid decrease of our musicians and the neglect of Irish airs, and advocated the stern repressing of English music-hall songs and return to and recultivation of our beautiful national melodies.

Finally I put in what may have seemed a rather quixotic plea on behalf of the jerseys of the Gaelic Athletic Association and our own homespun frieze in preference to wearing 'the cast off clothes of the English bourgeois'.

With regard to the last three points I found that the criticism of most of my hearers agreed with me, but with regard to the first and most important – the preservation and cultivation of Irish language and literature, I found much scepticism and opposition.[10]

He encountered the scepticism the very next evening at the Contemporary Club, most of the members of which had attended his lecture. The chairman of the Club's meeting on the occasion was W.F. Bailey, accounted one of the most brilliant men of the day, a friend of the Government, widely read in the law, an acknowledged authority on Irish affairs. When the subject of Hyde's lecture came up for discussion he dismissed it with contempt: 'Let us turn to something of importance and reality'.[11] He had no difficulty in getting the company to agree.

Foundation of the Gaelic League
Early the following year Hyde and W. B. Yeats travelled together to a meeting in Cork at which Denny Lane, an 1848 veteran, took the chair. Hyde listened with impatience as Lane proclaimed that if they were to wear the shackles of language he would wish them to be those of the English tongue, the jewelled key which opened the treasure-chest of the centuries from Chaucer up. Hyde spoke as he had in Dublin on the necessity of de-Anglicizing Ireland and countered the veteran with the riposte that the Gaelic Athletic Association had in five years done more for Ireland than the talkers had in sixty.[12] Hyde had little use for nationalists who disregarded the language.

The man to whom the honour is due for calling the Gaelic League into being is not Douglas Hyde, but Eoin MacNeill of Glenarm, Co Antrim.[13] To acknowledge this detracts in no way from the achievement of Douglas Hyde. At Hyde's inauguration as President of Ireland in 1938, MacNeill recalled the meeting forty-five years earlier at which Hyde had been elected President of the Gaelic League, the movement which aimed to restore the true personality of Ireland and resuscitate its fast-ebbing cultural traditions.

The meeting at which the League was born took place on 31 July 1893, in Martin O'Kelly's rooms at 9 Lower Sackville (now O'Connell) Street, its announced purpose being to preserve the Irish language as a spoken language in Ireland, *le haghaidh Teanga na Gaedhilge do choinneáil dá labhairt in Éirinn.*

Marriage

Douglas Hyde, for all that he was present at the founding of the Gaelic League and spoke at some length on the occasion, both in Irish and in English, had other things to engage his mind. He was occupied in the great human experience of love. His diary entries, normally so strictly kept, became quite erratic. He could not rightly remember what he did in July, a month during which he was paying all his attentions to Lucy Kurtz, 'until we arranged and settled firmly and irrevocably that we were to join in wedlock, and we made our engagement public'.[14]

In an end-of-year summary Hyde records that his marriage to Lucy Cometina Kurtz was for him the most important event of 1893, even of his whole life. *Leug na Gaedhilge* (as he called it – he did not like the word *Conradh*) he dismissed in a few words. The main workers in it, he says, were MacNeill, J. H. Lloyd, R. MacS. Gordon and O'Neill Russell. 'I did little. That was the year of least work and most importance I have yet experienced'.[15] In no way did he relate its importance to the Gaelic League.

Having married, Hyde settled down in Frenchpark to the life of a country gentleman. *Duine uasal thiar i Ros Comáin* was an tAthair Peadar's description of him.[16] There were shooting and fishing excursions with his neighbours the Lloyds, the O Conors of Clonalis and Lord de Freyne, often referred to by Hyde as *An Tiarna.* Social evenings were crowned with modest festivities amounting to a couple of cigars and a glass or two, sometimes more, of punch, or a bottle of hock, occasionally champagne. Despite impressions to the contrary that might be derived from his writings, Hyde's drinking was civilized and prudent. He wrote a great deal in these years.[17] His *Love Songs of Connacht* was published in 1893 and before the century was out he had some ten other publications to his credit including the *Literary History of Ireland,* published in 1899, a work of such latitude that its recent reprinting (London: E. Benn, 1967) finds two generations of brilliant Irish scholarship happy to pay it the tribute of leaving it without a rival. He was then nearing his fortieth year, the decade between 1890 and 1900 having been particularly fruitful in literary output.

There are people who insist, almost with vehemence, that Hyde was incapable of speaking or writing good Irish. It is wiser to avoid argument with them. Douglas Hyde's Irish may not have been impeccable, any more than St. Patrick's Latin, but he did have qualities of mind and imagination that touched what he wrote, even if ungrammatical, with the character that separates the poet, unbridgeably, from the grammarian. No one but a poet could have designed the *Love Songs of Connacht*. In the *Religious Songs of Connacht*, Hyde, a Protestant, produced a book of Roman Catholic content of which extensive tracts might have been written by a seventeenth-century Louvain friar. He was the most Roman Catholic of Protestants, or, put the other way around, the most Protestant of Roman Catholics. Entries in his diary telling us that he went to Mass on Sunday leave us wondering whether he attended Church of Ireland service. He does not seem to have been particular at what shrine he worshipped, and if he was in the company of Irish speakers, the part of humanity he considered nearest to God, all was well. If modern Ireland were to seek an ecumenical figure, Douglas Hyde would be ideal. His rectory background helped him to be quite at ease with priests and bishops, who were his great admirers and whose co-operation with him in the Gaelic League was one of the factors of its success.

The Gaelic League's Success

Many things helped to make the League a success far beyond the hopes of its founders. It did not take the shape they seemed to envisage for it, namely, to keep the language in its strength on the western perimeter where it was spoken. Although they announced their purpose of changing the venue of their work from Dublin to the Irish-speaking districts at the earliest opportunity, the course of events led in quite a different direction. The appeal of the League spread and took effect in the English-speaking parts of Ireland, where it called up feelings that Sir Horace Plunkett described as 'sentiments and thoughts which had been developed in Gaelic Ireland through hundreds of years, which no repression had obliterated entirely, but which remained a latent spiritual inheritance in the mind'.[18] In fact it was the extraordinary response of English-speaking Ireland, exhilarated at the discovery of its inner self, that made the League such a powerful influence.

Father O'Growney's grammars helped to make some knowledge of Irish widespread. The non-political character of the movement provided a neutral meeting-ground for people of different views; national politics were subdued, and the League provided an ideal alternative outlet for patriotic effort; the support of the influential Irish-American paper the *Irish World* was won by Hyde himself through persuasive correspondence with its formidable editor, Patrick Ford;[19] the final settlement of the land question, implicit in the Wyndham Act of 1903, cleared another field of contention;[20] the use of pageantry and processions lent colour and attraction to the Gaelic movement. The Boer War also helped, strange as it may seem, and its effect on Ireland is best related in Hyde's own words. He wrote:

> The Boer War had already, though nobody noticed it – openly at least – been the first public happening since the foundation of the Gaelic League to give a real impetus to the language movement ... For a couple of years the extraordinary courage and prowess of the Boers were steadily pumping hope and self reliance into Ireland; and it was the language movement which reaped most benefit from it. I took good care never to hint at this, scarcely even in private, but I was well aware of it at the time, and looking back now I do not think that I was mistaken.[21]

Hyde's own popularity was an invaluable asset. He had the appealing gifts of personality that attracted support. He never quarrelled with anyone – he was incapable of it. That was a great source of his strength. In controversy on behalf of the Irish language he was never less than courteous but at the same time he could be formidable. A case in point was the Commission on Intermediate Education in 1899 at which the Irish language as a subject of study came under discussion. A determined effort was made by a distinguished, but perhaps prejudiced, group of professors to have it struck off the education programme and so excluded from the schools. Hyde routed them in spectacular fashion. He sent copies of their evidence to such leading European Celticists as Heinrich Zimmer, Rudolf Thurneysen, Ernst Windisch, Ludwig Christian Stern, Holger Pedersen, Georges Dottin, Kuno Meyer and others, and the reasoned replies from these scholars were submitted by Hyde to the Commission. Their effect was crushing. Hyde's prestige soared.

To give some idea of the impact of the man and the movement on the public at the beginning of the present century let us go for a moment to the Gaiety Theatre in the heart of Dublin. *Diarmuid and Grania*, of which the joint authors were Yeats and George Moore, had just been performed. The scene is described by an eminent Belfast poet, James Cousins:

Then followed an event unique in the history of an imaginative and active people, the first performance on a regular stage by an Irish author in the Irish language performed by native Irish speakers. In a land of enthusiasm there have been few occasions to excel that one in the expression of a national hope ... It was a simple upsurge of a unifying wave from the depths of a race's consciousness, and it touched everyone with the joy of regeneration. Something had come to life, something that was experiencing birth in its body and rebirth in its soul. The play that thus opened up the authentic drama of Ireland, that is, drama dealing with the actual life and imagination of the people, written in the speech of the people by one of themselves and played by the people, was a one-act play, *The Twisting of the Rope*, by Dr. Douglas Hyde, the President of the Gaelic League, who himself played the part of Hanrahan ... A simple story; but its dressing and dialogue and the energy and delight of the actors were irresistible, and a scene of ungovernable enthusiasm followed...[22]

The League and Other Causes

In the years that followed, the Gaelic League, under the presidency of Douglas Hyde, advanced on the crest of a wave. It gave the breath of life to other movements. It was the progenitor of political Sinn Féin. It supported the Irish industrial revival. Sir Horace Plunkett found that the co-operative movement flourished best where the Gaelic League was active. It may well be asked – without the Gaelic League, would there have been an Anglo-Irish literary movement? Hyde toured America in 1905-6 on the invitation of his friend John Quinn. No cause could have a better advocate and by the end of his tour the prestige of the Gaelic League was consolidated in America. He returned home to a royal welcome, receiving the freedom of Cork, Kilkenny and Dublin. He wrote back to John Quinn: 'The whole of O'Connell Street was packed from side to side, and from the Rotunda to below Nelson's Pillar, with one solid mass of people ...'[23] Hyde would have been less than human had he not loved it. He brought back over £11,000 for the Gaelic League.

That year Hyde was appointed to the Fry Commission, which recommended the establishment of a National University for Ireland. After the university was brought into being by Augustine Birrell there began the great struggle as to whether Irish was to be an essential subject for entrance. The controversy raged throughout Ireland. Great meetings were held, culminating in the one held in Dublin which Hyde estimated was attended by about 100,000 people. There were two main factors which he believed won the day for 'essential Irish' in the university. The first was that the General Council of County Councils, which controlled an important source of finance, refused to give scholarships unless Irish was made essential. The second was the decisive voice in its favour of the United Irish League, the organization which represented John Redmond's Irish Nationalist Party through the country. Its attitude was announced at its Convention, what would now be called its Ardfheis, of 1909.

Although Douglas Hyde was not a member of the party, he had been asked to attend and was called on by John Redmond to speak after John Dillon. Hyde described what happened in a letter to Mrs. Alice Stopford Green:

> Today and yesterday I attended the National Convention of the U.I.L, where a motion was put on by Boland about 'Irish an essential'. John Dillon made a most powerful and emphatic speech against it, far the finest I ever heard him make. I followed him by special permission of John Redmond, and the division was taken when I had finished speaking, when Dillon was beaten by 2 to 1 in his own Convention! He did not like it!
> So powerfully and persuasively did he speak that if he had followed me I think he would have won.[24]

Hyde wrote to thank Redmond for allowing him to speak at the Convention:

> We are all very grateful to you for allowing the Gaelic League to be represented and to have a spokesman. It was very good of you too to allow me to follow Mr. Dillon.[25]

Let us pause for a moment to acknowledge that the debt owed by the Gaelic League to John Redmond for his gracious act was considerable. What Redmond may not have been aware of, however, was that behind Hyde's outward ingenuousness and simplicity of manner there lay hidden a superb and adroit capacity for making the best of an opportunity. One of the advantages Hyde had brought back out of his American experiences was an improved prowess in oratory. It is well to note also that his theological training may have contributed greatly to the civilized processes of argument of which he was a master. John Dillon, accomplished parliamentarian and sincere supporter of the Irish language though he was, started under handicap.

The significance of the Irish language victory in the Convention cannot be over-estimated. The United Irish League was the successor of Parnell's democratic machine and the predecessor of the present large-scale political organizations. It was not I.R.B. There was nothing revolutionary about it. But its ranks contained a great proportion of Gaelic Leaguers and provided a wide base of influential support for the Irish language. The result was that the National University Senate decided in favour of Irish forming an essential part of matriculation, although only by a majority of one – the casting vote of the Chancellor, Dr. William Walsh, Roman Catholic Archbishop of Dublin.

The Problems of Politics

This was the apex of the Gaelic League's success and of Douglas Hyde's active career. Henceforth Hyde and the League began to be confronted more and more with a problem that had raised its head from time to time since the beginning of the century, though not in any menacing way. This was the problem of keeping out politics. Horace Plunkett had long previous to this considered the danger of politics and forecast that if the League became political it would sink at once into insignificance.[26] Once he became a public figure Douglas Hyde never expressed a view on politics himself, not even to his own family. Long after the events he admits to have been at the back of his mind a Parnellite and therefore not drawn to Tim Healy.[27] He declined Redmond's offer of a place in parliament.[28] However, he did look forward to Home Rule and the advantages it might have in store for the language. He certainly did not consider a republic practical politics nor the demand for it expressive of the national ideal. He wrote to John Quinn on 9 July 1917:

> Colonial Home Rule would amply satisfy nineteen-twentieths of the race, and I don't care to see a republic preached lest, when real grievances are settled, the demand for it should persist and throw things into confusion.[29]

This was probably as close as he ever got to uttering a specific view on politics. Hyde did everything in his power to keep the League non-political and succeeded for many years. By doing so he earned the goodwill of everybody. He thus made it impossible for the Government to kill the League by sending out instructions to the education boards to strangle it as far as possible by hostile regulations. This he believed the Government would do if the League showed the least tendency to anti-English politics. 'The only reason I had for keeping politics out, was the desire to offend nobody, and get help from every party, which I did'.[30]

The formation of the Volunteers in 1913 drew away a certain amount of funds from the Gaelic League, to equip the military force. Hyde did not mind this, since the new feeling of nationhood that accompanied the rise of the Volunteers would, he considered, turn to the benefit of the language in the long run 'since nationality divorced from language is an absurd and impossible doctrine'.[31] He rejected the suggestion that the Gaelic League was a political society but did not deny that many of its supporters were politicians of an advanced kind. Because of this, said Hyde, many people identified the Gaelic League with advanced politics, and he was at pains to reject this view completely in a carefully-worded and realistic statement:

> The great bulk of Gaelic Leaguers through the country are pretty much of the ordinary type of politics current in their respective counties. I may call them the moderate men, whose ideas on political matters are much the same as those of their own County Councils. It is to these moderate men and to the County Councils of Ireland that we must look for support. When all is said and done, and in the last analysis, it is (in my opinion) in the hands of the rank and file of the tenant farmers and the shopkeepers of Ireland who elect the present County Councils … and who will … soon be electing members of the first Irish Parliament … that the government of this country will lie. And unless I am utterly wrong, I foresee that these men will be of a moderate and possibly even a conservative type, rather than of an extremist or revolutionary one.[32]

Here is a significant expression, by one who had given the matter deep and detached study, of the unregarded phenomenon that a nation is sustained by the people of moderate views whose unobtrusive and constant efforts receive no advertisement. It was on the people of moderate views that Hyde built his hopes for the Irish language. But his grave and quiet wisdom went unheeded. In the columns of *Irish Freedom*, well written, let no one doubt, the sentiment of John Mitchel was given fiery expression, 'Send us war in our time, O Lord!' The battlefield was romanticized, in emotions not confined to Ireland. It was the age of Rupert Brooke and Julian Grenfell.

> The fighting man shall from the sun
> Take warmth, and life from the glowing earth.[33]

The 1915 Oireachtas
When the Oireachtas of 1915 met in Dundalk the European war had been raging for a year. A great number of delegates were Volunteers. At the Ardfheis it was obvious that politics were in the air. Hyde saw many signs that he would have a disagreeable year of it, some items on

the agenda being, in his opinion, more or less directed at himself personally. He presided for two or three days and accomplished some useful work of harmony between Father Mat Maguire, who could not express himself effectively in Irish, and members of the Ardfheis, who insisted that he must use nothing else.

A resolution that the objects of the League be extended so as to include amongst them the further object of making Ireland 'free of foreign domination', was passed by a large majority, despite Hyde's protest that it was a political resolution. He stated, however, that he would treat it in a non-political sense throughout the year. It was not so much this resolution which made him uneasy as something else. This was the news that Seán Ó Murthuile, a member of the I.R.B., had received fifty proxies which, instead of being distributed to Irish speakers as would have been proper, were given to politically motivated people who did not know Irish and cared little for it. This proceeding helped to ensure that a predominantly political Coiste Gnótha would be elected. This was the result that really disturbed Hyde. He described his feelings:

> That night I did some furious thinking. About twelve o'clock at night I ascertained from O'Daly how the voting was going, and it was far enough advanced by that time to show that there would not be more than a dozen men on the new Coiste Gnótha who would support my consistently non-political attitude ... That decided me finally. I wrote out a letter addressed to Pádraig Ó Dálaigh to be read by him when the time for electing the President came on next day, in which, on grounds of health, I declined the honour of re-election if anyone should propose me ... I slipt away about 1 o'clock p.m. the following day after appearing as usual and talking to everybody, and arranging with Peadar MacGinley to take the chair at 2 o'clock. I got out my baggage from the hotel without anyone noticing it, got into the hotel bus and got to the train and was soon on my way to Dublin with a lighter heart than I had known for years.[34]

In effect, he had been forced out. The Gaelic League became identified with revolutionary politics. It is doubtful if the participants themselves realized the significance of what they had done or, though acting in perfect good faith, the harm they had brought on the Irish Language movement. It has been explained that their action was in the nature of a coup, or tactic, designed to offset the overwhelming influence of the parliamentary Nationalist Party.[35] The explanation, if it is the full one, is tragically jejune.

The Gaelic League, in its executive body, transferred its main interest from language to politics. As those who brought this about, or their successors, became engrossed in politics more and more, so inevitably their interest in the language became less and less, until in the end all their attention centred in politics. As the years passed, they persisted in offering the language, for political ends, the annihilating service of empty words. But this is to anticipate events.

The End of a Dream

In any case, perhaps Douglas Hyde's work was done by 1915. He was then 55 years old, having passed different phases of an extraordinarily active life promoting the language in work, thought and speech. He was in none too robust health, being exhausted with the uphill battle of recent years to keep the Gaelic League non-political. Perhaps he could have done no more. But the non-political years of the Gaelic League, coinciding with his presidency of it, were the era of its greatest success.

Far from being embittered, for indeed such feelings were alien to his nature, Hyde remained astonishingly clear and impartial in his view of what happened. He was not at all sure, he reflected, whether what had taken place was not in the best interests of the language, since now at least the movement had become homogeneous. But it put an end to his dream of making the Irish language a common bond between Irishmen of differing allegiances and made it seem the property of one section only.[36] This he regretted intensely.

When in 1923 he took a look at the political fact of an Irish Government sitting in Dublin, however, he recognized in its existence and character a logical consequence of the Gaelic League. He explained why nobody heeded the plea of Yeats that the Government should sit in the old Parliament House of College Green:

> It is because the movement which has resulted in the establishment of our own Government is the descendant of the Gaelic League, and the Gaelic League goes back to Gaelic Ireland, to ancient Ireland, for its inspiration. But Gaelic Ireland was a thing of which the 'old House in College Green' knew nothing, and for which it cared less. If it took cognisance of it at all it was only to despise it … The Gaelic League grew up and became the spiritual father of Sinn Féin, and Sinn Féin's progeny were the Volunteers who forced the English to make the Treaty. The Dáil is the child of the Volunteers, and thus it descends directly from the Gaelic League, whose traditions it inherits. And these are *not* the traditions of Grattan's Parliament but of something outside and beyond it.[37]

Hyde remains in many ways a subtle and unexplained character and it is by no means easy to get inside of him. There is no room in this sketch even to glance at his pioneer approaches to Irish folklore, his work for the Folklore Society of Ireland or his other academic pursuits. There is a statement of his which we might consider now since we can bring hindsight to bear on it. Making a comparison between the methods of militancy and the pacific methods of the Gaelic League in preserving the character of the Irish nation, he said, 'We were doing the only business that really counted'.[38] A view to ponder.

Choosing him by agreement as first President of Ireland was an imaginative act which by its doing raised the level of Irish politics above the commonplace. This writer has been told that he passed out of life in the full belief that the language was saved. For him there could have been no happier death.

References

Note: The author would like to thank particularly Captain Tadhg McGlinchey, publisher, Irish University Press, for permission to use the Diaries and other MSS. of Douglas Hyde; also the Department of Irish Folklore, University College, Belfield, for access to Hyde material.

1. An Craoibhín Aoibhinn; *Mo Thurus go hAmerice*, 178, Baile Átha Cliath, 1937.
2. Hyde, Diary, resumé of his career at end of 1878. Printed by Dominic O Dálaigh in 'Printiseacht an Chraoibhín i Litríocht na Gaeilge', *Éigse, a journal of Irish studies* 39-42, Samhradh 1971. Writer's translation.
3. *Ibid.*
4. Dubhglas de hÍde, *Mise agus an Connradh*, 67, Baile Átha Cliath, 1937.
5. Rossa first met Hyde in New York in June, 1891. Hyde had called to his office, and finding him out left a note, *Mo leun! Nach bhfaca mé thu...* Rossa comments characteristically – Sorry, and more than sorry were we at missing 'Craoibhín Aoibhinn' because we saw by his Irish writings for years past, he was one man in Ireland who was keeping the true faith alive there – even though that he was a black protestant. We wrote to Joe Cromien, the Irishman, asking Joe if he knew where Craoibhín Aoibhinn was stopping. Next morning we got a letter from Joe, and the same morning in walked Craoibhín, and found us reading Joe's letter. We had a walk and a talk about Ireland for a couple of hours. Of course we talked about Ireland and the Irish cause and the Irish people. These few words he spoke went sad and sorrowful to our heart. [Follows a statement of Hyde's deploring the emigration from Ireland of its best manhood] *United Irishman*, 20 June 1891 (New York).
6. Printed in *The Dublin Book of Irish Verse*, 530, ed. Cooke, Dublin, 1909.
7. An Craoibhín Aoibhinn: 'A plea for the Irish language', *Dublin University Review* August 1886, 675-6.
8. *The last three centuries of Gaelic literature*, 38, London, 1894. See also Hyde's preface to his *Story of early Gaelic literature*, Dublin and London, 1895, in which is expressed a pessimism that was no part of Hyde's later outlook. For example he refers to the language as 'that guarantee of nationality, Ireland, ... possessed ... but possesses no more' (vii) 'It has gone ... gone with its songs, ballads,

poems, folk-lore, romances and literature' (viii). In a footnote, page xx, he writes: 'The Gaelic League ... is now doing its utmost to keep our language, Ireland's noblest heritage, alive in those districts where it is spoken.' Hyde, no less than an tAthair Peadar Ó Laoghaire, seemed to believe at that stage that the language was approaching extinction.

9. *Mise agus an Connradh*, 40.
10. Hyde MSS. (McGlinchey Collection)
11. *Mise agus an Connradh*, 34.
12. *Ibid.*, 35.
13. Letter, headed 'MacNeill founded the Gaelic League' from Michael Tierney in *Irish Times* 25 Jan. 1971. MacNeill's bilingual call, published in the *Gaelic Journal,* March 1893, for the movement which brought the Gaelic League into being, deserves closer attention than it has received. In part of it MacNeill recommends methods of support for the language proposed by Michael Davitt ten years before, thus bringing Davitt into association with the genesis of the League.
14. Hyde, *Diary,* July, 1893.
15. *Diary,* 1893. End of year summary of important events.
16. In *An Claidheamh Soluis,* Iúl 8, 1899. An tAthair Peadar's relations with Dr. Hyde are discussed by Rev. Shan Ó Cuiv in his valuable unpublished study *An tAthair Peadar agus a Lucht Comh-Aimsire,* for reference to which I am indebted to the author.
17. For Hyde's publications, see 'A bibliography of Dr. Douglas Hyde' by P.S. O'Hegarty, *Dublin Magazine,* January-March, April-June, 1939; *The National University Handbook,* 182-5, Dublin 1932; R. de Hae, *Clár Litridheacht na Nua-Ghaedhilge,* I-III, 1938-40; T. de Bhaldraithe, 'Aguisin le clár saothair an Chraoibhín', *Galvia* IV, 18-24, 1957.
18. Horace Plunkett: *Ireland in the new century,* 153, Popular edn. London, 1905.
19. *Mise agus an Connradh,* 66-7.
20. Hyde, in the course of a lecture in Castlerea, April, 1903, said that 'with the land question settled, the work will be work for the uprising of the people'; report in *King's Co. Independent,* 11 April 1903.
21. Hyde: MS. *History.*
22. James H. Cousins and Margaret E. Cousins, *We two together,* 66-7, Madras, 1950.
23. Douglas Hyde to John Quinn 24 July 1906, in B.L. Reid, *The Man from New York,* 42, New York, 1968.
24. NLI MS. No. 15080 (1).
25. NLI MS. No. 15197 (6).
26. Plunkett, *Ireland in the new century,* 157.
27. *Mise agus an Connradh,* 166.
28. *Ibid.,* 121.
29. B.L. Reid, *The Man from New York,* 326.
30. Myles Dillon, 'Douglas Hyde', in *The Shaping of Modern Ireland,* 59-60, ed. Conor Cruise O'Brien, London 1960. The quotation is from Hyde's MS. *History.*
31. Douglas Hyde: *The Gaelic League and politics,* 1-2 [1915].
32. *Ibid.,* 3.
33. Grenfell, *Into Battle,* No. 962 in *The Oxford Book of English Verse,* ed. Quiller-Couch, Oxford, 1939.
34. Hyde, MS. *History.*
35. Earnán de Blaghd, 'Hyde in Conflict' in *The Gaelic League Idea,* 36-7, Thomas Davis Lectures, ed. Seán O Tuama, Cork and Dublin, 1972.

36. Cf. Myles Dillon, 'Douglas Hyde', in *The Shaping of Modern Ireland,* 59, where two extracts from Hyde's MS. *History* are quoted.

37. Douglas Hyde: 'The Irish language movement; some reminiscences', *Gaelic American,* 11 August 1923, from *Manchester Guardian Commercial.* The editor of the *Gaelic American,* John Devoy, has this to say of Hyde:

   In the Ireland of the future the name of Douglas Hyde will be enshrined in the hearts of the people as the restorer of the national language. Few men in any country have done so much to revolutionise the thoughts and habits of the people as An Craoibhín Aoibhinn. He disclaimed any political motive, saying that he had no *arrière-pensée,* and kept the League rigidly to the work of fighting for the language, but the movement had more decisive political results than if it had gone directly into politics. It stopped the process of anglicisation, then in full swing, revived interest in Irish sports and pastimes, arrested the decay of home industries and prevented the young men of Ireland from becoming imitation Englishmen. It undid in a few short years the reactionary work of several generations, and prepared the mind of Ireland for a new progressive future. (Leading article, *Gaelic American,* 18 December 1926)

38. From extract quoted by Myles Dillon, 'Douglas Hyde', *op. cit.,* 59.

Chapter 5

Robin Flower

The School of Irish Learning

Few scholarly correspondents have been as relaxed and discursive as the great Celtic scholar Kuno Meyer and by way of introduction to this essay it may be well to quote from a letter he wrote to Mrs. Alice Stopford Green dated at Thüringen, 19 July 1912. It concerned the School of Irish Learning and its programme of studies:

> ... I am to lecture in Dublin during the latter half of September [he writes]. Marstrander has left us for good; Pedersen cannot come, and the School must not let a whole session pass without some activity. If only Bergin would work more! He is most disappointing. On the other hand Irish studies have got a capital recruit in Mr. Robin Flower of the British Museum. Do you know him? He has made some fine discoveries amongst the MSS...[1]

Admirers of Osborn Bergin will bristle with indignation. Small blame to them. But Meyer's letter forms a suitable introduction to Robin Flower, who was then on the threshold of his fruitful and versatile career. Suitable also because Meyer was regarded in turn by Robin Flower for his courage and scholarship with an admiration that survived a great war fought between their two countries.

The School of Irish Learning was founded through the exertions of Kuno Meyer and his introductory lecture on the subject, delivered at the Dublin Rotunda in 1903, is one of the most important documents in the history of Irish scholarship. Flower was a disciple of Meyer, very sensible of the debt he owed the German scholar, a debt he acknowledges generously, as in his letter to Mrs. A.S. Green, 'There are few men to whom I (and the studies I serve) owe more than to Meyer. And I am in suspense ...', written in a moment of anxiety in 1915 following an injury to Meyer in a railway accident in California.[2] And when Flower was inclined to wander into other byways of research, Meyer recalled him to his Irish work, 'which is so much more important'.[3]

The Call of the Blaskets

Wide and diverse as the interests of Robin Flower were (he was for one thing an Anglo-Saxon scholar of eminence) it is with the Great Blasket Island that his name is inseparably associated. Working in a busy library, in the heart of London, his activities covered a range of mediaeval studies extending to every country in western Europe, yet he transferred his abiding attention to this long, lean backbone of island off the West Kerry coast. The logic of his choice was one that scholars would appreciate. Its more or less sheltered eastern ledge, facing the mainland, was inhabited by some hundred and fifty people who had preserved in their way of life a living pocket of the medieval culture that attracted him. Neolithic, said E. M. Forster, from the distance of London, an exaggeration to be pardoned in a novelist. The island fascinated Flower. It figured in his thoughts and dreams in London where he laboured daily in the Manuscripts Division of the British Museum, because every summer that he could, from 1910 onwards, the year of his first visit, he would return to study and record the life and oral literature of the Blaskets.

In the first chapter of *The Western Island* he has described the approach to the Blaskets which he took many times in his career thereafter, from Tralee across the old red sandstone peninsula dominated by Brandon Mountain. Time came when he could embellish every turn of the road from Dingle to Dunquin with a snatch of legend or folktale, blended with stories of personal experience. His car took him through Mám Clasach, the pass between Eagle Mountain and Cruach Mhárthain, a lonely lofty road around which in the gathering dusk the atmosphere is chillingly Gothic. He was not wholly unperturbed late one evening when driven through it by a drunken chauffeur, with a terrified girl passenger for company, uttering her prayers as the vehicle lurched on its way, for the blessings of tarmacadam were unknown in this part of Ireland until well after World War II and the road surfaces might be matched in Arabia Deserta. After that he relished the feel of the waves around the little craft that took him from Dunquin to the Island, 'deep in the sea', which gave him inspiration, poetry and vision, besides the most loveable of nicknames.

Family Tradition

Robin Ernest William Flower, or more affectionately Bláithín, was a Yorkshireman, born at Meanwood, near Leeds, on 16 October 1881. His mother was Jane Lynch, of Yorkshire birth but Galway family, and his father was Marmaduke Flower, who after an adventurous career which included soldiering in the American civil war, settled down to become in mature age the leading portrait painter of Leeds. Some of the ingredients that went to make Robin Flower's temperament are put down by his biographer Harold Idris Bell as 'a home near the Yorkshire moorlands and a strain of Yorkshire blood ... grit and sturdy independence, an Irish ancestry ... a tradition of scholarship from his grandfather ...'[4] which description echoes for us perhaps the characteristics of another great literary household of the neighbourhood. The Flower family also had North of Ireland connections.

His academic career was brilliant, from the time he entered Leeds Grammar School in 1894 to his graduation from Pembroke College, Oxford, in 1904 with a first in classical studies. Two years later he entered the Department of Manuscripts in the British Museum where he was to spend the rest of his official life. A colleague of his in the Museum was Harold Idris Bell, a classical scholar who was making a catalogue of the Museum's Greek papyri. He was studying Welsh. Their common interests, background and literary enthusiasms of classics, poetry and Celtic studies may have urged Flower to study Irish.

Soon after taking up employment in the Museum, Flower began to learn the language. There was a large holding of Irish manuscripts in the Museum which the adventurous Standish Hayes O'Grady had begun to catalogue in 1886 but never finished. The portion catalogued by O'Grady had in fact been printed and a few copies bound for the private use of the Museum. It formed a substantial volume of some 700 pages, but since it represented only a part of the Museum's collection it was thought better not to publish it. No one who studied O'Grady's fascinating catalogue could fail to be interested in Irish literature. From the wonderful fabric of learning, pungency, brilliant translation and rich historical footnotes, the personality of its author emerges with a unique authority. That it influenced Robin Flower is more than probable.

Flower, who had been taking private lessons in Irish and was making progress at it, conceived the plan of continuing and completing O'Grady's work. This would be a formidable task, requiring industry and talent, not to say an exact knowledge of Old and Middle Irish, but Sir George Warner, Keeper of the MSS division, when the suggestion was put to him by Flower, expressed full confidence in his capacity and asked the support of the Trustees on his behalf. So it came about that in June of 1910 Robin Flower received a small official subsidy and three weeks' special leave to attend the lectures in Old and Middle Irish language and literature being given in Dublin, in the School of Irish Learning, by Professor Carl Marstrander, as well as to become acquainted with the Irish manuscripts in the Royal Irish Academy.

Friendships and Common Interests

It was an important step in Flower's career. At the School he was introduced to a group of gifted men who had made Irish studies the interest of their lives. The School of Irish Learning had been founded in 1903 on the initiative of Kuno Meyer and the generous financial support of Alice Stopford Green in particular. The object of the School was to train native Irish scholars in the scientific investigation, study and publication of unedited Irish manuscripts, thus making available their literary and historical content, so that a true picture of Ireland's past might emerge. This work had been left to German and French universities until the arrival of Meyer, who considered that the centre of Irish studies should be in Ireland and laboured strenuously and successfully to create it there. Intensive courses were held in the Summer during university vacation, and it was one of these, conducted by Carl Marstrander, that Flower attended. He formed an enduring friendship with his teacher, an athlete and scholar, who had spent five months of 1908 in the Blaskets learning Irish from Tomás Ó Crithin. Flower's friendships with Irish scholars are represented even in the choice of godparents for his four children, for these were, in order of succession, Marstrander, Meyer, William Paton Ker jointly with Mrs. J.R. Green and Richard Irvine Best.

At the School he met other scholars whose interests coincided with his own. One such was Julius Pokorny of Prague, whose fruitful and lively imagination has enriched Celtic studies enormously. We are given a picture of what it was like to be there in that season of Flower's first attendance, by Richard Irvine Best, himself an Irish scholar and palaeographer of eminence, later the distinguished Director of the National Library, who writes –

> The School has been most successful this summer. Twenty students attend the various classes. The numbers are smaller than last year, but greater than in preceding years. We have Dr. Pokorny again from Vienna, Mr. Flower, Asst. in the Ms. Dept. British Museum, who is now completing the Irish MSS. Catalogue, who is a rising poet, of I think considerable merit. Mr. Fraser, lecturer in Latin at Aberdeen, Miss Mary Williams, who recently took her doctorate at Paris with a dissertation on Peredur, are also amongst the students. Mr. Marstrander gave a garden party on Saturday, at which most of the School were present. A photographer was in attendance! One and all are devoted to him. His amazing knowledge of the language and his profound philosophical explanations have made a deep impression. He takes a personal interest in the students and is getting them to prepare texts for *Ériu*.[5]

Carl Marstrander's Advice

Marstrander's scholarship and personality were a profound influence in the School. His estimate of Robin Flower, formed during that first term of instruction and communicated by him to Meyer, is worth recording here for its perspicacity and exactness – 'Mr. Flower also I find a solid fellow, on whose future conscientious and scientific work we may rely.'[6] On his advice Flower decided to visit the Great Blasket to learn Irish. He announced his departure to Richard Best in a brief note (on headed paper of *The School of Irish Learning*, 33 Dawson Street) a little apprehensively perhaps, 'I am about to entrain for the Blaskets. Go bhfóiridh Dia orm', for the island was over two hundred miles from Dublin, and the experience bound to be novel.

Thus he made his first acquaintance with the people who were to play such an important part in his life. He has epitomized the story of some twenty years' close association with them in his charming compendium of Blasket life, *The Western Island*, a book as Irish in its character as the *Acallamh na Senórach*, with its colourful mosaic of island poetry, prose, life, topography, mediaevalism and friendships. For instruction in Irish he placed himself under the tutelage of Tomás Ó Crithin, whose presence and address is invoked with all the enchantment of a Byzantine romance in Flower's recital of his appearance as...

> a slight but confident figure. The face takes your attention at once and holds it. This face is dark and thin, and there look out of it two quick and living eyes, the vivid witnesses of a fine and self-sufficing intelligence. He comes towards you, and with a grave and courteous intonation, and a picked and running phrase, bids you welcome.[7]

With a deal table between them, instruction commenced. First they discussed what method of teaching would be best, whether to proceed by way of isolated words and sentences, or by tales and poems. Since there had been an island poet, Seán Ó Duinnlé, whose poems Tomás knew by heart, they decided Flower should write down the poems and the circumstances in which they were composed. More than that, Tomás knew the island's history, some from personal experience, more from tradition. He suggested to his pupil, that they would do well to record the stories and poems lest they be lost. Sitting on one side of the deal table, chewing a mouthful of dilisk, Tomás taught and explained. He was not without experience, having tutored Carl Marstrander, 'An Lochlannach', who at their first day's session had addressed him as 'Master'. So between them, Tomás and Bláithín progressed as teacher and learner, while 'the picture of the Island's past grew from day to day under our hands'.[8] The account is Flower's. It is supplemented by Tomás Ó Crithin's recollection of how Flower visited the island yearly, spent two sessions a day writing together, spent a period every year from that first visit putting all they had written in proper editorial order and how the book thus written would contain an account of every misfortune and episode that ever happened in or about the Island.[9]

Blasket Culture and Legends

For Flower it became an adventure into the past which revealed to him the very essence of the civilization that had captivated him. His Blasket experiences formed the physical supplement to what he was learning out of the British Museum's Irish MSS. In the Blaskets he learned Irish and legends; in the Museum the literary manifestation of the same world unfolded from the pages of old writing. Others like him found enlightenment for their studies in the Blaskets. His friend Seoirse Mac Tomáis, whom Flower introduced to the Blaskets, has acknowledged his debt to the island civilization as a medium to the understanding of Homeric Greece.[10]

These Blasket holidays were the happiest times of Flower's life. In the account written from the King's house, Great Blasket, to his colleague Richard Best, he expresses a glowing delight with the island and its people –

> Dear Best,
>   I don't know if you are gone on your holidays yet. If not, perhaps you might think of coming here. I am enjoying myself wonderfully and by my thinking there is no place in the world like it. You could get a room in one of the new houses, if the King couldn't put you up, and you would hear the most delightful Irish and as a friend of Marstrander's and mine, I can promise you the best of welcomes. I am very busy reading and talking and listening. I have 100 pages of stories written down and hope for yet as many more before I leave. The people are good beyond belief to me.[11]

He writes about his progress on the collection of stories he was working on with Tomás.

> I have had a delightful holiday here and am much the better for it. Tomás and I have been working on the book of stories and it is getting into reasonably good order. I hope to start printing soon

after I get back. It is a fascinating collection with the whole life of the Island in the past generation in it, and talking over the tales again and again with Tomás, I have reached a fair understanding of that life which might too stand me in good stead in editing the collection. I am just going out to the land with my friend Seán an Rí and I hope to see Father Paddy Brown who is in Dunquin.[12]

Events of the world outside intervened and neither of them lived to see the published volume. It appeared in 1956, under the title *Seanchas ón Oileán Tiar*, edited with introduction and notes by Séamus Ó Duilearga who has suitably dedicated the volume to the memory of its joint authors. It is a fine collection of Blasket tradition, legend and history in Ó Crithin's classic style, and for its doing, which took them long periods of toil and application, its authors deserve the applause of posterity. Nor must we be unmindful of how much it is enhanced by the care and skill of its editor and especially by his valuable introductory essay on Flower. And we are left to ask, despite its excellence, how far does it correspond to what Bláithín and Tomás had planned.

On his first visit the Congested Districts Board were busy on the island, building new houses, making an access road to the turf banks and dividing the land for the best convenience of the inhabitants. Flower handled a pickaxe and worked on the road, learning scraps of conversation, taking part as best he might in the banter of the islanders, and resting between times when his bones ached. The men's conversation was full of intense argument about the benefits or otherwise of the Board's projects and Flower regretted keenly that he could not follow it.

Such was not the case for long. He returned the following year (1911) on his honeymoon, having got married to Ida Mary Streeter, sister of the Dean of Pembroke College, Oxford. 'We had a glorious time there' he tells Richard Best. 'The weather was too hot, and I was too tired for any serious work, but I got to be able to speak and understand pretty well'.[13] His wife had artistic talent and did some sketches of island scenes, four of which illustrate his book *The Western Island*. In the following year he was able to collect occasional items of folklore, and such was his perseverance, with the aid of his teacher and correspondent Tomás Ó Crithin, that by 1916 his grasp of the language was so good that he could produce creditable verse translations of the lyrics of Sir Thomas Wyatt the Elder, to judge by the two examples which he included in his Introduction to the first edition (1916) of *Dánta Grádha*, the anthology edited by his friend Tomás Ó Rathile. By that time his acquaintance with the literary language had also become so competent that he was engaged to teach Old Irish in London University, the course beginning on 27 May 1913.

Shadows of War

Bláithín was on holiday in the Blaskets in June 1914 when the tragic happening occurred that led to the First World War. He had gone down to meet the postman's little boat which he saw crossing the sound. The postman, who was also King, looked grave. An archduke had been killed in the east. Flower did not realize it then, but a train of events followed that changed all his plans and virtually deprived him for four years of the kind of scholarly work he would have liked to pursue. Although not interested in politics, Flower was a sincere supporter of his country in the war against Germany. He became a member of the Army reserve, and watched with apprehension the Zeppelins droning over his house, where his wife waited for him, while he sat in a stopped drain across the Thames 'and watched the shells bursting round that silvery beast. It was a beautiful and thrilling sight.'[14] The Great War played havoc with his plans for Irish literature and delayed the production of his Catalogue. Though not sent, as he feared he might be, to the War Office as censor or translator, 'a miserable fate', he was otherwise given duties to perform in which he had no interest. Towards the end of 1916 we find him writing –

> At present I am in despair under the weight of the Dutch and Belgian press. I have to read something between 100 and 150 newspapers in Dutch and French and German every week and write out reports on them, each report about as long as a review article. It is horrid work and leaves me played out. I never cared much for politics, and to have to write political articles is painful to me.[15]

There was a suggestion that he might be sent to the Netherlands. His friend T. F. O'Rahilly, in sending him best regards through Alice Stopford Green, expressed the hope, premature though it was, on 17 December 1916, that peace was not far off and that he would soon be back at his congenial work.[16] His visits to the Blaskets had perforce to cease and there was a long interval of absence from 1914 up to, as it appears, 1925.[17] On the other hand his home life was very happy and he was devoted to his children, 'an oasis in this bewildering desert of our time,'[18] for whom he wrote and dedicated the little set of poems entitled 'Monkey Music'. It is more than probable that he had his children in mind as well when he translated, exquisitely, from the ninth century Irish text in the *Thesaurus Palaeohibernicus* what is probably his best known poem, *Pangur Bán*, on the playful doings of the monastery cat, recorded in his manuscript by an Irish monk of St Paul's in Carinthia.

The Voice of the Manuscripts

Living among old writings all his working life, Flower acquired an almost uncanny sense of the manuscript's quality. Great libraries are offered items for which suspect claims are made and Flower came to be an expert in identifying between the genuine and the spurious. For Irish manuscripts he had almost a reverence and one hears accounts of the loving appreciation with which he would handle and appraise some great historic codex. With his mediaevalist's knowledge and wide learning he was able to trace to source, classify and put in context tales, poems, tracts and romances, until gradually the perspective and pattern of Irish literature unfolded to his investigations. He expressed his fascination with the task –

> The MSS [he wrote] are the living literature, the immediate voice of that vanished world, and as text succeeds text and cycles of legend alternate with homilies and translations we can watch the very movement of the Irish mind very much as a scientist pictures the past to himself from the fossil deposits in successive stratifications.[19]

Despite distractions he was able to devote time to revising his Catalogue throughout 1915, at which stage it began to assume a final shape, and he expressed the view to Best that, for the medieval period at any rate, his results added a considerable body of fact to the history of Irish literature.

> In the history of Irish literature everything remains to be done. We have only scratched the surface hitherto. And the first necessity to my mind is classification; and the second classification; and the third classification. And that classification must be based on the MSS ... I think that the most generally useful part of my work is the determination of Latin sources and influences for the period 600-1600. My Catalogue is necessarily delayed ...[20]

Achievement In Scholarship

It was in fact as late as 1926 when it appeared, in two volumes, the first, xii + 706 pages, being O'Grady's, the second, xxxvi + 634 pages, comprising the work of Robin Flower. The publication of their joint achievement forms an important landmark in the history of Irish studies. Critics were at one in according it the praise reserved for works of great scholarship. Flower's volume, differing in method and treatment from O'Grady's, is a forest of information on Irish literature, justifying the verdict of one of his scholarly correspondents, 'You have founded a solid basis for the future historian of Irish literature to build upon – tracing the sources for him of the various tracts you describe, and the centres of learning from which they have emanated'.[21] Bergin's review, in the *Irish Statesman*,[22] however, while praising Flower's work, was curiously disproportionate in that it was mainly devoted to O'Grady's personality and the qualities of his contribution which, though but newly published to the world, was long available privately to scholars. The rather less than generous treatment given by him to Flower prompted speculation. Did there lurk in Bergin's sub-conscious that anti-Saxon antipathy which is said to be stronger in the Protestant Gael than it is, if present at all, in his Catholic counterpart, causing him parochially to withhold from an Irish scholar of Yorkshire a full acknowledgement of his merit? That there did is the explanation received by the present writer from respected sources. Dom Louis Gougaud, on the other hand, after a brief mention of O'Grady, devotes his review in the *Revue d'Histoire Ecclésiastique*[23] entirely to Flower's work, *une oeuvre particulièrement remarquable par la quantité de matériaux mis à contribution*, and specially to its section on religious literature, and the illuminating results achieved by the author's comparative method.

This is the work on which Robin Flower's reputation as an Irish scholar firmly rests. Volume III did not appear until 1953, seven years after his death. Revised and passed through the press by Dr. Myles Dillon, it contains Flower's important essay, pages 1-40, on the history and acquisition of the Museum's holding of Irish manuscripts, and the indispensable index.

Difficulties and Distractions
Although his post in the British Museum gave Flower the opportunity to accomplish, on the spot as it were, his most important task, it is certain that he would be happier working in Dublin close to the main repositories of Irish MSS. With a note of longing he speculates 'What worlds beyond worlds open out in these Irish studies! I sometimes feel that we stand on the threshold of virgin continents. What treasures must lie hid in Dublin libraries. I ache to search them …'[24] He expresses a wish to work in the Royal Irish Academy,[25] where we can have no doubt that in the tranquil environment of the manuscripts he loved his happiness would be full.

A university chair might have been more congenial to him, and afford him leisure for his scholarly work. Meyer regretted that he was confined to a library. He considered applying for a vacant Chair of Celtic in Jesus College, Oxford but changed his mind because it would mean a reduction in his salary and was non-pensionable. This was important for him since he had a family of four young children. The Oxford post went to an old colleague, John Fraser, who has a place in Irish literature as 'the third man' in Bergin's lovely poem, *Wanderlust*. But what a pity that such a man as Flower had to occupy himself with the petty tasks of day to day administration and our sympathy goes out to him when we find him writing like this –

> I am myself thinking of retiring at the age of 60 to try and do some work. It is hopeless to attempt to do anything while I remain at the Museum. During the last week or so, for instance, I have been trying to write articles for our Museum Quarterly on a 14th cent. treatise in Italian on Chivalry and on the letters of Thomas Bewick, going into the Heron MSS, helping in a campaign for the acquisition of the letters of John Donne, discussing a bequest to the Museum of MSS of William Morris and Rossetti, making up my mind on some contested autographs of Shelley and Jane Austen and her family and reporting on a set of Elizabethan MSS which belong to an American collector, all this in addition to current business at the Museum and some anxious work in connection with German refugees. This kind of thing goes on all the time and fritters away all my energies. I have no conviction that this is my real work in life, though of course being paid for it I must do it. And I find it difficult nowadays to work in the evenings, tired after the distractions of the day.[26]

Relaxed Moments

By the end of 1925, however, when his Catalogue was with the printers, it was possible for him to feel more at ease and to look forward once again to visiting the Blaskets. There is a sense of freedom and anticipation in one of the rare jottings which he made, this time on Paddington station as he waited for the train to take him on the first stage of his island journey:

> 29 Márta 1927, 7.55 p.m.
> Go n'éirí an turas liom. Tá an obair a bhí le déanamh agam sa Mhusaem críochnaithe ar fad, [probably a reference to his Catalogue, published in 1926] agus tá sciatháin fúm chun bheith i gCiarraí ag labhairt na Gaoluinne agus ag éisteacht leis na daoine agus an chaint bhreá bhlasta ar siúl acu … Slán le Lúndain ghránna, cathair mhúchta an fhothraim go bhfuil mo chroí briste aici.[27]

The second period of his attachment to the Blaskets was relaxed and tranquil. The publication of his Catalogue had earned him world-wide recognition in Irish studies and his judgment was respected. When a Chair of Celtic Studies was being set up in Madison, Wisconsin, Flower was amongst the five persons consulted by Dean Sellery as to who should be appointed and his choice coincided with Best's in recommending Myles Dillon for the post. That distinguished Irish scholar was selected. He had mastered the Irish language and could converse in it freely. His family accompanied him on visits, during which he worked unceasingly at recording on the dictaphone tales of Island interest. He writes to Best in the spring of 1929:

> The girls and I will be in Dublin this weekend, Sunday and Monday, and hope to see you with Mrs. Best. They are having the time of their lives here, running about and dancing and picking up bits of Irish. The weather has been wonderful this last fortnight and now with the sun all day and a full moon over the island at night it is a heaven to be here.[28]

On one visit he was unluckily laid up with flu, but the ordeal was softened because 'the people have been incredibly kind to me and that has made things easier.'[29] He had endeared himself to one and all by being his natural and unaffected self. There are many references to him in the island literature, all in his praise. The islanders appreciated many unobtrusive acts of generosity on his part. Ó Crithin has written splendid words of appreciation. Three in particular were literary friends, Tomás Ó Crithin, Peig Sayers and Gobnait Ní Chinnéide. But every inhabitant of the island was his friend. As one of them said to Dr. Donal Binchy: 'I would confide things to Bláithín I would not reveal to the priest.'[30]

In 1934 he published *The Islandman,* a translation of *An tOileánach.* Gaunt and severe as a document of Tacitus, Tomás Ó Crithin's masterpiece is not easily done justice in translation. Flower explained in the *Preface* that 'it seemed best … to adopt a plain, straightforward style, aiming at the language of ordinary men who narrate the common experiences of their life frankly and without any cultivated mannerism'. He did not please everybody. Myles na Gopaleen in his *Irish Times* column did not think the translation was a success[31] and described it on another occasion as 'miserably botched'.[32] Respectfully, one has to disagree. Flower's version is a worthy and by no means unsuccessful effort to match the dignity of the original.

Health Problems
Apparently Bláithín's health was never robust. Richard Best feared that

the hardships of island life affected the health of John Synge and Carl Marstrander. The latter had indeed returned from his Blasket sojourn looking wretched and soon afterwards had fallen ill with the result that he had to abandon his lectures at the School of Irish Learning and betake himself to the South of France in search of health. But he lived to be 82, achieved great things in Celtic scholarship, fought the Nazis and only just escaped death at the hands of the Gestapo, a Viking hero and scholar, *ní fear go dtí é*, a man without peer. There is however no evidence that Bláithín's visits to 'the healthiest island in Ireland', Ó Críthin's phrase, had an adverse effect on his health. So much did he enjoy and benefit from his holidays there that the place had the dearest memories for him. But he did tax himself harder at times than his resources could stand up to. As early as June 1913 we find him writing to Meyer:

> I did a great deal on the Blaskets, took down stories three hours a day from Tomás, and hunted rabbits all day on the cliffs with Seán an Righ. The result of the double strain was that soon after coming home I was afflicted by an enemy of mine – cerebral anaemia the pedantic physicians call it, a most damnable depression is my own description of it. I was heavily overburdened with work, the classes [at London University] just starting and much besides to do. So that I went for some time on the verge of a complete breakdown. I think I have weathered it now … Sé an dream galrach lucht na Gaeluinne agus is dóigh liom go bhfuil cinneamhaint éigin anuas orainn, rud ná fuil tuillte againn ón bhfear atá thuas. Ach caithfimid foidhneamh leis …[33]

Lament for a Master

Robin Flower was one of a school, or team, drawn from many countries of Europe, dedicated to the pursuit of Irish learning, whose united achievements form a rich and monumental heritage. Flower's own contribution is considerable, as scholar, folklorist, literary historian, poet and stylist. His circle of fellow workers included Carl Marstrander, Osborn Bergin, John Fraser, Edward Gwynn, Tomás Ó Máille, Eoin Mac Neill, Richard Irvine Best, James G. O'Keeffe, T.F. O'Rahilly, Eleanor Knott, Gertrude Schoepperle, Julius Pokorny, and one can keep adding to the list. At the centre of the group was Meyer, the imperial. That great scholar's unexpected death in Leipzig in November 1919, at the early age of 61, was a calamitous blow to Irish studies, removing from the scene his great influence and inspiration, a loss represented in Flower's utterance of deep lament written to Richard Best in June 1920:

It will be long before we have so vivifying, so enriching an influence in all the branches of Irish work. I think we shall feel the lack of him more and more as time goes on and we miss that energy and enthusiasm that made him more than a fine worker himself, the source of fine work in others … I think we can serve his memory best by carrying on the work as far as possible in his spirit and to the ends designed by him. He was a great scholar, and this is the service to their memory that great scholars most desire. But I wish we had him back again. When I seem to myself to have made some small discovery or to have come nearer to the understanding of some text, I always find my mind turning insensibly to him, I wonder what Meyer would have thought, and I feel his loss again in realizing each time that he is beyond our question. It is a loss we shall never make good.[34]

Final Testament

One of Flower's cherished projects was to write a history of Irish literature. Meyer did not doubt his ability to do this, though Bergin, in whose nationalist strain there were puzzling inflexibilities, doubted whether a Yorkshireman could. About his literary plans he once confided to Best – 'I am full of dreams of these things, but I want time to realise any of them'.[35] This was one dream he did not live to realize. What its quality might have been is revealed to us in *The Irish Tradition*, a selection of essays published in 1947 after his death, in which he escorts his reader with erudition and style through centuries of literature, across many lands from West Kerry to the Levant, causing us to bewail the full achievement that was not to be, yet be thankful for its fragment.

For the second time in his life the havoc of war descended in 1939 to interrupt his studious world. He was transferred to Aberystwyth as senior officer in charge of the Museum's manuscript and other treasures sent to the National Library of Wales for safety, a charge which brought an increase of administrative duties. Never congenial to him, they now became a burden, and a steady decline in his health set in. But his enthusiasms remained very much alive and he continued to work, or rather overwork, and plan with the same spirit as ever. It could not last. After serious setbacks to his health he died on 16 January 1946. His final wish, that his ashes should be scattered on the Great Blasket, was carried out by his eldest daughter Barbara, on a September evening in 1946, under a grey and rainy sky. Though novel to the island's tradition, it must have been a moving and reverent occasion, as she walked at the head of a little procession of island people up the ridge to Claiseacha an Dúna, bearing in a bronze urn all that was mortal of

Bláithín, which she joined, clay to clay, in the hollow where he had often rested to look out over the Atlantic and dream of the great civilization which the island represented for him. Bláithín had come for the last time to his beloved Blasket.

References

1. NLI Ms No. 15091(1).
2. NLI Ms No. 15077(1)
3. H. Idris Bell: 'Robin Ernest William Flower 1881-1946.' *Proceedings of the British Academy,* XXXII, 13.
4. *Ibid.,* 3.
5. R.I. Best to Mrs. Alice Stopford Green, 20 July 1910. NLI Ms No. 10457(2).
6. Marstrander to Meyer 1/8/1910. TCD Ms No. 4224. No signature, but in its place a mini-photograph of Marstrander, holding a cup (of coffee?).
7. *The Western Island,* 12.
8. *Ibid.,* 16.
9. *An tOileánach* (1929), 260.
10. 'Sa Bhlascaod a fuaireas an eochair don gceist Hóiméarach', *An Blascaod a bhí,* 8.
11. NLI Ms No. 11,000(22). Letter undated.
12. *Ibid.* Letter undated but postmark, not wholly clear, appears to be 'Dunquin 19 Apr. '27 Dingle.
13. *Ibid.* Letter dated 9/8/11.
14. *Ibid.* To R.I. Best in twice dated letter 20/12/1915 and 12/1/1916.
15. *Ibid.* To R.I. Best 19/11/1916.
16. NLI Ms No. 10,457.
17. Cf. *An tOileánach* (1973), eagarthóir Pádraig Ua Maoileoin: 'Sa bhliain 1925 thainig sé arís', 248.
18. To R.I. Best 20/1/1916. NLI Ms No. 11,000(22)
19. *Ibid.* To R.I. Best 4/3/1913.
20. *Ibid.* To R.I. Best 20/12/1915 and 12/1/1916.
21. H. Idris Bell: 'Robin Ernest William Flower, 1881-1946.' *Proceedings of the British Academy,* XXXII, 16.
22. 9 July 1927.
23. XXII (1926) 813.
24. To R.I. Best 16/9/1914. NLI Ms No. 11,000(22).
25. *Ibid.* To R.I. Best 13/11/1914.
26. *Ibid.* To. R.I. Best 28/1/1939.
27. *Seanchas ón Oileán Tiar,* in eagar ag Séamus Ó Duilearga, Réamhrá XII. Baile Átha Cliath 1956.
28. 23/4/1929. NLI Ms No. 11,000(22).
29. *Ibid.* To R.I. Best, n.d.
30. Dr. D.A. Binchy in conversation with the present writer. Cf. 'Robin Flower, Oileánach agus Máistir Léinn' le Seán Ó Lúing, *Kerry Arch. & Hist. Soc. Journal* 10 (1977) 135.
31. *Irish Times,* 26/11/1962.
32. *Irish Times,* 9/12/1965.
33. Flower to Meyer, 12/6/1913, TCD Ms No. 4224.
34. 13/6/1920, NLI Ms No. 11,000(22)
35. *Ibid.* Letter undated but reference indicates it was written just after Easter 1916.

The title-pages of Marie-Louise Sjoestedt's two major works.

Marie-Louise Sjoestedt (on the right) waiting to make the crossing to the Blasket Islands. From *Bonniers Veckotidning* (Stockholm), 4 September, 1937.

110

Chapter 6

Marie-Louise Sjoestedt

It is to be hoped that interest in the literature of the Blaskets and Dunquin and in the scholars who visited the area will sometime lead to a full scale study of Marie-Louise Sjoestedt, whose name, as Máire Fhranncach, is legendary in the district and whose services to the Irish language are outstanding. For the present we have to rely mainly on a 79-page booklet published in Paris in 1941, shortly after her premature death, containing the memories and appreciations of her teachers and friends, and the present brief essay is based on this and on a selection of her writings. The fact that her death, on 26 December 1940, occurred during the war when communication was difficult meant that little news of the tragedy percolated through to Ireland. Even her obituary did not appear in *Études Celtiques,* publication of which was the while suspended, until eight years later.[1] The output and quality of her work had given promise of greater things to come and it was a cruel circumstance that her brilliant career was cut short.

Family
She was born on 20 September 1900 in Saint Thomas, a small town in the neighbourhood of Laon in Northeastern France where her parents owned property. Her father, Erik-Valentin Sjoestedt, special counsellor at the Swedish Embassy in Paris, was utterly devoted to France and for his services received the accolade of Commander of the Legion of Honour. Her mother was Léonie Bernardini, a novelist and essayist of talent, member of an old Corsican family. Marie's sister Yvonne was an accomplished artist. She also had a brother Armand.

Education
Marie-Louise was studious and brilliant, receiving her master's degree in Classics with distinction in 1920, and thereafter taking up linguistic and philological studies under scholars whose eminence was worldwide, Joseph Vendryes, de Bourguet, Antoine Meillet and Jules Bloch. She studied Russian and Czech in the School of Oriental Languages and for a while appeared to wish to specialize in the Slavic

languages, encouraged by her teacher and friend Paul Boyer. A period from June to October 1921 spent in Bohemia gave her the opportunity of acquiring practice in Czech. Overwork in the winter of 1921-1922 brought on an attack of pleurisy, followed by peritonitis which nearly caused her death.

It was Antoine Meillet who first urged her to choose a special subject for her researches and turned her attention to Celtic studies which opened up so many possibilities and which stood in need of young research workers. He recommended her to study under Vendryes, who became her master in the most direct sense, as she later became his assistant and associate in the editorship of *Revue Celtique* and *Études Celtiques.*

In Dublin

She first came to Ireland in 1924 and every summer thereafter until 1929. During a period as lecturer in Trinity College Dublin from October 1924 to August 1925 she became familiar with the life and people of Ireland. In Dublin she made contact for the first time with Osborn Bergin, Edward J. Gwynn, Tomás Ó Rathile and others prominent in Irish scholarship and it was there that she formed certain friendships which were to count among the most precious of her life. It would be fair to suppose that Seán Óg Kavanagh of Dunquin was one of the friends whose acquaintance she made at that period.

She became deeply interested in Ireland's history, development and future, and at a time when self-government was in its initial phase, in the contemporary politics and personalities of public life. In October 1929 she interviewed Maud Gonne, Michael Hayes, Ceann Comhairle of Dáil Éireann, Seán Lemass, briefly Éamon de Valera, and Ernest Blythe, Minister for Finance and beyond all else foremost champion of the Irish language in Dáil Éireann. Marie's query to him 'But now,' the future of the language?' he answered with characteristic conviction 'Ireland will become again an Irish-speaking country, there is no doubt about that' and went on to detail the measures being taken to that end.[2]

Marie was adventurous and intrepid, at close quarters with death many times, in a street accident in Dublin in 1925, some years later in a fall in the Savoy Alps. She excelled at winter and alpine sports, at which she was accounted valiant and indefatigable. 'I was fated to brush with catastrophe', she would say.

Attachment to West Kerry

She made further visits to Ireland in 1933 and 1936. 'She attached herself in particular to that part of Kerry which she had learned to love during the days of July 1925, where she found herself visiting for the first time the parish of Dunquin and the Blasket Island which stretches out to the extreme west of Ireland. She lived there for many months of winter and summer among the fishermen and peasants, partaking in their rugged toil and their hard won rewards, moulding her spirit close to theirs so as to understand and love them. All of her friends preserve, through her vision, as if they themselves had actually lived there, the memory of a land which was in truth the country of her choice'.[3] So writes her biographer Louis Renou. Joseph Vendryes in his appreciation speaks to the same effect in saying that the study of languages was for her no more than a means for getting to know people better.

> She overflowed with life and approached all manifestations of life with a sympathetic curiosity. She found it a genuine pleasure to live among the communities of the west of Ireland who are among the most disinherited of Europe. The simple and quasi-primitive life of the humble peasants of Dunquin or the fishermen of the Blaskets attracted her because it was a life at once innocent, wholesome and honest. She learned their language and collected from their lips the tales whose origin goes back to the distant past of their race and in which are also found, though mutilated or deformed, certain general themes of humanity.[4]

Letter from Dunquin

The following letter, translated from Irish, was written from Dunquin by Marie to Richard Best, Director of the National Library and distinguished Celtic scholar, who was friend, host and adviser to all students of Irish. It will be noted that it was not her first visit to the district.

> Dear friend,
> You told me not to write to you in English and I must do as you told me, although I am ashamed on account of my Irish – or, I should rather say, on account of the imperfect tongue which I have instead of Irish.
> I have spent three weeks here this time. I have only another week left before I return to France. Although I have a desire to see my family again, I cannot help but feel regretful at going away so soon. I am greatly taken with this place, lonely and wild as it is. I don't think I shall ever get tired of it. I do not know when I shall return, even. But if I am able to come, I shall go to the [Blasket] Island, and I shall remain here a couple of months. I was there one day last week. The people of the Island are companionable and joyous, very fond of music and dancing and company. No

doubt I shall get on with them very well, because the whole world knows I am full of roguery – just like themselves.

The day I arrived here, three weeks ago, I noticed the improvement in my Irish compared with when I was in Dublin. Isn't that strange? And without being working at all. I speak and understand better and I do not feel so foolish as I felt when I was here before. I do not rightly know whether to be pleased or not. I am fairly pleased with the amount of Irish I have now when I compare it with what I had three months ago. But when I compare it with the splendid soft language of this place, I get disgusted and pessimistic.

Will you write to me in France? Please tell your wife I send her my regards.

I remain, your friend

M.L. Sjoestedt

159 Avenue Malakoff, Paris, 16e[5]

Two Linguistic Studies

Marie-Louise Sjoestedt will be familiar to students of Irish dialects for her scholarly investigation of Dunquin and Blasket speech, about which she has written two studies. The first of these, *Phonétique d'un parler irlandais de Kerry* (Paris 1931) was favourably reviewed by the Norwegian celtist Alf Sommerfelt.[6] Himself a distinguished linguist, Sommerfelt could claim some familiarity with the Irish of West Kerry, having published a study of Ballyferriter speech in his *Munster Vowels and Consonants.*[7] In his review he observed that the language was very much alive in the whole district, where according to Coimisiún na Gaeltachta (1925), one hundred per cent of the population spoke Irish, and according to Marie Sjoestedt, the old people were unable to express themselves in English. There could still be found there some who had kept alive the old treasury of folklore. Mlle Sjoestedt had accordingly chosen well her area of inquiry. 'She has given us a complete description, clear and well-considered, of the speech, not limiting herself to the study of an isolated theme'.[8] Marie-Louise Sjoestedt's second study, *Description d'un parler irlandais de Kerry* (Paris 1938) was again reviewed by Sommerfelt in terms of high praise in *Études Celtiques,*[9] where he said her work would become one of the principal sources for a knowledge of spoken Irish.

The Influence of English

What may be considered as a supplement to these two studies was her 40-page essay on *The influence of English on a local Irish speech*[10] which she composed from notes made during her stay in Dunquin. 'All the examples cited come from that parish, or additionally from the neighbouring parishes, where Irish is equally the everyday speech and which in matter of dialect is no different from that of the parish of Dunquin'.[11] Her enumeration of the factors which had an effect on Irish is not without interest. These include the influence of small-town business people; bilingual school instruction by which most of the pupils have come to understand more or less English at the end of their studies, while the personal influence of the schoolmaster even among the grown-ups contributes to the anglicisation of the speech, principally by the introduction of learned words or ones considered elegant; the influence of the priest preaching in English tending in the same direction; emigrants who have returned from the United States to settle down in the district, who recover their usage of Irish and whose speech carries some traces of Anglo-American influence; the students who come on vacation among the fishermen and country people to acquire a knowledge of spoken Irish, about whom she says that 'often these students teach the inhabitants more of English than they learn from them of Irish'.[12] The influence of books and newspapers was negligible, apart from school texts.

Máire Fhranncach

Marie pays generous acknowledgement to the help she received in her investigation of Dunquin speech from Seán Óg Ó Caomhánaigh, her ever courteous guide and tutor.[13] Along with being scholarly, their association was warm and companionable, coloured with an aura of romance which has become absorbed into the folklore of the district, with Seán's affections genuine and serious, Marie's responsive but less than fully committed. In West Kerry she was called Máire Fhranncach, an appellation she cheerfully made her own, as in her presentation copy to Seán of *Description d'un parler irlandais de Kerry* (1938) which she inscribed *Do Sheán Óg ó Mháire Fhranncach*.[14]

Journey to Dunquin

Marie describes a journey she made from Paris via Cherbourg to Cork in September 1929 with the purpose of visiting Dunquin.[15] She may be numbered among the many famous who took the celebrated Dingle train to the otherworld of Corkaguiney West. Having arrived in Tralee, 'A little train on narrow track awaits me, the same which once took Synge on the journey in Kerry which resulted in the production of his masterpiece: *The Shadow of the Glen*. The way slopes gently westwards through the peninsula. Tralee Bay opens all round … There is no place more nostalgic than this coast',[16] her thoughts now prompted by the memory of Sir Roger Casement as, on his return to Ireland, he lay resting in the fort across the bay listening to the chant of birds. A winding, tortuous road, which she travels by car, succeeds the train journey. She is captivated by the changing scenery. At a bend of the road 'one sees suddenly revealed a magnificent chorus of islands, like the isles of Greece. The large island, a long-bodied beast, Inis Tuaisceart, a sharp-finned monster, An Tiaracht, a lofty flame, and the smaller islands scattered on the sea'.[17]

She arrives at Dunquin, where

> A semicycle of hills opening towards the sea shelters like a roadstead six or seven little villages, scattered amongst a motley of green and yellow fields. Here I am at my destination. The car slows down at a junction of paths, turns and comes to a stop in front of a low thatched house, with white limewashed walls, which is well known to me. A lady comes out and greets me with a hug: 'You are welcome here, Marie'. Her gentle voice lingering on the *here* lends it an affectionate emphasis.
>
> The elders rise with a familiar dignity to greet me: 'Dieu protège ta vie dans cette maison'. [Probably the old Irish greeting 'Dé do bheatha-sa chun an tí seo'].
>
> And here, by grace of the friendly welcome, the christian greetings, the gaelic chants experienced once again, there opens for me, with the door of the lowly house, the secret world of an ancient culture, humble today, yes indeed, and poor by the ways of the world, but rich in interior treasures.
>
> My hosts are a farming family who would be looked on as poor anywhere else, but who here – so differently are people's circumstances regarded – consider themselves to be well off. Which is to say that they live mainly on potatoes and salted fish, of both of which they have as much as they want. Nor do they fail to add Dieu en soit loué' [which was probably 'Buíochas le Dia dá chionn'].[18]

Her friends bring Marie up to date with the news: 'Bridget has another son; that woman is blest. As for weddings, there are hardly any here. And how could there be, when all the youth is swallowed up by the country over-the-water and there is not a girl of marriageable age left in the seven parishes. The King of the Island is dead: God have mercy on his soul …'[19]

Death of the King
That last piece of news came as a shock to Marie. She gave way to thought.

The King of the Island is dead. With him there has vanished a part of the past. I recall the grand old man whom everybody called the King without my being able to know whether it was genuine tradition or humour entered into the title. I recall him, just as I used to see him when, during the days of winter, alone in his canoe, handling the oar with powerful arm, he would bring ashore the Island mail. For the King of the Island was also its postman ... There was not a local legend, nor a traditional melody, that he did not know. He also enjoyed an unchallenged prestige, being tall in stature, a hardy seaman, a competent singer, a learned storyteller and man of good counsel.[20]

Christmas in Kerry

Two letters written to the Bests appear to belong to this period, one to Richard from Paris, the other to his wife Edith, from the house of Cáit an Ríogh in Dunquin. The first is trilingual, and dated 30.11.'29 from 159 Avenue Malakoff, Paris:

Dear friend

I do not know whether I should write to you in French, or in English or in Irish. Since I am a girl, and because a girl is a curious animal, I prefer writing to you in the language which I do *not* have, that is to say, in Irish.

I shall go to Ireland next week, with the help of God! Everybody in France is saying that things are in a disturbed state in Ireland, and that I shall be in great danger when there. But I do not believe them, *ambaiste*. [Irish]

I am going to stay a while in Trinity Hall, thanks to Miss Cunningham, and will leave in time to be in Kerry by Christmas. I intend to spend there a couple of months, studying the dialect. I am finishing a French translation of 'Forbuis Droma Damhgaire'. I am afraid I am doing an awful mess of it. Never mind. [English]

I am finishing my letter in French, since it is just as well to finish it. I hope to see you in Dublin, also Mrs. Best, and that the present situation will turn out to the best advantage of Irish interests. With kindest regards.

M.L. Sjoestedt.

I got a letter from Miss Young, who is, as you know, in Norway and seems satisfied, but does not forget Ireland. [Eng.][21]

The other letter, which is undated, is headed c/o Cáit an Ríogh – Baille in Tempuill Dunchaoin – Dingle – Co. Kerry, and is wholly in English:

Dear Mrs. Best,

Thank you ever so much for your nice present, 'awfully', well, let us say, 'reverentially' nice. It is so very kind of you not to have forgotten me, and the book is so interesting!

I read it almost entirely on my way to Kerry (it is a long journey) and I was delighted with it. It is somewhat different from what I had read from the same author, and is all the more interesting for it.

The weather is rather wild here, stormy and wet, though not very cold. I don't mind it. I enjoyed very much my Irish Christmas – except that I had to drink a little more than I would have liked to. My guests [hosts] would have been *too* sorry if I had not appreciated their costly 'brandy'.

I have not heard a word of English for the last few days, and I am afraid I am going to forget all about it.

Excuse please this dirty handwriting. I am seating near the fire, and don't feel like leaving the fire to go at the far end of the room, near the table. So I have got to write on my knees.

With many friendly thoughts and wishes I remain

Your affectionate,
M.L. Sjoestedt.[22]

On the Blasket Island

Marie's description of Blasket life is one of the most moving and sympathetic pieces ever written about the Island community:

Poor amongst the poor, these people have nevertheless the pride of their island. An island of saintly repute; here a man never died without the priest; here a young man never 'did wrong' to a young girl. Deprived of all material comfort they enjoy instead a social life more intense in this restricted community than in the scattered parishes of the coast. A social life in which are kept alive faithfully the customs and the musical and literary traditions of this people so admirably gifted with the things of the spirit.

All the elements of an old and rich popular culture; dance, dance music, vocal music, poems, stories and legends, are still alive and continue to flourish and to multiply, here as in every place where the Irish language is still spoken.

Individual dancers, virtuosos of the complex jig, musicians who accompany them on the violin or flute with variations heard a thousand times but always avidly listened to; traditional singers who, in sonorous and slightly nasal voice, phrase with such

118

purity, respectful of their meaning, the old jacobite ballads, the eternal songs of love or the verses of humorous character; storytellers who repeat, just as you would relate them, the legends that came down from their fathers, constantly refined by the effort of generations towards an ideal wholly literary in form; poets whose works, hardly less traditional, borrow the rhythm and the images of past compositions to exalt the heroes of independence, to celebrate the beauties of their native island, to lament the death of some loved one, or to call down the blessings of Heaven on the head of a host: how many times do you tell yet again the pride of Gaelic Ireland and the charm of its evenings?

Besides, practically all here are storytellers, poets and musicians without intending to be so. The attraction to what is powerful or strange, the faculty of looking beyond the utilitarian perception of the object, of evaluating it aesthetically, the gift of picturesque expression forever being recreated, the facility with which they manage words, all these gifts which go to the making of poets have widespread existence amongst this people.[23]

Peig Sayers

Ireland has two literatures, remarked Marie, that which Europe knows and that about which Europe knows nothing.[24] In her essay on contemporary Irish literature in *Études Celtiques* II (1937) she surveys the Blasket autobiographies in a general way, while she reserves Peig Sayers' autobiography for more detailed discussion in the following issue of the journal. As woman to woman, it might be surmised that Peig was her favourite among Blasket authors. In the course of her review, she notes, what George Thomson and other observers have drawn to our attention, that, under stimulation from outside, the island people, who up to then had found their mode of expression in traditional oral forms like story and popular song, were turning more and more to written expression, a process for which congratulation was due,

> and one to which we owe some of the most powerful and personal works of the young literature, and, at the same time, of precious documents, of a language sincere, enjoyable, rich in idiom and yet free of all pedantry. This is not the place to dwell on the literary and human importance of this varied and moving recital. The author, who is one of the best traditional storytellers of the district ... has a memory fully stocked with local folklore, of verse by poets of the region, of proverbs, with which her prose is sprinkled throughout. She has an innate sense of the resources of

her tongue. Those who do research on linguistics know that in every community there is to be found a born linguist, whose discovery will suffice for them to make their task very much facilitated. Those who have worked with Peig Sayers know that she is one of these, and that she possesses a feeling for the mechanism and the most delicate nuances of her language all the more assured in that it is not contaminated by any bookish influence. Her book therefore constitutes a document that is totally trustworthy for whoever wishes to study the syntax or stylistics of her speech. [25]

The Blasket Literature

Among Marie-Louise Sjoestedt's papers was found an essay bearing date 21 March 1937 which she had intended printing in some literary review. It was entitled *Essay on a national literature: contemporary Irish literature* and is printed in the memorial booklet, pp 53-78. It deals with the renascent Irish literature, beginning with Hyde's *Love Songs of Connaught*, taking in Peadar Ua Laoghaire's *Séadna* and *Mo Scéal Féin*, the writings of Pádraig Pearse, 'hero and saint', of Pádraig Ó Siochfhradha and later writers, touching on *Fánaí* (*Le vagabond*) of Seán Óg Ó Caomhánaigh, an Irish-American novel which is part of 'the colonial literature of Ireland', the novels of Séamus Ó Grianna and others, with some acute observations on each genre.

She comes to discuss the Blasket literature –

> And yet, it is from this gaelic milieu, so disparaged, so exploited, that there emerged the most original, most sincere book, one of the greatest books to be written in modern Irish. A book which stands apart from literary cadres and schools, which is simply the recital of the human experience of its author: three-quarters of a century of existence on an island a league long and a quarter league broad.
>
> Tomás Ó Criomhthain, author of *The Islandman*, who has just died, was one of the oldest of some hundred and fifty fishermen who inhabit the Blasket Island on the southwest coast. His book is his life, that is to say their life; their toil, their sufferings and their joys which land and sea, life and death can bring to men who are on a level with these forces. An authentic universe, and viewed through an authentic sensibility, in harmony with that life ... And the conclusion, which draws on human drama with the intensity of a chorus of elders from Aeschylus: 'I remember being a boy; a young man; in the flower of my ability and strength. There came scarcity and plenty, good fortune and bad, in the

course of my life up to the present. These things teach a great deal to the person who considers them'.[26]

From this 'little morsel of land cast in the middle of the Atlantic' there emerged two other life stories: *Twenty Years A-Growing* of Muiris Ó Súileabháin

> whose voice answers to that of Tomás like a chorus of the young to the chorus of elders, and following that, the book which Peig Sayers, a humble woman of the island, dictated, scarcely knowing how to write, to her son. A work which puts itself on the same human level as that of Tomás, and is nevertheless as different as two plants can be which have risen out of the same soil; because Tomás is of a serious spirit and because Peig, whose life has been but a long succession of sorrows, is a happy soul; because Tomás is a man and Peig a woman. The fullest hours of her life, the fullest pages of her book, were not about the first prey dispatched, nor about the first storm encountered. They were of the day when a little girl was sent into service far from her parents and the home of her childhood, by the will of the eldest son's wife, who was mistress in authority … and wept for her invalid mother and the sad life which the daughter-in-law ordained for her …[27]

The Islandman

She had no doubt that, when the new Irish literature emerged from its tentative and experimental stage, and the works of merit were sorted out from the rest, the distinction of being numbered amongst its classics would go to Tomás Ó Criomhthain's *Islandman* nor does she forget to point out that it was through the encouragement of Brian Kelly, a friend of the Gaeltacht, it came to be written. In her generous review of the book on its appearance in 1929, she thanked the editor, An Seabhac, for permitting her consult the original manuscript, and although fully understanding his reasons for normalising its orthography and nuances, she regretted that this had been done, as the traces of local dialect and expression had disappeared in the printed text. She gives examples of these and it may be noted that, true to linguistic standards, she gives priority of importance to the authentic spoken word as against editorial convention.[28]

Marriage and Travel

In July 1932 Marie married Michel Jonval, like herself an accomplished linguist. A student of Latvian literature, he had held a post as lecturer in

French at Riga University and was the author of *Chansons mythologiques lettones* (Paris 1929) translated from the Latvian. Together they travelled extensively in eastern regions, Russia, the Caucases, as far as Iran, in 1934-35, pursuing researches in folklore. Wherever she went Marie served as ambassador for Irish literature, knowledge of which she brought to faraway quarters, as in her essay on 'The Irish language and the language problem in the Ireland of today' contributed to a Latvian journal in 1934, copies of which are unlikely to reach the shores of Ireland.[29] Her husband died prematurely towards the end of 1935.

Marie spent the summers of 1936 and 1939 in Wales but was unable to elaborate on the linguistic materials she collected there, and her stay was cut short by the advent of war. She was also unable to sketch out a draft of a middle Irish grammar, for which she had made ample notes. The last important work of hers to be published was *Dieux et Héros des Celtes* (Paris 1940), a new and challenging approach to the problems of Celtic mythology, 'a book of profound originality, in its fact as in its presentation', (Vendryes), the appearance of which preceded her death only by some weeks.

Distress and Death

The war which broke out in the Autumn of 1939 brought on a series of crises in her life which in the end she did not survive. Like her father, her patriotism centred on France and her country's defeat in the early battles of the western front, and subsequent occupation, was for her a heartrending experience. The last phase of her life is described by her biographer with reticence and sympathy:

> Her ardent temperament, too prone to stretch to extremes and subject afterwards to profound depression, was unable to stand up to the anguish of the days of June [1940]. A too late departure from Paris, a return marked by tragic incidents, a whole lamentable succession of circumstances, led to a series of nervous crises: a kind of instability dragged her along by intervals towards death. On five occasions she came to be saved just in time.
>
> However she obtained a period of calm in November and December: there was a renewal of hope. It was at the end of that period that her second marriage took place to a man whom she loved and by whom she was loved.
>
> But on the evening of 26 December, following a fresh onset which gave no warning sign, on this occasion, to forestall it, she submitted herself to a cruel death, which at least did not allow her time to suffer. Her countenance became peaceful, the light of

youth returning at once to features that had long been under the duress of suffering.[30]

The name of her second husband is not given and the details of the tragedy have been shaded and softened. In reality she was a victim of the war. Among tributes paid to her one of the most touching was that of her teacher Joseph Vendryes. 'Marie-Louise Sjoestedt was the complete Celtiste. She encompassed the whole geographical expanse of the Celtic world, having also taken on recently the study of Scotch Gaelic and of Cornish, of which she had proposed in the near future to make a deeper study. She dominated the Celtic literatures … She was too much the Celt, alas! one might say', for he saw in her death something of the character of certain Celtic tales which ended poignantly in tragedy, 'Death roved ceaselessly round the heroes of Irish epic'.[31]

Myles Dillon was in Wisconsin when he heard from Kenneth Jackson 'that Madame Jonval died in Paris last year. Are these sad tidings true?' He was writing to Best. 'Someone should write a good notice of M-L Sjoestedt, for she did good work and was a charming girl.'[32]

His own tribute to her was his translation of *Gods and Heroes of the Celts*, performed 'as an act of piety to the memory of a friend whose death is a grave loss to Celtic studies'.[33]

A brief notice of her death was contributed by Professor Gerard Murphy to *Éigse: A journal of Irish Studies* III, pt IV [1943] 306 in which he considered that her death could not fail to retard the progress of Irish studies in France. One cannot help thinking that Seán an Chóta was much distressed by the news, having shared as they did a happy companionship.

Of the distinguished Celtic scholars associated with the Blasket Island she is the only woman. Readers of Máire Ní Ghuithín's *An tOileán a Bhí* will be aware of how much she enjoyed the island's social life. Her two books on the language of Dunquin and the Blasket are the only adequate scientific study of the popular speech of this premier milieu of the Irish language. Being of their time, their value now may be partly historic, as the local language has since then undergone changes.

References

1.   *Études Celtiques* IV (1948) 428-433. The obituary and appreciation by her professor Joseph Vendryes is a reprint from *Marie-Louise Sjoestedt (1900-1940): in memoriam* (Paris 1941) 17-24.
2.   'L'Irlande d'aujourd'hui, Dublin' in *Revue des Deux Mondes* (1 juillet 1930) 175. Vendryes comments that her judgements 'solid in their depth as moderate in

their form, would be for future historians a document of the first order'. *Revue Celtique* XLVII (1930) 471.

3. Louis Renou, 'Notice biographique' in *Marie-Louise Sjoestedt (1900-1940): in memoriam*, 9.

4. *Ibid.*, 21-2.

5. National Library of Ireland Ms. No. 11003 (22).

6. *Revue Celtique* L, 166-70.

7. Royal Irish Academy *Proceedings*, Vol XXXVII, Sect. C., p.195 *et seq.* Sommerfelt's study was made on the restricted basis of two native speakers, Domhnall Ó Mainnín of Ballyferriter and Dónall Ó Céilleachair of Coolea, both excellent, but interviewed in Dublin, September, 1923, away from their surroundings.

8. *Revue Celtique*, L, 167.

9. Vol III (1938-39) 381-3.

10. In *Étrennes offertes à Émile Benveniste* (Paris, 1938), 81-122.

11. *Ibid.*, 82.

12. *Ibid.*, 84.

13. Cf. *Phonétique d'un parler irlandais de Kerry* (Paris, 1931) Avant-propos ix-x.

14. I am grateful to Muiris Mac Conghail, in whose possession the volume now is, for drawing my attention to this.

15. She published a record of this journey and of her subsequent stay in Dunquin and the Blasket Island under the title of 'L'Irlande d'aujourd'hui: Gens de la terre et de la côte' in *Revue des Deux Mondes*, 15 juin 1930, pp 839-864, extracts from which are given in the course of this essay, under the reference 'Gens de la terre'.

16. 'Gens de la terre', p.843.

17. *Ibid.*, p.845.

18. *Ibid.*, p.846.

19. *Ibid.*, p.848-9.

20. *Ibid.*, p.849.

21. National Library of Ireland Ms No 11003 (22).

22. *Ibid.*

23. 'Gens de la terre', pp 857-58.

24. 'Essai sur une littérature nationale: la littérature irlandaise contemporaine' p.53. This essay is printed in *Marie-Louise Sjoestedt (1900-1940): in memoriam*, 53-78.

25. *Études Celtiques* III (juin 1938), 156-7.

26. *Marie-Louise Sjoestedt: in memoriam*, 68-70.

27. *Ibid.*, p.71.

28. *Revue Celtique* XLVII (1930), 211-214.

29. 'Iru valoda un valodas jautájums tragedéjá' *Irijá in Izglit, ministr. méneŝr.* (Riga), 1934, 1, pp 35-44.

30. L. Renou: 'Notice biographique' in *Marie-Louise Sjoestedt: in memoriam*, p.11.

31. *Ibid.*, p.23.

32. Myles Dillon to R.I. Best, 23. iii.1942 from the University of Wisconsin, Madison. NLI Ms No 11000 (17).

33. *Gods and Heroes of the Celts* (London 1949), Preface vi.

Chapter 7

Carl Marstrander

Carl Marstrander was a personality of some splendour. *Ní fear go dtí é –* he is without peer. In such pithy phrase did Tomás Ó Crithin describe the Norwegian Celtic scholar, *An Lochlannach,* to Professor D.A. Binchy on the Blasket Island.[1] The 'spare, tall, fair-skinned, blue-eyed' scholar has acquired an immortal niche in Irish literature through Ó Crithin's portrait of him in *The Islandman* as an Irish language student of great purpose and industry, and a friend of generous heart. *Beidh cion agam go deo air.*[2]

Carl Johan Sverdrup Marstrander was born a little over one hundred years ago (on 26 November 1883) in Kristiansand on the southern coast of Norway, although his surname, not characteristically Norwegian, is thought to derive from the town of Marstrand on the Swedish coast, north of Göteburg, whence in earlier times his family migrated to Norway.

A letter in archaic Irish from Marstrander to the great German Celtic scholar Kuno Meyer bearing the date *in seised laa fichett dabran 1909* is signed Carolus Mac Fredricc, puzzling until one remembers that his father was Fredric Marstrander and that the son was identifying himself according to Irish usage. His mother was Christiane Henriette, née Brodtkorb Sverdrup. Fredric Marstrander, principal of the local college, was a man of learning, with a library which included works on European linguistics. It is probable that Carl was influenced by these to study languages, in the Celtic branch of which he had already become interested before entering Kristiania (later Oslo) University at the age of 18. There his talent for languages was noted and encouraged by the Professor of Comparative Linguistics and Old Norse, Sophus Bugge, and by Alf Torp, the Professor of Sanskrit. So highly did they think of him that they procured a scholarship enabling him to go to Ireland to study spoken Irish.[3] Marstrander relates how he was called to the office of his professor, Sophus Bugge, to be told of the scholarship and how he was between two minds whether to accept it or go to represent Norway in the pole vault at the Olympic Games in Athens, an honour for which he had just been selected. Sophus Bugge, uttering a Latin phrase, prompted him to opt for Ireland, a choice he never regretted.

In Dublin he made the acquaintance of Richard Best, secretary to the School of Irish Learning, at whose house he was an honoured guest before setting out on the long journey to west Kerry to study the spoken Irish language. Marstrander believed that book learning by itself did not give one a complete view of the language and must be supplemented by an adequate knowledge of the spoken tongue.

The weather was at its worst when, writing from William Long's guesthouse in Ballyferriter on 17 July 1907, he gave an account of his adventures to Richard Best. He had set out from Dublin at 3 o'clock on Saturday (having to miss an earlier train simply because the driver did not turn up) and stayed overnight in Tralee. Travelling on next day about 11.30 by rail for Dingle, he left his suitcase on arrival at the station to be taken away in Mr. Long's cart, and walked the seven miles to Ballyferriter. There he had for pleasant company two people from Limerick, a brother and sister named Fitzgerald, who were studying in Dublin, and a young priest from Galway. He was very pleased with his place in Mr. Long's. 'He is himself a "native speaker" and his house is by far the best in this place.' However, he spoke the language too fast. But perhaps they could try to train him? On the previous day he had gone with Mr. Long on a remarkable fishing tour, passing by Carraig Bhréan (near Smerwick) and going along the foot of one of those steep, high mountains with two impressive natural peaks. There they fell in with a company of fishermen and others and there Marstrander had the most unusual meal of his life, consisting of fish, seaweed from the beach (which sounds like *duileasc*), thick sour milk, mussels which he had encountered in Norway under the name of *angel*, and *horribile dictu*, snails:

> I must however confess that the snails tasted very good, and that I would, with pleasure, if requested, procure a whole dishful for you. I am convinced that you and your wife would regard them as a delicacy once you had got used to them.[5]

Snails an article of food in west Kerry! They were not confused with the humble *báirneach* surely? But then Marstrander's *horribile dictu* can leave us in no doubt that they really were snails, of whatever variety. What an intriguing piece of research for social historians.

He had a long letter from Hermann Osthoff of Heidelberg, who was staying in Aran at Martin Concannon's, learning Irish, which he mastered well, and it was scholarship's loss that this great philologist was tragically soon to die, the fruits of his new learning unrealized. Of present sadness to Marstrander was the news just to hand of the death, on 8 July, of his revered professor, Sophus Bugge, a man truly great, who had raised a monument so enduring that his name would be cherished in Norway.

Marstrander enjoyed his stay in Ballyferriter but thought the Irish spoken there had too large an admixture of English. So he moved, in search of better, further west to the Great Blasket Island from where, on 6 August 1907, he sent a message by postcard to Best, who in the meantime had sent him on from Dublin the forgotten item of a razor to curb a sprouting beard:

> Gt. Blasket Isl. 6.viii.07
> Dear Mr. Best,
> Permit me to thank you belatedly for your letter and the trouble you took to obtain the razor.
> As you can see, I am now on the Blasket Island, and will certainly stay here for the coming months. Ballyferriter was a wonderful place, but the speech seemed to me too undisciplined. I made up my mind very quickly, and left Ballyferriter yesterday, with all my belongings. I have installed myself here in Mr. Patrick Keane's house, with whom I have evidently as good lodgings as I found in Ballyferriter. I am not quite sure yet how long I will remain here, perhaps two, perhaps four months. The dialect seems very interesting. With my best wishes to you and your wife.
> Yours truly, C.M.[6]

Marstrander had found his milieu. On another card he wrote: 'I very much like the Blasket Island and the language here. My conversation will now largely be conducted through Irish'.[7] This early correspondence of Marstrander with Best was in German, the language, after Norwegian, with which he seemed most familiar. But in a very short time after settling in the Blaskets we find him writing competent Irish and using it, with full assurance, for all his needs.

Before leaving Ballyferriter, Marstrander had in fact gone to the island to make enquiries and his arrival there, it appears, was expected. In later years he used to relate a story, which he may have embellished a little, about his reception on the island by the King, Pádraig Ó Catháin, who greeted him with a speech by way of civic ceremony. Marstrander did not understand a word of what the King said but, nothing daunted, he delivered in reply a prepared speech of his own, composed in archaic Irish, the only kind he then knew, to which the puzzled King made the courteous observation that the Norwegian was a fine language indeed![8]

So Marstrander installed himself in *seomra an Lochlannaigh*, as the King, in later correspondence, referred to it.[9] To his enquiry as to who might best teach him Irish, the King recommended Tomás Ó Crithin, and from Ó Crithin's classic autobiography we learn of Marstrander's diligence during an intensive learning course which must have made considerable demands on both men. Marstrander's personality made a profound impression on Ó Crithin, who in his autobiography and correspondence speaks of him with the greatest admiration.

Marstrander, for his part, found himself in total harmony with Blasket life. The Irish spoken there he considered the purest he had ever encountered. He enjoyed the good company and happy relaxed air of the island, mixing with the people as one of themselves, which was, he thought, the best way of acquiring the language. Writing in excellent Irish to Richard Best on 15 September 1907, he said he was now able to express anything he wanted in Irish, and that pleased him well, as he had hardly a word leaving Dublin. He thought he would remain on the island until near Christmas time, and expressed himself as being well in every respect. 'I must say that the finest thing I have heard and seen in Ireland has been the Irish language, the Irish music, the Irish song and the Irish dancing, which I found amongst the very poor people here'. His accord and best wishes went to the Gaelic people in all their activities.[10]

By the time he left the island, towards Christmas, Marstrander had mastered the language and become a fully competent Irish speaker. The knowledge proved useful to him in his scholarly career, balancing his already fine knowledge of Early and Middle Irish, extending his field of reference and comparison, and giving him the broadest vision of what was to him 'this wonderful language'.

> Did you hear anything on the part of our common Norwegian friend, the well-known Viking warrior Mr. Marstrander? Is he still retained by the charms of the Great Blasket Island, afar from all debauchings of culture and civilisation?[11]

This enquiry, addressed to Richard Best, came from Hermann Osthoff, and was dated at Heidelberg, 29 December 1907. Marstrander who had by then left the island was not looking well. Richard Best was worried about him and was later to speculate whether island life, with its inherent hardships, had done any good to Synge or Marstrander or Osthoff. 'I am sorry to hear of poor Marstrander's illness',[12] wrote Kuno Meyer on 2 January 1908, from a health resort in the Pyrenees, but things were better when he wrote again on 23 January from Paris that he had had a long letter from Marstrander, who had by then almost quite recovered. 'He gives an interesting account of his stay in the island and of his work.'[13]

Although he learned Blasket Irish so well, Marstrander never published a description of the language. That same year he won a scholarship in Comparative Linguistics at Oslo and continued his Celtic studies there, retaining his special interest in Irish literature, folklore and archaeology.

Throughout 1909 and the following years Richard Best and Kuno Meyer became preoccupied with the problems which the newly-established National University posed for the School of Irish Learning. The School, established in 1903 on the initiative of Kuno Meyer, offered summer courses of instruction in Early and Middle Irish as well as other branches of Celtic studies including Welsh, gave editorial training in manuscript reading and transcription and provided scholarships for outstanding students to study abroad. It employed Osborn Bergin on a modest salary as full-time professor throughout the year. Its excellent work was done on meagre resources which included a Government grant of £100, later withdrawn, and the generous financial support of Alice Stopford Green, whose name should never be forgotten by those who hold Irish scholarship dear. Osborn Bergin applied for the Chair of Old Irish in the National University at the persuasion of his friends –indeed he left his application till the last minute and even then he had to be urged to forward it – and was in due course chosen for the post.

On his appointment, he received a letter from his President, Dr. Coffey, suggesting that he discontinue his classes at the School of Irish Learning and get his pupils to attend the university, which Dr. Coffey hoped to develop into the major world centre for Celtic studies, a prospect about which Richard Best was, privately, in the highest degree dubious. Although Bergin wished to continue his teaching at the School of Irish Learning the necessities of his post in the National University compelled him to retire from the School. Bergin also had the task of editing materials for the comprehensive Dictionary of the Irish Language, a project of long existence, which the Royal Irish Academy proposed to publish.[14]

Bergin's departure raised the question of a successor, with Marstrander, if available, the obvious choice. He had been continuing his studies in Oslo, had sent to Best for books on the modern Irish language movement, including the writings of folk poets, for an article he was preparing, and had composed for the *Zeitschrift für celtische Philologie* what Meyer, its editor, described as 'a marvellous paper ... the like of which was never seen before ... If he sticks to Celtic', Meyer went on, 'our knowledge will advance with giant strides. I wish we could get a post for him, either here or elsewhere.'[15] Correspondence was opened with Marstrander. 'I have written to Marstrander sounding him on the Dictionary. If he will not come, I do not know what to propose', thus Meyer, writing to Best on 27 October 1909.[16] Marstrander's name was being mentioned in the premises of the Royal Irish Academy. 'Who is Marstrander?', Robert Lloyd Praeger, editor of Academy publications, wanted to know, a query that gave Best the opportunity of praising him in the highest terms. Best had no doubt that a worker of Marstrander's ability would complete the Dictionary in ten years under Meyer's directions and then be able to return home with a great reputation to a chair in Norway.[17] But by the end of October 1909 Marstrander had not replied and there were fears he would not come. One of the problems to be considered was whether the School on its slender resources could pay him an adequate salary. On 13 November Meyer lunched with Mrs. Green who promised to give as much money as the School required. 'I even hope' said Meyer, 'to be able to persuade Marstrander to come by proposing a good salary to him'.[18]

A brief note from Mrs. Green to Meyer has survived to which praise can add nothing. It reads:

> Most certainly I will guarantee the £100 for a year or two for Dr. Marstrander and am honoured to do so.[19]

Persuasion succeeded. Meyer crossed from Liverpool to Dublin in the first week of December 1909 to attend a meeting of the Governors of the School of Irish Learning, his sole business being to propose 'Marstrander's appointment as Professor of Comparative Philology, a title which he would like to have.'[20] On the 13th Meyer could announce that a telegram had just come from Marstrander who seemed delighted. In a season of storms the Viking scholar journeyed to Liverpool in the third week of February 1910 to have a discussion with Meyer and to be coached in the duties which he was to undertake in Dublin. 'He is willing to bind himself for three years and hopes to stay altogether.' Thus Meyer, highly pleased, to Best by letter of 17 February 1910.[21]

After his conversations with Meyer, Marstrander crossed to Dublin on 25 February 1910. Meyer's total satisfaction with him finds expression in a letter he wrote the same day to Best:

> M. leaves for Dublin this afternoon … I am delighted with him. He is wonderfully keen and eager and looks forward to his work with zest. He will reform the Dict[ionary]. Nothing escapes him. We went through the proof and Bergin's slips and he at once spotted every weak point and had the right thing ready. I feel that I can absolutely trust him and a great burden is off my mind. I hope in my absence you and Bergin will see him properly

installed at the R.I.A. I have told him to mention anything he wants to you in the first instance.[22]

Best as usual was given the task of finding suitable lodgings for the new staff member. It was suggested he might stay at the same address as R.A. Stewart Macalister, the archaeologist, but Best rejected the idea. Macalister was a militant and might try to recruit Marstrander for the new university, which Best would not want. 'We are now rivals'. Marstrander was satisfactorily lodged at 'Yeovil', Bushy Park Road, in Rathgar. Meyer sent instructions to Best on how Marstrander should be introduced gradually into his work. He should start after Easter and be let down easy at first with whatever he liked and could best do until he got a better grip of English.

> Then as to July, Marstrander must try to follow Bergin's old programme as best he can. There must be instruction in Old-Irish (especially for the foreigners), both elementary and advanced. That is the chief thing.[23]

Marstrander set to work with a will. Meyer, wandering in Italy in search of health, had news from him at Acqui a month later. Marstrander was working hard on the letter 'D' of the proposed dictionary. A word of explanation is necessary about the dictionary and the urgency which had come to attend it. The project had originated in 1852 when it was planned that it should be carried out by John O'Donovan and Eugene O'Curry. The early deaths of both these scholars left the plan unaccomplished and little progress was made until Meyer took over direction of the work in 1907 with Bergin as editor. A great and generous supporter of the Irish language, the Rev. Maxwell Henry Close, had left a bequest of £1,000 to the Royal Irish Academy on his death in September 1903 towards the expenses of an Irish dictionary. There was a condition attached to the bequest. A portion of the dictionary had to be in print within 10 years of his death or the money would be withdrawn.[24]

So Marstrander had to work to a dateline. This did not daunt him. But he was far from pleased at the state of things as he found them. The raw materials consisted of a collection of paper slips arranged alphabetically, 'defective and heterogeneous, gathered from east to west without any general plan, and to some extent by people who even lack the most elementary knowledge of older Irish'.[25]

Such was his later description. On his first survey he left Meyer in no doubt about what he thought of the situation. 'He has a very poor opinion of what has been done hitherto' wrote Meyer, who expressed as his own opinion that it was a thousand pities that they had to begin to print.[26] Meyer had complained about Bergin's slow progress with the dictionary and the fact that he answered letters not at all or only after long intervals, but not to Bergin himself, whom he held in great respect. He wished they could associate Charles Plummer with the dictionary, 'the *only* scholar who is working at lexicography'. Plummer at Corpus Christi College, Oxford, was known to be compiling his own early Irish dictionary.

In his new environment Marstrander made a profound impression. Naturally he was much in contact with Best, the secretary of the School of Irish Learning, who sent the following account of his new colleague to Meyer:

> Marstrander has been here constantly. He is assuredly a genius. I like him more every day. His knowledge is surprising, and his power of using it immense. He constantly tells me of his adventures among the slips and amazes me by the acuteness of his emendations. He has a most penetrative mind. The Dictionary will now begin to move, and promises to be a fine thing. I send M.'s praises daily to Praeger who is himself much impressed by his ability and his manner.[27]

'I am rejoiced to hear all this about the Norseman' wrote Meyer from Acqui by letter of 23 March 1910.[28] Marstrander was an immediate success as a teacher. He took his first class at the School of Irish Learning on 5 April 1910. We are fortunate to have a detailed account of it as related by Richard Best who wrote to Meyer on the following day:

> Marstrander opened his campaign yesterday evening. He had an auditoire of 14, and including the officers 17. T.P. O'Nowlan, Torna (ever loyal!), the faithful Purcell M.A., Miss Kennedy, Young Gwynn, and other old habitués turned up. I'm afraid some of the pre-Celtic explanations were beyond them; but he made a splendid impression; talked for an hour and a half without stopping. I learned a great deal and shall be henceforth a regular attendant. His knowledge is remarkable and the clear and lucid way in which he expressed himself in a tongue which he has never seriously studied filled me with wonder and admiration. Certainly there is no such scholar at present among us. We have a jewel of great price! He himself is greatly pleased. Many were struck by the purity of his modern Irish pronunciation, for he occasionally illustrated sound change by citing modern usage, and

they expressed a wish that he should lecture in Irish, using English words for the technical terms. I can see already that he will be very popular and will attract students. At present he is burning with eagerness to bring out *Ériu V,* which he intends shall be a *model* Celtic review. His interest and enthusiasm is a refreshing stimulus to us all. If only we may be permitted to retain him![29]

Meyer expressed his delight but, experienced editor that he was, thought Marstrander's ambitions with regard to *Ériu* would be hard to realize. 'He does not as yet know the bed of thorns of an editor'.[30]

Carl Marstrander and Seán Óg Ó Caomhánaigh of Dunquin, himself a future dictionary-maker, established a firm friendship. Indeed it is possible that the excellence of Marstrander's spoken Irish was due in part to Seán Óg's tuition or conversation, for Seán was an habitué of the School of Irish Learning and gave lessons in Irish to some of its students. He was also a columnist in Arthur Griffith's weekly *Sinn Féin* and it is probable that the description of the school containing the following paragraph came from his hand.

> Anois tá fear ann gur b'é a mhian 'An Lochlannach' do thabhairt air. Aon mholadh dob fhéidir linne do thabhairt dó níor dhóthanach é. Téidhidh chuige agus ní bheidh aithreachas oraibh. Rud ná raibh ag aon eachtaranach eile tá eolas iomlán aige ar Ghaedhling na haimsire seo.[31]

One can only regard with admiration the talented scholars who were drawn to the School of Irish Learning from different countries. How fortunate Dublin was in having them, commented Robin Flower, adding however, truly enough no doubt, that Dublin was unaware of its own good fortune. Some notion of their intellectual quality may be inferred from a letter to Mrs. Green from Best:

> The School has been most successful this summer. Twenty students attend the various classes. The numbers are smaller than last year, but greater than in preceding years. The quality is also on the whole fine. We have Dr. Pokorny again from Vienna. Mr. Flower, Assistant in the MS Department, British Museum, who is now completing the Irish MSS catalogue, who is a rising poet, of I think considerable merit, Mr. Fraser, lecturer in Latin at Aberdeen, Miss Mary Williams, who recently took her doctorate in Paris with a dissertation on Peredur, are also among the students. Mr. Marstrander gave a garden party on Saturday at which most of the

School were present. A photographer was in attendance! One and all are devoted to him. His amazing knowledge of the language and his profound philosophical explanations have made a deep impression. He takes a personal interest in the students and is getting them to prepare texts for *Ériu*.[32]

That account is dated 20 July 1910. It was Robin Flower's first term at the School. Later that summer, on the suggestion of his teacher Carl Marstrander, he (Flower) set out for the Blasket Island on the first of many journeys that were to have such important consequences for Irish literature and language. Marstrander's own comments on members of his class and reactions to his environment are put down by him in his characteristic way in a letter to Kuno Meyer that may be thought to have certain magisterial tones. These might, however, be related to his inexperience in the nuances of the English language. It is written from 'Yeovil', Bushy Park Road, on 1 August 1910:

> You will have heard from Mr. Best (which would be his duty as secretary) all about the class and our work in the summer course. I could not say I took up the work with much enthusiasm or expectation of profit or pleasure. I am happy to be able to say that I found both – for myself at least. For my pupils I am not able to speak. I had not realised before how it throws light on many obscure questions and fixes doubtful opinions for oneself, to make the great outlines of a difficult subject very clear and definite for a more or less intelligent audience! I may say that my knowledge *in rebus Celticis* has grown more in this month than in the previous six!
> Mr. Fraser from Aberdeen is a quite decent sort. He is hardly brilliant, but I think he works on a solid base, and that he may do good work in the future … Mr. Flower also I find a solid fellow on whose future conscientious and scientific work we may rely … To return to the other members of the school-menagerie, Miss Williams is a nice specimen! She will return in October and stay till after Christmas, attending my classes … Dr. Pokorny left yesterday for Belgium. He … was well satisfied with the course. I suppose you have heard through Mr. Best of his 'brilliant' thronged lecture in the Mansion House. It passed off with great éclat. How clever some people are in making an effect with the little they know….

And impishly he affixes in place of signature a mini-photograph of himself holding a cup, presumably of tea or coffee.[33] Whatever

Marstrander thought of Pokorny, the latter for his part wrote to Meyer that he was greatly pleased with Marstrander.[34]

Did Marstrander take on too much? His programme was formidable. He had to organize the letter 'D' for the projected Dictionary from imperfect materials and have at least part of it published by August 1913. He had to teach in the School of Irish Learning. He had a large part of the responsibility for editing the learned journal *Ériu*, his co-editor being Meyer. As if all this were not enough, he took on the immense task of preparing, in collaboration with Richard Best, a scholarly edition of the great codex *Lebor na Huidre* or Book of the Dun Cow, referred to in their correspondence as LU, at which he proposed they work together in the evenings, there being no time to spare for it during the day.

His youth – at 27 he was an acknowledged leader in the field of Celtic studies – his zeal and, possibly, his impulsiveness may have caused occasional difficulties with his more mature colleagues. There was, it appears, some friction relating to the journal *Ériu*, and the affable Best, who seems to have complained to Meyer, received a piece of advice on 10 November 1910 from the German scholar:

> Do not let, I beseech you, the present state of tension between M. and you continue. You are the older, the wiser, the more sure of yourself. Marstrander writes me in a temper that I deplore. I have just written eight pages to him trying to once more show him that when four people do not agree, all of them good friends, the thing is to try in the best of humour to arrive at some compromise...
>
> As to Marstrander's appointment, I have neither my letters to him nor his. The matter is however very simple and clear. He almost made it one of the conditions of his coming that he should be one of the editors of *Ériu* and I promised him that. As three editors would have been too many, Bergin like a good fellow retired without so much as a word being wasted over it.[35]

Five days later Meyer had words of praise for Marstrander's fine edition of Volume V of *Ériu*.[36] A possible explanation of the tensions is that Marstrander may have been overtaxing his health, not surprising in view of his multiple activities. An undated note from his Bushy Park Road address to Best reads:

> I am sorry to have to tell you that I don't feel at all well today and I could not possibly think of taking the class tonight. I think La Touche's splendid dinner has killed me.[37]

At the end of February 1911 he had to discontinue his classes because of a severe illness which was diagnosed as pleurisy. Meyer wrote from Liverpool expressing his anxiety:

> This is indeed sad and grave news. Is the doctor really capable? It seems odd his leaving him alone so long. However, I dare say nothing can be done meanwhile. Surely they know now how to treat consumption in its early stages – these new sanatoria are all over the place. I am anxiously awaiting further news. Meanwhile I have just written to Marstrander to cheer him up. His recovery is now the only question. If I should be needed in anything I would at once come over. Thank you for letting me know at once.[38]

Best, with equal concern, kept in close touch with the situation, sending news as it came of the scholar's condition to Meyer, who acknowledged by postcard on 26 February:

> Many thanks for your bulletins. I was greatly relieved to hear of the success of the operation and now hope to hear that nothing wrong is revealed by the examination.[39]

The serious nature of the operation may be inferred from a letter to Robin Flower from Tomás Ó Crithin who mentions receiving a postcard from Marstrander saying he was in a Dublin hospital, *'dúinsí(?) uisge bainte amach as a chliabh aige an liagh … tá eagla orm ina thaobh agus is oth liom soin dá mbeadh lias agam air'*.[40]

Marstrander was under treatment in Sir Patrick Dun's Hospital, and feeling better at the time he wrote the following undated note to Best, himself a victim of some ailment, perhaps influenza:

> So the gods have struck you down in the midst of your sins! I am exceedingly sorry to hear that you are sharing my sad fate as an invalid. I repeat your own admonition 'take care of yourself'.[41]

To recuperate he set out at the end of March to Monte Carlo, possibly on the advice of Meyer, who had often gone there himself for the good of his health. Some cheerful and extrovert letters he sent to Best show him in relaxed mood while not forgetful of future duties.

> I am sending you some hurried lines before going on an excursion to Mentone in an hour … I had a nice crossing to Holyhead, arriving in London at 11 p.m. after a rather wearisome journey. Mrs. Green was dining out that night and the following

... When I left for Newhaven Mrs. Green kindly presented me with a bottle of good wine and one of cold coffee. Now I love wine – and I am afraid I was in rather high spirits when arriving in Dieppe. But cold coffee is abominable. I managed to leave it in the Place de la République in Paris at the bottom of the great monument there. I have always been waiting for an opportunity of showing to the best of my ability my enthusiasm for the Revolution! I hope Mrs. Green will forgive me. How could she know I hated cold coffee so much.

Monte Carlo is a queer spot. All is first class here apart from the inhabitants and the visitors. I might be wrong – but I have never before seen such a vulgar lot of people ... Praise God – they have not been able to spoil the air and the sky and the blue sea ... Meyer will arrive on Monday next and probably remain for a fortnight ...[42]

Presently Meyer arrived and was accommodated at the Villa Médicis in the room next to Marstrander's. Naturally their conversation turned a great deal on Celtic studies, for which Marstrander was full of plans. He wanted Meyer to start a Celtic *Grundriss*, with the collaboration of Pedersen, Thurneysen, Bergin and Marstrander himself for grammar, Stern, Loth and Meyer for literature, Best for bibliography, Mac Neill and Macalister for archaeology. Although such a programme would take many years Meyer had no doubt that it would advance Celtic studies enormously if carried into effect.

The two scholars enjoyed themselves immensely, watching the motor-boat races, the superb fireworks over the bay at night, varying learned *immacallma* with visits to the gaming tables and leisurely promenades to look at the monde and demimonde. One day the King of Sweden appeared in the Club, looking very ill and haggard, 'with some lovely court ladies to whom Marstrander forthwith lost his heart so that I could hardly drag him away at midnight'.

Meyer, who had engagements to keep, left Monte Carlo on 24 April for Paris where, having missed an early train at the Gare du Nord on the morning of the 25th, he found himself with time to write Best 'an unvarnished account of the last fortnight'. He had left Marstrander the previous afternoon on the platform at Monaco, brown as a berry, and on the whole in good health and spirits. One of his brothers was coming to stay with him. Marstrander was finding life in Monte Carlo very pleasant, liked his quarters which were absurdly cheap, also the food, and if only he would not continue to play the tables as much as they both did during the last week all, said Meyer, would be well. He did not walk much owing to the heat and had to buy dark glasses for his eyes. He liked to stroll and sit on the terrace and listen to the band. Owing to sleeplessness he never got up much before 11 a.m. so that his day was short. Apart from the Norwegian papers he read little.[43]

On 30 April Marstrander wrote again to Best:

> A propos your letter: that soft spot in my heart is – I am afraid – an invention of yours! To imagine that you have known me now in four years and have not yet realised what an excellent specimen of a dry fossilised philologist I am! … I feel a good deal stronger than when leaving Dublin, heart function is quite normal and the left lung is gradually expanding; the slight catch which still is there, will it is to be hoped fully disappear after a couple of months. I am looking forward to the time I shall be able to take up work with renewed strength; but alas I am not yet the old; weariness and breathlessness often reminds me that something is wrong.
>
> My youngest brother is staying with me now. I am protecting him as well as I can against the perils of the Casino and the *malitiora gens feminarum*, as the prejudiced poet names them. He is a good young fellow.
>
> What about yourself and the LU? You have not spoken much of it lately. I hope you are firmly determined to carry the plan out. I 'intend' to live some years more (evil weeds never wither), and I should like to get that work out of hand before being gathered to my fathers. The heat will be intolerable here in a month. Don't you think it is a good idea to return to Dublin for one of the summer months to look after the Dictionary work and keep in contact with the Academy? …[44]

In a brief and hurried note of 14 May he wrote that he would be leaving for Dublin on the following morning. His brother had left for Norway the day before. After a short stay in Dublin he returned to Norway about mid-August 1911. On the 21st of that month we find him resident in Holmenkollen Sanatorium near Kristiania, from where he sends Best 'some hurried lines before I go down to have my dinner with the aged women of this place!' and bewails the loss on Liverpool station of his old winter coat, a calamity that almost broke his heart, for it had been with him through good and bad times and it would have been great fun to die in the old rag. Holmenkollen Sanatorium was not the place he first intended to go to …

> but the doctors unanimously advised me to spend two or – if required – even three months here, so that they might finally

decide whether my lungs are infected by tuberculosis or not. I am glad to say they have not yet found even the slightest trace of tuberculosis in spite of their careful examinations. They ignore me completely and treat me as a child of four, telling me when to arise and when to go to sleep, when to eat, walk, work – and how to do it. Of course – they are right and I am wrong – as usual.[45]

From this time on Marstrander spent much more of his time in Norway than in Dublin. He sent to Dublin for his books. As they had not yet arrived by 7 November 1911, although despatched from the Royal Irish Academy more than a fortnight earlier, he sent a reminder to Best from Omeyer's pensionat in Kristiania with a threat that if they did not turn up in a few days he would drown Macalister in a flood of wines,[46] doubtless aware of the archaeologist's horror of such beverages. They turned up soon after!

He was never a good correspondent. 'I have given up writing letters' he explains to Best in a note of 13 February 1912, wondering what Meyer and Mrs. Green thought of his silence, whether yet alive or gathered to his fathers. He was very busy with the Dictionary as well as with his contribution to the Miscellany or *Festschrift* which he and Bergin were preparing in tribute to Meyer who had been appointed in 1911 to the Chair of Celtic Philology in Berlin. This recently undertaken task was another sizeable addition to his responsibilities.

One result of his illness was that he had to discard certain of his activities. He wrote to Meyer saying his health would not allow him to carry on both the Dictionary and teaching at the School, so that he must at least temporarily retire from the School. He also spoke of retiring from the editorship of *Ériu*.[47] The Dictionary had to come first, and it was arranged between Meyer and himself that he should concentrate on that one object. Relations between the two scholars were becoming strained. Meyer thought Marstrander conceited, 'morbidly ambitious' and too indifferent a correspondent to have as fellow-editor of *Ériu*. There is a trace of acerbity in the message Marstrander sent to Best from Kristiania by postcard (postmark 1.IV.1912)

> I have written to Dr. Meyer about the School and I suppose he has informed you of my letter by this time. I received a strange letter from him the other day, which surprised me by a rudeness that I have never before detected in him. I am sorry he wrote it, for it is not pleasant to lose a friend, one has appreciated so highly...
> I am looking forward to seeing you in Dublin before three weeks

and work with you in the evenings on our common opus … The evenings are all that I can spare, as the whole day must be given to the Dictionary this year. With warmest regards to yourself and Mrs. Best.[48]

The coolness was temporary. At their discussion in Liverpool shortly afterwards, friendly relations were re-established, misunderstandings cleared up and Marstrander's immediate course of action defined. Meyer wrote to Best on 27 April 1912:

Before this reaches you Marstrander will probably have seen you. I was delighted to find him looking so well and in such good spirits – better than he ever seemed before. We spent the morning and afternoon together and talked over matters. His temporary resignation from the School and *Ériu*, until he had brought out D, was agreed upon. Even a summer course is impossible as he would lose a month for the Dictionary … He is at last going to devote all his time to this one object, and that is no doubt right.[49]

Marstrander came back to Dublin, but only for a brief stay. Evidently he decided to make Norway his base and work from there. He appears to have left Dublin at short notice without making his intention known to his friends. Best got a card from him on 18 May 1912 announcing his safe arrival in Kristiania where the weather was superb and 'one had no thought of one's health'. Best commented on the situation to Meyer:

If he can do the work as well in Norway he must of course live there. The Council (of the RIA) would not have stood in his way, their only concern is to get something printed – no matter where or how. And had M. consulted us we could have assured him of this, so that there had been no need to run away. E. Gwynn called to enquire of his whereabouts, anxious about his health and of course the Dictionary. Curious enough he too asked whether it was a case of *chercher la femme*. I do not think so but still you see people will think his sudden disappearance strange.[50]

Marstrander himself appreciated that his Dublin friends must have been puzzled and by letter of 4 November 1912 to Best is ready, in light-hearted mood, to express penitence to all concerned, including 'Maggee, the bashful lad'. This was William Kirkpatrick Magee, otherwise John Eglinton, of the National Library staff – 'my heart aches when I think of the enormous table he carried on his fragile back up to the third floor and down again all in vain. My eyes are getting wet.'

And so for the others:

> When I think of you, I hardly find one of you who has not (or
> fancied he has), some reason to be annoyed with me; you and
> Mrs. Best because of my inconsideration, selfishness and
> selfabsorption (which I guess you deem my most prominent
> virtues!), Bergin because I forgot about his coeditorship (and he of
> mine!) and Maggee ... I apologise most sincerely.[51]

He may have known that he would shortly be called to the Chair of
Celtic Philology in the University of Kristiania. His appointment to this
post was made in the summer of 1913 just before he returned to
Dublin but he was actually giving lectures there in 1912, according to
the following letter, which is dated 14.12.1912, not by Marstrander but
by Best, to whom it was written:

> I have to thank you for letters, received four or five months ago,
> it's a good while. It was very kind of you to write me such a
> friendly letter after my mysterious disappearance from Dublin. I
> felt convinced at the moment that in mentioning me to others and
> in discussing my person with others, your words would be
> marked by the same friendly spirit as was your letter – and so I
> suppose they have really been.
> The LU must be postponed ... at present I am too busy with the
> Dictionary to think of anything else. I am lecturing twice a week
> in the University for two students. One of them is very clever and
> has decided to give all his time to Celtic studies. I will secure him
> a scholarship next year and send him off to the Blaskets to my old
> friend Thomás Ó Crithin – providing the Princess is not there; she
> might disturb the piece of his heart, which according to his friends
> is of a very soft material...
> I am sorry to hear that Lucius Gwynn is worse. I have been
> thinking of him a good deal today. He is done, poor boy. I
> seldom met anyone I liked so well, his looks, his good nature and
> fine spirits...[52]

All through the late autumn of 1912 and early winter months of 1913
Marstrander worked ceaselessly in Kristiania, racing against the clock,
with the defective and heterogeneous materials out of which he was
expected to fashion the Dictionary. He was unable to take a holiday. 'I
would love to go to the mountains for a week but cannot'. The more
he worked the more it became clear to him that the raw material given
him was useless for all scholarly purposes. He made this plain to the

Royal Irish Academy by letter late in 1912.[53] At the eleventh hour he had to fill up numerous inadequacies. Later on he could point to the literal truth that never before had editor faced single-handed so gigantic a task. The high speed he worked at left him no time even to check proofs. But he produced the first part of the Dictionary for publication on 14 August 1913 and saved the £1,000. It was a fasciculus of 112 double column pages entitled *Dictionary of the Irish Language* and stated on the title page to be based mainly on Old and Middle Irish materials.

It was with a sense of relief that he wrote to Best on 4 September to say he would probably be in Dublin in a fortnight, was looking forward to the visit and the prospect of a chat with him in the DBC restaurant. 'I may even go to the Blaskets for a week'. He had no notion that a storm was brewing.

Osborn Bergin's first reaction to the Dictionary was to write to Best on August 24, ten days after publication:

> The great Dictionary is what we expected. It must have cost C.M. an amazing deal of hard work and it will be most useful. But for real information it is 50 pages too long.[54]

He referred to some 'howlers' he had detected and the large content of proper names, but from Bergin the words above are praise indeed and it is very clear that he looked on the result with approval. That he was qualified to judge goes without saying. Yet when controversy broke he failed to support Marstrander.

Criticism was led by Meyer who, apart from errors of detail, considered the scale of the work too elaborate and ambitious, in the light of the less than advanced state of existing Irish scholarship. His great influence and authority attracted the agreement to his views of other Celtic scholars. Bergin followed his lead. So did Best. There were exceptions, like Edward Gwynn of Trinity College who remained firm in his appreciation of Marstrander and, more than probably, John MacNeill. Marstrander attended a meeting of the Dictionary Committee of the Royal Irish Academy on 23 October 1913 – the proceedings of which have been described as stormy – and defended the order and method of his work. The Council of the Academy, accepting the criticisms of Meyer, pressed him to reduce the plan of the work for its future issues. This he declined to do. His equanimity never deserted him during this very difficult period and one cannot but admire the moderation with which he describes the parting of the ways between his colleagues and himself:

> As I have not succeeded in convincing the Council of the

Academy as to the impossibility of cramming the treatment of the work within the narrow confines designed, I have with great reluctance come to the conclusion that it was my duty to relinquish all connection with the conduct of the Dictionary.[55]

Marstrander's vision of Irish language lexicography placed him in advance of his contemporaries in the field, great though their talents were. Meyer found it difficult to accommodate himself to the independence of the man whom he acknowledged, even in the stress of controversy, to be a genius. As an instance of Marstrander's individual and independent ways of thought we might consider the memorable statement of how he approached his task:

The fundamental principles I have followed during the preparation of fasciculus 1 are simple and natural, and will, I am convinced, be followed by those who take up the work where I leave it. My aim has been to create an Irish dictionary that would reflect the most important periods in the history of that wonderful language, basing my work mainly upon Old and Middle Irish literature. It was my intention to trace, not only every word, but if possible every characteristic expression on its way forwards, whether it be first met with in the hard lines of the ogam stone or in Keating's graceful style; to reveal the meaning of words solely by the aid of literary sources and the living spoken language. My work was therefore quite independent of Cormac, O'Mulconry, O'Davoren, O'Donovan, Stokes, Windisch and Meyer. I have always tried to see with my own eyes, and to face difficulties without flinching. Therefore ... I bring a great deal that is new. But fresh ground is hard to till, and no one could be more ready to admit that I have often been mistaken with respect to details.[56]

Few Irish language scholars would have the daring to write in the fashion of the foregoing paragraph. This was not due to temerity on Marstrander's part, but to his all-inclusive view of 'that wonderful language', capable as he was of surveying it in the full range of historical perspective. His claim to see with his own eyes, and to face difficulties without flinching, proclaim the assurance and integrity of his scholarship.

Time, and his successors in the work, have vindicated him. It is a pity that the Dictionary Committee of the Academy did not see proper to print the Preface he had designed for the first issue. Rejecting it, they printed in its place a brief business-like statement. The whole regrettable chapter was a victory for the men of caution over the man of vision, for the conservatives over the pioneer of adventurous yet soundly-based scholarship. Nor was there a word of appreciation for his immense labour.

Marstrander, who just before the publication of the fasciculus, had been appointed to the chair of Celtic Philology in the University of Kristiania, now bade farewell to the Irish scene. We are left to speculate on the particular loss sustained through the severance of his immediate ties with Ireland. In his native land he entered on a new phase of a scholarly career that brought honour to his country through his brilliance in Celtic and diverse other fields. Any biography of Marstrander must be Norway-centred. There lay his main career and achievement.

In the chair of Celtic Philology, which he occupied until his retirement at 70 in 1953, he had little teaching to do, as not many students offered for Celtic or any of the other special fields in which he was an authority, but he availed of the great opportunities it afforded him for research. As far back as 1910 Richard Best had wondered whether he would devote himself entirely to Celtic or spread himself over the whole Indo-Germanic field. One thinks of Marstrander as having been driven by a restless intellectual urge which ranged and assumed authority not only over the Celtic languages but over such esoteric subjects as Hittite, Phrygian, Osco-Umbrian, Runic and Proto-Scandinavian, as well as Gothic and Indo-European studies, on any of which he would lecture to interested students. He spent three years in Brittany making himself thoroughly conversant with Breton. He published extensive studies on the history and language of the Isle of Man. Of the many tongues he was proudest of his own Norwegian. Of special interest to us in Ireland is his important work, published in 1915, *Contributions to the History of the Norwegian Language in Ireland*. One of his durable achievements was the foundation in 1928 of the *Norsk Tidsskrift for Sprogvidenskap* (Norwegian Journal of Linguistics) which stands to him as a monument, twenty substantial volumes of which he edited, providing a vehicle for the learned studies of Norway's leading linguists as well as for the bulk of his own scholarly output.

Marstrander got married in 1914 to Audhild Sverdrup. She died in 1932 and Marstrander did not remarry. There were three children of the marriage, two daughters Aud and Esther, and a son Kai, youngest of the family. Aud, who never married, may be living still. Esther became a famous Oslo socialite, made a rich marriage but died in early middle age, leaving a son born 1954. Kai, who was trained as a ship's engineer, now occupies an important technical post. Carl's brother Finn, born 1889, was also a philologist but his career was less spectacular. He taught Latin at an Oslo gymnasium and also gave lectures at University. His name appears in the current Norwegian telephone directory. A family relative is Sverre Marstrander, born 1910, Professor Emeritus of Archaeology at the University of Oslo and still resident in that city.

He did not forget his Irish friends at a significant crisis in Ireland's destiny. The voice of Marstrander intervenes to utter a dramatic message of support for John MacNeill:

Sandviken, Kristiania, 31.v.16
Dear Mrs. MacNeill,
On receiving the news of the judgement of the Court Martial in Dublin I beg to express to you and your children my heartfelt sympathy in the cruel fate which has befallen your husband. I do not know what has taken place behind the curtains; but I know this: that what John MacNeill has done, he has done for the country he loves beyond anything else in the world. May I ask you to remember me most respectfully to your husband? He is one of the tall trees in the wood and to fell him will be impossible. Tell him our admiration and love of him is unabated. Carl Marstrander.[57]

His favourite Irish author was An tAthair Peadar Ó Laoghaire. 'I am a devoted admirer of Father O'Leary. He is without rival the foremost stylist writing in Ireland today'. However he did not regard him as anything like a good novelist and was critical of the structure of *Séadna*. 'But his language is marvellous. In this field he is incontestably the master'. Father O'Leary, writing to him in December 1911, gave him the original story on which he based his great folktale, just as he had heard it 'from the lips of Peig Labhráis about 65 years ago'. Marstrander printed it along with a south Kerry folktale *Gabha an tSuic* in the *Miscellany presented to Kuno Meyer* (1912), with commentary and parallels in a study of classic thoroughness.

No one could blame Marstrander if he had retired in disillusion from Ireland in 1913. But such a feeling was no part of his make-up. Sooner or later he would have returned to his native land to which above all he preferred to give his service. He had won many friends and admirers in Ireland. One of these was the archaeologist E.C.R. Armstrong, 'the faithfullest of my faithful friends'. He kept in friendly touch with his Dictionary assistant, Eleanor Knott. A photograph she sent him through Alf Sommerfelt, shortly before the end of the School of Irish Learning in 1924, brought back memories:

It was not without emotion that I saw this little room again – so modest in appearance, but so important after all for our Celtic studies. Bergin looks exactly as he did 13 years ago. Do tell me what secret means he employs to carry his age as he does! I am afraid, though, they could not give me my lost hair back. At present my head is more like a billiard ball than anything else. Kindly remember me to our mutual friends in Dublin.[58]

He held occasional friendly correspondence with Best, who had failed to support him in the Dictionary controversy. One of the regrettable casualties of that episode was the edition of *Lebor na Huidre*, which they planned on the grand scale – 'a most interesting and most fascinating work. I am looking forward to it' – and was to be published with the aid of a grant agreed by the Academy of Science and Letters of Kristiania only after a pitched verbal battle against the men of science on that learned body, fought with resource by Marstrander and his great ally, Alf Torp. By formal correspondence between them Marstrander and Best parted company on the project. When *Lebor na Huidre* was published in a fine edition by the Royal Irish Academy in 1929 under the editorship of Best and Bergin, Marstrander generously wrote to Best from Oslo on 10 March 1930, 'Hearty congratulations on the great edition of LU.'

He returned to Ireland three times. The first was in 1917 on a private visit. The next was in 1936 to receive an honorary degree from Trinity College, Dublin. On this visit he renewed old acquaintance with Bergin and Best and it is pleasant to record that their warm regard for each other continued. He writes to Best from Oslo on 21 December 1936 to thank him for his card which reached him that day at the very moment when he returned from hospital where he had spent a couple of months with typhus. 'It was a great pleasure to meet you and Bergin again. Kindly remember me to Mrs. Best.' His last visit was in 1959, to the first International Congress of Celtic Studies, where he received a tremendous welcome. In effect it was an acclamation of his great achievements in Celtic studies and a compensatory gesture for the historical error of judgement committed earlier by his fellow-labourers in the field.

The second part of the *Dictionary of the Irish Language* did not appear until 1932 and it continued to be produced in parts by various scholars until its completion in 1976 as one of the major achievements in Irish language scholarship. The distinguished author Frank O'Connor, writing in December 1964 while, with 16 parts published, it was not yet complete, called it 'a project comparable in scale and possible importance to the Shannon Scheme … a great undertaking greatly carried out.'[59]

In the Historical Note to the completed work, Dr. E.G. Quin, who was General Editor from 1953 to 1975, points out that 'in fact Marstrander laid down the lines for the arrangement of the material which have been adhered to ever since', a vindication that justifies the faith in his vision of the great pioneer who was its first contributor.

Marstrander was more than a scholar, as we are reminded by Professor D. A. Binchy, who came to know him well when lecturing in Oslo in 1960. 'A fervent Norwegian patriot', recalls Dr. Binchy, 'he played an active part in the resistance to the invaders during the Nazi occupation of his country; at one time he was arrested by the Gestapo and narrowly escaped execution'.[60]

He was interned in a concentration camp at Grini near Oslo. While there he managed to smuggle out to his son Kai a diary written on toilet paper in Old Irish, which he could write with facility. Shortly afterwards Kai, who was in the resistance movement himself, was arrested and the diary discovered. It was sent for decoding to code and language experts in Berlin who, baffled, returned it to the Gestapo in Norway saying that the only person capable of translating this was Professor Marstrander of Oslo!

At his funeral in Oslo in 1965 the Irish Ambassador, Mr. Valentin Iremonger, spoke on behalf of Ireland an appreciation of his devoted services to the Irish language.

'It is seventeen years since I made the acquaintance of the Viking Marstrander' wrote Tomás Ó Crithin towards the end of his life story, published in 1929. Marstrander had no greater admirer. In an earlier poetic essay, Ó Crithin stated his regard for him in an expression of lofty grace that will be echoed by all who cherish the Irish language:

> Marstrander is ainm don Tréan-Fhear,
> Go raibh beannacht gheal Dé chuige uaim;
> Guidhim feasta saoghal fada óm béal dó
> Gan easpa gan déislin ná buadhirt.[61]

Acknowledgement
I should like to record my special obligation to Professor Dr. Magne Oftedal, Keltisk Institutt, University of Oslo, Carl Marstrander's successor in the Chair of Celtic, who very generously sent me material as cited above, which I have used in this essay. I am also grateful to Dr. Pádraig de Brún, Dublin Institute for Advanced Studies, and to Bríd Nic Craith for their kind assistance. — S. Ó L.

References
1. D.A. Binchy, 'Norse scholar whose Irish dictionary caused a furore'. *Sunday Independent,* 16 Jan. 1966.

2. Tomás Ó Criomhthain to Robin Flower, 29 Dec. 1911. (In Ó Criomhthain correspondence, Folklore Department, U.C.D. The writer is grateful to Professor Bo Almqvist for his kind permission to consult this correspondence).

3. Much biographical detail is taken from Dr. Magne Oftedal's obituary notices of Marstrander in *Studia Celtica* 11 (1967), 202-204, *Lochlann* IV (1969), 299-303, and the valuable paper 'Carl Marstrander's work with the Manx language' which he read at the ninth Viking Congress, Isle of Man 1981. Dr. Oftedal also kindly supplied the writer with further details by letter of 11 Oct. 1983.

4. M. Oftedal, 'Carl Marstrander's work with the Manx Language'. 1981.

5. National Library of Ireland MS 11001 (28). The writer has made considerable use of the correspondence in this file from Marstrander to Richard Irvine Best.

6. *Ibid.*

7. *Ibid.*

8. M. Oftedal, *Lochlann* IV, 300.

9. Pádraig Ó Catháin to Robin Flower 5/6/1911 (Letter in Ó Criomhthain correspondence, U.C.D.).

10. Carl Marstrander to R.I. Best from An tOileán Mór, 15 Sept. 1907. *Scríobh* 5 (Baile Átha Cliath 1981), 265-6. English translation in the *Cork Holly Bough* (1982) p.17.

11. NLI MS 11002.

12. *Ibid.* (Meyer to Best, writing from Amélie-les-Bains in the eastern Pyrenees, where he often went to recuperate.)

13. *Ibid.*

14. 'Poor Bergin seems overworked or fagged. He must, as he proposes, cut down the work at the School. What with teaching and meetings, he will have hardly any time for the Dictionary' – Meyer to Best, 2 Feb. 1909 (NLI MS 11002).

15. Meyer to Best, 12 Oct. 1909 (NLI MS 11002).

16. NLI MS 11002.

17. Best to Meyer, 26 Oct. 1909 (NLI MS 11002).

18. Meyer to Best from Euston Hotel, London, 13 Nov. 1909. (NLI MS 11002)

19. Alice Stopford Green to Meyer, dated 23 Jan. 1910, from 50 Grosvenor Road, Westminster. (NLI MS 2113. Cf. also note 20.).

20. Meyer to Best, 2 Dec. 1909. Earlier on 24 Nov., he had written: 'I forgot to say that the chief item for the Governor's meeting will be Marstrander's appointment. Mrs. G(reen) will finance him.' (NLI MS 11002).

21. *Ibid.*

22. Meyer to Best, 25 Feb. 1910. *Ibid.*

23. Meyer to Best, 1 Mar. 1910. *Ibid.*

24. See *Dictionary of the Irish Language,* Royal Irish Academy 1913-76, 'Historical Note' iii-vi, by E.G. Quin, General Editor 1953-75.

25. *Revue Celtique* xxxvii (1917-1919), 3.

26. Meyer to Best, from Terme, Acqui, 27 Mar. 1910 (NLI MS 11002).

27. Best to Meyer, undated. (NLI MS 11002).

28. *Ibid.*

29. Best to Meyer, 6 Apr. 1910. (NLI MS 11002). The last sentence may be explained by a letter from Meyer to Best dated at Bournemouth on 1 Jan. 1910 in which he says 'Priebsch tells me that they must soon fill up the post of Professor of Comparative Philology in London. He is on the committee and would greatly like to have Marstrander. The pay is however only £250, I think. I told him to select a stopgap, if necessary, and to wait three years or so for Marstrander.'

30. Meyer to Best, from San Remo, 12 Apr. 1910. (NLI MS 11002).

31. 'Scoil na Sean-Ghaedhilge' *Sinn Féin* 21 Ean. 1911.

32. Written from 35 Percy Place, Dublin, Best's residence for many years. (NLI MS 10457 (2)).

33. Marstrander to Meyer, 1 Aug. 1910. (T.C.D. MS 4224).

34. Meyer to Best, 7 July 1910. (NLI MS 11002).

34a. Marstrander set out the classic principles of manuscript editing in a letter to Best:
Skovveien 6
5.IV 1913
Dear Best,
… If our aim is to give as scholarly an edition of the LU as possible, it seems to me that we should follow the copyists all through as regards accents, separation of words, stops, capital letters, etc. If we introduce a normalising system of transcription, we at once produce a wrong picture of the LU and the men who wrote it. To me it almost seems as if some of the very spirit of the original has left all our ordinary looking editions of Irish texts. They don't recall the MSS at all. Gwynn's edition of the Monast. of Tallaght is better; it is thoroughly scholarly as far as the text is concerned. Our first plan was – as you remember – to reproduce the MS as closely as possible, keeping even the change of line and printing the interlinear glosses in posit between the lines. I have no doubt whatever that scholars to come will be far more grateful for a sober and minute edition of this kind than for an ordinary normalised one …
It seems to me that this is the worthiest way of editing our famous MS. Also it should be remembered that our edition – if carried on on these lines – will be the one used by scholars for always, while a normalised one would sooner or later be superseded by a new edition, based on some new and wonderful principles of editing Irish texts. (NLI MS 11101).

35. Meyer to Best, 10 Nov. 1910. *Ibid.*

36. Meyer to Best, 15 November 1910. *Ibid.* See also D.A. Binchy's essay on Marstrander, *Sunday Independent*, 16 Jan. 1966: 'Reading through it more than half a century later one is still overwhelmed by the breadth of his knowledge, … Already Marstrander was clearly marked as a rising star in the Celtic firmament.'

37. NLI MS 11101 (28).

38. Meyer to Best, 21 Feb. 1911, from 41 Huskisson Street, Liverpool. On the envelope of the letter is a pencilled note in Best's hand: 'Marstrander's' illness – pleurisy'. Another note from Meyer to Best, 23 Feb. reads: 'It is very good of you to keep me so fully informed and I am rejoiced to have so much better news. Perhaps with good care and a holiday he may not in the end be the worse for it. Like all of us he will have to buy his experience and wisdom. Give him my kind regards and tell him so from an old hand at making a mess of it', the latter reference obviously relating to Meyer's own imprudence in camping out in damp conditions which led to his arthritis. (NLI MS 11002).

39. *Ibid.*

40. Tomás Ó Criomhthain to Robin Flower, *an naomhadh lá fichead d'Abrán sa mbliadhain naoi gcéad-déag is aon déag.* (Ó Criomhthain correspondence, UCD).

41. NLI MS 11001 (28).

42. *Ibid.*

43. Account based on Meyer's letters to Best 10, 15, 25 Apr. 1911. (NLI MS 11002).

44. NLI MS 11001 (28).

45. *Ibid.* Letter dated 22 Aug. 1911.

46. *Ibid.* Date of letter supplied in Best's hand.

47. Meyer to Alice Stopford Green by letter dated Amélie-les-Bains, 19 Mar. 1912. (NLI MS 15091 (1)).

48. NLI MS 11001 (28).
49. NLI MS 11002. Written from Liverpool.
50. Best to Meyer, 19 May 1912. (NLI MS 11002).
51. NLI MS 11001 (28).
52. *Ibid.*
53. The following note from Marstrander to Best written on a postcard dated Kristiania 2.IX.11, may refer to his critical views about the Dictionary materials: 'I am going to speak seriously to the Council about the Dictionary, as soon as the 1. part is out and the £1,000 saved. There is no use in speaking now.' (NLI MS 11001 (28)).
54. NLI MS 11002.
55. *Revue Celtique* XXXVII (1917-1919), 4-5. Extract from Marstrander's article 'The Royal Irish Academy's Dictionary', pp. 1-23, 211-227, in which he gives a full statement of the problems attending the Dictionary in reply to Meyer's criticisms in *Zeitschrift für celtische Philologie* (1915), 361-83. Marstrander's reply is dated Kristiania, December 15th.
56. *Ibid.,* p.5.
57. NLI MS 10882.
58. RIA MS 12-0-28. Letter bearing address and date v.d. Lippes Gate 23, Kristiania 29.1.24.
59. 'The book nobody knows', *Sunday Independent,* 13 Dec. 1964.
60. *Ériu* XX (1966) 238.
61. From the poem 'Is fada mé im stad' l, NLI G 597, a MS of Seosamh Laoide's (J.H. Lloyd). The poem is printed in Seosamh Laoide's collection, *Tonn Tóime* (Baile Átha Cliath, 1915) 65-9. The extract quoted is on p. 67.

Chapter 8

Seán Óg MacMurrough Kavanagh, Lexicographer

Some two hundred yards from where the Atlantic caresses the shores of the parish nearest America lies the Kavanagh homestead, birthplace of Seán and Muiris (Kruger) Kavanagh, two members of a great Gaelic family who became distinguished for their personality, colour and talent. Some alchemy surely presides over this rib end of rugged peninsula that has nourished international scholars like Robin Flower, George Derwent Thomson and Kenneth Jackson, makers of learned books, and native writers like Maurice O'Sullivan who in the tradition of Alain Fournier caught and canvased the golden years of adolescence and youth in *Twenty Years A-Growing*, and Tomás Ó Crithin who in *The Islandman* recorded Blasket life in prose as intense and spare as a document of Tacitus.

Less well known than they, Seán Óg MacMurrough Kavanagh, otherwise Seán an Chóta, born in Dunquin in 1885, is of their company. Only that he was prevented by an alert father he might have enlisted under age in a British regiment bound for India and never have established links with the United States of America. Roving and adventurous by nature, he spent his early years working for the Gaelic League in different parts of Ireland before moving about 1910 to Dublin where, amongst other things, he became a student in the School of Irish Learning established by the celebrated Kuno Meyer. There he learned from Old Irish texts and taught modern Irish to Carl Marstrander and Julius Pokorny. What recollections might have been his had he committed them to writing, since he knew, and mixed with, many of the political and literary celebrities of the day. A friend and colleague of The O'Rahilly, at whose bungalow in Ventry he was a welcome visitor, he was likewise respected by Arthur Griffith to whose journals and Year Book he contributed. He explored the historic old places of Dublin City and wrote about them in Griffith's weekly *Sinn Féin* under the pseudonym of 'New Citizen' always in the rich and exuberant Irish that was his native tongue. Never at a loss for a word, be it English or Irish, part of the task Seán Óg set himself was to meet the challenge of adapting the Irish tongue, rural by tradition and usage, to the demands of an urban environment.

Stephen MacKenna, translator from Greek into English of the *Enneads* of Plotinus, when asked by Piaras Béaslaí what he thought of Seán Óg as a writer, acknowledged that he had fine Irish and a wealth of vocabulary, but lacked the creative instinct. 'He is an artist in life', said MacKenna, pointing at once to Seán Óg's spectacular gift of phrase, gesture, humour, jest, drollery and camaraderie. Dressed in kilts, in deference to the romantic spirit of the times, he appeared in his native parish to be promptly christened *'an Cóta'* by his neighbours, a title he cheerfully took up and signed to his correspondence. In the tradition of the legendary Pierce Ferriter, seventeenth century soldier, bard and lovemaker, he had, it was said, the gift of beguiling female hearts, so much so that Seamus O'Connolly, a Dublin wit and colleague of the poet Seamus O'Sullivan, doubtless in a flash of repartee, dubbed him 'Casanova'. His contemporary Helen Waddell has peopled her classic *Wandering Scholars* with such as Seán, brother in spirit to Guy Tabarie and François Villon. How she would have enjoyed his company, turned him perhaps into some immortal chapter.

As a member of the Irish Volunteers Seán Óg instructed the Ballyferriter company in the disciplines of drill, route march and manoeuvre, although one thinks that his innate humanity and artistic bent really unfitted him for the business of soldiering. Early in 1915 the urge to adventure led him to the United States, where he wandered nomadically for the next six or seven years, covering the land from coast to coast. He enlisted in the National Guard to learn military tactics, laboured in a Chicago steel mills and as riveter in a New Jersey shipyard. He toured the western and north western States making propaganda for the recognition of the Irish Republic. He campaigned for the acceptance of the Irish language as a subject of study in the universities of Chicago and Boston. He toiled as a harvest labourer on the Dakota ranches.

Out of his Dakota experiences was written his Irish language novel *Fánaí* (The Wanderer) which, taking all circumstances into account, is an unusual literary document. It is unique inasmuch as it is one of the earliest, if not indeed the first, Irish language novel to be based on first hand knowledge of United States life and background, with scenes and colour drawn from actual experience. As such the novel can be claimed to be truly American. The opening paragraph of Chapter 2 gives the setting of the story:

> Pembinea (Pembino on the map) is a small town, nowadays of little importance, in North Dakota, three miles from the Canadian

frontier. It is the final trainstop in United States territory on the north bound railway before one enters Canada. It stands on the banks of the Red River, the only large American river flowing northwards and probably the foulest river there is.

In this town and neighbourhood, and in Emerson, across the river in Minnesota, most of the action of the novel takes place. The story relates the adventures of Seán Lonergan, a thoughtful, quixotic, even bookish, young man, a reader of Oscar Wilde, forever roving from place to place in search of adventure, who having explored the secret haunts of New York, Boston, Chicago and many other cities, drifts west in response to the undefined promptings of his heart, turns to harvest labouring and in Pembinea meets and falls in love with Peg Roche, a local rancher's daughter. The course of their true love is thwarted by the machinations of a rival, an arrogant and unscrupulous neighbouring rancher. A tool of this man's, a half-breed who is drawn in lines of blackest hue, meditating murder, strikes a treacherous blow on the back of the hero's head which deprives him for a long period of his memory. The final denouément takes place in the Red River Tavern in Emerson, Minnesota, after which the story ends happily. There is plenty of action, with vivid descriptions of brawls and wrestling matches, and well observed accounts of ranch labourers' life and work. Hero and heroine are idealised in a tale where dialogue and situation are at times naïve and simplistic. It was, however, more an age of chivalry than ours. Many of the events and experiences are obviously autobiographical and the hero is endowed with ideas and qualities which might well be attributed to Seán Óg himself. Virtues and faults notwithstanding, it is a novel of America with landscape, background and location observed in close and authentic detail, written in rich and vigorous Irish, making it in the linguistic sense a unique contribution to the literature of the United States, in the romantic *genre* , which might possibly owe something to the influence of Zane Grey.

The civil war was being fought out in Ireland when Seán Óg returned, some time in 1922, and as a staunch republican, who had cheered and supported Éamon de Valera during his U.S. tour, he took up arms in defence of Dingle town on behalf of the Irish Republic. He also delighted audiences with recitals of de Valera's triumphant progress throughout America. Less a stubborn militant than a man of letters, however, he did not contest the occupation of Dingle against superior Free State forces. He was presently captured and placed in the Curragh internment camp where he wrote a prison diary and finished the manuscript of his American novel. Released in 1923, he gravitated towards Dublin, his favourite among cities.

His novel *Fánaí* was gladly accepted by the Government Publications Office and duly appeared in 1927, whereupon it almost immediately acquired a further claim to distinction. A disciple of Jansen and enemy of life protested to the Minister for Finance, the book's official publisher, that the idyllic love scenes depicted so tenderly in the novel were offensive and a danger to moral standards. So Seán Óg's novel became one of the earliest victims of the Irish censor. The book was withdrawn to be re-issued in 1928 minus the offending but innocuous passages. The pagination of the book was not affected, so that when the bibliography of modern Gaelic literature comes to be written the scholars will be set a pretty puzzle in identifying the differences between the two editions. But Seán Óg's likeness, drawn by his friend, the distinguished painter Seán O'Sullivan, enhances the dust jacket of both, showing him in relaxed and thoughtful profile, book in hand, the artist in repose.

Seán's brother, Maurice (Kruger) Kavanagh, also spent a number of years in the United States, mainly in New York, and he appears in photographs of the New York Kerry teams of the later 1920s. Kruger came back to settle in his native Dunquin and set up his celebrated guest house, and later hostelry, which became the rendezvous of visiting scholars and artists. More flamboyant and extrovert than Seán, he acquired in the United States the initiative of the entrepreneur. Unshackled by the timidities of life or the inhibitions of the respectable, he gave his personality its full freedom, enlivening the social scene of his native district with his wit and candour. Not to mention, if aroused, his crushing invective.

Seán Óg taught the Irish language in St. Andrew's College and the Masonic Boys' School in Dublin until 1937. His successful qualities as a teacher were highly appreciated and numerous students to whom he imparted his love of the Irish language remember him with gratitude. Ever a lover of company, his host of friends during this later period included Robert NM. Smyllie, editor of the *Irish Times*, the artists Seán O'Sullivan, Harry Kernoff, William Conor and the sculptor Jerome O'Connor.

Encouraged by the authorities of the Department of Education, who wished to provide some written record of his unique Irish language resources, he began in 1935 to compile a dictionary of words and phrases in use in his native West Kerry. He resigned his teaching posts in 1937 to give this project his full attention. The result was a massive compilation, finished in 1942, running to 2,200,000 words in 29 manuscript volumes, now in the National Library of Ireland. The vicissitudes of its accomplishment make a saga in themselves. It remains a monument to his industry and a valuable thesaurus of the Irish language.

Seán Óg survived its completion by five years. He died in Dublin in 1947 and was buried in his native Dunquin. Students of Irish language and literature remain immeasurably in his debt for the wealth which they inherit from him. His novel of the Dakotas will live, a literary link of absorbing interest between the old world and the new. His name has passed into legend.

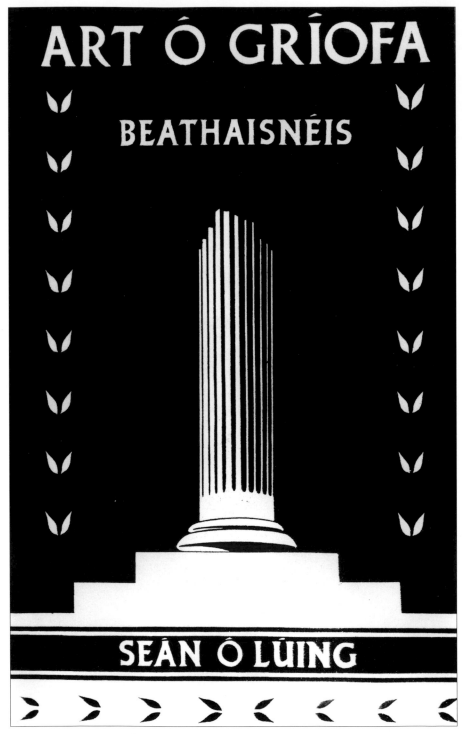

The front cover of *Art Ó Gríofa*.

Chapter 9

The making of a book: *Art Ó Gríofa*

My one-time colleague Máirtín Ó Cadhain called me a near native speaker of Irish. That is perfectly true. I might just as well have been called a near native speaker of English. Both tongues were spoken around my cradle and fireside in Ballyferriter. I have written a number of books, using both Irish and English. The two languages were familiar to me since childhood. My first major piece of writing was a biography of the national philosopher Arthur Griffith. In the lively times in which I grew up I heard his name mentioned in discussion, often enough in critical terms. When I obtained a teaching position in a Dublin commercial college in the early forties one of my duties was to teach Irish history, about which it gives me little pleasure to confess that at the time I knew little or nothing.

It became necessary for me to read widely on the subject so as to be able to stand before my classes with any confidence. In my reading of recent Irish history I tried to discover the influences that led to the Rising of 1916 and the contribution to them of Arthur Griffith.

My students were eager to know all about the period. Apart from vague and unspecific generalisations about Griffith's industrial policy the text books told me little. A search of the Dublin bookshops failed to turn up a biography. I did find, however, in Greene's celebrated bookstore in Clare Street, a little book on Griffith by the poet James Stephens, so finely written that it persuaded me to search further. I read Robert Mitchel Henry's *Evolution of Sinn Féin* and Shaw Desmond's stirring *Drama of Sinn Féin*. The absence of a life of Griffith I considered a major gap, however, and about this time the idea formed in my mind that I might try to fill it.

Pressure of teaching work in the evening hours prevented me from beginning this project at once and it was only when I entered the Oireachtas Translation Office late in 1943 that I was free at nights to frequent the National Library and read the journals Griffith edited and largely wrote. Their content was impressive.

I mentioned my interest to my translation colleagues and one of them suggested I should speak about it to Pádraig O'Keeffe, Assistant Secretary to Seanad Éireann whose office was on the floor under ours.

He was formerly Secretary of Sinn Féin. He was popularly known as Páidín O'Keeffe but I was advised not to address him as that. I called to his office to see him and he received me in a friendly way. 'You want to write the life of Arthur Griffith? There are about twenty people writing the life of Griffith'. This did not deter me as I had made up my mind nor did Pádraig try to discourage me, quite the opposite, for straightaway he began to tell me his recollections of Griffith, which I wrote down then and there as quickly as my hand could move across the page. These notes I later wrote out in a fair script. I thus began a task which I found myself eager to continue and wrote an initial chapter. Pádraig (by which name I shall call him) took a keen interest in my work, and would call me from time to time to ask: 'Have you any other chapter written?'. He gave me many leads and suggestions as to whom I should contact for further information. One of these was Dan McCarthy, who was a close colleague of Griffith, working with him in his office in 17 Fownes Street, 'on the inside' as Pádraig put it, 'the rest of us were on the outside'. Dan McCarthy lived in a high class local authority house on the Fairview end of Malahide Road and received me kindly. He gave me some valuable recollections of Griffith which I wrote down, first in rapid longhand and later in as careful and detailed way as was consonant with near total accuracy, with the aid of a memory that at the time was very good indeed.

My method was to examine Griffith's many printed papers, copy extracts from them and combine these with recollections of those who had known Griffith personally. Amongst the many people I interviewed was Earnán de Blaghd who was Director of the Abbey Theatre and lived in Kenilworth Square. Nobody could be more helpful and encouraging in my work than that man, whom I heard vilified by so many people so many times, but whom I found to be perfectly sympathetic, open and communicable, always ready with advice and suggestions. I knew something of his very controversial career in politics but in approaching my task I only considered the necessity of recording what was essential to it and never permitted myself to be swayed by anything else. I interviewed many people in this manner, working over years in my spare time. At a certain stage of the work I wrote to the Talbot Press to offer them the manuscript when completed. They wrote back expressing the hope that I had been in consultation with the Griffith family, without whose assistance the personal elements of Griffith's life, so essential to a biography, would be missing. I had not done so at that stage but later I did get in touch with Nevin his son and with Frank Griffith his brother who gave me valuable recollections. My task took me to every part of Dublin, then a much smaller and friendlier city, using my trusty Royal Enfield cycle for transport and I made the acquaintance of many interesting people. Amongst these I must mention Chrissie Doyle, a loveable lady then advanced in years who lived in St. Ita's Road, Glasnevin (I rely on memory). She might be called a pioneer feminist, of a very cultured and special kind, who had an interest in women in early Ireland. For Griffith, whom she knew well, she had a high regard. 'Arthur was the best of them all'.

I went to Galway to talk to Mrs. Máire Ó Brolcháin, who lived in Lenaboy Park. She was the widow of Pádraig Ó Brolcháin (Bradley) the first Secretary of the Department of Education. Meeting her and talking to her was like being transported back to an earlier and gentler age, so warm was her welcome and courtesy. She spoke freely of Griffith whom she knew well and remembered as 'Dan' living in a room surrounded by books. 'Dan seemed to belong to large book-filled rooms' she recalled which led me to ponder on what sort of books they were and what was the fate of his collection of books, which our National Library would be eager to acquire. She gave me immense encouragement. 'Is é Dia a chuir an treo tú'. I remember her as such a warm human person, so full of gentle and high character. I took down copious notes which, along with other notes accumulated in those years from various sources, I have placed in the keeping of the National Library.

The house of Sáirséal agus Dill, the proprietor of which was Seán Ó hÉigeartaigh, published my life of Griffith in 1953 with a Preface by Pádraig O'Keeffe. Bibliographically it was a splendid production, of stout and firm binding, finely printed by Fleet Printing Works in Times new-roman on antique Drimnagh paper, presented with pride in a format worthy of its great subject by a great publisher. Seán's father was P. S. O'Hegarty, one time Secretary of the Department of Posts and Telegraphs and an uncompromising critic of historical events of his time. Likewise a historian and book-collector, his large house in Highfield Road was crammed to the rafters with the literature and historical desiderata of his era.

He was hospitable in his support of the Irish language and its writers and held soirées in his residence, Highfield House, where all the young writers and personalities of the language were made welcome.

It is no exaggeration to say that his son Seán originated a significant and creative movement in Irish literature through the agency of his publishing house, Sáirséal agus Dill. He founded a free press for Irish writers. He set standards. Every book that carried his imprint was a model of good production, in clarity of print, in quality of paper, in design, in durability of binding. His pride in book production was obvious on every page. A particularly fine example, and now a collector's item, was *Scéalaíocht na Rithe*, (Stories of the Kings) with its attractive illustrations in colour. His work offered a challenge to some moribund publishing houses of Dublin. Writers of Irish were grateful for the courage he gave them. Sáirséal agus Dill takes its place in the tradition of the Cuala Press. Likewise it stands with the Dolmen Press for the tradition of fine book production. Above all, it stands out independent in its own achievement.

The writer in Irish must contend with the fact that comparatively few people will read his work, of whatever quality it may be, and that he is writing in the shadow of the universal English language, with which he has to compete on very very unequal terms. People have remarked to me in reference to my work on Griffith, 'Oh, I would love to read that in English'. I try to keep my writing in Irish separate from that in English. When a task stands done I leave it so, with no wish to translate it, and go on to the next. As a medium for historical writing Irish is the equal of any of the major European languages.

My life of Arthur Griffith was a success as Irish language books go. Griffith's message of national self-reliance had, and always will have, the merit of putting steel in a nation's character.

This is true even in the context of our merging into the European Union. A nation is respected for its own effort. Griffith's message to Ireland was one of hard, unremitting work. An event that caused me personally to reflect on the sacrifice demanded by our independence in the war years and our reliance on our Merchant Navy, to which we owe an immeasurable debt, was that on opening the *Irish Press* one morning I saw a photograph of my friend Joe O'Connor. He had gone down with his ship in bringing essential cargo to Ireland, the victim of hostile action. I first met Joe O'Connor in the West Kerry Gaeltacht, tall, bronzed, bony, pipe smoking. He was enjoying his holiday and improving his Irish. Such a marvellous companion. 'Ó a bhean a' tí tá mo chroí briste' he would say jokingly as he prepared to go back to his job, while times were peaceful yet. The photograph and the sad tidings it carried gave me a shock. Regrettably our Merchant Navy, a vision of Arthur Griffith, was disbanded by a government which claimed Griffith's inheritance.

Seán Ó hÉigeartaigh told me he would publish anything of mine after that. He was as good as his word. Sáirséal agus Dill published my two-volume life of O'Donovan Rossa with its striking jacket design by Anne Yeats, on which I had expended much labour, the details of which I describe elsewhere. His unexpected death at the age of fifty was a major tragedy. He was found in his office holding a book-proof in his hands. His whole life was given to service. Seán Ó hÉigeartaigh was a nation-builder, worthy to rank with Petrie, John O'Donovan and Eugene O'Curry or any of their great compeers in his contribution to Ireland's vital identity. He will never be forgotten.

Chapter 10

George Thomson (Seoirse Mac Tomáis)

Hardly ten colleges in Ireland now teach classical Greek. The study of the classical languages has diminished all over Europe, with the emphasis being placed in school and university on the teaching of modern vernaculars for the purpose of communication, and naturally Ireland, merged by her own full consent into the European Community, is obliged to follow the pattern. Latin, which was always more widely studied, has not reached a comparable point of contraction yet. But the abandonment of Latin as the language of public worship by the Catholic church was a shattering blow to the status of Latin studies in the modern world, from which no recovery is foreseeable. It is bound to become very much the language of the specialist. A strange turn indeed if the language that is the very cornerstone of European studies is to become the property of the exclusive few in university retreats.

Yet, although the study of classical Greek is vanishing off this island in common with the rest of Europe, paradoxically its future would seem to be more assured than its sister tongue. For the gulf between classical and modern Greek is not unbridgeable, as is the case between Latin and its closest descendant, Italian. Modern Greek is spoken by some ten million people and has the status of a working language in the European Community, even though this makes for headaches in the recruiting of translators. The Greek alphabet has never changed. The transfer of comprehension from the modern to the ancient language is not too formidable. One would not infer, from the classical catalogues published in recent years by Messrs. Basil Blackwell of Oxford and other centres that any diminution in Latin and Greek studies was taking place.

The above reflections, among others, were prompted by a conversation on the Birmingham-Oxford train between two donnish persons, of patently immense learning, at which this writer was a compulsory eavesdropper. They spoke of theses in progress, fragments, interpretations, of classical scholars and their achievements, with only a break in the highly civilised colloquy while one of them ate a meal which he produced from his briefcase. 'Do you mind if I have my lunch now' No, indeed, his companion did not, as he buried himself in study until, the repast over, they continued their talk. What most interested me, in the course of these learned exchanges between my travelling companions, was their ready agreement on the eminence, in the domain of his studies, of George Thomson, emeritus professor of Greek in the University of Birmingham. Here, to me, silent and anonymous in my seat, my wife Marie sitting beside me, was a fascinating junction in the mighty traffic of literature. Did my travelling companions know, I wondered, that George Thomson of Birmingham University was identical with Seoirse Mac Tomáis, a scholar of eminence in the Irish language, who had helped to embellish Irish literature by his influence on Maurice O'Sullivan, author of *Fiche Blian ag Fás* and by contributions of his own?

George Thomson was little more than a youth when, on what must have been one of his earliest visits to Ireland, he made the acquaintance of the author who describes him as 'a man neither too tall nor too short, with knee-breeches and a shoulder-cloak, his head bare and a shock of dark brown hair gathered straight back on it'. The rapid portrait is Maurice O'Sullivan's, in his classic *Twenty Years A-Growing* (pp. 238-9). O'Sullivan was afraid at first because 'There was not his like in the island.' For the encounter took place in the *ultima terra* of Europe, three miles off the headlands of Dunquin. Thomson had come to learn the Irish language, and O'Sullivan, his fears put aside, became his friend and tutor. 'George and I spent the next six weeks walking together on strand, hill and mountain, and after spending that time in my company he had fluent Irish.' (p.240) The year was 1923. Thus, fully equipped, George Thomson was later able to take up the post of Professor of Greek, through the Irish language, in Galway University, to the mystification, it would appear, of fellow-Hellenist E. R. Dodds.

It was the Chief Translator of Dáil Éireann, Liam Ó Rinn, himself a writer of talent, who introduced George Thomson to Stephen MacKenna, the translator of Plotinus. Hellenists both, they were also lovers of Irish literature and shared the ideal of enriching it with transfusions from classical sources, in much the same way as the great literatures of England and France had been developed, following the invention of printing, by translations and abstractions from Greek and Latin. The approximate time of Thomson's introduction to MacKenna may be placed as shortly after 17 May 1930, from a reference in a letter of that date of MacKenna's to Liam Ó Rinn, quoted in *Mo Chara Stiofán* (p.87).

MacKenna says he would be glad to meet the Professor. He had already read, and proposed to read again, *Breith Bháis ar Eagnuidhe*

(Sentence of Death on a Sage) and was grateful to the Professor for its doing. This was a translation into Irish of the three dialogues of Plato which tell of the trial, imprisonment and death of Socrates. It was published in 1920 by the Dublin firm of Fallon in association with the Stationery Office, in Gaelic type, 173 pages, including ten of introduction and thirteen of notes, and, for the delectation of bibliographers, a small erratum slip. The Irish is faultless and so easily read that one is unaware it is a translation. What is intriguing is the author's name, Seoirse Mac Laghmainn. This would translate as George Clements. Few would suspect that it concealed the identity of George Thomson, graduate of Cambridge, in time to become England's most distinguished Hellenist and interpreter of early Greek civilisation. The book is dedicated to Seán Mac Dáithi and carries the approbation of the Department of Education as being a suitable text for secondary schools. The imprimatur is likewise given to Thomson's next two contributions to Irish-Hellenic studies. These were the *Alcéstis* (1932) of Euripides and *Prométheus fé Chuibhreach* (Prometheus Bound) of Aeschylus (1933), published by the Stationery Office, Dublin. Both of these texts were edited to the most exacting standards of classical scholarship, even though the *Alcéstis* at least was produced under pressure. Thomson's preliminary note to this text is of interest:

> This is an effort at editing a Greek text in Irish. I did it in some haste and had I worked at a leisurely pace it might have less defects. But the need for textbooks in Irish is acute and accordingly I thought I had better get it done as quickly as possible. As for technical terms, it is my view that Irish is fortunate, in literary matters at any rate, in having so few of them. Should no particular term be available, the meaning must be expressed in clear and simple language, which will benefit both teacher and student; on the other hand, should there be an excess of such terms, it becomes all too easy for us to conceal a lack of knowledge behind a facade of learned speech. In the case of such terms as I had to invent, I considered it better to borrow from Latin, just as French, English and many other languages do, than have recourse to Old Irish, since it is more important, in my view, that they be easily understood than be dressed in a pure Irish garb.

The *Alcéstis* contains 24 pages of explanatory introduction in which he includes a brief discussion (pp. 18-20) of A.W. Verrall's controversial observations on the play in his book *Euripides the Rationalist* (Cambridge 1913). Printing was by Alex Thom and Co. in a beautifully clear Greek font. Notes, appendices and vocabulary take up 177 pages, making the whole an impressive achievement of scholarship. The same may be said for his next Greek-Irish publication *Prométheus fé Chuibhreach* (Prometheus Bound) Dublin 1933. This has a Foreword, an Introduction of 20 pages, a Commentary of 76 pages and a discussion on the metre and grammar of the text. It was the result of a study of the play which began six years before, which he considered had enabled him to arrive at a better interpretation than previous scholars.

This Irish edition was similar to the English one which he proposed to publish later, only it was simpler in detail so as to accommodate to the needs of those who were not yet *sár-oilte ar an nGréigis* (highly skilled in Greek). Much material which he thought might be unintelligible to them he omitted, along with proofs or evidence in support of the views he advanced. He pointed out, however, that some of these were to be found already in the *Classical Quarterly* xxiii (1929), 153-63 and *Classical Review* xliii (1929), 3-5, and the rest would appear in the forthcoming English edition. The English edition, October 1932, actually preceded the Irish one which had to contend with bureaucratic delays. No vocabulary was supplied, because the edition was not intended for beginners, but for the senior grades of secondary schools and university students, in order to encourage the use of the larger Liddell and Scott, the editor considering that the student should be weaned off the use of shorter vocabularies. Printing was done by Browne and Nolan, not in such fine and emphatic type as in the *Alcéstis* but clear and satisfactory. The print run for the *Alcéstis* was 1000, for *Prométheus fé Chuibhreach* 500.

It is doubtful if any scholar of comparable status to Thomson ever worked in the field of Gaelic-Hellenic studies or had his labours in this unusual area of scholarship marked by such conspicuous achievement. His pre-eminence in Hellenic studies is known, from his publications in English, throughout the wide world of classical scholarship. What is known only within a very limited sphere is his complete mastery of the Irish language. With his proficiency in Irish and Greek he represented what was to W. B. Yeats the ideal in education. What Thomson did was to make the language of Dunquin and the Blaskets the vehicle of commentary and exegesis in the most sophisticated area of the humanities and that he did this with perfect success makes him, if for no other reason, unique. He became involved, by his own consent and enthusiasm, in the task of revivifying Irish culture, and because he showed by his endeavour what could be done, the work of George Thomson remains for Ireland a beacon light.

George Thomson's friendship with Maurice O'Sullivan, who tutored him so well in spoken Irish, — 'it's the fine, rich Irish you have now' (p.257) — had an important literary sequel. Thomson persuaded the young man not to emigrate to America like his brother and sisters but to join the Garda Síochána, the Irish police force and go to the training depot in Dublin. Maurice left the island on the 15th March 1927, bound for Dublin, where he met his friend George, who introduced him to the ways of the city. In time he completed his training and was sent to take up duty at Indreabhán in West Galway. The life of a civic guard in Indreabhán was placid and O'Sullivan felt the winter long. He told Thomson he had time on his hands. Why not write about your youth on the island, suggested Thomson, who had noticed, not long after their first acquaintance, that O'Sullivan had qualities which go to make a writer, a talent for storytelling, imagination and a love of people. Stimulated by the example of his elder· neighbour Tomás Ó Criomhthain whose noted book *An tOileánach* (The Islandman) had appeared in 1929, and encouraged by Thomson, O'Sullivan wrote the book between 1929 and 1932, not for the wide world, but for the people of his own small island whom he remembered with such affection.

He sent the draft to Thomson, who had meantime taken up the chair of Greek in University College Galway, amounting to five hundred pages of bulky manuscript. The work was too long to publish in its entirety. Thomson edited, pruned and counselled, always in consultation with the author, until between them a satisfactory draft was produced. 'In my opinion' writes Thomson, 'what I mainly did to improve the book was to make it more compact in the telling. I added nothing but removed a word or two here and a line or a half-page there, as one might comb wool or clear the chaff from the grain. But I changed nothing without submitting it to the author.' (Editor's Introduction, 5-6, to the 1976 edition of *Fiche Blian ag Fás*). *Twenty Years A-Growing* has been criticised on the score of presenting an unreal picture of the Blasket Island as a never-never land where the sun shone perpetually. The character of the book, however, makes this criticism unreal itself. What O'Sullivan described was not so much the physical island as the aura of youth and wonder that is distilled into those magic, fleeting years that are lived before twenty. He has caught and registered the echoes of boyhood, its sense of wonder and the nostalgia of adolescence with all its candour. It is part of the literature of youth, an appeal to something that lies profound in the human heart, a composition of deep local feeling and affection. It continues to be reprinted and remains an enduring tribute to the co-operation and friendship of Maurice O'Sullivan and George Thomson.

Tosnú na Feallsúnachta (The Beginnings of Philosophy), in 76 pages, the last Irish language book of Thomson's to appear in print, was published by the Stationery Office, Dublin, in 1935, but the author's brief foreword is dated May, 1932. He offers the book as an account of Greek philosophy from its earliest times to Plato, with nothing new except in the way of its arrangement, nor any discussion of controversial details since it was a book intended for the common reader. It is a light, easy to read, account, unique in Irish, and Thomson is obviously in love with his subject and medium. He makes Greek philosophy and its context the property of everyman. Here is a brief passage from the last chapter of Section III which deals with Plato's philosophy:

> It is said that Socrates, when approaching the end of his life, dreamed one night that a swan, the bird of Apollo, came to him through the air piping sweetly, and that on the morrow he met a well-shaped personable young man named Plato, so that he understood he was the swan that he had seen in his dream. At any rate, but for Plato, we would know very little of Socrates; for he was always thinking of his master who had died in the cause of truth, and since it was from him that the light of truth had entered into his own soul, it was through the mouth of Socrates that he disclosed his thoughts to the world. No one has ever written prose more beautiful than that of Plato.

Our first meeting

Ever since I read *Fiche Blian ag Fás* I had been interested in George Thomson and his work and I looked forward to seeing him in person. I first met him a few days before his 80th birthday, in his Birmingham home, and had the pleasure of shaking his hand. He asked me about the position of the Irish language and its prospects. He went on to talk about the language, of how he had translated the dialogues of Plato into Irish, of how the beauty of Plato's prose transferred so easily into Irish, which had corresponding beauties, of how aptly and suitably both Greek and Irish transposed the one into the other. As he was speaking, he got up and paced the room, a light came into his eyes, his voice which at first had been weak, grew stronger, the years fell away, and I found myself listening to a man who spoke with the animation and fire of youth in a way that belied the calendar. I sensed I was in the presence of a most unusual person, who spoke with conviction and near passion about the matters in which he was interested. He talked about modern Greece and the huge audiences which had come to see the production of *Ajax* and *Agamemnon* in great open air theatres in Northern Greece, countrymen who had travelled miles to see these plays and had received them enthusiastically. He compared Greece with Ireland and talked of his Connemara experiences when he had attempted something similar.

His Irish language writings

I have the honour to be editor of a selection of George Thomson's Irish writings. He wrote on a variety of matters. Mainly they are drawn from two areas of experience, Greece and Ireland. Some are short stories, some are character sketches, some discuss the topics of the day. One thing that emerges is that George Thomson is very good at the art of storytelling. The Dancing Man (*An Rinceoir Fir*), is about a Dublin character who proclaimed he was a genius at dancing but was in reality very deft at the art of 'touching'. Phases of Thomson's own life are interwoven with the writings.

There is a fine account of his 1926 visit to Ithaca (modern Thiaki), birthplace of Odysseus, where he was the guest in the hilltop monastery of Brother Yannis, twenty years a monk and survivor of a community of three, who faithfully carried out his liturgy and gave shelter and hospitality to George and two poor retainers, a fisherman and swineherd, consisting of an omelette, a portion of octopus, goat's milk, cheese, olives, garlic, Turkish coffee and glass upon glass of 'fine spirited black wine', stimulating merriment, joy and the tempo of conversation. 'Let us rise now and drink a health to the stranger'. Midnight approached and grace was said, followed by prayers in the chapel. A description of classic charm. The Goat Boy (*Buachaill na nGabhar*) concerns a young goatherd who can produce sprightly music from the reed pipes, while George, who was not successful in getting a single note from the same instrument, watches the boy go off in the distance, like a reincarnation of Pan, making music as he went. There is a sketch, *Barra na Trá*, about the Blaskets (though he does not name it) and the observation of an elder about the future which corresponds to the prophecy of Tomás Ó Criomhthain ('Our likes will not be again').

Thomson is good at describing human situations – a young woman with her child abandoned by her lover, an army officer in gaudy red uniform, and the heroism with which she copes; the poor Connemara woman in the Galway train, grief-stricken but queenly in her dignity, in striking contrast to her mundane fellow-passengers. Many of the essays are on topics of the day, at a time in the late twenties when he lived in Watermill Cottage, Raheny, on the north side of Dublin Bay, and would walk around the curve of the shore to Trinity College where he was studying for a postgraduate degree. An absurd project was being given serious consideration, to build a Blue Lagoon, Hawaii-style, on the north shore of the Bay, a project which he scarified in an article headed *Blue Lagoon, mar dh'ea* as nothing more than a playground for the affluent and wealthy, possessors of yachts and motor cars, of no benefit to common humanity. Dublin City, which celebrated its millennium in 1988, should be grateful to George Thomson for his part in scotching the absurd proposition. It is good to know that the area is now a wildlife reserve and one of the most attractive of Dublin's environs.

George Thomson was also a fine Shakespearean scholar and has translated into Irish a number of the sonnets. Some of the material in the selection has been published in various journals; most, however, was made available through the kindness of Katharine, George's wife, to whom I take this occasion to acknowledge my gratitude for the readiness with which she gave of her time and help, and for the keen interest which she takes in George's Irish language work. George wrote in Irish on matters such as the use of the language in commercial life, on university education, how to enrich community life by taking learning to the people by way of University extension lectures, based on the principle that learning should be brought to the attention of the people and shared with them, that as a consequence of this the people would take an active interest in progress. He shared with Robin Flower the belief that great poetry and literature came up out of the thought and imagination of the people.

In Galway

In 1931 George Thomson was appointed lecturer in Greek through Irish at University College Galway, the first such appointment ever made. A special Act had been passed by the Oireachtas to legislate for it, providing also for a lecturer in Latin through Irish, a post to which Dr. Margaret Heavey was appointed. She and George Thomson were good friends and respected teachers. Besides teaching classes, George Thomson, whose appointment and educational projects had the favour of Ernest Blythe, Minister for Finance, had set himself two main tasks. One of these was the provision of textbooks and studies, of secondary and university standard, on classical Greek and related subjects, in the Irish language. In this field he did considerable work. His second task was to bring University extension lectures to the people of Connemara. His purpose was to introduce learning to the ranks of the people, to teach them about trade and economics, to bring the Irish language to bear on their everyday life and make it an agency of progress, to improve their lot and turn their attention to the future.

George Thomson considered that the Department of Education programmes for Irish concentrated too much on the past and ignored contemporary European thought. 'I conceived the idea of using the language as a means of giving them (i.e. the people of the Gaeltacht) a modern education so that they could adapt their culture to modern conditions'. In his efforts to bring University extension lectures to the people of Connemara he found himself up against an obstacle that no persuasion could surmount. The Connemara climate was not suitable for open-air lectures. The only feasible lecture halls were the school premises, the use of which was denied him by the uncooperative parish priests who managed them. He received no support from the government or any official source in his efforts. George Thomson was highly critical of Irish governments and did not mince his words. He said that in achieving political independence as a result of the national struggle they had got what they wanted, they had no ambitions for social progress and had designed their Irish language programmes with the view of turning back to the past.[1] After a successful performance in Galway of a play which he had organised, and which was acclaimed by the audience, a friendly critic of his policies, Professor Donegan, who was present, came to him and said 'I now see what you are trying to do and I agree with you'.

George Thomson found, at a certain stage of his progress, that the great programme he had envisaged, of providing edited texts, translations and studies of Greek plays and poetry, histories of Greek literature and philosophy, was being held up and inhibited, at official level. Ernest Blythe, who had backed and encouraged his plans for providing textbooks, was no longer in government. There came a point at which he lost patience and resigned his post at University College Galway, finding that the progress he had planned was being made impossible. He was in those days, as indeed he was at all times, a spirited and stubborn man, fiercely committed to the Irish revival, and he found the doors being closed against his efforts.

He left Galway, 'my mind in turmoil', and returned to Cambridge, where at King's College he held a Fellowship. The year was 1934. In the upset of his changing from Galway to Cambridge there was lost or mislaid his complete translation into Irish of Homer's *Odyssey*. It was a serious loss. Maurice O'Sullivan was to go through the text with him to give it an authentic Blasket Island flavour and it was to be illustrated by Gwen Raverat, grand-daughter of Charles Darwin and a talented artist. Enquiries to Cambridge confirm that it is not there. There is a hope that it may be somewhere in Galway. The twenty four books of the *Odyssey* would make a substantial manuscript. It shows the wholehearted commitment to the Irish language of George Thomson. It is our hope that it may be recovered, as something we would be proud to have in Irish.

This was the central reason why George Thomson left Galway. I have a very clear recollection of this, which George Thomson related to me in much detail twice, in his home in Birmingham. It has been suggested that his leaving Galway had something to do with his Marxist philosophy. That is not so. At that time George was definitely not a Marxist. His Marxism developed following his 1935 visit to Moscow and his appraisal of social and educational progress in the Soviet Union which he describes in a striking 'personal epilogue' to his essay on the Irish Language Revival (*Yorkshire Celtic Studies III*, pp. 10-12).

A fruitful association: George Thomson and Pádraig Ó Fiannachta
George Thomson's association in scholarhip with Father Pádraig Ó Fiannachta began in 1959. Professor Margaret Heavey, George Thomson's Latin colleague in the Classics Faculty of University College Galway, had forwarded his Irish translation of *Confessiones Sancti Augustini* to Maynooth College for appraisal and publication. There it was given to Pádraig Ó Fiannachta, of the Celtic Studies staff, who considered George's translation to be excellent. George had translated Books I-VII. Ó Fiannachta continued the translation to the end of Book X where a natural break occurs, a point at which the essence of the autobiography is complete. The text, *Mise Agaistín* (I am Augustine) of 252 pp., appeared under the imprint of *An Sagart*, Maynooth, 1967 with an introduction, pp. 9-24, by Fr. Seán Mac Riabhaigh and the imprimatur of Dionysius Episcopus Kerriensis. The sale cleared expenses and left a modest profit which Ó Fiannachta considered due to Thomson, who insisted however that it be credited to the funds of *An Sagart*, thus providing the first contribution to the enterprise that published in due course *An Leicseanáir, An Leabhar Aifrinn Romhánach* and *An Bíobla Naofa*. It is an entirely proper judgement that the name of the reader is consigned to oblivion who initially rejected George Thomson's translation of the Confessions because he was not a Catholic.

Thomson and Ó Fiannachta resumed their co-operation in 1975. *Fiche Blian ag Fás* had been out of print since 1941 and Thomson was having difficulty in finding a sympathetic publisher who would retain the unique native character of the author's text. Pádraig Ó Fiannachta, coming from the same milieu as Muiris Ó Súileabháin and familiar with the author's environment, was naturally interested in the book's fortunes and offered George his help in having it published. To ensure that editing would be sympathetic to the character of the book he crossed to Birmingham and after a week's collaboration they produced an acceptable text which is celebrated by Pádraig Ó Fiannachta, *'file agus fear léinn'*, Thomson's words, in a brief lyric in his collection *Donn Bó* (1977) much appreciated by George and his wife Katharine.

Thus the second edition of *Fiche Blian ag Fás* was launched at Listowel Writers' Week in June 1976, which George and Katharine attended, with George signalising the event in an elegant Irish address in a local tavern. Travelling to West Kerry he gave a striking interview to Proinsias Mac Aonghusa on the verge of a Dunquin cliff against the backdrop of the Blaskets which was filmed to appear in a later dramatisation of the book on the stage of the Peacock Theatre.

George's Greek and Irish language interests are so intertwined that to disengage them is impossible. In three important contributions to the Maynooth literary journals *Léachtaí Cholm Cille* and *Irisleabhar Mhá Nuad* Pádraig Ó Fiannachta has printed, out of George's *Nachlass*, a number of translations from the Greek in his fluent and lucid Irish.[2] These, which were found in Galway University, evidently related to his University lectures and his efforts to supply adult education to the Connemara public in his belief, as Pádraig Ó Fiannachta observes, 'that knowledge of the classics with their philosophical thought, their literary art and imaginative content would benefit the mind and soul of the Gaeltacht people who had not for aeons of time received their educational rights from clergy or laity, Gael or Gall.' (*Léachtaí Cholm Chille* XVIII, 162. *An Sagart,* Maigh Nuad (1988)).

George's translation from the History of Herodotus of stories which were appreciated by the Blasket fishermen appeared serially in the monthly journal *An Phoblacht* between 21 January and 19 May 1928 under the general title *An Seana-shaol Gréagach* (Life in Ancient Greece).

Fiche Blian ag Fás and the Talbot Press

In preliminary notes to the manuscript of *Fiche Blian ag Fás*, which he presented to the National Library, George gives an interesting account of his negotiations with the Talbot Press about his efforts to persuade them to publish it. Apart from causing him much editorial trouble, they kept raising difficulties. 'They said at first they would not publish it without a subsidy, but, after I had made it known that an English translation was being published by Chatto and Windus, with a foreword by E.M. Forster, they changed their minds, accepting instead a guarantee.' The guarantee had the support of Lennox Robinson, Edward Gwynn, Lord Longford and others, with Lennox Robinson urging him to go ahead and publish the English version, leaving the Talbot Press to its own devices and discomfiture. In the event George Thomson financed the publication at his own expense. The Irish edition was dedicated to Ernest Blythe, because it was through his influence that Maurice was accepted into the Garda Síochána. Maurice's own wish had been to dedicate it to George Thomson.

Other Irish language writings of George, as yet unpublished, are mentioned by him in these preliminary notes. 'I wrote a Greek Grammar and a *Tosnú na Sibhialtachta* (based on lectures given at University College, Galway).' These were also rejected, 'the first because of my spelling, the second because I was suspected of believing in the Darwinian theory', once more the identity of the editorial Boeotians being mercifully wrapped in oblivion. In collaboration with Osborn Bergin George translated an abridged Book of Common Prayer for the Church of Ireland which was published in 1935.

A comrade spirit

It is proper that the name of the North Kerry classical and Irish scholar Tim Enright should be mentioned as a friend and disciple of George Thomson. A primary school pupil of Bryan MacMahon, he graduated from Trinity College and went on to become classical master of Brooksbank Comprehensive School, Elland, in Yorkshire. When he retired in 1981, the Department of Classics, under the influence of his teaching, was ranked one of the top twelve in England. Sharing a love of Classics and Irish with George Thomson he also shared his Marxist convictions and campaigned on behalf of the underprivileged on the hustings of Yorkshire. A born teacher, he believed that the classical world was part of every child's heritage. He is one of the distinguished group of translators and interpreters of Blasket literature whose work has been published by Oxford University Press. Of George Thomson he wrote to me: *'Níl aon teora leis an sár-fhear sin'* – 'There are no bounds to that great man'.

The best account of George Thomson is Tim's *Memoir* of him which forms the last part, pp. 119-150, of *Island Home, the Blasket Heritage*, George Thomson's own profound interpretation of the Blasket way of life, and his final book (Brandon, Dingle, Co Kerry, 1988).

The heritage of George Thomson

We might ask what did George Thomson bring to the Irish language. First of all he brought his positive conviction that its revival could be accomplished. He brought his talents of scholarship, by which he produced textbooks of the highest quality, using the language of the Blaskets and Dunquin to bear on the most sophisticated area of scholarship in the world. His career in Galway marked the zenith of achievement in Irish-Hellenic Studies. He brought to the Irish language a spirit of adventure and freshness. He inspired a young islander to produce a classic in the literature of youth, *Twenty Years A-Growing*, which may be cited as an example of his belief that great literature came up from the people. He identified for us the intellectual wealth that is present in the speech of the people. On the other hand he contributed to Irish a history of Greek Philosophy and translations from Greek masterpieces that sounded in Irish as natural as if produced by a Blasket islander. He enriched the Irish language with a new classical content, and showed how it could be enriched further. It is to be hoped that his Irish translation of the *Odyssey* will turn up. His familiarity with Greek influenced his style in Irish, which he wrote with Attic precision. In the Gaelic Pantheon he is a versatile and distinguished member.

From: *Classics Ireland,* vol.3, 1996.

References

1. See George Thomson's illuminating essay 'The Irish Language Revival' in *Yorkshire Celtic Studies III* Transactions 1940-46, pp 3-12.
2. Theocritus, *Idyll* 15, except vv. 100-149 (supplied by Pádraig Ó Fiannachta) in *Léachtaí Cholm Cille XVIII* pp. 164-169. *The Iliad,* Book 1, *Ibid,* pp. 169-182. Plato, *The Symposium,* in *Irisleabhar Mhá Nuad* 1988, pp. 161-189, continued and concluded in *Irisleabhar Mhá Nuad* 1989, pp. 76-102. The foregoing appeared under the imprint of *An Sagart,* Maynooth, as did George's study of the Blasket culture *An Blascaod a bhí* (1977) and its expanded English version *The Blasket that was* (1982) in which were revealed parallels between Blasket life and the Homeric world. Pádraig Ó Fiannachta, now Canon and Parish Priest of Dingle, is the editor of *An Sagart.* He is distinguished as a lecturer, poet and writer, with a phenomenal range of work to his credit, chiefly the organisation and editing of *An Bíobla Naofa* (1981) of which he was part-translator. He recently purchased the library of the late President Cearbhall Ó Dálaigh (2500 volumes) and presented it to the Great Blasket Centre in Dunquin. There is a brief biography of him in *Stair na Gaeilge* (Maigh Nuad 1994) 1-21. His full-scale biography by Risteárd Ó Glaisne has been published by *An Sagart* (1996).

George Thomson on his first visit to the Great Blasket, Summer 1923. Left to right: Peig 'Buffer' Keane, Hannah Kearney, Mary Kearney (later Sr. Mary Clemens), George Thomson. (Courtesy of Mrs. Katharine Thomson).

Chapter 11

Tim Enright, scholar and Marxist

The death of Tim Enright on 7 December 1993, at the Halifax Royal Infirmary, will be felt in places as far apart as Yorkshire West Riding and County Kerry. Irish and classical scholar, socialist campaigner, schoolteacher, translator of Blasket Island literature, good friend and companion, Tim's cheerful company will be missed at literary gatherings in the Dingle Peninsula as will his fiery eloquence on behalf of the underprivileged on the hustings of Yorkshire. He was a combination of idealist, scholar and fighter.

Tim Enright joins the distinguished group of translators and interpreters who have brought the Blasket Island's native literature to the attention of the world, and have given the little island, so often beleaguered by storms and lashing seas, a status and permanence in every place throughout the world where thought and culture are prized. By his work he has widened the perception of the Blasket culture for readers of English and has done this with learning and style.

I Early years and background

Tim Enright was born in Listowel, North Kerry, at the beginning of 1926. Political antagonisms at that time were tense, in the aftermath of the short and bitter civil war of 1922-23. Tim's father had been in the British Army and, like many others who had similarly served, transferred his conscience and loyalty to the cause of the Irish Republic, fighting against the Black and Tans and later against the Irish Free State, having declined to accept the Anglo-Irish Treaty of December 1921. Tim's uncle Daniel likewise gave his commitment, and finally his life, to the Republic. Tim's father and uncle Daniel were captured and interned. In March 1923 Daniel Enright was one of four young men executed at Drumboe in Co. Donegal by the Free State forces, in the most distressing and tragic period of the young State's experience.[1]

The tragedy of family history made an indelible impression on Tim Enright and turned him into an uncompromising and resolute youth. At the age of seven he joined the Republican Boy Scouts, an organisation that did not have the favour of authority, and never deviated from his republican ideals throughout his life.

In the emerging Irish state the aftermath of civil war gave rise to many features that were far from consonant with freedom. The basic principles of civil liberty as enunciated for example in the classic definition of John Stuart Mill were given little room to flourish. A rigid censorship continued for decades to curb the creative instincts of Ireland's writers. Although governments changed, the restrictions did not. A joyless aura of Jansenism denounced such innocent amusements as the kitchen set-dance. The happy jollity of the crossroads dance was proscribed and pressurised out of social life. These were recreations which had preserved the traditional music of reel, jig and hornpipe. The merest whiff of socialism was considered immoral by the establishment interests.

Tim Enright the young student read and admired the works of Ireland's greatest socialist, James Connolly. He introduced their message to a circle of fellow students. His teachers disapproved. This was rank communism. He must sign a pledge of renunciation or face expulsion. He chose expulsion. He could not continue study for his Leaving Certificate nor avail of such educational avenues as it might open up. Of necessity he took a job cutting turf for the County Council. In seeking other outlets for his talent he won a scholarship to Trinity College Dublin where he spent four happy years in the study of Celtic languages. Joining the Cumann Gaelach (The College Gaelic Society) he would bring in to this rather conservative body matters of topical urgency for debate, such as the necessity of providing work for the Gaeltacht population which was being whitened by emigration to Great Britain in search of the living denied it at home. The exodus from the Gaeltacht numbered thousands. This was a generation deceived and betrayed by the promises of its platform instructors. Tim Enright was becoming a rebel.

He was no stranger to the Gaeltacht. He spent all his summer holidays in West Kerry, immersing himself in the culture of the region, its rich language, folklore, traditional music and song. He loved the music of the fiddle, the whistle, the flute and the Irish pipes, and the lively rhythm of the figure dances. He played the tin whistle himself. In this milieu Tim found himself in communion with his psyche and heritage. His native North Kerry nurtured writers like his teacher Bryan MacMahon and Maurice Walsh, storytellers both, John B. Keane the playwright, and Thomas MacGreevy, art critic and translator of French literature, who early recognised the genius of Samuel Beckett, the O'Rahilly brothers, Thomas F., Celtic scholar and Alfred, mathematician and economist, born controversialists. Two generations earlier the area

Plate 1 Johann Kaspar Zeuss (courtesy of the Royal Irish Academy).

Plate 2   Rudolf Thomas Siegfried (by kind permission of the Royal Irish Academy).

Plate 3   Hermann Ebel (by
           kind permission of
           the Royal Irish
           Academy).

Plate 4   Ernst Windisch
           (courtesy of the
           Department of
           Manuscripts, Trinity
           College Library,
           Dublin).

Plate 5   Heinrich Zimmer (by
kind permission of
the Royal Irish
Academy).

Plate 6   Kuno Meyer aged
seventeen,
Edinburgh, 1875 (by
kind permission of
the Royal Irish
Academy).

Plate 7   Kuno Meyer
            (courtesy of the
            National Library of
            Ireland).

Plate 8   Rudolf Thurneysen
            (courtesy of the
            National Library of
            Ireland).

Plate 9   Ludwig Christian
Stern (courtesy of the
National Library of
Ireland).

Plate 10   Henri Gaidoz
(courtesy of the
National Library of
Ireland).

Plate 11   Henri d'Arbois de Jubainville (courtesy of the National Library of Ireland).

Plate 12   Joseph Loth (courtesy of the National Library of Ireland).

Plate 13   Graziadio Isaia Ascoli
            (courtesy of the
            National Library of
            Ireland).

Plate 14   John Strachan
            (courtesy of the
            Royal Irish
            Academy).

Plate 15   Carl Marstrander
(courtesy of Verdens
Gang, Oslo).

Plate 16   Julius Pokorny
(courtesy of the
National Library of
Ireland).

Plate 17   Whitley Stokes (courtesy of the National Library of Ireland).

Plate 18   William Maunsell Hennessy (courtesy of the Royal Irish Academy).

Plate 19   Richard Irvine Best in
1917 (courtesy of the
National Library of
Ireland).

Plate 20   Douglas Hyde
(photograph by
Chancellor).

Plate 21   Robin Flower (by
kind permission of
the British Academy).

Plate 22   George Thomson
(courtesy of Mrs.
Katharine Thomson).

Plate 23   George Thomson's study (photograph by Gearóid Ó Lúing).

Plate 24   Tim Enright (courtesy
of Mrs. Trudy
Enright).

Plate 25   Dr. Patrick Henchy (courtesy of the National Library of Ireland).

Plate 26   Donn Sigerson Piatt.   Plate 27   Kaspar Zeuss Gymnasium, Kronach
(courtesy of the Headmaster).

Plate 28   Seán Ó Lúing in the garden
            of Eduard Meyer's house in
            Berlin (photograph by John
            Marin).

Plate 29   Tomás and Seán Ó Crithin
            (courtesy of Mrs. Katharine
            Thomson).

Plate 30   R. A. S. Macalister (courtesy of the Royal
            Society of Antiquaries of Ireland).

had poets of merit whose language was Irish. Listowel has its Writers' Week every Summer with the object of developing creative writing. This was Tim Enright's native environment.

II   Teacher and social activist

When Tim graduated in Celtic Studies he might have expected to secure congenial employment in his own country but his radical views debarred such a prospect. His tutor helped him obtain a teaching post in England. Emigrating there in January 1949 he spent his first night of slumber directly under what was believed to be Cromwell's tomb in Newburgh Priory, Coxwold, where his school was situated. It was an uneasy sleep for an Irish republican and Marxist in such nearness to England's formidable first republican.

Tim remained but a short while in this first job. Being attracted to the comprehensive school system, he resigned and took up the post of Latin master in a small mixed grammar school in Yorkshire West Riding, an area in which, under the enlightened direction of Sir Alec Clegg, there flourished one of the most progressive regional authorities in the country. This school, having merged into the comprehensive system, became the Brooksbank Comprehensive School, Elland. Beginning in 1951, Tim taught Latin to O-level and presently extended the standard to A-level. When he retired in 1981, the Department of Classics, under the influence of his teaching, was ranked one of the top twelve in England.

As well as having a degree in Celtic Studies, Tim was a brilliant Classical scholar, familiar with the literature and culture of the early Mediterranean world, and would quote appositely from Vergil or Homer as context required. Far from considering that Classical studies should be the preserve of an élite and the peculiar garden of the academic he believed that the Classical world was part of every child's heritage and introduced them to it without distinction. He made its learning a pleasure, producing Greek plays, for which he provided incidental music with his tin whistle. He was a born teacher and there is tribute and testimony from his pupils at Elland to the profound human qualities and educational merit of his work in the classroom. A pupil wrote: 'I will never forget my schooldays at Elland; the profound human qualities of a teacher who knew the true meaning of education; the liveliness of his teaching; the generosity of his spirit.'

With his marriage to Trudy, England became his permanent home. There were numerous social and political problems around him in Yorkshire and farther afield which he did not hesitate to address with full commitment, taking for his guiding principle the creative radicalism of James Connolly. He began his campaign as a member of the Labour

Left, but finding it less progressive than he wished he joined the Communist Party in 1955, having come to believe that Marxism was the most forward agency for achieving the progress and happiness of the human being. His work with the Communist Party brought him into close association and friendship with George Thomson, the Classical and Irish scholar who was the foremost intellectual and interpreter of British Marxism. Their unity of thought on economics is expressed in *Island Home* (p. 85): 'This paradox of poverty in the midst of plenty has been the law of a monetary economy ever since men first went to market, but in our day it has become catastrophic. The free play of market forces must be brought under control'.

No freeman of Athens proclaimed his thoughts in favour of man's rights with such fervour as Tim. He protested against the closure of industries, campaigned against job losses and welfare cuts, called for Nuclear Disarmament, campaigned against the war in Vietnam and against racism, combining his teaching with his political activism, pressing for improvements in education, leaving untouched no feature of public life that called for attention. His diary was constantly full. He appreciated that freedom of thought and liberty of expression were fully respected in England.

Following early retirement in 1981, Tim's life continued as active as ever. He took his stand in solidarity with the miners in their great strike, translated the Irish language works of the Blasket Island authors and persevered in his firm support of Marxist principles. As Press Officer for the Calderdale Pensioners Association he campaigned for the welfare and security of the aged and infirm, opposed cutbacks in their essential services, contested the notorious VAT on fuel, and strenuously resisted the notion that would deny a decent pension to the aged. Ever the champion of the weak, he lived his life to the standard proclaimed by one of his beloved classical authors – I am a human being, I consider nothing human outside my ken.

III Master and disciple: George Thomson and Tim Enright

It was Ray Stagles who first told me of the communion of ideas between George Thomson and Tim. I came to know of it later at first hand. I recall meeting Tim and Ron Ogden on 12 February 1987 at Birmingham Airport, whither I had travelled with Muiris Mac Conghail, maker of a splendid film on the Blaskets, and Colm Luibhéid, Professor of Classics in University College Galway. We had come to attend George Thomson's funeral. He had been to us an inspiration and a leader. Ron drove us directly to his own house, where we met his wife Elizabeth and Trudy, in an atmosphere that radiated friendliness. We discoursed on George's work, amongst other things, and after drinks and a meal, we went in two cars, Tim's and Ron's, to the Robinhood Crematorium, where the funeral service was to be held. It was a day when thought ran deep. The Irish language had lost a devoted friend and humanity at large mourned its champion. It was a moving ceremony. I well remember Tim Enright's address. 'Comrades!' his voice rang through the oratory, in a clear and well-delivered piece in his North Kerry accent, in which he spoke about George's connection with the Blaskets, his contributions to Irish scholarship, his identification with the Blasket people and his espousal of the interests of humanity, introducing or quoting with translation, Irish phrases, and quoting Máire Ní Ghuithín's description of him, duine uasal, íseal, a noble person, he loved the people. It was a sensitive and well-appreciated tribute, taking up four minutes, for the time was brief.

The best account of George Thomson is a Memoir by Tim Enright forming the last part of *Island Home, the Blasket Heritage,* George Thomson's own profound interpretation of the Blasket and Gaelic way of life, and his final book (Brandon, Dingle, Co. Kerry 1988). It occupies pages 119-150. This review of George Thomson's life and work was clearly a labour of love. In fact it is difficult to consider George and Tim apart from each other, so close did their interests coincide and Tim may be considered as the disciple and successor of his friend.

Tim's close association with George and his family enabled him to supply new or little known information which is incorporated in his memoir, for instance George's deep understanding of music, his interest in the Clarion Singers of Birmingham, a choir of Midland workers who brought their experience of factory and workshop into their interpretations of operatic roles. Katharine was an active member of the choir as accompanist and conductor. It was founded in 1940 by Dr. Colin Bradsworth, who had been a medical officer with the International Brigade in Spain. Paul Robeson was its President for many years and when Tim was writing in 1988, the office was held by the distinguished English composer Alan Bush, author of *Wat Tyler* and other operas. Ralph Vaughan Williams was a strong supporter of the choir and came to hear their performance of his composition *Sir John in love,* based on *The Merry Wives of Windsor* and, although ill at the time, went home delighted and restored to health and spirits. Tim records George's friendship with the celebrated Hungarian composer Zoltán Kodály (1882-1967), collector of folksongs out of which he fashioned a strongly national idiom.

Of George Thomson, Tim wrote to me, 'Níl aon teora leis an sár-fhear sin' – There are no bounds to that great man. The expression is contained in a letter which he sent to me along with his translation of

Tomás O'Crohan's *Allagar na hInise* which is titled *Island Cross-talk, pages from a diary*. In it he deprecates his own translation as compared to what Robin Flower, who knew Tomás O'Crohan, might produce. He had no need to do so. His translation is excellent. I am proud to have received a copy from his hand with a warm and generous inscription.

IV   The western island

> My island lies deep in the sea and nearer the west than its neighbours which rather face the dawning and the sun. It is a harsh land, yet it breeds good youths.

The quotation is from the *Odyssey* in Lawrence of Arabia's striking translation (which has not escaped the reproof of scholars like Benjamin Farrington). It describes the island of Ithaca, and the topography puzzles Homeric scholars. It has received a second identity from the celebrated Hellenist George Thomson, better known as Seoirse Mac Tomáis to readers of Irish, as the Great Blasket Island which lies, too, deep in the sea, doimhin sa bhfarraige, in the words of a local quatrain about the island fishermen. To Seoirse, as to his colleague and disciple Tim Enright, the Blasket and its language was the focus of study and devotion that rivalled their love of Greek literature.

Tim Enright's name is joined with that of George Thomson, Robin Flower, Moya Llewellyn Davies, Bryan MacMahon and Seamus Ennis as a translator of the Blasket Island authors. The first book he translated was *Is trua ná fanann an óige,* the reminiscences of Micheál O'Guiheen, the last of the Great Blasket poets and storytellers, under the title *A pity youth does not last.* In this Tim used his own Kerry English, the language Micheál O'Guiheen would have used if Irish had disappeared from the Great Blasket, as it had from Tim's own part of Kerry long before he was born. In this he followed the example of his old schoolmaster Bryan MacMahon, translator of *Peig,* the notable autobiography of Peig Sayers, who was Micheál O'Guiheen's mother and, in Tim Enright's phrase, 'the queen of Gaelic storytelling'. George Thomson contributed a foreword to the translation. He had met Micheál in 1923 on his first visit to the Blasket and they had formed a close friendship, which was renewed in 1966 following Micheál's career of wanderings in America and return to Dunquin.

'My love to God, isn't youth the grand thing!' So begins his story. Tim Enright, in his Introduction, fills in the background to Micheál's experience in a pithy history of the Island. Micheál was also 'The Poet', An File, representing a profession honoured in Gaelic Ireland, and was the author of *Coinnle Corra,* 'Wild Hyacinths', a collection of poems, personal thoughts, regrets and apprehensions, ten of which have been translated by Tim Enright and included in this book, in one of which the poet sings in Horatian echo

My spirit will be in a book
I will live there forever.

Micheál O'Guiheen was a well read man, studious and introspective, who hoped that he might go to college following his primary education. It was not to be. A living repository of folklore, he had contributed many thousands of pages to the Irish Folklore Commission in his distinctive hand, of which one can see a specimen in Seamus Stewart's *Boccaccio in the Blaskets* (introduction, XII). Micheál O'Guiheen translated a number of tales of Boccaccio which came his way in an English version on the Blasket Island.

Tim Enright's introductory essay is an epitome of the island's history. He sees Micheál O'Guiheen as recording the decline of his native island, the main cause being an economic whirlwind in the shape of the deep sea trawlers which came to comb the sea-beds around the Blaskets of the fish harvests on which the islanders depended. Their frail currachs could not compete with the giants of capital. Springfield, Massachusetts, that other Ireland, beckoned and there many of the Blasket youth made for themselves a new habitation. Tim Enright's translation matches well the grace and idiom of the original, echoing its sadness and pathos, for the book, as he says, is a sombre recitation by a man steeped in the island culture of song and story, of the death of that community and culture.

Two more translations followed. The first was *Island Cross-talk, pages from a diary*, from Tomás O'Crohan's *Allagar na hInise*. The title accurately represents the character of O'Crohan's diary, which consists of the conversations, banter, wit, repartee, view of life and comments of island folk who loved the thrust and parry of words, an exercise which was part of their age-long oral tradition. In his Introduction Tim explains the genesis of the text, how Bryan O'Kelly, a graduate of Trinity College Dublin, learning Irish from the author, and noting his talent, urged him to put his thoughts on paper and with this purpose supplied him with pens, ink and paper, with the result described by Tim:

Tomás thought to amuse as well as instruct his pupil by recounting the cross-talk of Islanders whose quirks and oddities of behaviour and expression he had come to know during his story. Comments on the weather, of daily concern on the Island three miles out, often grew into lyrical descriptions of natural phenomena, penned simply and swiftly, his seabird's eye darting on the essential.

The diary adds up to a picture of Blasket life from the end of 1919 to the beginning of 1923. Tim Enright's racy English translation is a faithful mirror of the original and is in itself a writing of quality. The translation is of the first (1928) edition, a selection which comprises but a third of the original diary, but judiciously chosen and representing a full chapter of Blasket life. Tim's Introduction, prefaced by appositely chosen lines from the *Iliad* and *Aeneid* in lament for Troy, is a model of compressed prologue. O'Crohan had in the diary expressed the wish 'Wouldn't it delight my heart to be able to read a book of my own before I died', a wish more than fulfilled for, as Tim points out, 'he had placed his small island, three miles by one, on the literary map of the world'. Tim had good help from Trudy and George Thomson in the making of the book, which is enhanced by some very interesting photographs.

Seán O'Crohan, son of Tomás, author of *The Islandman*, lived on the Great Blasket Island until 1942, when the exigencies of life compelled him to abandon the island and move with his wife and family to the mainland. He told the story of his experience in *Lá dár Saol*. The translation by Tim Enright is entitled *A day in our life*. Published by Oxford University Press in 1992, it is dedicated 'In memory of George Thomson (1903-1987)'. As an example of book production it deserves praise for its binding, paper, clear print and attractive dust jacket.

At this point it is suitable to applaud Oxford University Press for its services to Irish language and literature. Twice in his classic study of Irish literature Douglas Hyde commended Oxford University 'which has given noble assistance to the cause of Celtic studies' and again 'Oxford deserves splendidly of Celtic scholars' (*The Literary History of Ireland* xii and 414, footnote 2). Tim Enright, in his Acknowledgements to *A day in our life*, pays a deserved tribute to Oxford University Press, for its active encouragement and the care it took with the production of his books. In 1989 the Great Blasket was declared a National Historic Park by the Irish Government and placed under the care of the Office of Public Works. This was a development for which some of the credit was quite correctly attributed by Tim to the Oxford University Press which kept translations of the Blasket books in print down the years, giving the island's literature and the island itself recognition throughout the world.

Tim Enright provides a 14 page Introduction to his translation. In it we find evidence of his own acquaintance with the great personalities of the island, as for example his recollection of Peig Sayers telling him about her son, Micheál O'Guiheen, poet and author, sitting with a copybook on his knee composing poetry, and her regret that it had not been a young woman on his knee instead. Micheál remained a bachelor in a narrowing society where weddings had declined to non-existence. Seán O'Crohan, author of *A day in our life*, was the rare exception, who married Eibhlís O'Sullivan, writer of a thirty year correspondence with George Chambers, in English, in a transfer of language that was inexorably gaining ground amongst the dwindling number of native Irish speakers.

Eibhlís's correspondent was a Londoner who came periodically to check on the operation of the Tiaracht lighthouse on a rocky inch west of the Great Blasket. Tim Enright quotes from her correspondence which foreshadows the final leaving of the Island of her husband Seán and their growing child who must soon attend school, there being none on the Island. 'Times are changed.' They moved to the mainland in 1942, only ten miles away, into the same Gaelic culture, but a milieu which meant, in Jane Austen's words, quoted by Tim from *Persuasion*, 'a total change of conversation, opinion and idea'. Seán O'Crohan relates, not without grim humour, the pressing circumstances which caused his removal from his beloved island to Muiríoch on the shores of Smerwick Harbour, where with his family he settled into his new house, and earned his living as fisherman and casual labourer. Inheriting his father's talent for language, he wrote a series of letters to his nephew Pádraig Ua Maoileoin, officer of the Garda Síochána in Dublin, giving an account of his mainland life. These letters form the basis of his book. He has a sharp and critical eye and writes the Irish language with distinction, in a manner not unworthy of his remarkable father.

V   Letters of Friendship

Tim and I corresponded from the first time we came to know each other. Our letters were in Irish and ranged over a number of years, exchanging news about books and publications, such matters as the progress of the Blasket Heritage Centre, the establishment of the Island as a National Park, an idea cherished by Ray Stagles and promoted by the prestige of George Thomson. His letters, in fluent, lucid Irish and a clear and firm hand, were a pleasure to read. As he kept in constant touch with George Thomson he sent me news of him regularly, such as the tidings that 'On Wednesday [16 April 1986] he will receive the honorary citizenship of Eleusis, the birthplace of Aeschylus, a great honour well-deserved.'

In a letter of 2 March 1987, he mentions having written an essay on

George for *History Workshop*. 'I was able to say something you did not previously know, I would think, which is that George was the only person on the Executive Council of the Communist Party who stood out against the new policy of the Party 'The British Road to Socialism' in 1950. 'Revisionism' he called it! He was ever a fearless man, as we know.' Regarding George's translations from Greek to Irish, he mentions that Plato's *Symposium*, the *Iliad* Book 1 and *Idyll* XV of Theocritus would be published in the coming year in *Irisleabhar Mhá Nuad* (Maynooth Journal) and *Léachtaí Cholm Cille* (Colmcille Lectures) which would have as theme the Gaeltacht writers. Of the Editor of these publications, Fr. Pádraig Ó Fiannachta, he writes 'Pádraig Ó Fiannachta is a splendid man without a doubt and he well understands how to edit the Irish of the Blaskets which is in these translations. That was a fine essay on George which he had in *Anois* and there was lovely poetry in it as well.'

Tim and all friends of George were deeply concerned at the loss of George's Irish translation of the *Odyssey* which went missing in the upset of George's moving from Galway to Cambridge in 1934. It is to be hoped that this translation, which would be an important accession to Irish literature, will turn up eventually. When Colm Luibhéid, Professor of Classics in Galway University, reported the discovery in Galway of an Irish translation of the *Odyssey*, it was hoped it might be George's, but it proved to be the work of Monsignor Pádraig de Brún. George's version would be of unique value, as he planned to have the aid of Maurice O'Sullivan in giving it an authentically Blasket Island character and of Charles Darwin's grand-daughter, the artist Gwen Raverat, in designing suitable illustrations for the text.

'How did George manage to achieve all he did at all?' asked Tim, writing to me on 25 October 1987. 'He was highly thought of in Birmingham if anywhere. Next month he will be commemorated in a concert by the 'Clarion Singers'. They have planned an excellent programme in honour of Katharine as well because she has been participating in the Clarion performances for a very long time. Furthermore there is a prospect that a young classical scholar will do a Ph.D. on the subject of George's work and that a biography will ensue. We shall see. It is a good thing that Katharine has been constantly occupied in that regard. It is true that George would not be able to accomplish all he did without Katharine's sympathy and support for his work and her perfect understanding in relation to it as well. You probably know that Katharine herself obtained first class honours in the Classics in Cambridge. Following that she studied music in Germany.'

The distinguished Irish author Risteárd Ó Glaisne and Tim were fellow students in Trinity College Dublin and kept in touch by correspondence. Risteárd would send him his books as published, 'the most recent one on the splendid Gael, Cardinal Tomás Ó Fiaich. Like the Craoibhín [Douglas Hyde] – another Protestant – Risteárd has done Trojan work these many years for the language' (19 March 1991) and Tim admired Risteárd's biography of Douglas Hyde for its wealth of information and general excellence.

He lamented the link with the Blaskets broken by the death of Mrs. Cáit Mulkerrins, widow of Maurice O'Sullivan. After Maurice's death she left for England to find work and settled in Bradford where she met and married her second husband Pádraig Mulkerrins from Connemara. Tim who was at their wedding in 1955 wrote a touching obituary of her for the Cork *Evening Echo* (19. vii. 1990) in which he recalled 'Her strong voice which soared into sweetness [and] brought to mind the bare rocky land of Connemara and, at the same time, Paul Henry's beautiful paintings of that landscape'.

In a letter of 9 July 1991 Tim told me he had no plans to go to Ireland that year, since recently he had not been well, but that he had every hope to be on his ancestral soil the following year for the opening of the Blasket National Park. With his family he used visit the historic city of Whitby, of Celtic association, on the Yorkshire coast, from where he would send me postcards. 'But of course my usual place of abode is Kerry, especially the Western Island. Now my mind is travelling away back on the little road of thought because I am leisurely reading Maidhc Dainín Ó Sé's *Tae le Tae* and I take great delight in it, as my thoughts go back to the '40s when I used make the journey west year after year to Corkaguiney, as a servant boy! for James Moriarty'.

This letter touched a chord. For James Moriarty was my cousin and next door neighbour in my native village of Ballyferriter. Jameseen, as he was familiarly known, had unusual qualities of character and intelligence inherited from a family that had in its generations given priests and nuns to the American and Australian missions. His grandfather Tomás was a scribe and collector of Irish books and manuscripts, some of which I remember were treasured in his house. In the middle of the last century Tomás took a cow from his herd and drove her in the early hours of the morning the eight miles of road to the fair of Dingle where he sold her. With the proceeds he bought in the nearby village of Ventry the seven volumes of *The Annals of the Kingdom of Ireland*, a much prized work of Irish history and genealogy recently edited by the Irish scholar John O'Donovan. From this episode he was called Tomás na Bó, Tomás of the Cow. Jameseen, who derived much of his character and imagination from this grandfather, took a delight in the nuances of the Irish language in which he was a master, as well as in the wonders of science and of the firmament and would spend hours of the day in discussing them, in a field or by the fireside.

Jameseen had spent some years in Chicago where he met and married Margaret (Mag) Kennedy from Baile Móir in a neighbouring parish. She was a charming and hospitable hostess in their Ballyferriter home. Jameseen farmed a holding of some 50 or 60 acres on which Tim worked along with him in summertime. 'Work!' wrote Tim. 'A ten year old boy would do as much in one day as we used do in a week. Jameseen was the Professor, I the student listening to him, as I told you before. At night we would have other company – Seán de hÓra, Séamas Mac Gearailt (Séamas na Jackies), Seán Ó Cinnéide (now Professor of Chemistry) and the other lads – the crack, songs, music, dance. No wonder I cannot forget those days!'

It is probably safe to say that the nightly gatherings took place in Dónall Ó Catháin's tavern in Ballyferriter, a favourite rendezvous of discussion, gaiety and kitchen dancing. Seán de hÓra was a traditional singer of quality, Séamas Mac Gearailt was noted for his ready wit and repartee, Seán Ó Cinnéide, formerly on the staff of Harwell, was Professor of Chemistry in Galway University and author of massive textbooks who would be appealed to by Jameseen to solve some question of atomic energy or physics. In this congenial environment Tim was immensely happy. Just as he was in the Wellington pub in Halifax with his colleagues of the 68 Club, in more serious vein perhaps, as he would expound his thoughts on politics and society and the betterment of humanity.

He loved the great classical authors as he did the rich literature of the West Kerry Gaeltacht and would compare them text with text. He would recall that Macaulay praised Book 7 of Thucydides as the finest work of prose he ever read and would contrast Thucydides' text with Tomás O'Crohan's *Islandman* as a comparable example of style and powerful compression. He marvelled at the constant flow of literature from the rockbound Blasket region. He had looked forward ever so eagerly to being present at the official opening of the Blasket Heritage Centre. Sadly, death came to him too early, after a sudden brief illness, at the Halifax Royal Infirmary, on 7 December 1993. He was aged 67. Tim was favoured by nature with the happy gift of friendship. His hosts of friends will mourn him. So will the underprivileged whose fearless advocate he was. The loss to his family, whom he deeply loved, is irreparable.

Tim was by conscience a humanist and his funeral, on 14 December 1993, was a secular one. It took place at the Co-operative Chapel of Repose, Clare Road, Halifax, followed by cremation at Parkwood, Elland. Tributes were paid at the funeral service to his lifelong struggle for justice to the exploited and oppressed. The integrity of his life was celebrated in his favourite music, Beethoven, in Mozart's lovely *Eine kleine Nachtmusik* and the traditional Irish strains of the Chieftains. The Birmingham *Morning Star* carried tributes from his loyal friends Elizabeth and Ron Ogden and family (13 December 1993) and from the family of his special associate and friend George Thomson which reads:

In memory of our dear friend and comrade Tim Enright, Marxist, scholar, fighter against oppression. He was a noble person, he loved the people.
Katherine, Lis, Dimitris and Family (14 Dec. 1994).

References

1.   This tragedy is related by James Quinn in *The Story of the Drumboe Martyrs*, printed in Letterkenny [1956?] The execution took place on 14 March 1923 of Charlie Daly, Seán Larkin, Tim O'Sullivan and Daniel Enright. Daniel Enright's last letters to his mother and brother are printed on pp. 50-53. A memorial to their memory erected in Drumboe in 1956 brought a characteristic letter from Tim Enright, pp. 7-10 in support of their republican convictions and in appreciation of the memorial. It is dated at Halifax, Yorkshire, January 1956.

John Robb (photograph courtesy of Colm Ó Torna).

Chapter 12

The present position of the Irish language (1995)

Language is not just a method of communication; it is the repository of values, interpretation, ways of looking at things, the means of storing in an appropriately unique manner the heritage of a people. Language is precious and necessary if we are to preserve the diversity on which man's social as well as his biological and psychological survival is so dependent. This has never been more true than today. The right of people to be different must ensure the right of people to preserve and use the means of communicating the colour and nuances of life which are unique to them. With our ancient language, the very rocks come alive through their descriptive names. The stories light up with new dimension in their telling.

John Robb
in *The Irish Times*
16 September 1988[1a]

Historical

Ireland is facing a crisis. Not of trade, finance or economics, or anything so mundane, but of language. Her native tongue, the Celtic language spoken throughout the island for two thousand or more years, has its back, literally, to the Atlantic and is holding on as a vernacular in fragments of land on the western coast. The same era that saw the sack of Rome by the Celtic armies in 390 B.C. witnessed the invasion of Ireland by Celtic forces speaking a cognate tongue with the invaders of Rome. Ever since 52 B.C., when the Celtic nation of Gaul, under its chieftain Vercingétorix, challenged the might of Rome under Julius Caesar in final conflict, on the uplands of Alesia, and failed, the Celtic tongues have been fighting a rearguard action. Gaul became thoroughly Romanised, even though pockets of Celtic speech survived there until the fourth century, as noted by Sulpicius Severus (363-425).

Insular Celtic survived, in Britain but more notably in Ireland where it was reinforced by a developing and highly significant literature which continued to flourish. In 1601, at Kinsale on the south Irish coast, the expansionist Elizabethan power, ruthless as Rome, overcame the Irish forces under their chieftain Hugh O'Neill, island successor to Vercingétorix. The parallel with Celtic Gaul is striking. Thereafter, English administration was imposed and the development of the Irish language was stifled. Outlawed from education and denied the printing press, its position in mid-17th century is thus outlined by the Earl of Longford, translator of Irish Bardic poetry:

> In Irish Bardic poems we see reflected the life of mediaeval and renaissance Ireland. We find here the expression of a culture cut short just as it was about to expand under the influences that made the literature of the modern world. We find in them not only the ancient Gaelic tradition, but constant reminiscences of the classics, of mediaeval Latin literature and of the contemporary writers of England and the Continent. All this is finally wiped out by the devastating wars of Elizabeth's and Cromwell's days: a unique culture, as interesting in its potentialities as in its achievements, goes down without reaching its fulfilment; and the last of the bards sing of its ruin, before they die and leave no heirs. Most of what follows is folksong and artificial revival.[1]

Regression

The all but total change of language from Irish to English continued apace during the 19th century. In 1801, the unrepresentative Irish Parliament, the language of which was English, became merged by the Act of Union with that of Westminster. With the passing of Catholic emancipation in 1829 the Westminster parliament, thenceforward open to Catholics, became the centre of political attention for the emerging Irish democracy under Daniel O'Connell and ability in English became the essential passport for parliamentary and professional success, besides carrying the stamp of prestige. O'Connell, whose maternal tongue was Irish and who was educated in France, used his formidable command of English as the vehicle of communication to great popular gatherings. The process was continued under later national leaders like Parnell. Many of the great statements of Irish patriotism were henceforth in English, culminating in the striking Proclamation of 1916 which became the central document of modern Irish nationality.

The Education Act of 1831 established English as the sole medium of instruction in the national schools while Irish was penalised. Weekly and daily papers used English exclusively. The Great Famine of 1847 had a disastrous effect on the Irish language since it ravaged chiefly the poorer western regions where Irish was mainly spoken. Pre-famine Ireland had a probable population of 8,500,000 in 1845. By the Census of 1851 it was reduced to 6,552,365 of whom 319,602 are returned as speaking Irish only; 1,204,684 spoke Irish and English.[2] Large-scale emigration from the stricken western areas hastened the attenuation of the language. The tragedy is recorded in passionate verse by Francesca Lady Wilde in her poem *The Exodus:*

> *'A Million a decade!' Calmly and cold*
> *The units are read by our statesmen sage;*
> *Little they think of a Nation old,*
> *Fading away from history's page;*
> *Outcast weeds by a desolate sea –*
> *Fallen leaves of humanity.*[3]

Linguistic maps and statistics of the 19th century show the steady progression westward across the country of the English language and the corresponding contraction of Irish.[4] It seemed as if the shadows were finally closing in on the language when an event occurred which promised to reverse the disastrous process and guarantee it a fresh lease of life.

The Gaelic League 1893-1993

This was the foundation in 1893 of the Gaelic League which last year celebrated 100 years of its existence. It was inaugurated in Dublin by a group of idealists who included Douglas Hyde and Eoin MacNeill 'to preserve and spread the Gaelic language in Ireland'. At that time Irish was spoken by nearly 700,000 persons and was the language of 100,000 Irish homes, but the number speaking it was diminishing at the rate of 20,000 a year.[5]

The success of the Gaelic League went far beyond the hopes of its founders. It did not take the shape they seemed to envisage for it, namely, to keep the language in its strength on the western perimeter where it was spoken. The League spread and took effect in the *English*-speaking parts of Ireland, where it called up feelings that Sir Horace Plunkett described as 'sentiments and thoughts which had been developed in Gaelic Ireland through hundreds of years, which no repression had obliterated entirely, but which remained a latent spiritual inheritance in the mind'.[6]

The time was favourable. Political life and prospects were moribund following Parnell's death in 1891 and it would seem that the lacuna in public interest called for something that was uplifting and idealist. The Gaelic League gathered strength and support. As Kuno Meyer observed in 1903, it was one of the most remarkable and unexpected movements of the time, 'one of those almost elemental phenomena, the suddenness and force of which seemed to carry everything before it,' the object at stake being nothing less than 'the salvation of a nationality at the eleventh hour'.[7]

Some idea of the progress and influence of the Gaelic League may be gleaned from what the distinguished Orientalist, Stanley Edward Lane-Poole, had to say, writing in the *Fortnightly Review* in June 1907:

> ... no one who has lived in Ireland of late is under any illusion about the vitality of Gaelic. Whatever it was ten years ago, it is very much alive now. One might fill pages with statistics but they are needless. Anyone who knows Ireland is fully aware that at this moment there is no question which is exciting the intelligence of the people more than this question of the language. You see Gaelic inscriptions over the shops, Gaelic on the street labels, Gaelic in advertisements, a Gaelic column in newspapers ... The Gaelic League is everywhere, and on 'Language Day' in Dublin, when the disciples of the Irish tongue march in their thousands with Gaelic banners and strange devices, the main streets at some points are almost impassable ... The fact remains that Irish boys and girls and their teachers as a rule do not care a fig for French or German, but they do care a great deal for Irish. They want to learn Irish, as they want no other language on earth ... They want it because it contains their national literature.[8]

Writing a few years earlier, Frederick York Powell, Professor of Modern History in the University of Oxford, could envisage a future in which the influence of Irish literature would shape what was characteristic and best in Irish writing to come:

> ... there is one thing I am confident about, and that is that the very best that Irishmen have been able to do in English is necessarily inferior to what Irishmen have done in Irish. The greatest names in Irish literature in the future, when we can judge better of it than we can today, will be the names of persons very little known at present, even to the majority of people of Irish blood and Irish names. This points to the fact that the first study of literary importance for an Irishman is the real Irish literature. It is only from the real Irish literature that the Irishman can draw the inspiration which differentiates him and makes his impress on literature really peculiar and valuable.[9]

The foregoing statements by outstanding scholars, neither of them nationalist, give some idea of the intense enthusiasm and support for the language in the full tide of the Gaelic League movement.

Independence and State Policy

With the establishment of political independence in 1922, the revival of the Irish language became state policy and the language was given explicit national recognition in the Constitution. Henri Hubert, in his great history of the Celts, voiced a general hope when saying 'C'est l'État irlandais qui sauvera la langue'.[10] Many of the political leaders active in government had been members of the Gaelic League and Douglas Hyde in his writings traced the foundation of Dáil Éireann, the Irish parliament, back to the League's influence.[11] Eoin MacNeill, who had called the League into being, became Minister for Education and declared his full support for the revival of the language. But the most resolute and unbending champion of the language in government, and the real architect of language policy, was a North of Ireland Presbyterian, Ernest Blythe. He it was who modelled state policy in favour of the language and was the author of the many measures introduced to establish it as a significant element in Irish education, promoting all-Irish elementary and secondary schools, the Gaelicisation of Galway University, the provision of scholarships for Gaeltacht students and a pool of fluent Irish-speaking entrants to the teacher-training colleges who on qualifying would strengthen and promote the language in the national schools, and many other measures helpful to the language.

The momentum he created was not sustained. Conservative elements within the key public departments of Education and Finance were critical and dismissive of the measures adopted. The Preparatory Colleges, which were pivotal to success, were closed, one in 1939, the rest in 1961, marking a strangely retrograde step. Uniform effort was not maintained. There was vacillation and incoherence, with different governments taking differing attitudes. An interested American observer, viewing the position in the early sixties, discerned the weaknesses: 'the State has been so slow, so awkward, and so timid in regard to the language that the charge of sit-down sabotage has been made several times against it ... superior officers, out of sympathy with much of the nationalist outlook, were able quietly to impede language progress'.[12] The official steps taken for the advancement of Irish in the educational system during the first 60 years of independence and the factors that impeded them are detailed in an impressive study by Dr. Séamus Ó Buachalla, Professor of Comparative Education in Trinity College Dublin and former schools inspector.[13]

Vernacular Irish in the early 1950s. 'The ruins of a language.'

In 1958 the Dublin School of Celtic Studies published the first of four volumes of a comprehensive survey of Irish dialects made in 1949 and the following years. It was the work of Dr. Heinrich Wagner, Professor of German in the University of Basel and a pupil of the Celtic scholar Julius Pokorny. Although he approached his task with a sympathetic mind, Dr. Wagner produced an objective and clinical report, the accuracy of which gave small comfort to those committed to reviving the language. In his investigations he was concerned only with the areas in which Irish was the everyday tongue of the community. He wrote:

> There is no place in Ireland where English is not now understood by the majority of adults; monoglots, apart from small children, have become extremely rare ... My main problem was to find out where native Irish was still available. Irish is rapidly dying out everywhere despite having been fostered strongly by Irish governments. There is no Irish left in the province of Leinster ... We are not dealing with a language spoken over a wide area, but rather with the ruins of a language. We compare our work with the archaeologist's task of reconstructing an old building from a few heaps of stones, lying here and there in the place where the original building stood ... The change of civilisation ... taking place since the first world war, has brought the final decline of the language and the victory of English even in the last strongholds of this Celtic language.[14]

Wagner learned Irish in Dunquin, the only parish in the southwest of Ireland where it was a firmly based community language. A patriarchal figure of the same parish, noted for his poetical speech, when asked how stood the language in Dunquin, replied, 'My friend, there is the height of the gable-end of grass growing over the best of the Irish language.'[15]

On the other hand, the position of acquired Irish, as learned at school and college by thousands of young people, might reasonably be called encouraging, although the difficulty persisted of linking school-Irish with the post-school world where the universal language was English. Writing in 1963, Eoin MacKiernan was impressed by the overall result: 'Nevertheless, the achievement is unparalleled. Virtually every person under 30 has a reasonable ability in Irish – and it is beyond belief, almost, that thousands have attained an absolute bilingualism.'[16]

Following independence, successive governments integrated the language firmly into the educational system, making it essential for public examinations and entry into the Civil Service. But the legislators who did this notoriously exempted themselves from the requirement, marking the contrast, for example, between the meagre pay, barely sufficient to keep body and soul together, of the humble Writing Assistant, and the amply remunerated Dáil Deputy, Minister, Senator, director of semi-state bodies and other well-paid official posts, whose occupants might have been expected to give the example, a circumstance that was not lost on the public and generated no little comment and cynicism. As a general comment on the present status of Irish in Dáil Éireann, it is legitimate to say that a legislature which does not consider it worthwhile to record in Irish any more than two per cent annually of its discussions has already conceded defeat. Among the nation's elected representatives surely the reaction should be one of dismay.

Critical Voices

The Marxist scholar George Thomson, who taught Greek through Irish in Galway University, and cooperated with Ernest Blythe in his policy, was a strong critic of Irish government attitudes to the language. Having achieved political autonomy, he contended, and got what they wanted, they set their face against further change. The Irish language and literature became a means of turning the eyes of the people away from their future to their past, weakening its value as a progressive force.[17] In recent years the position of Irish has come under searching discussion in the wake of two publications which survey it critically. One is in English, a substantial study, replete with statistics, entitled *The death of the Irish Language,* but subtitled, *A qualified obituary.*[18] The author, Reg Hindley, a geographer in the University of Bradford, has dedicated the volume 'To those who work to keep Irish a living language'. An honest appraisal, it carries no message of cheer, its general import, supported by an array of figures, being that the spoken tongue, in the *Gaeltacht,* faces inevitable extinction, a consummation which its author would sincerely regret, but to which he would seem to have conditioned his mind.

The other publication, in Irish, is the work of a distinguished bilingual writer, Breandán Ó hEithir, novelist and long-time journalist, a native of the cliffbound Irish-speaking Aranmore Island. Prompted evidently by the publication of Reg Hindley's study, Bord na Gaeilge (The Irish Language Board) asked him to report on the position of the language and make recommendations for its promotion. Ó hEithir had a lifetime association with the Irish language movement and his report has the character of a philippic. In acidulous, cutting commentary he estimates the actual number of native speakers of the language at about 10,000, like Hindley, equal to the attendance at a county football final and hardly greater than the present membership of the British

Communist Party. 'You are counting houses at this point.' He scarifies the State attitude as being neutral, indifferent or covertly hostile and recommends for the promotion of the language a carefully planned co-ordination of all bodies and elements in its favour.[19] There are those committed to the language who thought his criticisms too harsh, and he may well have been motivated by the wish to awaken public opinion to the desperate position of the language.

Reg Hindley's book drew a vigorous and well-reasoned reply, *Buried Alive*, a 28-page pamphlet[20] written by Éamon Ó Ciosáin, a lecturer in French and scholar in Breton. Challenging the 'death-theme' of Hindley, he strongly denies the objectivity claimed for his book and argues that its methodology is inconsistent and its picture incomplete. The author typifies the fierce resilience of the youthful pro-Irish elements.

Intellectual debate

Hindley's book drew forth echoes. In a documentary film of unusual interest shown on Irish national television on 3 December 1990 and on the BBC 'Bookmark' programme on 9 January 1991, the precarious position of Irish was brought visually and dramatically into national focus. It was seen as confirming Hindley's thesis. The documentary, 'One fond embrace', centred on the career of Thomas Kinsella, a leading poet who writes in English, but is influenced by Irish literature from which he has translated extensively and who has been described as a poet between two traditions. In so far as it pertained to the Irish language, the message of the film was one which recognised its quality and lamented its loss. A series of linguistic maps flashed on the screen showed how its position as a nation-wide speech had progressively declined to its present-day position of occupying fragmented and scattered footholds on the Atlantic coast. As an exposition of Thomas Kinsella's views, that he is obliged by his environment as a Dubliner to choose English, the programme was brilliant and instructive. For the Irish language by contrast it was permeated with the sense of impending loss, discontinuity, fractured tradition, and the note of defeat. To the viewers committed to the future of the language, it came like a shock. The import of the programme was immediately challenged by the Irish poet Gabriel Rosenstock who rejected Kinsella's suggestion that the Irish language no longer ranked as a vehicle of literature, asking who were those people who won literary prizes every year at the Oireachtas festival for stage, TV and radio drama, for criticism, poetry, translation, novels, stories and the rest, a valid rejoinder considering that more than 60 books in Irish were published in a good year (*Irish Times* 11 Dec 1990).[21] To this might be added the claim that the most distinguished verse contributed to the current literary scene is the work in Irish of poetess Nuala Ní Dhomhnaill.

Although critics contend that what is happening in Kinsella's context is a fusion of cultures, this is literally, and linguistically, untrue. To the argument that Irish was a source from which writers of English might draw inspiration for their work, Ernest Blythe contended that such a development would become exhausted with time and the process of becoming integrated with, and indistinguishable from, mainstream English literature, was inevitable. In a closely argued essay on the significance of the Irish language for the future of the Nation[22] he wrote: 'I believe that if the language were to be allowed to perish as a living speech, there could be no possible future for the Irish Nation, as such ... What is questionable is whether the Irish people of the future will merely be that section of the British people which happens to reside in the western island or whether they will constitute a distinct Nation'.[23]

To believers in the future of the Irish language such a possibility would bring into vision the nightmare of the 17th century Irish poet, 'New Saxonland called Ireland.'[24]

The climate which was in being in Stanley Lane-Poole's time has changed and many issues that were then important have folded down into the pages of history. This does not alter the fact that the Irish language is of supreme importance amongst the title-deeds of the modern Irish state. The entire Irish community, through the political agency of the United Irish League, fought hard and successfully in 1909 to have the Irish language made essential for entry into the newly-created National University. It remains essential to the present day. But recent voices have been heard to decry this position and to challenge it. There is a body of thought which regards the Irish language as a relic of a past age which has no present-day relevance and argues that lingual requirements must be geared to the commercial importance of the major European tongues. Eight decades have passed since their materialist precursors were anathemised by the national philosopher, Arthur Griffith, for claiming a stand in the market place at the expense of the Irish language.

Professor Aidan Moran, Registrar of University College Cork, made a strong protest against the trend which would reduce or ignore the language requirement for university entry:

> It is no longer possible to ignore what is happening. If it has been decided that Irish should progressively disappear from our educational system and die from the top down, it must not happen quietly. The truth needs to be spoken and the issue

publicly addressed. The State must be asked to define its policy with regard to the Irish language, and to Irish culture in general, in the educational system: it cannot be allowed to pretend to be unaware of the issue or to wash its hands of responsibility for it.

And by the State one ultimately means the Irish people who, though now unable perhaps to repossess the language, must still decide what it is they do want for themselves and their children by way of identity and how they might achieve it.[25]

The national teachers of Ireland, who labour in the country's primary schools, have been in the front line of battle for the language revival. The latest issue of their organisation's education magazine, in its editorial and other contributions, voices the anxieties, questionings and difficulties facing the profession in its task. Whereas previously the aim was for literacy, the aim now is for oral proficiency, but the teachers have not been provided with the modern technology which is necessary to this purpose. 'Gaeilge (Irish)', states the editorial, 'is at the very core of our cultural heritage but outside the culture set of the vast majority of our pupils ... As educationalists we know that the language must be presented in an interesting and effective way.' To this end resources, materials and equipment were urgently needed. The magazine contains contrasting views on the teaching of Irish, many of them favourable and helpful.[26]

Identity

The debate on 'identity', which has been in progress for years, must be of a character unique to Ireland. It has been discussed at length in periodicals, some of which, like *The Crane Bag*, are defunct, others, like *The Irish Review*, in progress. Writers and philosophers have contributed to it at large and its solution occupies them mightily. It is virtually related to the threatened diminution or demise of the Irish language and the absence of a substitute. It is discussed only by writers of English who appear to be at their wits' end in their search for a definition that seems to take the shape of a pluralised amalgam. Writers of Irish do not discuss it. They never mention it for they have no need. It is inherent in the language they write. *Bord na Gaeilge*, while admitting there are few if any obvious pragmatic reasons for maintaining the language, suggests that the Irish language has an integrating and stimulating role to play in refurbishing Irish identity and providing a sense of confidence in our uniqueness within a polyethnic Europe.[27]

Rays of Hope

In spite of all the necrological predictions, and in flat defiance of the statistics, there are positive and heartening circumstances in favour of the language. Amongst these can be mentioned a substantial background of popular support and sympathy as indicated by the public-opinion polls; the successful project of Raidio na Gaeltachta which caters primarily for the western Irish-speaking areas but has a much wider audience, presenting a full range of material, news, music, commentary, sport including coverage of the British soccer results, and discussion of all current problems; a lively and vibrant modern literature, novels, poetry, history, children's books and translations.

Publishing in Irish has expanded significantly, with private publishers taking the initiative and competing with the Government Publications Office, *An Gúm*. Over 120 new titles are now published yearly, the standard and variety of which reflect an improvement, according to *Áis*, the distributing agency for Irish books, stating the position in 1993. This is in contrast with a figure of 30 titles a year ten years previously. They receive little publicity, being for the most part ignored by the media. Poetry output is phenomenal. There is much poetic translation from the other Community languages, stemming from Ireland's membership of the European Union.

The support for the language of the President, Mary Robinson, is a factor of exceptional encouragement. She gives a lead by spirit and example. In her message to mark the 100th anniversary of the Gaelic League she said:

> In my address to the Oireachtas[28] I made reference back to that mysterious point of time at which a nation comes into being. I stated that the Irish language was interwoven with that event and that it is always the symbol and distinguishing mark of our nationality … Let us also take support and courage for Irish and for the culture enshrined in it from the varieties of language cultures in Europe. The success of the Gaelic League since its inception one hundred years ago has been great. Let that splendid beginning give us courage and inspiration to compose strategies which will be imaginative, suitable and effective to build on the firm foundation laid down for us by the League's founders.[29]

Gaelscoileanna

A remarkable source of optimism for the future of the language is the rise of *Gaelscoileanna*, that is to say, schools where Irish is the language of instruction and communication among teachers, children and management. Since 1973 a voluntary organisation, the National Committee of All-Irish Schools, has operated. In the last twenty years, 81 all-Irish primary schools have been opened in cities and towns throughout Ireland, outside of Gaeltacht areas. At the beginning of the 1993-94 school year there were 24 second-level all-Irish schools functioning outside Gaeltacht areas.[30] It is a mark of their growth that in October 1993 fourteen more Gaelscoileanna opened their doors for the first time, eight primary and six secondary.

Tributes to the high standard of education in these schools come from people in different walks of public life, politicians, radio and TV personalities, actors and singers.[31] The growth of Gaelscoileanna has been significant over the last ten years and shows every sign of increasing. The encouraging factor about it is that this movement comes up from the people and owes no part of its origin to official or state action. Some of the most successful of these schools have been established in suburban areas of Dublin City that are anything but élitist and in actual fact disadvantaged, like Ballymun, where in the local all-Irish school '250 little children, each more spotless than the next in their neat uniforms, played and studied in the language of their forebears. As the free choice of their parents.'[32] When the school could take no more, a second all-Irish school was opened. 'Parents who couldn't get their kids in there could have sent them to one of the excellent local English-language schools. But they wouldn't. Rather than educate them through English, they raised money and borrowed a site and got a teacher themselves.'[33]

The literary background
The sheet-anchor of the Irish language is its literature, the manuscript tradition of which goes back to the sixth century. This is a robust and vital creation. For centuries consigned to manuscript, denied the printing press, it circulated in copies handwritten by scribes. From the middle of the 19th century it began to be published to the learned world. Its great treasures were edited and printed by European philologists, mainly German, during the latter quarter of the 19th century and the early decades of the 20th. The early Irish epic tale, *Táin Bó Cualgne*, was edited by Ernst Windisch, who wrote of it 'Irland darf stolz sein auf seine alte Heldensage'.

Stephen MacKenna, the translator of the *Enneads* of Plotinus, in a review of an anthology of Irish love poetry rescued from the manuscripts, wrote in 1916:

> ... our Irish literature will not die but will, rather, come to a vigorous, an immortal new life.
> Irish literature has entered into the purview of world-wide scholarship; it will never be forgotten again; it will live as long as the Greek literature, as long as the Hebrew; Anthropology,

Comparative Religion, History, Philosophy, a score of sciences, will know it for ever; and the purely artistic sense will, here and there at the very least, find, during centuries to come, the matter of a high pleasure in what was so long despised and might so easily have utterly perished in a general illiterate contempt. In ages to come and in many countries speaking in many dialects, there will be found students lingering with delight over passages here and there of Irish verse and prose savoured for their beauty or wit or depth, if only as chance cups of wine unexpectedly refreshing the pilgrim as he plods the dusty roads of exact scholarship ... In the peculiar position of our land and language to-day our scholars are doing a greater service – to art no less than to knowledge – than any poet, unless an Aeschylus or a Dante – could do.[34]

Present-day efforts are underwritten by a great past. The essays in building a modern Irish literature appeal to a proud and sustaining history.

In 1899 Douglas Hyde dedicated his *Literary History of Ireland* to the members of the recently founded Gaelic League, 'the only body in Ireland which seeks to render the present a rational continuation of the past'. ... Stephen MacKenna in 1916 saw signs that 'the language of Ireland through all her days even until today, may still be saved alive ... by a fire in the heart of the people'.[35] This fire is imponderable. It is youthful and resilient. It is resonant in the playgrounds of Ballymun and Clondalkin on Dublin City's perimeter.

Political Awakening?

There is a hopeful awakening on the political front. Too often in the past it has been the custom of governments to delegate promotion of the language to an individual member, while the remainder averted their eyes from responsibility. In a document headed *Programme for a Partnership Government 1993-1994, Fostering our Language, Culture and Heritage*, the Minister for Arts, Culture and the Gaeltacht, Michael D. Higgins, set out guidelines for the support and progress of the language. The document states (p.5) that

the Irish language has an integral and creative role to play in defining Irish identity. We accept that the state must play a leading role in expanding the degree of bilingualism in Irish society and, in particular, in achieving greater usage in Irish.

One of the projects planned is the establishment of an Irish

Television Service – Telefís na Gaeilge – with limited broadcasting hours. The document goes on to say (p.6) 'The linguistic, cultural, social, physical and economic development of the Gaeltacht will be intensified, particularly with the aid of EC Structural Funds'. As representing the combined policy of two major parties in Dáil Éireann, this is a studied and elaborate plan. It will be watched with keen interest, given that it is not without precedent. At the launching of a history of the Gaelic League in the Yeats Room of the Mont Clare Hotel, Dublin, on 13 December 1993, the Minister gave an undertaking that Telefís na Gaeilge would be operative in 1995.[36]

The views of the Irish-speaking community were reflected in a leading article in a national daily[37] that the Government's much delayed decision was welcome not least because it marked a significant development in public service broadcasting at a time of what might be described as cultural invasion. It pointed out the overwhelming dominance in Europe of American-made television programmes and videos, which are causing concern to European ministers of culture. 'Telefís na Gaeilge arrives at a crucial time for the Irish language. In many parts of the Gaeltacht it has gone into serious, perhaps terminal, decline. The next 20 years should decide once and for all whether it is to survive as a living language. This places a heavy burden of responsibility on the generation which at present holds power; its indifference or neglect could easily snuff out the last chances of survival.'

So the debate, re-appraisal and soul-searching continues. The next twenty years? The statistics are grim. Population 3,500,000. Cushion of popular support for the language, which could include those with minimal to fair to good knowledge of it, slightly over 1,000,000. Actual number of habitual speakers in Gaeltacht areas, between ten and twenty thousand. The figures are approximate.

And the imponderables? A fierce attachment to the Gaelic psyche. The Will of a Nation? 'As if by fire' – the phrase is Stephen MacKenna's. The resilience of the Gael? In its centenary year the spokesmen of the Gaelic League predicted that the language would flourish in its strength to its second centenary, and there was no note of pessimism or defeat. *Utinam fiat* will be the prayer of many. Is human effort equal to the task? The drama goes on. The fate of a language over two thousand years old, carrying the history of a nation in its literature, is in the balance. The curtain is suspended. It may not fall.

References
1a.   For John Robb see *Saol* (Iúil 1999) 14.

1. The Earl of Longford: *More poems from the Irish* (Dublin and Oxford 1945) Introduction IX-X.

2. T.W. Freeman: *Pre-Famine Ireland. A study in historical geography.* (Manchester University Press 1957) 13,138-9.

3. Reprinted in John Cooke (ed.) *The Dublin Book of Irish Verse 1728-1909* (Dublin and London 1909) 324-6. The author was Oscar Wilde's mother.

4. Cf. Brian Ó Cuív (ed.) *A view of the Irish Language* (Dublin 1969) 137-140; Máirtín Ó Murchú: *The Irish Language* (Dublin 1985) 26 *et seq.* – '19th century Havoc' with maps and statistics; Garret Fitzgerald, statistician and former Taoiseach: 'Estimates for baronies of minimum level of Irish-speaking amongst successive decennial cohorts:1779-1781 to 1861-1871' in *Proceedings* of the Royal Irish Academy (Dublin 1984) Vol. 84. The figures indicate a decline amongst younger Irish speakers, greatest in eastern and central counties.

5. The plan and objects of the Gaelic League were outlined in Irish and English in *The Gaelic Journal* (Dublin, March 1893). The actual figures for Irish speakers, by Census of 1891 were:
    Irish only   38,120
    Total Irish speakers   680,174

6. Sir Horace Plunkett: *Ireland in the new century* (London 1905) 153.

7. *Celtia* (Dublin) May-June 1903.

8. Stanley Edward Lane-Poole (1854-1931). Orientalist and historian. Educated Corpus Christi College Oxford. Prepared the *Catalogue of Oriental and Indian Coins in the British Museum* (14 vols.) 1875-92. Professor of Arabic in Trinity College Dublin 1898-1904. Prolific writer. It might be noted that at the present time, with the influence and requirements of the European Union, instruction in French and German and other Community languages is eagerly pursued in Ireland.

9. Oliver Elton: *Frederick York Powell. A Life and a selection from his letters.* 2 vols. I. *Memoir and letters.* II *Occasional Writings.* Oxford 1906. The quotation is from Vol. II 'Irish influence on our literature' p.301. York Powell (1850-1904) was born in London and educated in Oxford, where he became Professor of Modern History, 1894-1904. He wrote important studies in English history. An outstanding Scandinavian scholar, he helped to edit the *Corpus Poeticum Boreale* (1881).

10. *Les Celtes et la civilisation celtique depuis l'époque de La Tène.* (Éditions Albin Michel 1974) 294. Reprint from 1932.

11. Douglas Hyde: 'Who were those who sat in the first Dáil? They were the children of Sinn Féin. Who were Sinn Féin? They were practically all children of the Gaelic League'. *Mise agus an Connradh* (Myself and the League). Dublin 1937. Foreword p.5. Writer's translation from the Irish.

12. Eoin MacKiernan: *The will of a nation. Ireland's crisis* (Butler Family Foundation – Saint Paul, Minnesota 1963) 9. The author was Professor of English at the College of St. Thomas, Saint Paul, Minnesota.

13. *Education policy in twentieth century Ireland* (Dublin 1988). Cf. especially pp. 341-356 regarding the Irish language. Also, by the same author, 'Polasaí teanga an Stáit' (State language policy) *Irish Times* 12 August 1986, on the support of Ernest Blythe for the language.

14. Heinrich Wagner: *Linguistic atlas and survey of Irish Dialects* (Dublin 1958) Introduction IX-X.

15. Pádraig Ua Maoileoin: *Na hAird Ó Thuaidh* (Dublin 1960) 111.

16. *The will of a nation. Ireland's crisis* 6. That there was a high level of competency in the early 1940s is the experience of the present writer, who taught in a

commercial, non-state, college in Dublin between 1941 and 1943. The college prepared students for matriculation and civil service entrance examinations and instruction included evening classes. Many of the students had been to all-Irish schools and proficiency was remarkably high. Debating classes in Irish and English were formed on the students' own initiative.

17. George Thomson: 'The Irish Language Revival' *Yorkshire Celtic Studies III*, Transactions 1940-46 p.9.

18. Published London and New York 1990. Reprinted 1991.

19. The text, dated June 1990, 'Report on the present position of Irish' (translation) is printed in the Irish language monthly *Combar* June 1991 pp 6-16.

20. Published Dublin 1991.

21. Gabriel Rosenstock's protest has become an annual event. Writing to the *Irish Times* again on 5 January 1994 he takes a contributor to task for ignoring in her 1993 literary survey the hundred-odd Irish language titles published during the year and denounces 'this insidious form of cultural and linguistic apartheid' of the Irish media.

22. *University Review* (Dublin) Vol. 2. No. 2. (n.d. [1957]) 3-21.

23. *Ibid.* p.3.

24. The Irish poem of which this is the general theme is printed in Thomas F. O'Rahilly: *Measgra Dánta II* (Miscellany of Poems II) Cork University Press, 1927, pp.144-147. Written about 1612.

25. 'Decision time for the Irish language', *Irish Times,* 11 June 1991.

26. *Education today* Spring 1994.

27. *The Irish language in a changing society. Shaping the future. Bord na Gaeilge* (the Irish Language Board), (Dublin n.d. 1988?) XXXIV and p.91.

28. The annual festival of the Gaelic League, at which prizes are awarded for success in literature and drama.

29. Extract from original, in Irish, printed in *Irish Press* (Dublin), *Special Supplement* 30 July 1993. Writer's translation.

30. The primary schools cater for 14,782 pupils, representing 9,746 households. The secondary schools cater for 3,745 pupils, representing 2,758 households. Figures (dated 26.1.1994) courtesy of the Irish Language Board, *Bord na Gaeilge.* Latest figures, for 1996-1997, are: Primary Schools 17,627, representing 11,906 households. Secondary Schools 4,626, representing 3,649 households. Figures supplied by *Bord na Gaeilge,* to whom the writer expresses thanks.

31. *Education and living.* Supplement to *Irish Times,* 5 Oct. 1993.

32. Nuala Ó Faoláin, *Irish Times* 13 Sept. 1993.

33. *Ibid.*

34. *Irish Opinion* (Dublin 15 November 1916) 5.

35. *Ibid.*

36. The history, entitled *Ar son na Gaeilge* (For the Irish language) 464 pp., was written by Proinsias Mac Aonghusa, President of the Gaelic League. Telefís na Gaeilge became operative in 1996. The quality and variety of its programmes have earned widespread appreciation.

37. *Irish Times* 26 November 1993.

A version of the above paper was read to the Translation/Interpretation students of the Johannes Gutenberg-Universität Mainz at Germersheim on 18 May 1995.

Chapter 13

Donn Sigerson Piatt agus an Oidhreacht Úgónach

Bhí aithne agam ar Dhonn Sigerson Piatt le seacht mbliana fichead, ó Dheireadh Fomhair 1943, tráth a ceapadh an bheirt againn ar fhoireann aistriúcháin an Oireachtais. Aon duine riamh dá chomhluadar a chuir aithne ar Dhonn Piatt, d'fhéadfadh sé a rá gur chuir sé aithne ar uaisleacht agus ar ionracas. Fear é a bhí lán de léann, lán freisin de shaontacht chneasta an linbh. Fear é de mhuintir a bhronn tairbhe a n-intleachta, cuid acu ar Éirinn abhus, cuid acu ar Mheiriceá thall.

Ó shinsireacht, agus ó thaobh athar agus máthar, bhí mianach na litríochta i nDonn Sigerson Piatt. Bhí táipéis fhairsing idirnáisiúnta de dhúchas laistiar de, ag sroichint ón bhFrainc go dtí na Stáit Aontaithe go Críoch Lochlann ó thuaidh agus go dtí fóid éagsúla d'oileán na hÉireann. Bhí Donn mórtasach as iolarthacht a phréamhacha agus thug sé tuairisc fhileata air mar a leanas:

> **Fréamhacha**
> Sinsear sin m'athar ón Oileán Úr,
> Tháinig a sinsear sin anoir ón bhFrainc,
> Sinsear mo mháthar ó Thír Eoghain aduaidh
> Is ó Chorcaigh chuanmhar chaoin chois Laoi na Sreabh.
> Dúchas dom tuaisceart fhearúil is deisceart mín,
> Meiriceá thiar is thoir thar muir an Fhrainc,
> Dúchas dom Lochlann bhorb na ngaoth is na sreabh,
> Dauphine ó dheas: ón ithir sin mo dhream.
> Tuaisceart is Deisceart: Eoraip's an Domhan Thiar,
> An Fhrainc ró-mhín, Críoch Lochlann fhuar na bhfear,
> Corcaigh 's Tír Eoghain, Áth Cliath 's an Srath Bán
> Ainmníodh mo dhán mar thiomna uaim anocht.[1]

Muintir Phiatt
De shliocht Úgónach na Fraince ab ea é ó shloinne athar. B'éigean dá shinsear Jean Piatt teitheadh ó ghéarleanúint chun na hOllainne, mar ar

phós sé Frances Wykoff. Chuadarsan ar imirce go dtí na hIndiacha Thiar ar dtús agus d'aistríodar as sin, tuairim 1670 nó roimhe, go mórchríoch Mheiriceá, mar ar lonnaíodar i New Jersey. Shíolraigh uathusan clann agus clann clainne agus áirítear ar a shliocht Donn Piatt (1819-1891), a saolaíodh i Cincinnati, Ohio, an naoú leanbh d'ál deichniúr clainne. Bhain an fear sin ardghradam amach agus bíonn trácht air i stair na Stát.[2]

Col seisir dósan ab ea John James Piatt (1835-1917), fear le cumas filíochta agus iriseoireachta, a saolaíodh in Indiana, agus a bhfuil tagairt mhinic dá shaothar ag Walt Whitman. Phós seisean Sarah Morgan Bryan ó Lexington, Kentucky (1836-1919), banfhile a bhfuil áireamh mór saothair lena hainm agus meas nach beag uirthi sna Stáit, bean leis a raibh sinsireacht spéisiúil aici, sa mhéid go raibh gaol ag a seanathair Morgan Bryan le Daniel Boone.[3]

Sa bhliain 1882, ceapadh John James Piatt ina Chonsal Meiriceánach i gCorcaigh. Ligfimid anseo do Dhonn Piatt leanúint de scéal a shinsear:

M'athair mór ó thaobh m'athar, John James Piatt, an file as Gleann Ohio … tháinig sé go hÉirinn in ochtóidí an chéid seo caite … i dteaghlach mhuintir Piatt, sa Phríóireacht, i gCóbh Chorcaí, thóg John James Piatt agus a bhean Sarah, mo mháthair mhór ó thaobh m'athar, agus file dea-chlú, thógadar lán an tí de mhic agus iníon amháin, Fred, Cecil, Marion, Guy, Victor agus Louis a bádh in aois a naoi mbliana agus é ag bádóireacht i gCuan Chorcaí agus, ar deireadh thiar, an té nach lú tábhacht agamsa, m'athair féin, Arthur Donn Piatt, Leas-Chonsal Mheiriceá i mBaile Átha Cliath ar feadh áireamh maith blianta sula bhfuair sé bás, an 12 Aibreán 1914. Tá a chorp i nGlas Naíon ag feitheamh leis an aiséirí.

Dob í Hester Varian ó Thobar Rí an Domhnaigh mo sheanmháthair ó thaobh mo mháthar … d'éirigh sí suas i gCorcaigh, mar a raibh athair mo mháthar, an Dr. Seoirse Sigerson, ina mhac léinn i gColáiste na Banríona. Scríbhneoirí ab ea iad araon agus spéis acu sna rudaí céanna. Phósadar agus, ar a shon gur aistríodar go Baile Átha Cliath, choinníodar suas an ceangal le Corcaigh, áit a raibh saol bríomhar litríochta agus cultúir ina mbíodh na Meiriceánaigh éirimiúla, muintir Piatt, páirteach.[4]

Saolaíodh beirt iníon do Sheoirse Sigerson agus Hester Varian, Dora agus Hester. Phós Dora an t-iriseoir Sasanach, Clement Shorter. Phós Hester mac de chlann Piatt, Arthur Donn Piatt, sa bhliain 1900. Faoin am sin, bhí glaoite ar ais go Meiriceá ar John James Piatt ag an Uachtarán Grover Cleveland ar an ábhar go raibh sé *persona non grata* ag an mBreatain mar gheall ar a chairdeas le náisiúnaigh na hÉireann.[5] Saolaíodh mac, Donn, agus iníon, Síle, d'Arthur Donn Piatt agus Hester Sigerson.

Bhíodh ceist á cur ag Donn Piatt air féin – cé mhéad atá fágtha den Mheiriceánachas ionam? Cuid mhaith, dhealródh sé. Ag caint liom san oifig lá, thagair sé don mhórshiúl a ghluaiseann gach Lá Fhéile Pádraig trí Fifth Avenue i Nua-Eabhrac agus d'airíos an bród ag nochtadh trína chaint ag trácht dó ar bhrí dhoimhin agus comharthaíocht na hócáide. Bhí an Meiriceánachas tréan sa teaghlach úd i gCóbh Chorcaí. *Americana* ar fud na háite go líonmhar, litreacha ó dhaoine ardchlú sna Stáit, Longfellow san áireamh, bratach Mheiriceá ar crochadh faoi onóir, clann óg an tí agus saol polaitíochta na Stát á chaibidil acu go hardghlórach, iad go huaibhreach ar leith Mheiriceá agus go lántréan in aghaidh Shasana. Sin é tuairisc an údair Katharine Tynan ar shaol an tí.[6] Bhíodh sise ar cuairt mhuintearais ann. Mar atá ráite, is duine de na stócaigh sin a tháinig chun bheith ina athair do Dhonn Sigerson Piatt.

Muintir Shigerson

Bhí Sigersúnaigh i mBaile Átha Cliath ón 11ú céad agus iad ag éirí maoinmhar sa tsaol. Bhí fearann agus caisleáin acu in áiteanna éagsúla i gCúige Laighean. Chuir concas Shasana in oirthear na tíre iachall orthu aistriú ó dheas go hUíbh Ráthach. Lonnaíodar ansin agus bhíodar ceannasach, gaol agus cóngas acu le muintir Mhathúna agus muintir Chonaill agus iad ag gabháil faróta do thrádáil smuigléireachta leis an bhFrainc. Bhí nath cainte ann – muintir Mhathúna a bhí, muintir Shigerson atá, muintir Chonaill a bheas.

Ionnarbadh Risteard agus Críostóir Sigerson ó Bhaile an Sceilg ó thuaidh thar Sionainn i 1653 mar gheall ar iad a bheith ar thaobh na nGael sa chogadh i gcoinne an *Phrotector*. Ach fós sa bhliain 1704, i réim na Banríona Anna, bhí seilbh ag Tomás Sigerson Bhaile an Sceilg ar thigh measúil i gCathair Bhaile Átha Cliath ar an taobh theas de Rae na gCraicneoirí, tigh a lig sé ar cíos don Alderman French.[7]

Scríobh seanathair Dhoinn, an Dr. Seoirse Sigerson, stair a mhuintire ón am a thángadar ó thír Lochlann go hÉirinn. Chuige sin, chuardaigh sé an *Domesday Book* agus gach foinse dhóchúil eile. Bhíodh Donn ag cabhrú leis cois leapan i ndeireadh a shaoil ag déanamh ceartuithe air. De réir na staire sin, is mar seo a rianaítear an ceangal idir é féin agus Sigersúnaigh Chiarraí:

Throid cuid de mhuintir Shigerson Bhaile an Sceilg i gCath Eachdhroma in arm na nGael, agus maraíodh iad go léir ach duine amháin, buachaill dhá bhliain déag. Tar éis an chatha, ghlac sagart paróiste in Eachdhroim an buachaill sin faoina chúram. Ó

Thír Eoghain ab ea an sagart agus chuir sé an buachaill óg ó thuaidh go Tír Eoghain chun cónaithe i dteaghlach a thuismitheoirí. Tá sé ráite go ndeachaigh capaill na bhfear marbh ar ais go Baile an Sceilg uathu féin, eachtra ar ar scríobh an Dr. Sigerson an dán 'They come, great God, all riderless, the horses of the dead'.

Ba é Uilliam Sigerson ó Dhoire athair Sheoirse Sigerson. Nancy Neilson ab ainm dá mháthair. Col ceathar ab ea í do Samuel Neilson, an tÉireannach Aontaithe, agus b'é Holyhill a hionad cónaithe. Protastúnaigh ab ea muintir Neilson. Ar eagla, is dócha, nach bhfaighidís toil a dtuismitheoirí lena bpósadh, d'fhág Nancy Neilson an baile os íseal fara le Uilliam Sigerson agus d'fhilleadar pósta. Fuaireadar cead ó mhuintir Neilson cur fúthu i Holyhill agus is ann a rugadh Seoirse, an 11 Eanáir 1837.

Cuireadh Seoirse Sigerson ar scoil go Montrouge sa Fhrainc. D'fhoghlaim sé Gaeilge i dtimpeallacht a bhaile féin, ó chainteoirí dúchais Thír Chonaill agus freisin óna athair Uilliam, fear a chleacht an teanga le toil ghrámhar di agus a fuair leabhair Ghaeilge ó Bhéal Feirste. Ar theacht abhaile ón bhFrainc do Sheoirse, cuireadh go Coláiste na Banríona i nGaillimh é ach nuair a bhris an calar amach ann chuir a athair ó dheas é go Coláiste Banríona Chorcaí, ag foghlaim leighis. D'iarr sé go mbunófaí rang Gaeilge sa Choláiste, ach ní fhéadfadh sé ach fear amháin eile a fháil a bhí toilteanach bheith fairis á foghlaim agus Sasanach ab ea é sin. Snobairí ab ea na Muimhnigh i gcónaí a dúirt sé agus bhíodh Donn ag aithris an scéil sin dom féin le sult mór. Ach is iad daoine saibhre na Mumhan a bhí i gceist aige, agus níorbh iad an chosmhuintir mar bhí go leor Gaeilge á labhairt sa chathair, agus bhíodh sí á labhairt coitianta i gcistin a sheanmháthar Hester Varian, a deir Donn.

Ultach de chine Viking a thug an Dr. Sigerson air féin.[8] Phós sé Hester Varian, Úinitéarach i gcreideamh, a d'iompaigh ina Caitliceach. De bhunadh Úgónach na Fraince ab ea í.

Ní gá cur síos anseo ar an bhfear ildánach Seoirse Sigerson, ach ní miste an meas a bhí ag Donn ar a sheanathair a lua ina bhriathra féin:

I am proud of the nineteenth century Irishman, the man born in the century of the Great Famine and the evictions, when the Irish nation was so near to death, who could hurl intellectual as well as political defiance at the enemy in the darkest days of our history. Proud of his haughty stand, his noble brow, his kindly words, his poetic vision – and he wrote verse and translated it in both of the languages spoken in Ireland.[9]

Arbh aon iontas, nuair a dúirt fear leis nach raibh aon Ghaeilge ag a sheanathair, gur tháinig racht feirge ar Dhonn?

Is dóigh gur trína mheas ar Ultachas a sheanathar a roghnaigh Donn Piatt Gaeilge Thír Chonaill a chleachtadh in go leor dá shaothar agus ba léir gur sa Ghaeilge Chonallach ab fhearr leis comhrá a dhéanamh. Is minic a chuala ag caint ar an bhfón é sa chanúint bhríomhar sin. Ach bhí gach canúint ar a thoil aige. Ag tracht dó ar a mhuintir, dúirt sé liom uair go raibh sé i mbéaloideas mhuintir Shigerson gur bhuaigh duine acu óigbhean mar dhuais i gcluiche cártaí, bean a ghlac sé chuige féin mar bhanchéile.

Óige agus Oiliúint

Ní nach ionadh, bhí ardmheas ag Donn ar a shinsireacht, ó thaobh athar agus máthar. Ba Mheiriceánach a athair agus tógadh é féin ina leath-Mheiriceánach nó go raibh sé naoi mbliana d'aois. Bhíodh sé cóngarach do na dualgais a bhain le post a athar mar Leas-Chonsal Mheiriceá i mBaile Átha Cliath, an urraim do bhrat náisiúnta na Stát ar an 4 Iúil, cuairteanna oifigiúla a thabhairt ar longa Meiriceánacha a thagadh go Baile Átha Cliath agus Dún Laoghaire. Bhí cónaí orthu i mBóthar Ráth Luirc agus bhíodh aontachtóirí Ráth Maonais ag déanamh gearáin in aghaidh ainm a athar a bheith ar chlár na dtoghthóirí, á rá go mba eachtrannach é.

Mhair dáimh nádúrtha a mháthar Hester le tír a fir go dtí gur tháinig na Stáit Aontaithe isteach sa Chogadh Mór ar thaobh Shasana i 1917. Tháinig laghdú ar an dáimh ansin. Cuireadh Donn go Scoil Íte faoin bPiarsach nuair a bhí sé an-óg, áit a bhfuair sé an chéad bhlaise den Ghaeilge. Bhí óige an-sona aige agus cion croí aige ar a athair is a mháthair. Níor cuireadh smacht air ach dhá uair, ócáid amháin nuair a dúirt sé an focal 'Hell' i láthair mná a bhí cineál sean-mhaighdeanúil. Dar le Donn gurbh iontach an focal é – nach raibh sé sa Teagasc Críostaí!

An dara huair, ócáid a bhfuair sé 'gréasáil mhaith', tharla sé tuairim 1909, nuair a chuaigh sé i bhfochair a athar is a mháthar anonn go Sasana ar cuireadh go dtí a aintín Dora. Thugadar an gluaisteán leo. D'fhanadar oíche i dteach ósta agus cuireadh Donn óg a chodladh go luath. Cheithre bliana a bhí sé ag an am. Níor thit a chodladh air agus d'éirigh sé amach as a leaba agus bhí ag póirseáil roimis go dtáinig sé go doras gloine. Chonaic sé a athair is a mháthair ag ól dí, iad suite chun boird, agus a athair ag cur lámh thart ar a mháthair is á pógadh. Bhíodar mar a bheadh beirt shuiríoch ann agus iad imithe ar ais go mí na meala. Ní raibh a fhios acu go raibh a maicín óg ag gliúcaíl orthu. Nuair a thugadar faoi ndeara é, 'bhí m'athair ar daoraí'. Cuireadh ar ais chun a leapan é, 'faoi tharcaisne náisiúnta.'

Ag breathnú siar dó ar bhlianta caite, chuir an chuimhne sin aiteas ar chroí Dhoinn.

'Buíochas le Dia go bhfaca, nó is méadú measa agus urraime dom ar chuimhne na beirte – go ndéana Dia a mhaith orthu araon – go bhfaca mé cruthaithe é gur ghráigh siad a chéile, díreach mar a ghráíos mé féin agus mo bhean chéile a chéile, díreach mar a ghráíos gach glúin fear gach glúin ban ó bhí Deirdre in Eamhain.'

Fuair a athair bás an 12 Aibreán 1914, agus d'fhág san tocht uaignis ar Dhonn. 'Bhí gnúis na gréine báite orm.' Fágadh an teaghlach bocht dealbh, a mháthair ag brath ar phunt sa tseachtain chun a clann óg a thógáil. Chaoin sí a fear céile i bhfilíocht agus sa bhliain 1931 scríobh Donn dán á chaoineadh mar mhair an t-uaigneas i bhfad. Tar éis a bháis, chuaigh Donn agus a mháthair go Sasana ar cuairt go dtí a aintín Dora. Chonaic sé ceannlíne nuachta sa Charraig Dhubh, go raibh Ard-Diúc na hOstaire dúnmharaithe ach níor chuir sé suntas ann le cumha a athar. Bhí cónaí ar Dora Sigerson i sráidbhaile Great Missenden, fiche míle ó Londain. Nuair a bhris an Cogadh Mór amach, d'athraigh meon Shasana don Ghearmáin agus ag Aifreann Domhnaigh in Aylesbury chuala Donn seanmóir 'nar cheart a thabhairt'. Ní deir sé cad dúradh, ach chuir sé a aintín ar crith le feirg. Bhí sise pósta le Clement Shorter, eagarthóir an *Sphere*, Sasanach a bhí dílis dá thír agus rí-cheanúil ar a bhanchéile. B'ise a scríobh *Sixteen Dead Men*. Ar fhilleadh ar Éirinn dó, cuireadh Donn ar scoil chónaithe agus is beag eile a chuala sé faoin gcogadh ach amháin nuair a thagadh a mháthair dá fhiosrú. Bhí sí go tréan in aghaidh Shasana. Aon bhliain déag a bhí sé nuair a scaoileadh saor é, Céadaoin an Bhraith 1916. Fuair sé iompar go Baile Átha Cliath i gceann de na seanchóistí agus chuir a mháthair na fáiltí geala roimhe ina seomra suí-is-leapan i dtigh a sheanathar, 3 Sráid Chliara.

Bhí a athair dhá bhliain marbh ag an am sin, agus ba bhuille trom é sin ar a mháthair, mar bhí úire agus beocht na hóige inti fós. Ní raibh a fhios ag Donn go ceann míosa ina dhiaidh sin go raibh ardmheas agus ardchion aici ar Sheán Mac Diarmada, 'an t-aon fhear amháin, tar éis m'athar, a d'fhéadfadh sí pósadh', mar a dúirt sí le Donn ar ball tar éis an Éirí Amach, 'glóir na Bealtaine' ag taitneamh, agus í cúramach leis an *National Aid Association*.

Déardaoin na Comaoineach, 1916, chuaigh Donn agus a mháthair ar thuras na seacht dteampall mar ba ghnách i mBaile Átha Cliath, ócáid comhluadair agus deabhóide ar aon. Bhuaileadar le Con Curran agus dúirt seisean leo gur ghearr uathu Éirí Amach ach é a choimeád ina rún. Luan Cásca dá éis sin, chuaigh Donn agus a mháthair amach go Deilginis ag fiosrú a gcol ceathracha, muintir Varian, cuid den dream céanna a dhéanann na scuaba. Bhíodar i 'gCúil Ghréine', tigh mhuintir Varian, le linn do mhuintir an tí féin a bheith ar saoire i gCorcaigh. Bhí dhá theaghlach eile de mhuintir Varian i ndeisceart an chontae, ceann i Stigh Lorgán agus ceann i mBaile na Manach. Bhí lucht Varian Bhaile na Manach taobhach le Sasana. Fuair máthair Dhoinn scéala an tráthnóna sin go raibh an tÉirí Amach tosnaithe. 'Buíochas le Dia na Glóire!' ar sise. Níos déanaí sa tseachtain tháinig Uaitéar Varian, col ceathar Dhoinn, isteach chucu. Dúirt sé go raibh ardspórt aige féin is a chairde in O.T.C. Choláiste na Tríonóide ag caitheamh ar na reibiliúnaigh. Chuir máthair Dhoinn in iúl dó, le hamharc agus is dóigh le briathra, nach fáilte a bhí roimh a ndúirt sé. Ghabh sé leithscéal agus shín amach a lámh chun lámh a chroitheadh léi. Dhiúltaigh sí lámh dó. Shín sé a lámh chuig Donn. Choimeád Donn a lámha ina phócaí. D'imigh Uaitéar Varian leis go brónach. Sar i bhfad , bhí sé sínte marbh i mbéal catha i bhFlóndras, 'faoi éide ár namhad'. Ghoill sé ar Dhonn go mór gur scaradar leis, faoi fheirg, gan é d'fheiscint go deo arís. Ní dhearna sé ach an ceart, de réir an teagaisc a fuair sé.

Chuaigh Donn ar ais go dtí an scoil chónaithe trí chathair scriosta. An chéad rud eile ba chuimhin leis, gur tosnaíodh ar Ghaeilge a theagasc sa scoil. Bhí beagán Gaeilge ag Donn cheana féin a d'fhoghlaim sé in aois a sé bliana i Scoil an Phiarsaigh in Ascaill Feadha Chuilinn, áit a raibh brainse de Scoil Éanna fá choinne bhuachaillí beaga. Scoil do bhuachaillí óga faoi bhun dhá bhliain déag ab ea an scoil ina raibh sé agus mná rialta ar fad a bhí ag múineadh inti.

Cailín as an gclocharscoil a cuireadh chucu mar mháistreás Gaeilge. Thaitin an cailín go mór leo mar mhalairt ar na mná rialta. 'An solas sa dorchadas' ab ea í, dar le Donn, agus do gheal sí an saol dóibh. Ní raibh ach Donn agus buachaill ó Chorcaigh sa rang tosaigh. Scríobh suas le leathchéad buachaillí abhaile ag lorg cead ar a dtuismitheoirí Gaeilge a fhoghlaim. Fuair suas le daichead acu diúltú. Ar ball, bhí seachtar sa rang Gaeilge. Bhí rudaí eile ag athrú. Ní bhfuaireadar a thuilleadh léachtaí ó shéiplínigh d'arm Shasana a bhíodh ag teacht roimhe sin ag caint ar an mBeilg. Nuair a tháinig laethanta saoire an tsamhraidh, 1917, bhí bratach trídhath na Poblachta le feiscint gach áit.[10]

Tugann Donn fios dúinn ar an gcion a bhí aige ar a mháthair leis an toirbheart seo a rinne sé di ar a leabhar filíochta *Dánta ón Oirthear* – 'do mo mháthair. Ós tú dháil gach maitheas ó aois linbh dom: ós tú freisin a thug misneach agus oiliúint dom le scríobh, agus ós tú a chlóbhuail mo chéadiarracht; is duit a thoirbhrim an leabhar beag seo.'

Bhí máthair Dhoinn ag obair ar an *Weekly Freeman* faoin ainm 'Uncle Remus' ar chúinne na n-óg ag stiúrú comórtaisí litríochta d'óganaigh. Is í a d'fhoilsigh céad iarrachtaí filíochta Dhoinn. I mBéarla a bhíodar sin. Sa tsaol a bhí ann, ní fhéadfadh Donn gan spéis a chur i gcúrsaí na haimsire. Le linn Chogadh na Saoirse, in aois a sé déag dó, scríobh sé dán ar bhású Phádraig Uí Mhóráin agus cúigear eile óigfhear i bPríosún Mhoinseó. Foilsíodh i *Misneach* é. Sa bhliain 1919, scríobh a mháthair an dán 'In Leinster Lawn' tar éis di féachaint amach ó fhuinneog chúil uimhir 3 Sráid Chliara agus Mícheál Ó Coileáin d'fheiscint ag siúl go rábach trasna Faiche Laighean.[12] Seo é an dara véarsa:

> Then swiftly passed me, with no ghostly tread
> A living man, one of our world to-day,
> Youth in his strength and bearing, and his glance
> Went past me, proud and confident and gay.
> Did he too see the vision? He could tell
> Better than I, for he had fought the fight
> And so would answer – Comrade, all goes well,
> Near, and yet nearer, breaks the dawning light.

Taisteal agus Foghlaim

Gaeilge, Fraincis agus Breathnais na hábhair a rinne Donn dá chúrsa ollscoile. Bhain sé a chéim M.A. amach sa bhliain 1928 i gColáiste Ollscoile Bhaile Átha Cliath. Ní haon ionadh go raibh páirtíocht aigne aige don Fhrainc, tír shinseartha a shloinne. Bhí dlúthbhaint leis an bhFrainc ag a sheanathair Seoirse Sigerson. Fuair sé scolaíocht ann. Rinne sé taighde agus staidéar iarchéime ann. Sa tslí go raibh gaol intinne ag Donn leis an náisiún sin ó thaobh na dtaobhann. Rinne sé cúrsa léinn i Spáinnis agus Iodáilis in Ollscoil Phoitiers i 1927-28. D'aistrigh sé Ronsard agus Émile Verhaeren go Gaeilge. D'aistrigh sé go Fraincis cuid d'amhráin tíre na hÉireann, Chansons Populaires d'Irlande. Ar cheann acusan, bhí 'An Réiltean Leanbach', 'L' Étoile Enfantile.' B'iad na tréimhsí a chaith sé sa Fhrainc an chuid ba shona agus ba scaoilte dá shaol. D'fhoghlaim sé ansin ceachtanna tairbheacha don Ghaeilge seachas gur bhain sé sásamh as sibhialtacht éagsúil a thaitin go mór leis, sibhialtacht tinteáin agus teaghlaigh féin. Seo mar a scríobh sé:

> French enables me to look across the Boulevard at Saint Germain des Prés Church and feel I am no stranger in a strange land, but part of it all, knowing the French language since I was a kid at school. French has become a part of me for over forty years, and I can still thrill to its message.[13]

'Tabhair leat *Dánta Grádha Uí Rathaile*' an chomhairle do bheir Donn don té a bheadh ag triall ar Phrovence, 'an tír ghrianmhar' as ar shíolraigh cuid de na laoithe áille ceana. Tráchtann sé go heolgaiseach ar údair agus stair na dúiche. Lá dó in Avignon, cathair na bPápaí tráth, agus 'béile deas agus fíon breá blasta deas agus sin go saor', mar bhí Donn chomh dúilmhear le haon i dtaitneamhachtaí na beatha agus cá mb'fháth nach mbeadh? Cuairt ar theach Phetrarca, Domhnach breá i lár na Bealtaine, damhsa ag girseacha Avignon agus a gcuid stócach. I Hyères cois cuain 'bheir an oíche dhubh orm agus mé ag iarraidh dán a chumadh cois trá. Dán Gaeilge a choinneodh áilleacht na hoíche ag teacht, áilleacht na gcnoc fána gcuid crann olóige, áilleacht na bpailm ndíreach, áilleacht an eitleáin a chuaigh siar bealach Nice, os sléibhte an Esterel agus crónán codlatach aige, a choinneodh sin i mo chuimhne fhaid is mhairfinn.'

Bhuail ocras é. Thaispeáin seanduine bistró dó, teach beag adhmaid, inar tairgeadh béile dó, fíon, feoil fhuarbhruite agus olaí. Déanfaidh sé mo ghnaithe, bia blasta le fíon rosé, ar chúig franc déag, agus ní raibh sé sin saor, ach cér mhiste é? La vie est belle.[14] Sea, bhí Donn sona saor sa Fhrainc.

An Félibrige agus an Ghaeilge

Chuir Donn spéis go háirithe sa chuid theas den Fhrainc, An Phroibhinse, Provence, sa chanúint áitiúil a bhí á labhairt sa dúiche sin agus san fhile Frédéric Mistral, a fuair clú agus cáil agus duais Nobel as anam agus uaisleacht a thuilleamh don chanúint lena shaothar filíochta. Ní raibh sé ina aonar. Bhí chomhluadar filí ag scríobh ina theannta leis an aidhmeannas céanna. Bhí an ghluaiseacht Félibrige ina múnla do ghluaiseacht na Gaeilge.

> Tá stair fíor uasal ag teanga na Proibhinse, mar atá ag ár dteanga Ghaeilge féin agus saibhreas fairsing litríochta. An ghluaiseacht do chothú teanga na Proibhinse agus na teanga Gaeilge, is iarrachtaí iad ar son cearta an duine, ar son áilleacht agus aoibhneas na beatha, mar níl aon tubaist níos measa ná daoine a dheighilt óna n-ancaire nádúrtha, mar ní bhíonn fios ar a hanam féin ag an nádúir daonna nuair atá gach rud a bhí ar eolas ag athair agus seanathair imithe gan tásc ná tuairisc, go fiú a litríocht, a n-ealaí agus a dteanga. Sin í an chúis gan ligean don Fhraincis an Phroibhinsis a bháthadh, gan ligean don Bhéarla an Ghaeilge a chloí.[15]

Sa bhliain 1932 nuair a bhí caint ar Ghníomhaíocht Chaitliceach Thuata in Éirinn bhí barúla á lua ag Donn ar an gceartbhrí a bhí le baint as an abairt sin:

> Ó mo thaithí ar an nGaeltacht so againne, (ar seisean), agus ó mo chleachtadh ar dhúichí i dtuath na Fraince atá gach uile phioc

chomh doimhin-Chaitliceach céanna – Anjou agus Vendée – bhí a fhios agam cén múnla a bhí ar thuathmhuintir fhíorghlan Chaitliceach agus bhí ardmheas agam air.

Is é an tslat tomhais a mheas Donn do Ghníomlaíocht Chaitliceach in Éirinn, í a bheith toilteanach luí isteach ar an gcrua-obair a bhain le sábháil na coda a bhí fágtha den tsean-Éire a bhí Caitliceach, agus a milleadh sa seachtú céad déag.

Má bhíonn aon duine nó dream, tráth ar bith, ag lorg eolais atá ar mo chumas-sa a thabhairt i ndáil le fadhb shóisialta – agus fadhb Chaitliceach féin – den tábhacht is airde, is é sin, slánú na Gaeltachta, agus *gach uile rud a ghabhas* leis sin, beidh mo dhícheall-sa cabhrach acu agus fáilte.[16]

Lena chur in iúl do lucht Béarla an meon agus an cháilíocht a bhí i gcultúr na Gaeltachta sular milleadh í, rinne sé aistriú ar thrí dhán le Pádraigín Haicéad, a saolaíodh i dTiobraid Árann tuairim 1600 agus a fuair oideachas ar an mór-roinn. 'Má tá file ag Éirinn is ionchomortais le Pierre de Ronsard na Fraince, is é Pádraigín Haicéad é',[17] a deir Donn. 'Tabharfaidh a chuid filíochta fionscladh éigin ar chultúr na hÉireann mar a bhí trí chéad bliain ó shin.'

Seo véarsa amháin as an iarracht álainn. 'A Pity', aistriú ar 'Is mairg thug Searc'. Tá an file ag impí ar an Maighdean Mhuire cabhrú le peacaigh:

Milk-fruitful, gracious nurse, warm-hearted woman, you
In Heaven, Mary Virgin, come at once
And help them out to carry shifting loads
Of sin, or else, these people are undone,
And must go down, with shame upon each brow,
Hell, soon, must have them, or you save them, now.[18]

Caitliceacht chruthaitheach, shibhialta, intleachtúil, a bhí i gcré Dhoinn.

Ag féachaint don mhéid atá ráite roimhe seo, is ar éigin a chreidfeadh duine an rud atá le lua agam anois. Sa bhliain 1935, do foilsíodh leabhrán dár theideal *Could Ireland Become Communist?* B'ionann Cumannach a ghairm de dhuine san am sin agus a rá go raibh crúba agus adharca air. Seo sliocht as an leabhrán:

... a so-called Workers' College ... established in Eccles Street ... to train Communist agitators ... had on its governing committee such I.R.A. leaders as David Fitzgerald, Seán Mulgrew, DONN PIATT, Seán McCool and Peadar O'Donnell.[19]

Ollamh le Stair in Ollscoil Chorcaí, Séamas Ó hÓgáin, a scríobh an leabhrán. Bhíodh an tagairt sin á caitheamh san aghaidh ar Dhonn, mar mhagadh ar uairibh, i ndáiríre uaire eile. Chuala féin é á rá go raibh an tagairt sin de shíor ag teacht ina choinne. Bíonn iarsmaí fada ar an bhfocal éagórach.

I Rannóg an Aistriúcháin

Fear trom leathan ab ea Donn Piatt, fionnchnis, fionnghruaige, leathanéadain, ar meánairde, ceannuasal, an-líofacht chainte aige agus glib nó dhó gruaige ag titim le haill a éadain nuair a bhíodh rith lena dhúthracht.

Tuairim an ama chéanna liom féin a fostaíodh Donn i Rannóg an Aistriúcháin sa Dáil, is é sin, Deireadh Fómhair 1943. Ní raibh sé deacair muintearas a dhéanamh leis. Mo chéad chomhrá leis i dtaobh focail agus leaganacha, conas a deirinn a leithéid seo nó siúd. Ina chomhrá dó, shiúlaíodh sé síos agus suas. Dá mbeadh spéis doimhin aige in aon rud, thiocfadh corraí air agus ansin thiocfadh racht casachtaigh air. Bhíodh an múchadh air agus b'fhéidir freisin go raibh baint aige sin le liogaí. Rinne sé iarrachtaí arís agus arís leigheas a fháil nó cóireáil a mhaolódh an múchadh. Amanna bhíodh cúrsa instealladh á fháil aige féachaint an bhféadfaí teacht ar an gcúis áirithe ba thrúig leis an ngalar. Is cuimhin liom go ndeachaigh sé don Fhrainc go dtí láthair nó clinic sláinte ina mbíodh cóireáil á cur ar lucht múchta, cúrsaí folctha nó tumadh coirp in ábhar éiginnteach te, réim cóireála a bhí dian go maith ar an duine. Tar éis dul faoi chúrsa cóireála mar sin, tháinig sé abhaile agus shíleamar go raibh feabhas air ach tar éis tamaill bhí an galar ar ais air chomh trom agus a bhí riamh. Ní foláir nó bhí na rachtanna casachtaigh an-dian ar a chliabh.

I gcaitheamh na mblianta a raibh caidreamh agam air, fuaireas corrphíosa eolais ar a shaol roimh é theacht isteach sa Rannóg. Bhí sé tréimhse ina Oifigeach Fiosrúcháin. Sa ghnó sin bheadh sé riachtanach tástáil maoine a chur ar dhuine sula bhfaigheadh sé teideal do phinsean. Cheapamar nach raibh Donn ró-dhian ag cur na gcoinníollacha i bhfeidhm mar bhí croí daonna bog aige. Scéal a d'inis sé féin mar gheall ar fhiosrú maoine a bhí á dhéanamh aige i gContae Longfoirt ar bhean a bhí ag cur isteach ar an bpinsean seanaoise. Theastaigh ó Dhonn dul síos go dtí an móinéar féachaint cé mhéid bó a bhí aici ach níor theastaigh uaithise ligint dó, mar, ar sise, 'Ní fhaca mo chuid bó fear ariamh!'

Bhí spéis an domhain ag Donn i logainmneacha agus eolas aige orthu. Bhí sé freisin pas so-chreidmheach agus bhítí ag cumadh scéalta dó. Thugadh Donn géilleadh do na scéalta áiféiseacha ar dtús mar cheap sé go raibh gach éinne chomh saonta fírinneach leis féin, ach, tar éis tamaill, tháinig fios dó nach raibh iontu ach bréag. Shiúladh sé amach as an seomra nuair a bhíodh bréag éigin áiféiseach á insint ina láthair. Bhí Donn uasal. Bhí d'uaisleacht ann nach ndearna sé riamh agairt ar lucht inste na scéal ach neamhaird. Uaisleacht shaonta a bhí ann. Uair amháin riamh le linn m'aithne air a tháinig tréanchorraí, nó an rud ba ghaire d'fhearg, ar Dhonn. Tharla sé sin nuair a dúirt duine leis nach raibh aon Ghaeilge ag a sheanathair, an Dr. Sigerson. Bhí Donn an-mhórálach as a sheanathair, ní nach ionadh, agus ghlac sé leis mar mhasla agus an ceart aige. Tháinig tocht ina ghlór.

Bhí meabhair gan chuimse sa chloigeann uasal úd, agus bhí filíocht. Tharla, lá, ar é bheith tamall amuigh as an seomra, gur chuireas suntas i ngiota páipéir le scríbhinn a bhí ar a bhord. D'fhéachas air. Blúire filíochta a bhí scríofa air leis an teideal 'Saol an Mhada Bháin.' Is cinnte go bhféadfadh Donn an saol sin a léiriú le tuiscint mar bhíodh dhá pheata bheag madra de mhianach Peke aige féin. Bhí an mada bán san fhilíocht ag labhairt ar an dóigh inar mhaith leis féin an saol a bheith leagtha amach agus ina dheireadh thiar bhí an líne amháin Béarla 'To hell with the cat/Babh-bhabha, babh-bhabha, babh-bhabha.' Tá súil agam go bhfuil an blúire filíochta sin slán, mar nuair a chuireas ceist faoi ar Dhonn ina dhiaidh sin bhí sé imithe glan as a cheann go raibh a leithéid scríofa aige. Sa tslí sin, bhí Donn cosúil lena athair is a mháthair mhór sa Chóbh, de réir na tuairisce a thugann Katharine Tynan orthu, iad a bheith ar fud an tí agus a n-aigne san aer lasmuigh agus lastuas díobh féin agus gan suim acu sa tsaol nithiúil ina dtimpeall.

Bhíodh gluaisteán ag Donn de sheandéanamh le cúinní, cosúil le bosca. Ní raibh gluaisteáin ar na bóithre i rith an chogaidh mar ní raibh peitreal le fáil. Nuair a bhí sé le fáil arís ar ciondáil dian agus é fíorghann, fuair Donn amach go raibh dhá ghalún fágtha fós san umar peitril aige.

Ní gá a rá go raibh Donn fial. Bhí dídean agus fáilte le fáil ina thigh cónaithe ag díbeartaigh Cheilteacha ó thíortha eile, agus go háirithe, le linn an chogaidh dhomhanda agus ina dhiaidh, ag scoláirí agus lucht ealaíne ón mBriotáin a bhí ar a dteitheadh óna dtír dhúchais.

Scoil Bhríde

I Rannóg an Aistriúcháin, ní fhéadfaimís gan spéis a chur i ngnóthaí a chéile agus níor ghá bheith fiosrach in aon chor le haithint go raibh aigne Dhoinn suaite le ceist mhórthábhachta lenar chuir sé dícheall a chroí. Tuairim na bliana 1959 é sin, b'fhéidir. Dob í an cheist sin Scoil

Bhríde a athbhunú, mar bhí an chéad scoil in Ardán Phort an Iarla le dúnadh toisc an léas a bheith ag dul in éag. Scoil lán-Ghaelach ab ea í. 'De thoradh dianiarrachta,' de réir thuairisc Dhoinn, bunaíodh Scoil Bhríde arís mar scoil lán-Ghaelach i láthair nua i Raghnallach in aice le Teach Feadha Chuilinn. Ní raibh sé éasca. Bíodh Donn mar fhinné: 'Is éachtach na deacrachtaí atá roimh scoil lán-Ghaelach.' Bunaíodh coiste tuismitheoirí, Donn ar dhuine acu, rinneadar diantroid agus fuaireadar tacaíocht mhaith. Thug Donn creidiúint mhór don Aire Airgeadais, An Dr. Séamas Ó Riain, a fuair an suíomh dóibh. Mura mbeadh é, ní bheadh a leithéid le fáil. Tógadh scoil nua a raibh spás inti do bhreis agus 400 páiste, agus amharclann le haghaidh drámaí agus maise ró-bhreá ar gach rud agus fós, cúlra stairiúil leis an áit, mar bhíodh Pádraig Mac Piarais ag saothrú ann agus Bartholomew Mosse ina chónaí ann, rudaí a chuir méadú bróid ar Dhonn Piatt mar staraí ar Baile Átha Cliath.

Rinne Donn go tréan ag cur an tionscail sin chun cinn. Bhí lucht mí-ghnaoi ag drannadh leo. 'Tosóimid' ar seisean, '... agus slua naimhde timpeall orainn... Trí mhí ó shin, d'iarr roinnt naimhde orainn balla ard ... a chur thart ar an scoil le nach mbeadh orthu a bheith ag féachaint ar pháistí ag súgradh agus ag screadach (i nGaeilge).'

Ba léir go raibh rímhéad ar Dhonn an obair sin a chur i gcrích go séanmhar.[20]

Bleácliathach bródúil

Scríobh Donn mórán aistí ar *An tUltach* agus tá sé soiléir gurbh í Gaeilge Thír Chonaill ab fhearr leis cleachtadh. Ach de chionn gur i mBaile Átha Cliath a rugadh is a tógadh é bhí a ghnaoi agus a chion go léir á mbronnadh aige ar a chathair dhúchais agus ar Chúige Laighean ina timpeall, mar a deir sé sa dán 'Mo Chúigeadh Féin':

Laighneach mise ó Linn Life
Sean-phort oinigh Bhaile Átha Cliath
Dúchas dúinne taobh na mara
Saoghal na cathrach ba linn riamh.
Mór mo chathair go na soillse
Soillse geala teacht na h-oidhch';
Cathair álainn – deacair a fágáil
Is seacht ngreama ar mo chroidhe![21]

Sin é an Bleácliathach bródúil ag caint. Ní ar an gcathair a bhí sé ag trácht ach ar an gcontae, sílim, nuair a thagair sé do 'Baile Átha Cliath, ... áit a bhfuil an talamh is measa agus an Galldachas is mó i gCúige Laighean'.[22] San aiste chéanna, faoin teideal 'Litríocht Réigiúnach,' deir sé.

217

Domhaineach mise, is Eorpach, is Éireannach, is Laighneach. Sé mo thír féin is mo chúige dúchais is deise do mo chroí ar fad. Ar Laighnibh ba mhaith liom labhairt. Agus mo Chúige Laighean-sa, caidé mar bheas sí amach anseo.

Tugann sé fios dúinn ar an aisling a bhí aige. Na Gaeil a theacht ina gceart, agus litríocht mhór a fhás in Éirinn. A chúige féin a bheith rannpháirteach inti, ó Ros Láir go Ceatharlach is fríd Sléibhte Chill Mhantáin go Baile Átha Cliath. 'Tá tréithe na ndaoine sin gan scríobh go fóill. Daoine a bhfuil eadar mín is garbh iontu, a bhfuil greann dá gcuid féin acu is a dtréithe féin.'[23]

As a dhúthracht do Chúige Laighean i gcoitinne a chuir sé le chéile an leabhrán spéisiúil *Gaelic Dialects of Leinster* ina bhfuil, mar a deir an fotheideal, an iliomad logainmneacha mar atá siad i mbéal na ndaoine agus roinnt céadta focal Ghaeilge a labhartar go háitiúil maille lena bhfoghraíocht. Le linn dó a bheith ag obair ar an saothar sin, léigh sé na Litreacha Suirbhéireachta Ordanáis a bhain le gach contae Laighneach, scrúdaigh sé na léarscáileanna Suirbhéireachta Staidrimh a bhain le tosach an naoú céad déag agus na léarscáileanna orlach agus sé orlach, mar iarracht chun Gaeilge chaillte Chúige Laighean Thoir a chur ina hathchruth le cabhair na gcéadta focal a mhaireann sa Bhéarla. Chríochnaigh sé an saothar sin mí na Samhna 1933.

Donas Deich mBliana

Déarfainn gurbh é 'Máire', Séamus Mac Grianna, an scríbhneoir Gaeilge is mó a raibh meas ag Donn air. Aigesean a bhí scoth Ghaeilge Thír Chonaill. Gaeilge Thír Chonaill ba rogha le Donn. Go Tír Chonaill a théadh sé le haghaidh athnuachan spioraid agus meanman. Chruinnigh sé ann na hamhráin áitiúla agus ba chabhair dó go raibh cluas mhaith cheoil aige. Tá toradh a chuardaigh le fáil ó am go chéile san *Ultach*. Go Tír Chonaill a chuaigh sé tráth ar lorg sóláis tar éis tréimhse fada cruatain, mar a deir sé linn i bhfilíocht:

Leigheasadh créachta mo chroidhe
Nuair phill mé fá chríoch seo Chonaill
D'éirigh mé fileamhanta ar ais
I ndiaidh tost fada an donais.

Fiafraímid, cad é an donas a bhain dó? Ní fhéadaim é sin a fhreagairt. Ach caithfidh gur thit an donas air go trom agus gur fhulaing sé, nó ní scríobhfadh sé mar seo:

Donas deich mbliana gan ghó
A rabh mé fá bhrón croidhe
'Nar chaill mé dóchas as an tsaoghal
Is dóchas nach mór as Dia.
Muna mbeadh mo mhuintir féin
Is mo chéile chaoin chumainn,
Ar éigin mhairfinn beo
'S an saoghal mór liom i gcogadh.[24]

A mhuintir féin agus a chéile chaoin chumainn a bhí cúntach tacúil dó. Bhí Donn pósta le hEilís (Elsie) Ní Cholgáin agus bhí beirt iníon acu. Is tuigthe as litir ón gCraoibhín atá i measc scríbhinní Dhoinn sa Leabharlann Náisiúnta go raibh Donn tráth ag beartú ar dhul go Meiriceá go post éigin agus go raibh an Craoibhín lánsásta é a mholadh, ós é ab fhearr a bhí ina theideal as an mbaint mhuintire a bhí aige le Meiriceá.

Sa bhliain 1937 chuir Donn isteach ar phost i Rannóg na Seirbhísí Sóisialta de Rúnaíocht Chonradh na Náisiún. Chuige sin fuair sé teastas molta ón Ollamh T. Rudmose-Brown, Coláiste na Tríonóide. Is eol gurbh eisean ollamh Fraincíse fir cháiliúil eile ó Bhaile Átha Cliath, Samuel Beckett. Dáta an teastais, 4 Feabhra 1937. Is é seo é:

> I understand that Mr. D. S. Piatt is applying for a post as member of section in the Social Services Section of the League of Nations Secretariat.
>
> It gives me great pleasure to recommend him very strongly, both on account of his knowledge of French and his experience of Social Service under the Free State Government. He has an excellent Honours Degree in Modern Languages. I can speak from my own knowledge of his fluency and accuracy in spoken and written French.
>
> I came into contact with him when I was Irish correspondent of a Provincial Review published at Avignon to which he contributed and I heard him speak most eloquently and fluently, and with a perfect command of French at a recent opening meeting of our Modern Languages Society. I know of him as an enthusiastic student of French Literature, of the French Provincial and Irish Languages. He is a gentleman of high culture and most engaging manners, with a very strong sense of responsibility and the duties of a Citizen. I wish him all success.
>
>   T. Rudmose-Brown
>   Professor of Romance Languages in the University of Dublin.[25]

Postanna gearraimsire a bhí á bhfáil ag Donn nó gur tháinig sé isteach i Rannóg Aistriúcháin an Oireachtais i 1943. Chuir sé isteach ar phost mar Chúntóir le Gaeilge i gColáiste Ollscoile na Gaillimhe ach ní bhfuair. Chaith sé tréimhse mar mheánmhúinteoir i gColáiste na Dea-Chomhairle i Ros Mhic Treoin ó 1928 go Feabhra 1930. I 1930-1931, bhí sé fostaithe mar Aistritheoir Sóisearach ar Fhoireann Aistriúcháin an Oireachtais. I 1934-1935 bhí sé ag múineadh i gColáiste Cholm Cille (Saint Columba's) i Ráth Fearnáin. Ó 1936 go 1940, bhí sé ag saothrú mar Oifigeach Fiosrúcháin faoi na Coimisinéirí Ioncaim. I 1937 a chuir sé isteach ar an bpost i Rannóg Seirbhísí Sóisialta na Náisiún Aontaithe a bhfuair sé an teastas molta ina leith ón Ollamh Rudmose-Brown. I 1942 bhí post sealadach aige in Oifig Aistriúcháin an Oireachtais agus thug tréimhse an bhliain chéanna mar Chúntóir Páirtaimsire i Scoil an Léinn Cheiltigh. Seachas iad sin go léir, thug sé tamall oibre i mionphostanna nó ag saothrú ar ghnéithe áirithe den Ghaeilge. D'fhoghlaim sé an Córas Fuaime Idirnáisiúnta d'fhonn comharthaí teangan a bhreacadh síos go beacht. Bhí sé tamall ag saothrú ar an gcuid fuaimeolais de Ghraiméar Gaeilge i bhFraincis ina raibh sé ag comhoibriú leis an Ollamh Gherard Haes as Ghent.

D'fhéadfadh Donn barr aitheantais a bhaint amach sa Bhéarla nó sa Fhraincis, mar bhí an dá mhórtheanga sin ar a thoil aige. Bhí de gheallúint ann go bhféadfadh sé a bheith chun tosaigh i bhfilíocht Bhéarla na tíre seo. Sí an Ghaeilge a roghnaigh sé. Tá saothar fairsing scríofa aige sa Ghaeilge, cé nach bhfuil mórán de bailithe idir clúdaigh leabhair. Tá dhá leabhar againn óna láimh, *Mhaireadar san Ardchathair* agus *Cois Life Fadó*, trácht ghrámhar ar a chathair féin agus bíodh sé le rá nárbh é Donn Piatt an staraí ba lú tábhacht ar Bhaile Átha Cliath. Tá neart aistí dá chuid, go háirithe in *Inniu*, atá le foilsiú fós. Deir Seosamh Mac Dónaill liom go bhfuil ceithre aiste is caoga eile ar láimh aige ag feitheamh le foilsitheoir agus ina theannta sin sraith eile dhá aiste dhéag ar an téama *As measc mo leabhar*. Tá cuid mhór eile dá scríobh báite in irisí agus tréimhseacháin áitiúla, san *Ultach, Fáinne an Lae, Scéala Éireann, Humanitas, An Sguab, An Phoblacht, An Réult agus* eile.

D'aistrigh sé ón bhFraincis dánta le Pierre de Ronsard a foilsíodh sa *Phoblacht* agus le Émile Verhaeren a foilsíodh i *Humanitas*. D'aistrigh sé saothar le Joseph Bédier, *Scéal fileamhanta Thristan agus Iseut* (1935) agus freisin, le Joseph Bédier agus Louis Artus, *Tristan agus Iseut* – dráma trí ghníomh agus ocht dtableau (1934). An Gúm a d'fhoilsigh.

D'aistrigh sé ón mbun-Ghearmáinis go Gaeilge Thír Chonaill an Chéad Chuid de *Faust* le Goethe gan de chabhair aige chuige ach an leagan Fraincise a rinne Gérard de Nerval. Tá sé sin i gclóscríbhinn sa Leabharlann Náisiúnta.

Sa Lámhscríbhinn G 1076 sa Leabharlann Náisiúnta, tá cnuasach de leabhair nótaí, cóipleabhair agus sracleabhair ina bhfuil ábhar éagsúil le Donn Piatt. Tá cuid den ábhar sin luachmhar le seasamh Dhoinn mar scríbhneoir a mheas, ach níor mhór cúram agus foighne chun an chuid is fearr substaint a roghnú agus a chur in eagar. Ní raibh Donn cúramach ná críochnúil ag féachaint i ndiaidh a chuid scríbhinní féin. I measc na leabhar nótaí, tá ceann ina bhfuil meascán d'fhilíocht bhunaidh, logainmneacha, sloinnte, aiste spéisiúil i mBéarla 'The Gaedhealtacht'; i leabhar nótaí eile tá 'Amhráin Ghaedhilge a rinne mé is mé sa Fhrainc', filíocht phearsanta, e.g. 'Pósta', aistriú Béarla ar 'Cuirim séad suirghe chun seise'; taobh istigh de chlúdach tosaigh leabhair eile tá: 'Donn Sigerson Piatt 1918 – Poems (March 1918)'. Iarrachtaí fileata iad sin a foilsíodh san *Irish Fireside Corner* agus áiteanna eile, aistí a foilsíodh i *Saint Enda's,* san *Independent, Irish Fun,* srl. Tá leabhar téagartha gan chlúdach ina bhfuil aistí greamaithe isteach a scríobh sé don *Phoblacht* agus *Scéala Éireann*. Tá litreacha ó lucht comhfhreagrais greamaithe isteach freisin, ag trácht ar an nGaeilge i gCill Mhantáin agus ábhair eile. Tá aiste ó Dhonn sa *Phoblacht,* 17 Meán Fómhair 1932, ag géarghearán ar *Humanitas* ar chuir sé aistriú Gaeilge chuige ar 'La Nuit d'Octobre' le Alfred de Musset. Chailleadar é agus ní raibh an dara chóip aige. Fuair sé lochtaí eile ar *Humanitas.* Tá trí chóipleabhar tógtha suas le haistriú Gaeilge atá luaite ar na clúdaigh mar 'Dráma Saunders Lewis' ach measaim go bhfuil cuid de in easnamh. Tá leabhar nótaí ina bhfuil aistriúcháin Ghaeilge ar Amhráin Náisiúnta na hEorpa. Agus go leor eile. Theastódh aga agus foighne chun an plúr a roghnú, a scagadh agus a chur in ord.

Bhí Donn ag scríobh coitianta ó 1918 go dtí go bhfuair sé bás i 1970. Rinne an bás slad nuair a rug sé leis Donn. Bhí sé chun scríobh ar a shaol. D'fhéadfadh sé léargas a thabhairt ar shraitheanna sóisialta a bhí ar eolas aige féin agus ar phearsana spéisiúla mná agus fir ab aithin dó féin agus a bhain le timpeallacht a mhuintire.

Ag trácht dúinn ar Dhonn Piatt agus a léargas ar an litríocht agus ar an saol, ní foláir a chúlra a chur san áireamh. Ní mór féachaint siar ar a réamhtheachtaithe Úgónacha a theith as an bhFrainc ón ngéarleanúint, muintir le mianach saoirsiúil agus saorchoinsias nár ghlac le cuing agus a thug a n-aghaidh thar muir siar chun cónaithe i ndúiche nua. Smaoinímis ar a dhúchas Meiriceánach agus ar na glúinte dá mhuintir a bhain amach lonnaíocht agus céim i bpoblacht na Stát Aontaithe, ar an bhfear dá shinsear a thug tacaíocht d'Abraham Lincoln, ar a mhisneach agus a spiorad poiblí, ar Mheiriceánachas agus tréithe fileata Sarah Morgan Bryan Piatt agus John James Piatt, agus gurbh é Donn Sigerson Piatt an chéad duine den treabhchas tréithiúil sin a ghlac chuige féin an Ghaeilge, agus an teanga sin amháin, mar mheán scríbhneoireachta agus saothair.

Ag féachaint ar a phréamhacha ón taobh eile a shroich ó Thír Lochlann i leith go hÉirinn, ar a sheanathair Lochlannach – Éireannach agus a chumas ealaíne agus éigse a thug dúinn *Bards of the Gael and Gall*, ar a aintín Dora Sigerson a scríobh *Sixteen Dead Men*, ar a mháthair Hester a thug Lord Edward agus Mícheál Ó Coileáin i gcóngar a chéile sa dán *In Leinster Lawn*, tá gach uile chúis againn le bheith bródúil as an bhfear a raibh na sruthán éirime sin ag gluaiseacht ó dhúchas isteach ina chuisleanna agus a d'iompair dhá shloinne onóracha ina ainm féin, Donn Sigerson Piatt, fear uasal a bhronn a liobrálacht agus a intleacht go léir ar an teanga Ghaeilge.

Notaí

1. *Dánta ón Oirthear*, 32.
2. *Dictionary of American Biography.* C.G. Miller: *Donn Piatt: His work and his ways* (1893). James Bayard Taylor: *Critical Essays and Literary Notes* (Londain 1880).
3. *Dictionary of American Biography*, 304-308.
4. Leabharlann Náisiúnta na hÉireann. LS. G 1077. Ó chúntas i mBéarla le Donn Sigerson Piatt.
5. *Ibid.*
6. Katharine Tynan: *Twenty Five years: Reminiscences* (Londain 1913), 274-278.
   Bhí Katharine Tynan an-mhór le beirt iníon Sheoirse Sigerson. Ise a chuir an iníon ab óige acu, Hester, in aithne d'Arthur Donn Piatt. Phósadar ina dhiaidh sin. Is tríthise freisin a cuireadh an dara hiníon, Dora, in aithne do Clement Shorter roinnt blianta ina dhiaidh sin arís agus phósadarsan. Deir sí go mba chailín fíormhaisiúil í Dora, í oilte ar dhathadóireacht agus dealbhóireacht, óigbhean éagsúil thar ghnáth.
7. Níor ionnarbadh muintir Shigerson go léir as Uíbh Ráthach in aimsir Chromail. Bhíodar láidir ann arís ina dhiaidh sin. Ba den chlann an file Sigerson de Cliford. Dúirt Donn liom go raibh a sheanathair an-bhródúil as an marbhna ar Froinseas Seigearson a scríobh Diarmuid Ó Sé (na Bolgaí). Seo ceathrú as:
   > Dob fhearr thú ná a lán acu dá bhfacthas fós,
   > A sheabhaic álainn a tháinig ó Sheigearson Mhór:
   > Ní raibh caim ort ód mháthair d'fhuil Chonallaigh Chóir,
   > A rábaire an áthais, a bhronnadh an t-ór.

   Agus seo mar a d'aistrigh an Dr. Sigerson é:
   > O handsome Hawk, who towered the country o'er!
   > Top-spray of all who sprang from Segerson More!
   > And pure thy mother's blood, Clann Connell's old, –
   > Thou dashing chief – thou joyous hand with gold.

   Bards of the Gael and Gall (Nua Eabhrac 1974) 342.
   Tá tuairisc mhuintir Shigerson le fáil in dhá léacht a thug Donn Piatt do Chumann Seandachta Bhaile Átha Cliath agus a foilsíodh faoin teideal 'A Pale Family and Old Dublin' sa *Dublin Historical Record* vol. xviii (December 1962 – September 1963) lgh 91 – 100, 122 – 126; Cuntas le Donn Sigerson Piatt i LNÉ: LS G 1077; 'George Sigerson … A Memorial Preface' le Dubhglas de hÍde in *Bards of the Gael and Gall*, athchló den 3ú heagrán, Comhlacht Phoenix, Baile Átha

Cliath, v – xxii; C.P. Curran: *Under the Receding Wave* (Baile Átha Cliath 1970) 82 – 95. 1837 bliain a shaolaithe, de réir D.S.P. *Dublin Historical Record* réamhluaite, 126.

8. *The Poets and Poetry of Munster* … with metrical translations by Erionnach (i.e. Seoirse Sigerson). Second Series (Baile Átha Cliath 1860), Introduction xxvii.
9. LNÉ: LS G 1077.
10. Tá na heachtraí seo agus tuilleadh ábhair le fáil in *Cois Life Fadó* le Donn Piatt, Baile Átha Cliath, 1985.
11. 2 Aibreán 1921.
12. Hester Sigerson Piatt: *The Passing Years,* (Baile Átha Cliath 1935) 29. Terence O'Hanlon: *The Minstrel of Éirinn* (Baile Átha Cliath 1930).
13. LNÉ: LS G 1077.
14. 'Provence' in *Humanitas* (Márta 1930) 5-7.
15. 'The Provencal Movement' in *Outlook*, 5 Márta 1932.
16. 'Anglicisation through Irish' in *Outlook*, 13 Feabhra 1932.
17. *Outlook*, 27 Feabhra 1932, 9.
18. 'A Pity'. Aistriú ar 'Is mairg thug Searc' le Pádraigín Haicéad, *Outlook*, 9 Márta 1932.
    Cf. freisin, 'As the Sweet Daisy', aistriú ar 'Dála an Nóinín', *Outlook*, 27 Feabhra 1932; 'On the Death of Mary', aistriú ar 'A Shuaircfhir Sháimh' – iar gclos báis Mháire, *Outlook*, 9 Aibreán 1932. Tá na bundánta i *Saothar Filidheacht an Athar Pádraigín Haicéad,* in eagar ag 'Torna', Baile Átha Cliath 1916.
19. Lch 64.
20. *Cois Life Fadó*, 169 – 172.
21. *Dánta ón Oirthear*, 26.
22. *An tUltach*, Uimh. 1, 1929, lch 3.
23. *Ibid.*
24. *Dánta ón Oirthear*, 15.
25. LNÉ: LS G 1077.

Tugadh an aiste thuas mar léacht i Halla na dTáilliúirí i 1993 agus cuireadh i gcló é i *Féile Zozimus* iml. 3, Baile Átha Cliath 1994.

E. H. W. Meyerstein.

A view of Magdalen College, Oxford.

Chapter 14

An Unusual Blaskets Visitor;
E. H. W. Meyerstein

I had a heart, and all its waking dreams were poetry.
E.H.W.M. 19.6.44

Of the many distinguished visitors to the Blasket Island few could have been more unusual than Edward Harry William Meyerstein. The friend and colleague of Robin Flower, he worked in the Department of Manuscripts of the British Museum from August 1913 until November 1918, except for a brief interlude in 1914 when he was a private in the 3rd Battalion Royal Dublin Fusiliers at Cork, from which he was discharged, not surprisingly, as 'Not likely to become an efficient soldier.'

He was a frequent visitor at Robin Flower's home, where he spent practically every New Year's Eve, joining in the children's fun and games like an overgrown child. When Flower's brilliant daughter Barbara won the Craven Scholarship to Cambridge in 1932 and the effort resulted in nervous collapse which left her exhausted, Meyerstein wrote her a letter couched in soothing verse (printed after his death in *Verse letters to Five Friends*, London 1954, pp 2-5).

Born in Hampstead, London, in 1889, the eldest son of a wealthy financier and a talented, artistic mother, he spent an unhappy childhood before going to Harrow and Magdalen College, Oxford, where he did not achieve the primary academic success that his enormous capacity for learning warranted. He wrote ten novels and a considerable body of verse, attaining a distinction that earned him an appreciative study by Lionel Butler in the *Proceedings of the British Academy* under the heading 'Chatterton Lecture on an English Poet', fittingly since he had written a *Life of Chatterton*, 'the work of a fine scholar, of a polymath of English poetry', Lionel Butler's appraisal. That he was a brilliant Latinist his translation of Rimbaud's *Le Bateau ivre* is testimony. His knowledge of Classical, French and English literature was extensive. He was a strange mix of human being, solitary, melancholy, eccentric, throbbing with interior distress, a mass of contradictions, who would ruthlessly rebuff a friend and soon after express his sincerest regret. His friend, editor and literary executor, Rowland Watson, must have been gifted with saintly patience to bear the brunt of his changing humours. Writing to Barbara Flower (23 October 1933) he ends his letter: 'Pray that peace comes to this wretched outcast heart; it needs it' (*Letters*, p. 156). His place in the literary world is assured but perhaps as yet undefined. In person he was heavily built and walked with an awkward shambling gait. His countenance was distorted by Bell's Palsy which caused a squint in one eye. When relaxed and among friends his face would settle into repose. Averse to machines, he never drove a car or rode a bicycle. Radio and cinema were unfavoured things. It was no doubt at Robin Flower's suggestion, as it was in his company, that Meyerstein made his visit to the Blasket Island in April 1931, 'one more grotesque episode in my quaint career', as he wrote to his friend Rowland Watson from the Island on 8 April. It was a change for a city habitant and he was not without apprehensions. The constant sitting and standing about in draughts had not improved his facial trouble and he thought he would be lucky to get back home as well as he came. It was a custom of the islanders to have nightly singsongs and in his desire to please them, he 'buffooned', as he puts it, this involving putting on expressions which made his facial trouble worse. It was typical of him, this part of the child in his make-up. 'And I *have* pleased them'.

The scenery reminded him of South-West Cornwall, though here it was more broken and island-studded. There were no trees and no growth higher than heather. Part of his island company, besides Flower, was a German student and a Dublin chemistry man, young and charming, both studying the language. 'We feed together, and Flower spreads the wealth of his ripe and varied knowledge on our bread and marmalade. To him this place is a dream of his youth; everybody loves him and runs up to shake his hand, and he teases the girls to his heart's content — all is laughing and merriment. Physical spirits are a great thing.'

He was having introspective doubts about whether it was prudent to have come to the island but suspected there was a reason for doing so not unrelated to his mental progress and he needed all this faith now. In an undated letter from the Great Blasket island written about the same time, to T.N. Green-Armytage, he relates that he is writing in a pitch-roofed cottage, where eight people were grouped around a turf fire on which a kettle swung from a sort of gallows. 'Irish is being spoken and there is much laughter.' Neither donkey nor hen, not to mention a sheep, had intruded through the front door on this talk as they did on previous ones. It was some years since he had been in Ireland but it still struck him as the place where the unexpected always happened. He tells his friend about the crossing which had been rough. A bridge near Rosslare had been declared unsafe due to the floods and the train had to go two-thirds round Tipperary. A swift glance at Killarney was all he had, and the train from there to Tralee left an hour late. At 9 p.m. on Thursday, after a mountain climb in a local train, they reached Dingle, where they slept. No doubt they were tired. He describes their arrival on the island:

> Yesterday was a day of great calm and blueness, and this naked and deserted stretch of Kerry stood out carved against sky and sea. We crossed the Atlantic (only a gentle swell) in the afternoon; and most of the 130-odd islanders met us at the harbour. It was a *joyous* sight to see twenty or so children, all girls, with hair glistening in the sun, gathered like puffins – the gulls are not here in number yet – on the undercliff.

There were four visitors in all. Meyerstein himself and Flower, though he would hardly describe Flower as a visitor, rather an Irish-speaking omniscience who, in the absence of telephone and wireless, kept the islanders acquainted with the doings of the great world outside, a young student of Trinity College, Dublin and a privatdocent from Berlin, both come to speak and study Irish, with the Berliner preparing a work on the origin of the genitive case, which seems a curious subject, and is perhaps a fancy of Meyerstein's. His interest in the island life was intense.

> It is a beautiful sight to watch the men gathering the long strips of seaweed and stuffing them into panniers on donkeys, to be used as manure, and a still more beautiful one to see an old woman, with a black shawl enveloping her head, blowing up a fire with her lips, while the light from the kindled turf invests her eye with a sort of prophetic glow.
>
> The language – which, to an uninstructed ear, differs more in sound, according to the tone of the speaker, than most languages do – I am making no attempt to learn. The people have that grave courtesy that goes with removal from a social world – a fact, by the way, which Wordsworth very fully appreciated. I have the *Prelude* with me (no other book). They laugh a great deal, in a happy childish way, and yesterday evening I amused them in a cottage, where the son played reels on a fiddle – by executing an improvised series of dances, in and out of the door. The fact that I

do not understand a word they say does not make me feel suspicious or lonely.

Perhaps the exertion of dancing brought on a feeling of tiredness, which caused his face to be drawn down under his right eye, but he had learned to expect this symptom of his affliction in strange surroundings.

Flower – who needed a holiday badly – has thrown off all the cares of the British Museum and jests with everyone. This morning (except for a short walk to an ancient earthwork) was spent entirely in handshaking and renewing friendships. A community of simple hearts – where it is necessary for a priest to come once a year only!

Meyerstein was back in his rooms, 3 Gray's Inn Place, London, on 19 April 1931, after a fortnight in the Blaskets.

Yes, [he wrote to his friend, T. N Green-Armytage], it has been a valuable experience this fortnight on the Great Blasket Island, for it has shown me very clearly what is wrong with me. I suppose I have never seen so many girls at close quarters and with such happy familiarity in my life. They like me because I behaved like a grimacing ragamuffin – which is, I suppose, my attitude to civilization. These folk have precious few diversions – no telephone, wireless, cinema; a human being has only to amuse them off and on to win their affection. It is very natural in me to talk nonsense and to behave grotesquely. I had only to recite the first fable of La Fontaine, with exaggerated gesture, to be asked for 'Fox and Crow' every evening and when I pretended the old widow, huddled by the hearth, in whose house these gatherings took place, was 'Maître Corbeau', and tried to charm the imaginary cheese out of her mouth by amorous gestures, the whole house was with me, and the girls were shouting my Christian name with an acute accent 'Edie Edie'. There is no masculine jealousy, even if you make up to any particular girl – as everybody on the island is related, and they all marry off the mainland. So for once in my life that horrible distrust of women and their practical ways was lifted from my brain, and I could, as I thought, be an affectionate natural being, without love, perhaps, but certainly without fear.

It was an occasion of auto-therapy for Meyerstein. 'This is what I have learnt, that by hook or by crook I must throw off this introspection, which (native to my temperament) has been aggravated by living alone, and go out, forget myself, and mix with the world . . . I must make a start of looking out instead of in . . . I thought this jaunt would be an experience, and it has proved one . . .'

Robin Flower he described as 'a wonderfully learned man, and much loved by the islanders as he actually contributes to their support. He carries his knowledge very lightly, and is the most purely detached intelligence I know'.

On leaving the Blaskets he had an adventure, recorded in his volume of poems *The Delphic Charioteer* (London 1951) pp 22-26 in cryptic verse as 'Fortune of Dunquin'. The landing on Dunquin pier is described:

> The black and orange painted
> Coracle
> From the great Blasket Island
> By the swell
> Buffeted, lolled against the
> Kerry Coast.

The passengers were helped up the steep incline above the pier by the boatmen. A friendship between a young lady and her male companion who 'had been bosom friends a week at least upon that treeless isle . . . ceased as suddenly as it began'.

The incalculable fortune appears to be that the young lady transferred her interest and converse to the poet. Most of the poem is taken up with the light and fleeting friendship, which included a meal together of raisined biscuits, while waiting for the train out of Dingle, which he boards exulting in the 'incalculable fortune of Dunquin'. There is a priest in the cryptic drama, and an intrusive cat. But the drift of the poem is not easy to follow. Meyerstein lived the life of a recluse in his rooms at 3 Gray's Inn Place, London. In the early years of the Second World War he was bombed out and returned to live in Magdalen College, Oxford. After the war he went back to Gray's Inn where he died on 12 September 1952. His last years were made comfortable by the care of his relations and friends who looked after his every need.

This essay is based mainly on three letters, numbered 102, 103 and 104, pages 125-129, in *Some letters of E. H. W. Meyerstein* (London, Nevill Spearman 1959) edited by Rowland Watson. Neville Spearman Publishers are incorporated in the C. W. Daniel Company Ltd., 1 Church Path, Saffron Walden, Essex 1JP, England. I gratefully acknowledge the permission of Mrs. Jane Miller on behalf of the C. W. Daniel Company Ltd. for the use of this material. I have been unable to trace Rowland Watson.

Other sources consulted include *World Authors 1950-1970* (New York 1975) edited by John Wakeman, for the entry on Meyerstein, pp 988-9, and Lionel Butler's essay on Meyerstein in *Proceedings of the British Academy* 1955, pp 141-169. An Irish friend of Meyerstein's was Nora Ní Shúilliobháin of Valentia Island, who recalls him by his familiar name Eddie Marstein in her interesting essay 'Valentia Fireside – yesterday' (in the *Capuchin Annual* 1976) as a reader of his novel *Robin Wastraw* and their shared fondness for fishes' eyes and marrowbones. Meyerstein inscribed for her his Latin translation of *Le Bateau ivre.*

Chapter 15

Leabharlann Náisiúnta na hÉireann

Réamhrá

Tá an léiriú is fearr ar thréithe tíre le fáil ins na bunachais náisiúnta arb é a gcúram bail a chur agus a choinneáil ar mhaoin intleachtúil na tíre sin, ar na cnuasaigh mhóra ealaíne agus leabhar, ar na hearraí saíochta agus léinn, ar na taiscí lámhscríbhinní agus taifead a thugann an léargas is glaine agus is bunúsaí dúinn ar phearsantacht agus doimhneas agus anam na tíre. Sa deireadh thiar, sin iad guth na tíre: sin iad an teachtaireacht atá á cur ag an tír le hannála na sibhialtachta.

Má fhéachaimid in ár dtimpeall, tá go leor den chineál sin againn le bheith bródúil astu. Féadaimid a bheith bródúil sa chéill is airde agus is mórálaí as Leabharlann Náisiúnta na hÉireann atá i dtrácht san aiste ina dhiaidh seo ag Pádraig Ó hInnse. Tar éis dó a bheith ag saothrú sa Leabharlann ar feadh chúig bliana is tríocha (1941-1976) agus a bheith ina Stiúrthóir ar feadh na naoi mbliana deireannacha díobhsan labhrann sé le heolas agus údarás.

Mar a mhíníonn sé dúinn, tá sé de chúram ar Leabharlann Náisiúnta scríbhinní agus taifid na tíre a chruinniú, pé foirm nó riocht ina bhfuilid, agus iad a chur ar fáil le haghaidh lucht staidéir nó taighde. Ós í príomhionad leabharlannaíochta na tíre í, is cuid dá gnó catalóga, cláir saothair agus liostaí foinsí a sholáthar. Tagann gach uile ábhar agus gné a bhaineas le saíocht agus sibhialtacht na tíre faoi raon a cúraim. Samhlaíocht, grinneas, fadamharc, súile an iolair geall leis, a déarfá nár mhór a bheith ag lucht a stiúrtha agus iad a bheith san airdeall de shíor ag faire ar gach ócáid agus ceaint agus loc inar dhóigh go mbeadh duais le soláthar, ó chaisleán go bothán.

Mar is léir ó chuntas Phádraig Uí Innse, bhí na cáilíochtaí sin ag an bhfear ceannasach Risteard de Hae, a shaothraigh chomh feidhmiúil sin chun an Leabharlann a shaibhriú agus a fhorbairt. Bhí an tréith soláthairte sin ann, fara le hinspioráid, nuair a scríobh sé an nóta gairid spreagúil úd go dtí George Bernard Shaw agus gur thug an saoi toradh air láithreach. Níl ansin ach mír luachmhar amháin den mhaoin intleachta a tháinig i seilbh na Leabharlainne lena linn agus gheofar eolas ar a thuilleadh mór dá leithéid sa chuntas seo istigh, cuntas atá thar a bheith spéisiúil sa mhéid go léiríonn sé mar a dhéanann oibrithe ciúine na bearta is fearr tairbhe gan phoiblíocht ná gleo. Tá an Clár Beathaisnéise Náisiúnta le tiomsú fós ach de thoradh tuisceana agus dea-bhreithiúnais an Dochtúra de Hae tá an t-ullmhú is riachtanach ina chomhair leagtha síos mar bhunsraith sa dá mhór-liosta, *Foinsí Lámhscríbhinne ar Shibhialtacht na hÉireann* agus *Aistí i dTréimhseacháin Éireannacha.*

Bhí bua na taidhleoireachta ag Pádraig Ó hInnse agus acmhainn muintearthais agus ba luachmhar mar a chuaigh na cáilíochtaí sin chun tairbhe don Leabharlainn. De thoradh an chairdis idir é féin agus Patrick Kavanagh bhí ar a chumas margadh a dhéanamh leis an ardfhile sin chun dlús tábhachtach lámhscríbhinní dá chuid a chur i dtaisce na Leabharlainne agus faighimid léargas spéisiúil uaidh ar an modh oibre a bhíodh ag an bhfile agus seod litríochta á chumadh aige. Is cuí freisin mar a thagraíonn sé don mbronntanas fairsing scríbhinní a fuair an Leabharlann ó mhuintir Yeats, bailiúchán atá thar luach, agus mar aitheantas ar a bhféile, bhí beartaithe ag an Dr. de Hae agus Pádraig Ó hInnse Seomra Yeats a bhunú sa Leabharlann. A leithéid a bheith ann fós ní foláir a bheith ina dhóchas dúinn. Tá tagairtí spéisiúla anseo do phearsana a bhí dícheallach ar son na Leabharlainne cosúil leis an ildánach Éamonn Mac Giolla Iasachta, údar ar ghinealach, agus John Ainsworth ar a mbíodh de chúram dul i dtadhall le muintir na dTithe Móra agus a gcuid lámhscríbhinní a shealbhú don Leabharlann agus beidh lucht taighde buíoch go bhfuil cnuasach stairiúil áirithe a bhreithnigh sé, Lámhscríbhinní Thiarna Inse Chuinn, curtha go slán sábháilte i dtaisce na Leabharlainne. Is trua gur éiríodh as an Treoir leis an *Freeman's Journal (1763-1924)* a bhí á dhéanamh ag príosúnaigh Phort Laoise.

Bíonn spás, agus bíonn cion ceart foirne, ag teastáil le haghaidh ábhair a bhíonn de shíor ag teacht isteach agus le haghaidh freastal ar lucht taighde a bhíonn i gcónaí ag méadú. Nuair a ghlac Pádraig Ó hInnse ceannas na Leabharlainne i 1967 chuir sé roimis go háirithe cóiríocht agus spás breise agus líon ceart foirne a sholáthar. Bhí Iontaobhaithe na Leabharlainne ar aon aigne leis sa chuspóir sin agus tá an fhírinne bheacht chiallmhar acu nuair a deir siad nach féidir dualgas na Leabharlainne Náisiúnta a chomhlíonadh gan a riar ceart spáis, airgid cheannaigh agus foirne a bheith aici.

Bíonn ar an Leabharlann Náisiúnta bheith de shíor ag soláthar. Ní foláir di faireachas a dhéanamh ar dhíolacháin agus ceainteanna agus ócáidí eile ar a mbíonn leabhair, lámhscríbhinní, litreacha, léarscáileanna agus earraí eile a bhíonn tábhachtach do shaol an náisiúin á ndíol. Ar ócáidí mar sin bíonn an Leabharlann ag iomaíocht le forais agus le daoine eile a bhfuil neart airgid le caitheamh acu. Is léir dá bhrí sin nach foláir bonn chomh tacúil a bheith ag an Leabharlann ó thaobh airgid go bhféadfaidh sí dul ar an margadh le dóchas cinnte ceannaigh. Ba laghdú ar mhórtas na tíre go mbeadh lón intleachta dúchais ag dul go háit éigin eile seachas an láthair is dual dó. Tá sé de theagasc ró-dhearfa le baint as an aiste seo go bhfuil an Leabharlann Náisiúnta i dteideal an fáltas is flaithiúla a fháil is féidir le tír na nÉireann a thairiscint di chun go mbeidh sí in acmhainn dul ar aghaidh leis an saothar tairbheach atá ceaptha di agus na haicmí éagsúla dualgais atá uirthi a chomhlíonadh.

Ábhar mórtais agus misnigh is ea an tuairisc a thugann Pádraig Ó hInnse dúinn ar a thréimhse sa Leabharlann Náisiúnta. Tá eachtraí le hinsint aige ar na pearsana a casadh air, mar atá Joseph Holloway, fear a labhair beagán, agus Bulmer Hobson, fear a labhair mórán, nuair a bhí a gcuid scríbhinní araon á nglacadh aige mar mhaoin don Leabharlann. Tá scéal aige ar a thuras go Cill Chainnigh chun lán leoraí doiciméidí mórluacha ina raibh insint ar sheacht gcéad bliain de stair na hÉireann a iompar ó Chaisleán Mharcas Urmhumhan chun na Leabharlainne Náisiúnta. Fuair sé dea-thoil go fairsing ina chuid saothair. Dob iad a chairde-sean cairde na Leabharlainne chomh maith agus tá buíochas agus onóir ag dul do leithéidí Sybil le Brocquy as a síor-dhúthracht ag soláthar ar son na Leabharlainne. Bhí an Leabharlann ina teaghlach spioradálta ag a chara Richard Ellmann a bhfuil saothar bunúsach foilsithe aige ar scríbhneoirí móra na hÉireann.

Rud áirithe a bhí tábhachtach do leas na Leabharlainne ab ea gur bunaíodh Cumann Leabharlann Náisiúnta na hÉireann i 1969 le haird a tharraingt ar bhail na Leabharlainne. Uirlis fheidhmiúil ab ea an Cumann sin do chabhrú le cáil agus cuspóirí na Leabharlainne. Obair uasal is ea í agus bhí agus tá cairde uaisle ag an Leabharlann. Ar áireamh na gcarad sin bhí Barry Brown agus a bhanchéile (nach maireann) a d'fhág le tiomnacht suim £30,000 ar mhaithe le cuspóirí an Chumainn. Is faoi choimirce an Chumainn a thug Pádraig Ó hInnse an léacht atá i bprionta ina dhiaidh seo. Bhí sé d'ádh ar an scríbhneoir seo a bheith i láthair agus féadann sé a rá go raibh toil agus meon an lucht éisteachta go tréan leis an méid a bhí le rá aige.

Réamhrá é seo don pháipéar *The National Library of Ireland 1941-1976* a léigh Pádraig Ó hInnse do Chumann Leabharlann Náisiúnta na hÉireann an 22 Deireadh Fómhair 1985.

Darnaway Street, Edinburgh, where Kuno Meyer lived from 1874 to 1876.

Chapter 16

In the footsteps of Kuno Meyer

Kuno Meyer wrote to his friend Whitley Stokes in 1882 that he hoped to take up the study of the Irish language and literature as the principal object of his life's work. He was then twenty-four years of age. He kept his resolution faithfully and spent the rest of his life in pursuit of it. In his search for the manuscript materials of Irish literature he travelled widely throughout Europe. I have called this talk 'In the footsteps of Kuno Meyer'. It is a far from accurate title. In it I propose to relate my own modest travels to places frequented by Kuno Meyer or in search of documents which would tell the story of his life. This talk has neither system nor order and I shall begin it here in Germany, at the lovely peaceful village of Morenhoven not far from Bonn.

My friend John Marin, from the *Deutsch-Irische Gesellschaft,* and I left Morenhoven at 9.00 on the morning of 28 May 1990 on our way south-eastwards to the city of Kronach, our object being to visit the grave of Johann Kaspar Zeuss, the founder of Celtic Philology, *Begründer der Keltologie.* We made one stop on the way for petrol and to feast on a meal of mineral water and frankfurters and reached Kronach at 17. 10, just ten minutes after schedule, a tribute to the excellence of John's driving on the 400 kilometre journey on a close and sultry day. We had an appointment at the Hotel Bauer, Kulmbacher Strasse 7, with Heinz Müller, the Head of the City Tourist Information Office, and Hermann Wich, the City Archivist, the preparatory diplomatic work having been done in advance by John who had written to the Mayor of Kronach about our proposed visit.

We duly met our friends, who greeted us warmly and took us to the *Kaspar-Zeuss Gymnasium* where we met the Headmaster who received us with the greatest of courtesy and bade us be seated. An enormous tray of buns was brought in, with coffee, and the conversation turned on Zeuss, whose importance in language history was recognised and who now was honoured in Kronach as one of its most distinguished sons along with the painter Lucas Cranach. What had helped to bring this recognition about was that the city boundaries had been extended to bring within its limits the little village of Vogtendorf, some kilometres outside, with the result, for one thing, that a few weeks before our arrival, Zeuss had been honoured in a ceremony at a small central city park when the Mayor had unveiled a statue of him, in scholarly pose, book in hand, beside a placid little lake, a place for rest and reflection. A portrait of Zeuss in oils was brought in, a copy of the original, now in Munich, which a student of the Arts class had made and with it as centrepiece and our party grouped around it, a photographer appeared to take a record of the occasion.

Our friends took us to the cemetery where Zeuss is buried. This was close by and well within the city precincts. The Zeuss family plot is just inside the gate and is carefully tended and maintained. It is surmounted by a statue of the scholar, book in hand. John and I were very conscious that we had come on a pilgrimage. Our hosts had bought a bouquet at a local flower shop and I, coming from distant Ireland, was thought to be the most suitable person for the duty of laying it on his grave. This I did reverentially with the words in Irish, 'Leagaim na bláthanna seo ar uaigh Johann Kaspar Zeuss, in ainm mhuintir na hÉireann, le hardmheas air agus le hómós dá chuimhne', repeating them in English 'I lay these flowers on the grave of Johann Kaspar Zeuss, in the name of the Irish people, in honour of his person and in homage to his memory'. As the four of us stood there together I recited in Irish and in Latin, the two languages honoured by Zeuss, a Pater, Ave and Gloria. Halfway through the Ave Maria, with the feeling and emotion of the occasion, I suffered a memory block and turned back to Irish, finishing with the Gloria. Indeed it was with difficulty that words came to me at all. We all participated in the intense feeling of the occasion.

We were, indeed, following in the footsteps of Kuno Meyer. Seventy-four years earlier, in July 1906, the centenary of Zeuss's birth was celebrated in Bamberg in a commemoration in which Kuno Meyer was a participant if not the prime mover. The occasion then was enhanced with music. After the performance of Gluck's *Overture to Iphigenia in Aulis,* Kuno Meyer gave an outline of Zeuss's life and achievement in what was the principal oration of the day, 'Johann Kaspar Zeuss as Philologist', to an audience that included Windisch, Thurneysen, Osthoff and the great linguists of the era. In the cemetery of Kronach Joseph O'Neill laid a wreath on Zeuss's grave on behalf of the Gaelic League of Ireland, speaking a tribute in Irish in what was described as the most emotional moment of the whole commemoration.

On the following day John and I met the Mayor, who kindly took time off from his busy routine, for the influx of newcomers from East Germany, seeking to establish business connections, placed a heavy burden on himself and his staff. We thanked him for the hospitality of his friendly city and after a pleasant exchange of courtesies we set out, laden with a stock of brochures, for Bamberg where Zeuss had been a student and later a teacher. It is a lovely city, with over 2000 listed buildings, crowned by the impressive Cathedral, which it was our special object to visit. We were filled with wonder at its interior where there are examples of the exquisite woodcraft of Tilmann Riemenschneider when our attention was drawn by a rare and unexpected delight. High up in the nave of the Cathedral was a balcony where the organ was located, which an unseen hand began to play, filling the Cathedral with sound. A beautiful voice sang the *Panis Angelicus* in accompaniment, probably rehearsing for some ceremony. John and I sat down to listen and remained in rapt attention while the singing lasted, which was only for a minute. Then silence.

We continued our journey to Würzburg, city of St. Kilian, where we were expected, but that is a story for another day.

In Berlin-Lichterfelde, No. 7/8 Mommsenstrasse, is the home of Eduard Meyer, successor to Mommsen as the historian of the Ancient World. There is a plaque in his memory on the wall beside the front door and inside, in one of the rooms, there is a framed display board showing the Meyer family ancestry. Kuno Meyer traced his family back to Christian Meyer, born 1686. Direct descent was through Johann Gottlieb Meyer (1722-1781), Johann Heinrich Meyer (1770-1837) born in Dresden, who had a family of five sons, born between 1797 and 1806, all with artistic talent. The fourth son was Eduard, who became assistant master in the Johanneum in Hamburg, and whose life span was 1804-1884. He married twice. His second wife was Johanna Henrietta Dessau, of a Hamburg family. These were the parents of Eduard, Kuno, Antonie and Albrecht.

At the time of our visit to Berlin, in June 1993, we were fortunate to have the good offices of Dr. Christhard Hoffmann, a young scholar of the *Technische Universität Berlin,* who has made a special study of Eduard Meyer.

The present owner of Mommsenstrasse 7/8 is Barbara, daughter of Hans Eduard Meyer and granddaughter of the historian. She was away on holiday, but by the help of Dr. Hoffmann, we were given access to the house and were received by its very cheerful tenant, a lady who is a musician. We were given access to all parts of the house, including the attic. We climbed up to the attic which was full of trunks which presumably contained the historian's records and writings, but these were covered with bags and boxes and various other things, which would require patience and energy to remove, not to mention disturbing the dust. There was a large press containing framed family photographs in which we rummaged without success, in search of a portrait of Kuno Meyer which Christhard Hoffmann had seen on a former occasion. Looking around I could not help thinking of the Grimm brothers who might have described such mysterious places as this, of such strange and secret atmosphere. What knowledge was stored in those trunks? What secrets of family or history held within? For the researcher it is a place of beckoning and anticipation. We would have wished to remain but our time was limited.

Downstairs again, we took a photograph of Eduard Meyer's splendid portrait in oils by Lovis Corinth. It is a house of character, the habitation of a scholar, lined with books, furnished for comfort, with all the appurtenances for the promotion of study and thought. Comparisons between Eduard and his brother Kuno came to mind. Eduard moved in circles of influence, was familiar with the high politics of his day. Sir Roger Casement and Admiral Tirpitz were guests at his house. Of a serious cast of mind, he was inclined to the company of the important. Though an outstanding historian of the Ancient World, his mind was very much occupied with the world of his own present. He would invite his senior history students to functions in his spacious garden at the rear of the house. Lacking the imagination of his younger brother, his mind was devoted to the direct and undeviating path. He is considered to be a less interesting study and a less attractive subject for biography than his brother Kuno. This is the view of the scholar who is in the best position to judge, Dr. Christhard Hoffmann.

It would not be true to say that our search for documents relating to Kuno Meyer was speculative. We knew that there were Meyer documents in the old-established *Akademie der Wissenschaften* but we went first to the *Staatsbibliothek zu Berlin, Preussischer Kulturbesitz,* on the Potsdamer Strasse in the hope that we might also discover materials. Arriving there shortly after 10.00 on the morning of 2 June 1993, John, without whose negotiating skills and knowledge of German I would have been utterly handicapped, made known our purpose at the entrance to the manuscripts department, which was to consult whatever *Nachlass* there was of Kuno Meyer.

Two boxes of documents were placed before us, to which we turned our attention. We were hardly prepared for what they contained. Turning over document on document, diaries, poems, sketches, Italian and Spanish itineraries, stories, letters, photographs, translations, histories, reviews, drawings, genealogy, it began to dawn on us that the author of all this was a very precocious boy, whom we could see in the documents developing into a studious, creative and adventurous young man, who recorded and wrote down every experience of his life. We had no previous idea that we would come on such a treasury of knowledge. Here was source material which would be of primary importance in filling out the chapters of his early life story in particular and essential for providing a fully rounded and satisfying portrait of an obviously gifted individual.

As discovery followed on discovery, and we came upon something significant, as for example, The Hamburg Diary, *Die Gaelen in Irland,* a bound collection of *Briefe aus Schottland,* a particularly illuminating series which would document Meyer's introduction to the Gaelic world, we would utter our surprise almost out loud, to be reproved by black looks and 'Shh' from fellow-readers, for the rule of silence was meant to be observed.

We decided to have copies made of the most important documents, in particular those relating to Irish history and literature, since these were the mainspring of Kuno Meyer's life. There were copying facilities in the library for our convenience. We had to work quickly for our time was limited. Most documents were in German, some in English. We appraised each document, decided quickly what was useful to us, to note its contents and identify it for copying. By closing time we had noted a considerable number of items for copying, though we were still very far from the end of the *Nachlass.* John placed his carefully noted list on top of the box, to be continued next day.

Next morning, on opening the box, to our dismay, our list was not there. We made urgent and thorough inquiries, without result. Undeterred we went again through the task of examining the documents and at the end of the day John put our collection of notes in his case, not trusting to the gremlins, sprites or others who had caused the mischief of our labour's disappearance.

On the following day we set out for the *Akademie der Wissenschaften* in the Jägerruh 22/23, which we found after some difficulty, as construction works were under way in the area and we had to go around them. The *Akademie* was probably the premier institution of learning in the world in its greatest period, before the First World War. The list of its members, as published some years ago, makes up a roll of prodigiously learned persons. We found it, with the sculpted medallion-shaped outline of Alexander Humboldt inset in the outer wall, and entered to be introduced to Dr. Klauss in his office. Having introduced me, John explained our purpose. Dr. Klauss was no less than astonished to see me because well over ten years before, in 1981, it was he who had signed his name to a letter giving me permission to do research in the *Akademie* which, at that time, was in East Berlin jurisdiction. John had with him his copy of *Kuno Meyer* in which Dr. Klauss was very interested since Kuno Meyer was a member of the *Akademie.* In the unsettled last year of his life, 1919, Meyer was given two rooms in the *Akademie,* where he could both work and sleep, and he had planned to transfer his books there.

We were highly impressed by the efficiency and courtesy of the staff. We were not long seated when they brought us two long-shaped containers of card-indexes, clearly the basic material for an Irish language dictionary. The handwriting on the entries I had long been familiar with. It was Kuno Meyer's. Lexicography was only one of the many areas to which Meyer was constantly contributing. The entries were excerpts, with meanings in English, from Irish language sources, both manuscript and printed, the sources being indicated in all cases. I considered these to be the basic work for Meyer's *Contributions to Irish Lexicography*, his unfinished Dictionary, of which the letters A to D had been printed. Following his differences with Carl Marstrander, to whose dictionary work he had been contributing, Meyer proposed to hand over all his own dictionary slips to the young scholar Hans Hessen who had been assembling an independent Irish Dictionary from printed sources. It would appear that he never got around to doing this. Hessen was killed early in the First World War and although his dictionary work was later edited and published by a group of scholars, Meyer's work was not included in it.

There are twelve long-shaped boxes of those dictionary slips in the *Akademie*. We only had time to make a cursory examination of two. The *Akademie* itself did not know what was in them, or what language they were written in, and had even considered disposing of them. They had brought them to our attention in the hope that we might explain what they were and suggest some place which might wish to have them. We pointed out their significance and John supplied them with a description in German of their nature and importance. I said I would bring them to the attention of the National Library of Ireland which already possessed the most important collection in Ireland of Kuno Meyer material and would I believed be the most suitable destination. They were perfectly prepared, willing and happy, to let them go to an interested Irish institution.

Meantime the very efficient staff had put on our table, in their separate envelopes, all the other materials of Kuno Meyer interest which they had and we selected our choice of these for copying and what we selected was copied on the spot. There was some correspondence of Sir Roger Casement whom we see writing to Eduard Meyer in a cheerless mood from Dresden on 4 January 1916:

> I have been so unwell of late – my heart troubling me – that I have not been able to write or do anything but brood. And that is very bad. I want to move and do something in the open air – as of old in Africa where the happiest days of my life were spent ... I wish to God I were in Ireland ... Maybe I shall go by submarine.

His letters to Eduard Meyer seem written in a hurried and urgent hand. In reading them we are conducted through emotional avenues of history. There is his account of the Howth arms landing for the Irish Volunteers and its sequel, and there is a detailed document in German on the subject of Casement signed by Eduard Meyer, dated 13 August 1916, whose handwriting biographers will not find easy reading. Regarding the economics of copying, the charge per page was about 60 Pf. By comparison, the *Staatsbibliothek* charged I DM per page. The entire cost of what we copied in the *Akademie* came to just over 72 DM, very reasonable indeed. In due course, on my return to Dublin, I explained to the National Library that the *Akademie* possessed this important collection of Kuno Meyer dictionary slips of Early and Mediaeval Irish which they were prepared to let go to an interested Irish institution. I supplied the details which were included in a letter forwarded by the Library saying they would be very glad to have them and would pay any cost of purchase and transport. In the circumstances we were sure there would be no difficulty or hesitation about receiving possession of them on these terms. In a very short space of time there came from the *Akademie* a brief reply saying in effect that this was artistic property of the State and its export was prohibited by law. That decided that. John and I were perforce to be happy in the satisfaction that we had identified for the *Akademie* this important item which, before our arrival, had been a mystery.

On looking through Antonie (Toni) Meyer's correspondence we find in one of her letters confirmation that our identification was correct. Writing to Richard Irvine Best on 24 November 1919 she says:

> Kuno bequeathed all his slips for the Dictionary to the Academy when they offered to give him a study within their precincts [NLI 11002 (46)]

The Royal Irish Academy's *Dictionary of the Irish Language* was completed a number of years ago, lacking the benefit which might accrue to it through the use of Meyer's Dictionary slips. A future revision of the Dictionary will accordingly have available for its editors the Meyer material which is housed in the *Akademie der Wissenschaften*.

Talking of Kuno Meyer leads us naturally to his sister Toni. They were very close together. After his death she took up a post as matron or manageress of a boarding school for boys at Templin near Hamburg. She retired from this position towards the end of 1922 and went to live in the *Johannesstift*, Heilwigstrasse 160, Hamburg. It is a residence for retired people. She seemed to have her own private quarters there and was able to follow her interests. 'My time is filled up with all sorts of things in the house ... reading, music, paying visits etc.'. And of course writing to her friends, letters that are full of musical allusions and are a delight to read, for music was her whole life. She had a number of pupils to whom she gave lessons in English. What they chiefly wanted was everyday English for practical purposes (to Edith Best 23.X. 1922) and would use the *Manchester Guardian* as their reading matter (31.XII. 1922) [NLI 11002(5)]. She viewed the future with equanimity. She said that when she died she wished her ashes to be spread over the Alster. This however was not to be her last resting place.

Patricia Wimberger had discovered that a friend of hers in Leverkusen, Frau Oda Kiesselbach, was the daughter of a niece of Toni Meyer. She was Frau Elisabet Beselin and was living in Hamburg.

John and I decided to visit Hamburg in the expectation that our journey might provide some discovery about Kuno Meyer, and an appointment was made on our behalf with Frau Beselin who lived in a house in the Maienweg, Hamburg, where we were to arrive at a certain time. We set out, with John at the wheel as usual, stopping overnight at Osnabrück where we met our friends Máire and Jerome Morris and were guided by them through the historic places of that attractive city where was signed the treaty ending the 30 Years War.

Reaching Hamburg we put up at the Hotel Ibis, all popular hotels being full because of an important function in the city, and on a Saturday afternoon we navigated our way to the Maienweg where we were received by Frau Beselin. Kuno Meyer's American colleague Gertrude Schoepperle had once described him as being of aristocratic and conservative mind and certainly the niece whom we met was, in my impression, a genuine aristocrat. She was 87 years of age but active and vigorous of mind, clear and decisive in speech. Her grand-daughter Maya had arrived on her bicycle at the same time as ourselves and introduced us. We sat down to coffee and a tasty cake, baked by Maya, and chatted. Frau Beselin told us her Aunt Toni often came to visit her at the house in the Maienweg, always appearing unannounced, quite unconcerned about the war and interested mainly in family and music. The house in which Frau Beselin lived was built in 1936. She had ready for me a typescript of four pages giving an account of Kuno Meyer, which was part of a larger account of the Meyer family and tradition.

After coffee we drove out to the Ohlsdorf Cemetery to see the family grave in which Toni was buried, guided expertly by the directions of Frau Beselin, 'move over to the left-hand lane... watch out for fast cars coming round that concealed bend', who had given up driving no more than a year or two ago. Ohlsdorf Cemetery is extensive and if a cemetery may be described as beautiful, as Toni once did, it is truly so, with wide avenues flanked by splendid old trees. The Meyer family plot is enclosed in a circle of shrubs and dominated by the huge stone monument in which is inset the plaque of Franz Andreas Meyer, the celebrated architect of many Hamburg buildings, and here, quite obviously, the local Patriarch of the family. At the foot of the monument were the stone tablets bearing the names of various members of the family and we found the tablet commemorating Toni Meyer. It was not possible to photograph it because it was obscured by the growth of ground plants. Here then was the final resting place of Toni Meyer's ashes, not, as she had fancied it might be, scattered over the expanse of the Alster but deposited in the shadow of the great trees of the Ohlsdorf Cemetery on a cold November day of 1945, after her peaceful death in the *Johannesstift*. My effort at taking photographs turned out to be a failure, through my unskilful knowledge of the camera. Places such as this invoke thoughts and silences. We returned to the house in the Maienweg, taking leave of Frau Beselin, hoping we had not tired her too much, and very conscious that we had been in the company of a striking and memorable person.

Since Kuno Meyer spent the best part of his working life in Liverpool, twenty-seven years, it was only to be expected that some correspondence of his was to be found there and in consulting this I was greatly aided by the Assistant Archivist Mr. Adrian Allan, to whose help and courtesy I wish to pay tribute. The main content of Meyer material in Liverpool University consists of his letters to Glyn Davies, who lectured on Welsh. It is well to remember that Meyer's encouragement of Welsh language and literature in Liverpool University was pioneer work which has earned for him the appreciation and gratitude of all lovers of Welsh tradition and literature. In recognition of this the University of Wales honoured him with a Doctorate. One of the students, David Evans, spoke for many when he said that 'We Celts have lost part of our soul if we do not acknowledge him for the man he was'.

During the 1914-18 war and for many years afterwards, because of the acrimonies of the time, Kuno Meyer's name was under a shadow in Liverpool University, but with the softening influence of time and because his distinction as a scholar called for recognition, his name has undergone a rehabilitation there. In April 1993 I had the honour to give a lecture on his life under the auspices of the Institute of Irish Studies of the University as part of the celebration of the Gaelic League's centenary. I was guided through the rooms in Victoria Buildings in the oldest part of the university complex where he lectured on German and was enabled to savour the ambience of his daily labours of a century ago. His Liverpool years were full of camaraderie and friendship and it was one of his life's regrets that these were sundered by the shadows of war.

At the beginning of the First World War Kuno Meyer was given, and he accepted, the task of representing Germany's position to the United States public. Osborn Bergin commented that as a Berlin professor he had tasks thrust on him from which he did not shrink, but which surely must have been uncongenial. In correspondence with John Sampson, the Librarian of Liverpool University, Meyer explained that it was most natural that he should place his services unreservedly at the disposal of his government, 'especially' he added, 'when called upon to do so'. This, then, is a clear admission that he was officially instructed. How happy was he in this duty? He performed his services as propagandist faithfully. Osborn Bergin tells us that he felt, and said at the time, that his lifework was ruined. We do not know Bergin's source. On the other hand we read in Meyer's correspondence (21.5.1915) his own asseveration: 'The weapons with which I fight are clean ... I rejoice that I am allowed to take part in this fight'. We did not come across the 'kind of political diary' which Meyer kept and which he told a correspondent he had been keeping since 1896. It is something which would be likely to be included in the effects of his brother Eduard, who wrote on political matters. If it never turns up, we do not need to lament its loss. It is bound to be quite unrelated to the matter of Celtic language and literature to which Kuno Meyer had dedicated his life.

Meyer had been visiting Ireland for many years between say 1880 and 1895 before he came to have sympathy with Irish national aspirations. By 1895 he had come to support the notion of Home Rule, as he admits in correspondence with his colleague John Sampson to whom he wrote: 'I became an ardent Home Ruler in the nineties, when I really first began to understand the Irish better'. He may very well have become a Home Ruler due to the influence of the Gaelic League, which was founded in 1893, a movement which in 1903 he described as arriving to save Irish nationality at the eleventh hour.

What of the man himself? How did he mix and get on with his fellow men? Meyer was a sociable person who liked company. He liked a good cigar, and enjoyed a drink in the company of fellow spirits. On his many travels to spas and clinics throughout Europe he made interesting friends. He found it difficult to adjust to life in Berlin since there were not many in the University who shared his interests and his colleagues, who were enormously learned in many spheres, seemed to pursue their own studies in isolation from their fellows. In fact he came to Berlin too late to form serious friendships and the early death of his fellow-celtologue Ludwig Christian Stern deprived him of a congenial link. He admitted that he missed the friendly intercourse of Liverpool and it was this desire for a social milieu that led him to plan a University Club for Berlin. He was making good progress with this until the plan was interrupted by the First World War.

His late marriage in California to the nurse who took care of him when recovering from a railway accident came as a complete surprise to his friends. One cannot help thinking that it was hasty and impulsive. In the event, it did not turn out happily. She was many years younger and had no sympathy with his scholarly interests. She was divorced, with a young daughter, Margaret. His friend Alice Stopford Green cryptically commented 'The poor man' and hoped the lady would not experiment on him as she had on her first husband, whatever she meant by that. We cannot help thinking that Mrs. Green, a widow herself, and his friend and admirer for many years, might have been the ideal companion for Kuno. Their interests broadly coincided. He had invited her to accompany him to America, away from the troubles of Europe. 'We could accomplish much together' he said. It is possible to have regrets that she did not. One can only speculate what the outcome might be. Regrettably perhaps our speculations would have to dismiss any notion of marriage. The disparity of their ages excluded that. She was born in 1847, he in 1858. She was aware that there had been an earlier love affair in Meyer's life, this being, as she puts it, 'an old and desperate love affair', which he had confided only to his friend Whitley Stokes who, for all we know, kept the knowledge secret to the end. The phraseology would suggest that Meyer's feelings were deeply committed. Up to now, we know nothing of this love affair. It is possible that there exists, in undisclosed correspondence or records somewhere, some knowledge that would enlighten us. Otherwise an element of mystery remains in the human portrait of Kuno Meyer. But his emotional life was not happy.

To follow all the movements of Kuno Meyer one would need the seven leagued boots of the fairytale. It is fortunate that almost all of his correspondence relating to Irish studies is centred in Dublin, mainly in the National Library of Ireland and to a lesser extent in Trinity College. We might follow him to Cracow, where he spent three very interesting days, meeting most of the University professors at a *Kneipe* and explaining to them about Ireland and the Gaelic Movement till he was hoarse. They were a curious mixture and largely composed of counts or priests. He was in several monasteries calling on some of them. Their manners were charming. All the lady academics smoked like chimney-stacks. But what astonished him greatly was that some of the most learned could not speak German though of course they read it.

Or we might follow him to the United States which he travelled from coast to coast. One of the interests which he shared with John Sampson of Liverpool was the culture of the gypsies and his American experience led him to suggest that Sampson might undertake a survey of the North American gypsies. Meyer came across gypsy settlements in all parts of America, most of them near Chicago and San Francisco. They were of all stocks and varieties. Meyer made tours of Ireland during which he made the acquaintance of wandering tinkers who spoke Shelta and whose jargon was at least as old as the eleventh century. He was disappointed in his efforts to find speakers of Shelta in Co. Wicklow in 1891 despite two weeks there in search of them. He concluded he had not been asking the right questions.

During his three years stay in the United States from 1914 to 1917 it is certain that he made many contacts and friendships and wrote correspondence which has yet to see the light. I understand that a student of the German faculty of Trinity College Dublin is doing research in that sphere. We may remember that Kuno Meyer's American wife returned to the United States with her daughter Margaret after the war. Toni Meyer was much relieved at her safe arrival there, because Kuno's friends in the States would thenceforward look after her.

I believe Kuno Meyer would re-establish friendly contact with former friends from whom the war separated him. One of these was Sir Walter Raleigh. I quote a few sentences from a letter Meyer wrote to him one month before his death.

> My dear friend
> I must sit down at once to reply to your delightful friendly sensible letter ... I believe there are a number of curious myths about me and my doings ... You know I am not a pessimist, but the future to me is pitch-dark. During these 5 years elements have come to the front and a generation has grown up that cause one to shudder. I shall retire to two rooms, which the Prussian Academy has placed at my disposal, there work at Irish poetry and my dictionary, receive the few friends I have (for I came too late to Berlin to make many) and only regret that you and other old friends cannot look in upon me ... I regret that I shall probably never be able to visit England again, nor Ireland, unless she succeeds in making herself independent of English laws. When I came back from my last visit to England (in May 1914) 1 remember saying to my sister when I saw her again – I am more in love with England than ever ... It is 2 o'clock in the night, late even for me, and I must close ...
> Always yours
> Kuno Meyer

This was dated 12 September 1919. In exactly one month, Meyer was dead.

As time passes we can see Kuno Meyer's accomplishment in clearer perspective. He was one of a great movement of scholarship which, beginning with Zeuss, produced Windisch, Ebel, Zimmer, Stokes, Rhys, Loth, Strachan, Stern, Thurneysen, Pokorny, Holder and many more, an era which Kenneth Jackson, eminent himself, called the Heroic Age of Celtic Learning. He put Irish learning on the path of self-reliance. He left behind him a body of disciples, which was less numerous than he would have wished, who staffed the newly-founded National University. He was the first to appreciate Irish as a great historical literature. Gifted by nature with a deep poetic sense, he revealed to the world the beauties of early Irish poetry. Had he written only *Selections from Early Irish Poetry*, his praise would still be great. He brought to Irish studies the concept of the Science of Antiquity, of investigating and recording the early civilisation of Ireland in all its aspects, language, metrics, archaeology, poetry, customs and literature. Only thus could a complete picture of early Ireland be built up. It was a concept which had been applied to Classical Studies in Germany. Meyer is to Celtic literature what Theodor Mommsen is to Classical.

He had many far reaching plans for Ireland, not all of which came to fruition. Amongst these he mentioned the foundation of an Irish National Academy, a School of Irish History, which he designed for Belfast, the Organisation of the National University, all of which he advocated and sketched and laid before the people as well as the authorities. 'They did not come off' (Meyer to John Sampson, 26.1.1915, from Hotel Willard, New York). But the School of Irish Learning, on which he lavished all his energy, was a complete success. It revolutionized the study of Irish literature and learning. It was an echo of the Golden Age of Irish learning, when in the seventh century students came in numbers from the mainland of Europe to Ireland in pursuit of knowledge and Irish missionaries travelled abroad. Meyer was an evangelist on behalf of Irish literature. He believed and maintained that the study of Irish should be put on a par with that of the Classics, that it was an essential key to understanding the civilisation of mediaeval Europe. He never tired of urging young Irish scholars to study and publish the manuscripts which were gathering dust in the libraries. Ireland, he urged, should be the centre of Celtic Studies and the task of editing its ancient manuscripts was one for her native scholars. Some distinguished pupils there were who answered his call, but until the end of his days he was disappointed at how few took up the task.

The learned journal *Ériu* which he founded and edited in

partnership with John Strachan, was the first journal in Ireland to cater for the scientific investigation of the Irish language. It still flourishes and has carried valuable contributions from the disciples who followed his lead. It was the precedent for other journals like *Celtica*, the journal of the Dublin School of Celtic Studies, and *Éigse*, a journal of Irish Studies of the National University. So too the celebrated *Zeitschrift für celtische Philologie* which he founded continues to the present day to enlighten the domain of Celtic studies. He accomplished pioneer and essential groundwork in Irish lexicography and continued all his life to add to the immense vocabulary which he accumulated and which he planned to enlarge further in the *Akademie der Wissenschaften.*

When Kuno Meyer first put the project of a School of Irish Learning before the Irish public in 1903 he appealed for a capital sum of ten to twelve thousand pounds to provide for the School 'a home and habitation of its own' (his words). In fact he received a few hundred pounds, mainly from sympathisers, and after much negotiation, an official pittance of one hundred pounds, later withdrawn. With this tiny sum he literally accomplished miracles. A generous Irish-American benefactor paid the rent of the School's accommodation. During Kuno Meyer's time and for years after the School never had a home and habitation of its own, having to move from one location in central Dublin to another throughout its existence.

Kuno Meyer would have been pleased with the establishment in 1940 of the present School of Celtic Studies which now has a home and habitation of its own, a solid spacious building at No. 10 Burlington Road, in an easily accessible location. It is known as the Dublin School of Celtic Studies and is in effect the lineal successor of the School founded by Meyer in 1903 with functions outlined in the Act of Parliament that virtually correspond to those proposed by Meyer. It represents his ambitions for Irish studies.

For more than half a century it has been producing works of importance in every branch of Celtic studies. To take one instance, the field of Early Irish Law. One of Ireland's leading jurists, who is also a distinguished Celtic scholar, Dr. Daniel A. Binchy, has produced a diplomatic edition of all the extant vellum manuscripts of early Irish law. It is entitled *Corpus Juris Hibernici,* in six volumes, with Introduction and text totalling over 2,300 pages, published in 1979.

Another individual item we might note is a diplomatic edition of the 12th century Irish manuscript, the Book of Leinster, an important repository of romances, genealogy, topography and poetry. The six published volumes, edited by four leading Celtic scholars, amount to more than 1,800 pages.

The importance of this School for Ireland's intellectual image and prestige is of incalculable value. With a small and dedicated staff, it has for over fifty years been publishing works of literature, bardic poetry, studies of early Irish law and genealogy, volumes of Ireland's Latin literature (edited by the distinguished mediaevalist Ludwig Bieler), studies in Welsh and Breton literature, for it caters for all the Celtic countries on the lines designed by Kuno Meyer for the original School of Irish Learning, adding steadily to the fabric of early Irish history and civilisation. Many pressing tasks remain, for one thing, in the words of Professor Donnchadh Ó Corráin of University College Cork, 'A multi-volume history of the Irish language and literature, from the beginning to the nineteenth century'.

I shall bring this talk to a close with a quotation from the *United Irishman* (Dublin) of 23 May 1903, reporting Kuno Meyer's celebrated address in the Dublin Rotunda proposing the establishment of a School of Irish Learning.

The words are those of Ireland's national philosopher, Arthur Griffith:

> Perhaps a future generation may honour the seventh Oireachtas most of all for the lecture which Dr. Kuno Meyer delivered to it – the seed he sowed to grow, we trust, into a mighty tree.

- Oireachtas, meaning Assembly, was the festival held annually by the Gaelic League at which prizes were awarded for works of poetry, prose and drama and which was attended by many recreational events.

The above essay was delivered as a talk to the *Deutsch-Irische Gesellschaft,* Bonn, on 16 May 1995.

Karl-Ludwig Wimberger and John Marin, to whom this book is dedicated.

Chapter 17

A window on Germany

I had been looking forward to visiting Germany in February 1997 in the expectation of seeing the Karneval, which my friend Karl Wimberger told me was a uniquely German happening which would give me cause for wonder. My son Gearóid had engaged to give a talk to the German-Irish Society of Bonn and I took the occasion to travel with him to Düsseldorf on the 6th of February by Aer Lingus, a flight of one and a half hours from Dublin. At the luggage reclaim in Düsseldorf we were unexpectedly faced by one of those odd problems which have neither rhyme nor reason. Looking for a trolley to carry our luggage we found one could not be released from its anchorage without inserting a two-mark coin into a slot. Not all travellers landing in Düsseldorf are fortunate enough to have a two-mark coin. We managed our bags by hand, happily for no great distance because just outside the exit there was Karl who helped us with our luggage and took us in his car on the 40 minute journey to Köln where he lives. Karl is the best of travelling companions for, knowing and loving his native Germany as he does, he enlightens every kilometre of the road by his rich knowledge of its interesting places. Although night was setting in we got an outline impression of the Brauweiler Monastery and church and many of the towns and villages that, in a sense, 'shortened the road'.

It was a two-stage journey, since my own destination was Bonn where, on the Venusberg, high over the city, my friend John Marin lived. Gearóid stayed in Köln where he was the guest of Karl and his family. Karl brought me on the half hour's further distance to the Venusberg, a considerable road journey which caused me to admire his driving skill and patience. I was warmly received by John who had been my host on many previous occasions.

Bonn is industry-free. On the banks of the Rhine, for more than forty years the capital of Germany, and forever linked by association and history with Konrad Adenauer, regenerator of the modern state, Bonn's status as the seat of government has furnished it with an extensive complex of administrative buildings. Bonn University is an important centre of learning and the city is given a youthful dimension with its thousands of students, who use the cycling paths along the streets with a verve that must be carefully respected by fussgängers like myself. Beethoven above all gives Bonn its native personality and fame. The Beethovenhaus is the centre of attraction for his numberless admirers who come to see the memorabilia of his career located on its several floors and wonder at the sad serious face of the composer in his portraits. His statue stands in the Münsterplatz, the city's main square, in front of the Postamt, a dignified building now protected by planning law. Dominating the Platz is the Münster of Bonn, profiled clear across the unimpeded square, a shrine of dignified balance and proportion with a lofty central spire, an exterior of rather dullish grey, and by contrast an interior of mellow and appealing colours designed for reflection and prayer.

A place of special interest to us in Bonn was the Sprachwissenschaftliches Institut der Universität Bonn, in other words the Linguistics Institute which has a language library where all the tongues of Europe are represented in terms of study and scholarship but which has for students of Celtic an extensive collection of the great books of Ireland, Scotland, Wales, Brittany and lesser Celtic regions. To browse through the shelves of this great collection is to get lost in the thought and time of the centuries. For bibliographers this is a house of dreams. One can turn over the pages of John O'Donovan's large paper *Annals of the Kingdom of Ireland* or of the *Book of Armagh*, a treasured repository of information on Saint Patrick, edited by Edward Gwynn, or of any of the thousands of volumes that stock the shelves, and ponder on the civilisation by which this wealth was produced.

Great scholars laboured in these rooms. The portrait of one of the greatest, Rudolf Thurneysen, looks down in benign dignity from a wall, presiding, as it were, over the learned activity going on beneath. His collected essays, in three substantial volumes, have been edited by Patrizia de Bernardo Stempel and Rolf Ködderitzsch and published by Niemeyer of Tübingen between 1991 and 1995. Their contents explain, in the words of Patrick Sims-Williams, 'the unassailable position in Irish studies which Thurneysen gained long before his death in 1940'.[1] The Thurneysen family stemmed from Nürnberg whence a forebear arrived to settle in Basel in mid-fifteenth century, where his descendants came to occupy important civic and business positions. Eduard Rudolf Thurneysen was born in Basel on 14 March 1857, married Elisabeth Knebel of Munich in 1897 and had a family of four daughters.[2] His fellow-Celtist Osborn Bergin wrote a metre-strict poem in his praise, a tribute richly earned, for Thurneysen is the author of the master-survey *Die irische Helden- und Königsage*. My friend and neighbour Séamus

Kavanagh of the celebrated Dunquin family studied here and made the acquaintance amongst others of Ernst Robert Curtius, forming a link between that great scholar and West Kerry. Anton Gerard Van Hamel, who came to learn Irish in Ballyferriter, lectured here during the First World War.

Karl Horst Schmidt has retired from his post in the Sprachwissenschaftliches Institut but continues to edit the *Zeitschrift für celtische Philologie*, which reached its centenary year in 1996. Since its beginnings in 1896 the ZCP has been indispensable, through many vicissitudes, to the study of Celtic (largely Irish) literature. Pioneer chapters of Celtic prose and verse and literary history have appeared in its pages, opening up fresh paths to the knowledge of mediaeval Europe. There is every prospect that it will achieve a new lease of life. Karl Horst Schmidt's successor is Dr. Stefan Zimmer, a youthful and eager Celticist, brilliant in his special area of Welsh and looking to expand, update and renew the field of Celtic studies, to include in its ambit modern Irish literature and other kindred extensions. *Floreant.*

A special focus of Irish interest in Bonn is the German-Irish Society. This is a social and cultural body which provides a friendly link between the two countries. Lectures covering all facets of Irish life are given, by Irish writers, or by authorities on special matters of Irish interest. Some of these talks are intriguing. In June 1997 two members of the Sherlock Holmes Society of London spoke on the subject of Conan Doyle, Sherlock Holmes and the Irish and paid homage to the great storyteller who features in his tales the arch-villain Professor Moriarty of possibly Kerry provenance. Talented Irish musicians give performances, Irish national festivals are suitably celebrated by romantic candlelight and there is continuing cultural liaison with Ireland.

It was surely no accident of planning that situated a major bookshop across the street from the main university building. Bouvier sounds French but that is the name of one of the great bookshops of Germany, if not indeed the greatest. Here you may browse for hours, on ground floor and upstairs, in alleys and by-rooms, among myriads of books on all subjects and languages, and lose count of time. It offers the browser a complete range of entertainment and there are willing assistants to help him track down his literary quarry. Here I have bought a reprint of Rudolf Thurneysen's prized *Die irische Helden- und Königsage* and of the finely illustrated and boxed two volumes of Hermann Von Pückler-Muskau's *Reisebriefe aus England und Irland*, a weighty production in the literal sense.

Why, one might ask, is Köln not the capital of Germany? It is the greatest city of the Rhineland, with all the attributes of a capital, throbbing with a native warmth and humanity. It has fine streets and period architecture. Köln has the famous address of 4711 given to a beauty aid by which the French version of the city's name is known across the world. 'Cologne' springs more readily to the mind than the native 'Köln'. The glory of Köln is its Cathedral. The magnificent Gothic shrine dominates the city. Seven centuries or more of loving craft and skill have gone into its making. This is the 'glorious temple' of Petrarch. You gaze and marvel at the symmetry of its twin spires which cleave the heavens. In Köln you cannot go astray. Wherever you go in the city it beckons, rising to your view from all around.

Köln has a recorded history of over two thousand years, dating from its Roman foundation of Colonia Agrippina early in the first century. Extensive Roman remains testify to its importance. There is a Roman-Germanic Museum, situated near the Cathedral, full of the riches of its early history. I walked around it with Karl as my guide, rapt in wonder at the power of the Roman empire which left such solid evidence in stone and wall and tower and sepulchre.

In February of this year 1997 I was fortunate to be in Köln with my son for the Karneval, which is held on 'Rose Monday', preceding Ash Wednesday, in the Rhineland cities. It is a special Rhenish tradition, celebrating with a flourish the freedoms of everyday life before ushering in the rigours of Lent. For 175 years the Karneval has been an integral part of the civic and religious life of the city. It was solemnized by a Festival Mass in the Cathedral celebrated by Cardinal Archbishop Joachim Meisner with a retinue of twenty clergy of Köln attired in topical dress and headgear. They would presently be assimilated into the vast procession through the city. We were in Karl's house in Köln on Rose Monday. To take part in the Karneval as one should, it was necessary to be suitably dressed or, I should say, accoutred. Some attention was given to this and I emerged from the process wearing an outsize Mexican-style hat, with mayoral decorations around my neck and blobs of red paint, liberally applied by Fidelma, colouring my cheeks. Karl and Gearóid and Patricia, each decorated in their various styles and colours, and I set out as a group, with Karl as chauffeur and guide, towards the city centre where Karl had a special parking place. Our plan was to go to an upper room with a bird's-eye view of the Karneval route which had been specially provided for us by friends. But when we reached the city centre, such was the density of the throng that we could not make our way through. So we mingled with the festive crowds. This was preferable because we got a better feeling of the occasion and its immediate excitement. It brought us into closer contact with the heart pulse of the teeming city.

Karl had prepared me to expect something unusual. But Karneval in Köln was fantastic beyond belief. I take some details from the *Kölner-*

Stadt Anzeiger of 11 February 1997. More than one and a half million human beings in motley dress swayed, hummed, trilled and forgot the serious things of life as they lined the six kilometres of the centre city streets through which the Karneval procession passed. 'Winter had itself dressed as spring', the sun shining brightly as if it were in the spirit of the occasion. In the late morning the 74 gorgeously decorated Festival wagons began to move, along with 111 bands, the equitation groups, the standard and colour bearers, under the motto in Köln dialect 'Nix bliev wie et es – aber wir werden dat Kind schon schaukeln' – nothing will be as it is, but we will rock the baby after all. The Karneval people make politics in Köln, Germany and Europe the target of their remarks, but criticism is good natured.

It was a joyous and extrovert demonstration. And imaginative. To children it brought the magic world of the fairytale. Great white steeds, mechanised and richly accoutred, with fiery eyes and waving plumes gave the procession a fairytale appearance, while real, handsome and well-groomed animals, well mounted, moved with equine deportment, each in charge of an attendant. There were headgears which were works of art. At corners and angles along the route were built platforms occupied by chanting groups who kept up a continuous harmony of sound and song, hearty rather than musical, but filling the air with a cheerful symphony.

To shouts from the crowded streets of 'Alaaf! Kamelle!' and a forest of upraised hands, showers of caramels, toffees, chocolates, sweets of various kinds, even tidy packs of sausage, or, for contrast, bunches of flowers, were showered on the crowds from the passing floats. A rectangular-shaped confection, in a wrapper bearing the legend 'Bürgergarde "blau-gold" Präsident: Hans Wallpott' bounded off the bridge of my nose, a reminder of the pleasant hazards of the day.

Politicians and dignitaries were represented in kindly vein. Helmut Kohl sported a long white beard as he was proclaimed Chancellor for the year 2022. I am sure this contained a message but as a visitor I could not say what it was. Rita Süssmouth figures with her Rita-Arlines, carrying a message understood by the throng but obscure to me. Fantasyland, and a day of special joy for children, family groups of whom were gorgeously decked in matching outfits which must have cost time and a labour of love to produce. The rear was taken up with the Prinzenwagen, on which Prince Thomas I presided over the jubilation of his people. Echoes of a Roman triumph? Köln is after all a Roman foundation. But the Roman triumph was a celebration of conquest. The Karneval was a display of joyous exuberance, built on the tradition of a peace-loving community. It was in some ways like our Saint Patrick's Day parade.

The procession over, the street cleaning vehicles moved in. These had been mobilised in a long rank, strategically placed on the fringes of the Karneval area. They now advanced with military precision in the wake of the dispersing crowds. From the foreground of the Cathedral we had a view of the cleaning up process which left spotlessly clean and washed streets, with order restored where there had been accumulations of mull, plastics and litter.

Part of the pride and splendour of Köln consists of its Romanesque churches, twelve in number, which date back to 1200 and earlier. These were, every one, reduced to starkest ruin by aerial bombing during the Second World War, in which the city was almost completely destroyed. The great Cathedral itself suffered severe bomb damage and is still under repair.

St. Gereon is the largest of the Romanesque churches. Named after the saint who was martyred about the year 300 along with his companions, and thrown into a well which has still not been found, it was chosen in the Merovingian era as a church for coronations and ceremonial events. After the Cathedral, it is the most important church in Köln, its present structure dating back to 1219-1227. So badly was it destroyed in the second World War, practically to its foundations, that it was seriously thought it could not possibly be restored. It took a mighty act of faith, and the skilled hands of the mason, for it to rise again to its former splendour, true in every detail of its building to what it had been, and today it stands, impressive in its Romanesque grandeur as a place of worship and prayer.

It was in this church we attended Sunday mass with Karl and his family and John Marin. The church was full. In the vestibule we noted a photograph of what little was left of it by the desecrating bombs. There was a choir which sang in Latin and German; in fact Latin was largely used, appropriately in a Romanesque church, with the Credo in an arrangement with which I was not familiar. What thoughts of prayer I had were distracted by the beauty of the interior, the marvellous decor of which had been restored by leading artists. 'The beauty of Thy house' was a reality before our eyes.

Not far away was Jameson's Irish Pub where we had a substantial brunch in friendly surroundings. Was this place sponsored by the famous distillery whose name is synonymous with the finest Dublin whiskey? For there were tavern artifacts all around bearing its name. Or have Jamesons of Dublin come to cater as well for all kinds of drinks and excellent food? Or have they just lent their name to the enterprise? I wondered but did not ask. I chose a full Irish breakfast, while my companions had their own choice from a varied menu, which included items like salmon and oysters, most unJameson-like but accounted delicious. There are a number of Irish pubs in Köln serving traditional Irish dishes, and while it would have been nice to tarry and sample what they offered, our time was short, for we were to return to Dublin that evening from Düsseldorf. We returned to Karl's home in An der Ronne where we rested for the afternoon.

References

1. *Cambrian Mediaeval Celtic Studies* No 32, Winter 1996, 123-25.
2. *Schweiz-Geschlechterbuch*, 6 Jahrg. Basel 1936.

Seán Ó Lúing at Vogtendorf (Photograph by John Marin).

Chapter 18

R. A. S. Macalister

Robert Alexander Stewart Macalister, the name resounds like the skirl of Highland bagpipes. Physically he can hardly have been more than a few inches over five feet, but was broad-shouldered and chested as any countryman and looked like one to whom walking the outdoors and wide spaces was a lifelong habit, solid and well-based as one of those dolmen pillars amidst which much of his life was spent. His head was strong and noble, mounted on a secure foundation of neck and shoulder, his cast of face intellectual, not unlike portraits I have seen of David Lloyd George, only with a frank and enquiring expression, free of the sorcery that glinted even photographically from the statesman's countenance. A generous brush of moustache gave his profile an added distinction.

This solid figure was seen to move, like an animated Epstein sculpture, through the corridors of University College Dublin, Earlsfort Terrace, one afternoon a week on his way to lecture on Celtic Archaeology. Ever punctual, for me he could not arrive too soon, so absorbing did I find his lectures. Archaeology from its earliest phases was his abiding love. I can see him now in the half-shadows of the darkened room in Earlsfort Terrace where he described and illustrated with lantern-slides the earliest traces of man's development, jumbled since in my memory by the caprices of time, Mousterians and Beakers, Hallstatt and La Tène, in his cultured voice, spoken with easy delivery, such a good communicator of learning was he. The hour flew.

From time to time he would tap the floor with his pointer and his assistant would put in a change of slides and away he would talk, not talk really, but instruct, fascinatingly, bringing the materials of archaeology to life and garnishing them with theory, for he was never afraid to put forward his own thoughts and reflections, nor ever hesitant to discard them if new evidence compelled. He was taken in, like many a distinguished colleague, by the Piltdown forgery (bad piece of humour that!) as is clear from his foreword to the second edition of his discursive *Archaeology of Ireland* (1949).

Inspired by his lectures, I became an enthusiastic student of archaeology, practically committing to memory his earlier *Archaeology of Ireland* (1928) and I believe I might have specialised in it, had not some talk I had heard on the matter discouraged me. With a group of fellow-students I fell to discussing the prospects of archaeology as a career and someone remarked that Dr. Macalister encouraged none of his students to specialise in it. To anyone wishing to take his interest in it beyond degree standard he would say 'Has someone left you a legacy?' So I was told. Someone added that he did not wish to admit future rivals into his own domain, but this I found hard to believe. His own range of learning was so wide that few aspirants could be held in fear of approaching it. In any case, in the twilight years before the 1939-45 holocaust there was a chill and forbidding humour in the air that withered archaeological enterprise. One afternoon I listened for two hours in the crowded Physics Theatre to a lecture by Paul Jacobstahl on Celtic Art, the entrancement of which not even his poor command of English could diminish. A refugee from a regime of fear, the great scholar took his learning to other lands and audiences. His case was a symptom of the unsettlement of the times. Macalister lectured once a week. On a few occasions he took us to the National Museum in Kildare Street to see the originals of some of the antiquities he had described to us in lectures. On such occasions he would be less formal, and we had glimpses of his intense patriotism as he spoke with feeling of the country's antiquarian wealth and the Museum's riches.

Never timorous in his speculations, he was not short of critics. A professor of archaeology in an institute of learning I find it discreet not to name observed to me once of Macalister that 'of course his theories are very much out of date now' with a lofty air of dismissal, a notion generally put forward by critics whose own theories, if any such they had, have been kept securely locked in their occipital cupboards. Macalister demonstrated with the publication of his *Ancient Ireland* (1936) that he was not afraid to contribute a piece to the theatre of Irish archaeology more stimulating than the measuring tape. This work he wrote to complement his *Archaeology of Ireland* (1928).

Ancient Ireland was no text for chauvinists. Of the theories in it that gave offence to the sensitive was one which proposed that the Gulf Stream and its warm air current had a soporific effect on Ireland that poisoned human energy 'with the mechanical efficiency of a leaky gaspipe', the effects of which however did not touch the progressive northeastern corner of the island. Worse than this could not be said in the context of a polity committed to industrialise the country but Macalister was immune to timidity. Going further, he announced that human sacrifice was not unknown in early Ireland. Aodh de Blácam, who contributed a daily feature to the *Irish Press* under the pseudonym of Roddy the Rover, took umbrage at the notion of human sacrifice in ancient Ireland. Macalister replied. No doubt it was an error on his part to do so. Newspaper readers are not interested in erudition. In the field of serious discussion de Blácam would have been hard put to match Macalister. But he used irony, at which he was more than good. I cannot now remember with any clearness the details of the combat, but I believe he proposed to his readers a menu which included slices of cooked human being, a sally that brought chuckles from his readers. Macalister retired from the fray, realising that there could be no common factor in argument of this kind. The possessor of a daily newspaper column has advantages that need not be stressed when jousting with an opponent with a case no matter how good.

His course of lectures to us should have run to two years. I had completed the first, and about four lectures of the second when, to my intense regret, it came to a sudden end. What happened was that, through some oversight, no reference to the second year course appeared in the college syllabus, so that, unless you had taken the trouble to find out, you might well suppose no second year course was provided. The situation gave two busybodies an opportunity to approach the college authorities with the request that, because the second year course did not appear on the syllabus, there should be no obligation to do it. The request, which was an impertinence, was granted, and those interested were denied the pleasure of further lectures from Macalister. What he thought of the matter himself was not revealed, but his comment could be suitably devastating. One of the quibblers even suggested to me that I should be grateful for his intervention. This I was not.

In order to confirm the material of his lectures, I read some of the books on archaeology that Macalister had written, to find that they differed in many respects from what he had told us in class. I think that this was because he was constantly discarding older views in favour of new ones. His massive *Textbook of European Archaeology*, planned in Teutonic detail, was described as a series of lectures to students at University College, Dublin, but I must say that his lectures to us on the same subject were simpler and untrammelled by the prodigious assembly of learning in that volume. When a full assessment of his work appears it is certain, I believe, to place him high in the records of scholarship. As preliminary to any such survey a bibliography of his writings is essential and a beginning of this kind has been made in the *Journal of the Royal Society of Antiquaries of Ireland*.

His *Secret Languages of Ireland* (1937) is an entertaining amalgam, based mainly on the collections of John Sampson, sometime Librarian of the University of Liverpool and leading authority on Gypsy traditions. The materials were placed in Macalister's hands by Sampson's literary executor, Miss Dora Yates, Secretary of the Gypsy Lore Society. The chapter heads, which give an indication of the book's content, include Ogham, Cryptology, Hisperic, Bog-Latin, the Vagrants of Ireland, Shelta and Béarlagar na Saer. Some of the contributions are Macalister's own and his discussion of that oddest of Latin compositions *Hisperica Famina,* which may well be an ancient exercise in leg-pulling, earned the commendation of the great Bollandist scholar Paul Grosjean. See his essay 'Confusa Caligo' in *Celtica* III (1956) 53, footnote 2. Incidentally, attention to this text could have dire consequences, since the history of editorial necrology in its wake is alarming. As Père Grosjean observes, Henry Bradshaw was on the point of publishing a study of it when he died, the great Latinist Max Niedermeyer was about to give the world the fruits of his study of it when death intervened, Macalister had completed his examination of it and was to make it public when he too, alas, departed life, all leaving the puzzle unravelled. Nor, may we observe, did Grosjean himself (and no one more than he would have enjoyed a joke however grim) survive publication of his brilliant essay all that long. So detrimental to scholarly life has been the study of that intractable and outrageous piece of Latin. The moral, though not conclusive, is disconcerting. Scholars of this curiosity would be well advised to proceed cautiously, although it is a comforting thought that some editors who tussled with it are happily alive and well.

In his *History of Western Europe* (1928) Macalister draws his historical perspective with an archaeologist's hand, weaving the Irish experience deftly into its broader European context. Critical of the Roman world, he was an obvious admirer of the Celts and their traditions, 'which have ever been hostile to Imperialism', and one sees Vercingétorix as his great hero. Nor was he ever timorous in obtruding a strong personal judgement into his arguments. The destruction of the Public Record Office in 1922 he denounced as 'the most gigantic crime against the country which was ever committed since the dissolution of the monasteries by Henry VIII' (p.215). Ending his review of what was then recent Irish history he concludes on a note of optimism. 'As we write, six years have elapsed and the Free State in that short time has done wonders', forecasting that 'it will not be long before the country will be able to compete educationally with any other country in the world'. A strong advocate of the Irish language revival, he considered that the restoration of the national language to its rightful place in the national life was in the nature of things a task of tremendous difficulty, but that 'the extraordinary success of the Jews in Palestine, who have made the Hebrew language, dead for some two thousand years, the mother-tongue of the rising generation, shows that nothing of the kind is impossible' (p.216).

His correspondence with Eoin MacNeill attests that he wrote the Irish language reasonably well. But with the gravity of years his ardour cooled. Presently he came to see virtue in *imperialism* (his italics) as the agency for the planting and fostering of civilisation.

The Macalister family was not originally of Dublin, the archaeologist's grandfather having come from Paisley in 1829 to succeed the writer William Carleton as secretary of the Sunday School Society. His son Alexander became Professor of Zoology and later of Anatomy in Trinity College Dublin from where he progressed to the Chair of Anatomy in Cambridge and was elected a Fellow of St. John's College. Robert was born in Dublin in 1870. Educated at Rathmines School and Cambridge, he went out to Palestine where he held the position of Director of Excavations, Palestine Exploration Fund, from 1900 to 1909 and 1923 to 1924. From 1909 to 1943 he held the Professorship of Celtic Archaeology in University College Dublin.

He gave long and devoted service to the Presbyterian Church in Dublin. Ordained in 1920 to the Eldership of the Adelaide Road Congregation he took a deep interest in the life and work of the Congregation, acting as voluntary Organist and Choirmaster for seven years. On his departure for Cambridge in 1943, his Congregation gave him a grateful farewell.[1] In regarding his distinction as an archaeologist one is disposed to overlook his talent for music and his profound knowledge of musical history. His lecture on 'Early Metrical Psalmody in the Presbyterian Churches' given on 23 June 1933 in Belfast delighted his audience.[2]

His address on 'The Present and Future of Archaeology in Ireland' to the Royal Society of Antiquaries on 27 January 1925 bears re-reading for its vision. 'Retrospective and prospective', it covers a wide field within its 24-page span in a commentary that on occasion can be pungent and critical. As a design for the future, delivered shortly after independence, it took in more than pure archaeology, proclaiming the value of education, hand in hand with legislation and planning, a full survey of the whole country, the calendaring of every document in existence that had a bearing on the religious, political, artistic, social or cultural history of Ireland and of the Irish people, all to be performed to the standards of scientific truth. In our European-conscious present, the message it had to impart some three-quarters of a century ago speaks to us yet: '… the paramount and supreme importance of Irish antiquities is not so much national as extra-national… Ireland was one of the very few countries of Europe whose originality was not crushed by Roman domination. In Ireland we may see how Europe would have developed, had Julius Caesar kept to his own side of the Alps. The preservation of Irish antiquities thus becomes a duty that we owe to Europe, and not merely to ourselves.'[3] He died in Cambridge on 26 April 1949.

His name may be ranked not least amongst the distinguished group of archaeologists to whom he dedicated his book *The Archaeology of Ireland* (1928) and its noncomformist successor, the edition of 1949.[4]

References

1. I have taken the details of his Church career from an article by Very Rev. R.K. Hanna, M.A., D.D. entitled 'Dr. R.A.S. Macalister's departure from Dublin' pasted onto the front fly leaf of my copy of *Ancient Ireland*. The book formerly belonged to E.H. Paul, College Park East, Belfast, whose slight annotations therein and other presscuttings indicate that he was a careful student of Macalister. In due acknowledgement I bless his memory.

2. *Proceedings* of the Fourteenth General Council of the Alliance of Reformed Churches holding the Presbyterian System, held at Belfast, Northern Ireland 1933. Edinburgh 1933, pp 150-160.

3. *The Present and Future of Archaeology in Ireland*, p.13. Falconer, Dublin (1925).

4. These are: George Coffey, Thomas Johnson Westropp, Walther Emanuel Friedrich Bremer, Edmund Clarence Richard Armstrong and Henry Saxton Crawford 'who rendered high service in the quest for hidden truth.'

Appendix 1

An Claidheamh Soluis Mí na Nodlag 19, 1908

Open letter to every patriotic Irishman, and especially to the priesthood of Ireland. By Julius Pokorny, Vienna IX., Schwartspahterhof, Austria.

Vienna, December 6th, 1908

Sir,

As I have followed the Irish University movement with considerable interest for a long time, you may permit me to make a few remarks on some essential points. It has been opposed to the efforts of the Gaelic League of making Irish compulsory at the Entrance examination on the ridiculous ground that such a thing would keep out foreign students.

Myself being a foreigner, and thoroughly acquainted with the university affairs throughout England, France, Germany and Austria, I think I have the right of speaking about things I am very well acquainted with.

To say that foreign students would be kept out because of the thoroughly Celtic character of your university, is ridiculous and absurd, and those who dare say such a thing, seem either to be struck with blindness or to speak consciously and purposely false things to conceal the truth – that they are but instruments of a higher power standing behind them.

In former times such people were called traitors.

Firstly, do you really believe, that any foreign student, intending to learn English, would come to Ireland? (I don't speak at all of the students of Latin or Greek, as these hav'nt it necessary to go to the British Islands for a teaching that they can have better on the Continent.)

You may as well send some Englishman, who wishes to study French, to Alsace-Lorraine instead of Paris.

Not only lies Ireland much out of way and has not many material attractions for foreigners (except the scenery) especially compared with the many amusements and other luxurious things, that are to be found in English towns – and who, if he has to choose between a far country without these attractions and a nearer country provided with all modern comfort, will not choose the former – but you don't seem to realise that Ireland is not England, and everyone who wishes to learn perfectly well English, will go to England. I know myself personally hundreds and hundreds of students who went over to England for learning English, to Cambridge, to Oxford or London, and no one of them ever was in Ireland or came upon the idea of going thither for learning English.

As well I know of nobody, intending to study English, who went to the Welsh Universities of Aberystwyth or Bangor, though alas!! – these universities, that are called 'National' Universities are really English ones, where Welsh is taught only as a dead language. Such a university would but be a ridiculous puppet with the resemblance only of a national institution.

Wilt thou never remember, poor Irish people, that thou never canst become real English, and trying to do so, thou wilt be only a wretched imitation, as England will never regard thee as her equal, and so thou wilt be neither Irish nor English – a poor nothing.

The other day I had some discussion with another scholar about English phonetics. Do you know what he replied to me, when strongly insisting upon some fact? 'Oh, you have been only in *Ireland* and therefore you have no right of speaking about *English* phonetics!'

Many cases, I remember where some friends of mine who wished to learn English had to choose between an English and an Irish teacher. Always preference was given to the Englishman.

But while Ireland has not many material attractions for the foreigner, there are spiritual ones, greater and nobler than in any other country, and these attractions you must keep alive – they would perish together with the native language and the national character.

It has been said a Celtic university would keep out foreign students, but just the reverse would be the case.

We know almost everything about the old literatures of Europe. There is hardly a corner, that has not been yet explored. But there has been opened a new fountain of lore and legend and literature, almost inexhaustible, belonging to the eldest Aryan nation of Europe, to the Celts, to the Irish Celts. The scholars of Europe have long ago begun to recognise the immense importance of Celtic studies. Schools begin to spring up – slowly but steadily – and in fifty years the students of Celtic will be as numerous as those of Latin or Greek. Then every university will have its school of Celtic – students will go, as wont, to Berlin, to Freiburg, to Paris – only Ireland will stand alone, a laughing-stock for England and for the whole world.

I won't speak of my own humble personality, of myself who went to Ireland this summer to study the language I love so much, as if Gaelic and not German were my mother-tongue, who went to the Connacht College to learn there from the lips of native speakers the famous tongue of the Gael, no, I'll speak only of the great continental scholars who visited Ireland during the last years. There were Professor Pedersen, Dr. Sarauw and Dr. Marstrander from Scandinavia, Professor Dottin from France, the Professors Dr. Zimmer, Dr. Osthoff and Dr. Finck from Germany and others: all these – did they go to Trinity College or to the Royal University of Ireland? Ask John Long the schoolmaster of Ballyferriter, ask the simple peasants of the Arran Islands! No, they went among the poor people, they endured often great privations only for learning the native Irish tongue.

And how many students that don't have the energy of living among the poor peasantry, would come to Dublin, if there would be a great Gaelic University! From the whole British Empire Celts would come to Dublin, to the university, as they are beginning already to come to the School of Irish Learning. From the whole continent students will come to Ireland. Perhaps not the first year, but in short time.

That an English university would not attract any foreign student I have shown sufficiently, I think: that a Gaelic university will attract many foreigners [you] may be quite sure, for the recognition of the importance of Celtic studies is growing from year to year. The only reason why they have been advancing so slowly is, that we must first lay the foundation for scientific study, that only just the last years good elementary works have begun to come out.

People of Ireland!

The twentieth century is the century of the nations, the century of artistic and national individuality. The Hungarian people, the Slavonic nations, peoples that have no great past, no great literature, peoples that are much inferior in culture to the Teutonic or Celtic races have attended [attained?] national independence as to their language and education. (I don't mean to say that you should follow their often bad and disreputable means!) And you, with your great past, with your fascinating literature, should allow your nationality to be killed?

Arise at least [last?] from your long sleep, and remember that, 'the people that cannot fight will die.'

To the priesthood of Ireland I would say:-

Remember, that in the past the Irish language played such a prominent part in keeping amongst the Irish people the faith for which their forefathers suffered so much.

Remember, that you have to atone for the mistake that was made when the ecclesiastical colleges of Ireland were Anglicised, when the priests that went out to administer to the people were no longer able to speak their own language, and instead of preserving the sacred national tongue of St. Patrick and St. Columba fostered amongst the people the language of a hostile nation. You only can do for Ireland, what the Protestant clergy of Wales and Scotland have done for their nations, so that in times to come the people may never accuse their religion of being the cause of the loss of their national language and characteristics. You have now the power to make your name as immortal in the annals of the national history as it already is in those of the Catholic religion!

It has been often said, that the Irish have initiative but no tenacity?

Now you have occasion to show the world that this reproach is wrong, and that the Gaelic movement in Ireland is

> 'Like a great tide
> That moving seems to speak
> Too full for sound or song!'

Is mise,
Le meas mór,
Julius Pokorny

Appendix II

An Appeal for a Gaelic Academy
By Kuno Meyer

'An Appeal for a Gaelic Academy' is described as being an Address delivered to the Liverpool Branch of the Gaelic League on October 26th, 1904. This appeal was printed in *An Claidheamh Soluis*, the Gaelic League weekly, between 3 and 31 December 1904. The 'Appeal' is doubtless identical with the lecture on 'The Future of the Irish Language and Literature' noticed in Arthur Griffith's *United Irishman* of 5 November 1904 as having been delivered by Dr. Kuno Meyer at St. Francis Xavier's College, Liverpool, for the local Gaelic League.

In a letter to John Sampson dated 26.1.1915 from Hotel Willard, New York, Meyer mentions certain plans which he had advocated for Ireland. Amongst these were the foundation of an Irish National Academy, a School of History designed for Belfast and the organisation of the National University, all of which he sketched and laid before the people concerned. 'They did not come off.' We may take it that the Irish National Academy was what he outlined to the Gaelic League of Liverpool.

When I received the invitation of your Committee to deliver an address before this branch of the Gaelic League, I happened to find myself in Eastern Europe in a country which has often been compared to Ireland, and has sometimes been held up to her as a model and example to follow (the Kingdom of Hungary). Indeed, the fate of the two countries has been in many respects so similar that the student of their history or the traveller visiting them is constantly reminded by one of the other. Nor can it be denied that the victorious struggle of the Hungarians for their national existence affords many lessons which may usefully serve the cause of an Irish Ireland. A series of brilliantly-written and instructive articles on the recent history of Hungary in the columns of the *United Irishman* has but lately drawn the attention of its readers to the subject.[1] These articles dwelt almost exclusively on the political aspect of the development of Hungary, and drew numerous parallels between Hungarian history and Irish politics. As a student of languages and as one who wishes well to the Gaelic movement, I was even more interested in the story of the revival of the Hungarian language and literature; and during a stay of several months I began to study the history of that movement, and to note the various steps and stages which led to the rehabilitation of Magyar, or Hungarian, as the national language of the country in which I found myself.

Here again comparisons with the Gaelic movement forced themselves upon me at every turn. The more I read and the more I saw and heard what was going on around me, the more I became convinced that the successful career of Hungary contained some fruitful lessons for the Irish to follow, lessons at no moment perhaps more opportune that at the present. So when your summons came, it seemed to me I could hardly do better than to put together some of the facts which I had learnt and to point out their bearing upon the future of the Irish language and literature. In laying these remarks before you tonight, I desire most earnestly to promote the cause of the Gaelic movement which, from its inception, has had my heartfelt sympathy, and, so far as I have been enabled to give it, my co-operation.

Of course, in the short time at my disposal, I cannot give you more than a rapid and meagre sketch. It would be a most useful task if one thoroughly acquainted with the present state and the needs of the Gaelic movement were to find leisure and opportunity to study the Hungarian revival on the spot, and to report on it to the League.

One of the first things that struck me in studying the history of the national development of Hungary was the remarkable fact that the language movement had preceded by half a century the political struggles which brought about autonomy. It seems as if the Hungarian people had first intended to establish their claim to be considered 'a nation once again'. It was a period of preparation, of rallying their strength and forces, a period during which they became thoroughly imbued with the national idea, while in the process they acquired that unity and solidity, that fusion of hitherto discordant elements which, when the great struggle for national independence arrived, found them united to a man and ready for any sacrifice.

The eighteenth century saw the deepest decay of the national spirit in Hungary. The nation which had so often victoriously withstood foreign invaders had lost its independence under Austrian rule. A process of Germanisation was going on apace in all departments of national life. A generation had grown up in degeneracy brought about by apathy or despair. It had allowed the language and literature to decay, so that for a time a revival seemed almost as hopeless as it did in Ireland a few years ago. Yet the situation was not quite the same as in Ireland before the Gaelic League began its work. In some aspects it was perhaps worse, but in others far better. While the Irish language, e.g. has always had one rival only, *viz.*, English, Hungarian had three, German, French and Latin. On the whole, this proved to be an advantage when Hungarian began to assert itself, for none of the three languages had obtained such firm root on the soil of Hungary as

English has obtained in Ireland, and the enemy's forces, so to speak, were divided, and could be the more easily attacked and beaten separately.

By the middle of the eighteenth century the neglect of Hungarian as a spoken language had reached its lowest level. It had fallen into general disuse among the upper classes, and all those who laid claim to education and culture. Left to the lowest orders, it threatened to degenerate into a mere patois. Latin was the language used in the schools, in all public business, and in the county courts, while German or French had become the language of the home, society at large, and of the stage. There was no living literature in Hungarian, so that in 1764 the patriotic Jesuit, Illei, could write: 'Our language has indeed been carried to its grave, though it is not yet wholly dead'.

In spite, however, of this almost general neglect, Hungarian has never come so near extinction as Irish had through such successive calamities as the settlement of foreigners throughout the country, the dispossession of the native land owners, the penal laws, the famine, and the constant drain of emigration. In Hungary, the upper classes, though they disdained to employ their native language, could yet understand it, much as Frederick the Great could speak and write German after a barbarous fashion, though he preferred to use French.

On the whole then, the difficulties of reviving the language were not nearly so great as they are in Ireland at present.

The first indications of a coming change are found towards the end of the eighteenth century. A reaction set in which first showed itself in the homes and private life of patriotic citizens of all classes, more especially among the nobility, students and the priesthood, a number of whom began once more to cultivate the native language. There was in this no political object. These men were simply filled with shame and regret that such a fine language should sink to the level of a mere spoken jargon and be left to die out in a few generations.

They realised that Hungarian had all the possibilities of becoming the medium and vehicle of a great modern literature, as it had already in the past produced some fine prose and poetry. But to achieve this the language had first to be cultivated; and many branches of literary expression had to be created. Its claim to be considered one of the civilised languages of Europe had first to be made good. Here indeed their task was much more difficult than that which lies before the Gaelic League. You know that the Hungarian language was a late arrival among the great civilised languages of Europe, with which it was not connected.

No written records exist of it before the 12th century (a time when the Irish language and literature had already had their golden age). It swarmed with foreign words mostly taken from Latin, German, or the surrounding Slavonic languages, which threatened to choke the native element more and more. So little was Hungarian as it then stood adapted to be used, e.g. for purposes of scientific expression in writing or teaching, that as late as 1847 physics, logic, astronomy, and most other sciences had to be taught in the schools through the medium of Latin. But the men who started the movement did not lose heart. They knew that other national languages also had been in the same state, and had equally to fight their way against Latin and other foreign tongues. Had not the development of German been delayed for centuries by the predominance first of Latin, then of French? Why should it not be possible to do in a small country like Hungary what had been done throughout the length and breadth of a huge country like Germany, with its numberless dialects, its Universities, and learned men biased in favour of Latin, its courts and society equally prejudiced for French language and literature.

I will now shortly sketch the history of the movement from the first separate efforts of individual reformers to the triumphant re-establishment of the national language, and you will note for yourselves how almost each initial step and phase through which the movement passed closely resembles what has been going on under our eyes in Ireland for the past ten years.

There is, however, one marked difference at the outset. In Hungary the desire to reinstate the old language remained for a long time confined to a few enthusiasts, who worked on in isolation or in small groups before they arrived at any concerted action. No such large and popular body as the Gaelic League came to their help. Perhaps the earliest outward sign of a coming change was the foundation in 1780 of the first newspaper in Hungarian, which was published by one Matthew Rath, in the town of Pressburg, or Pozsony, as the Hungarians call it. This was the 'Fáinne an Lae' of Hungary. As it proved an unexpected success, it was soon followed by a number of non-political papers which opened their columns to literature and poetry, and every interest of national life.

The smaller groups of enthusiastic young men now began to form into societies for the purpose of cultivating the language, studying the older literature and the history of their country. Under the leadership of John Kis in Oedenburg, Anton Cziráky in Pesth, and George Aranka in Transylvania, they gradually obtained a wider influence, especially among the aristocracy of the country.

The period from 1807-1830 in Hungary bears in many respects a striking resemblance to the present state of the Gaelic movement. It was a period of preparation, of laying the foundations, of learning and of criticism. But the most gifted among the groups which I have mentioned began also to write and publish, and to show by example what the language was capable of achieving in literature.

Some translated and adapted the masterpieces of ancient and modern literature, others took for their model the old native songs and epics, others again more boldly struck out new lines and enriched Hungarian literature by original compositions.

You can almost in reading the history of this period single out individual writers and compare them to men now working on similar lines in Ireland. There was, e.g., the Hungarian Aesop, as he was popularly called, one Andrew Fay, who, like Father Peter O'Leary, reproduced the Fables of Aesop in the native language. But perhaps the closest parallel is to be found in the first attempts made to found a national drama. Up to this time there had been no national stage. Only French or German plays were performed. But now a large number of plays were written in Hungarian and on Hungarian subjects; travelling companies of amateur and professional actors were formed and set up their stage in many towns of the country. A rich repertoire of native dramatic literature gradually arose. Apart from all other advantages, this migratory theatre had the effect of setting a model of correct pronunciation before the people. But all these efforts, much good as they did in some ways, were still felt to fall short of their aim. They did not lay hold of the younger generation that was growing up; nor did they work for unification, but rather for separation. For the disintegrating effect of the dialects began to show itself. The need of a centre to organise and direct the necessary work, the creation of a standard language, and the introduction of the movement into the schools and colleges, were now felt to be the most urgent needs. Two proposals which had already been made at an earlier stage, though they had not then been acted upon, now took effect.

As early as 1793, at a literary soirée, Joseph Kármán had pointed out to his fellow-workers the necessity of making the capital of Pesth the centre of the movement. Some remarks of his are worth quoting literally. After having mentioned what their cause owed to patriotic men in Vienna, Komorn, Kaschan, Debreczin, Transylvania, and other places, he proceeded as follows:

> Unless a common centre is now created to unite all those local efforts, the dialects will never merge into a universal uniform standard language; nor will these isolated provincial efforts produce a national literature which alone is able to level and harmonise the differences of language, taste, and individualism.

He then pointed out the claims which Pesth possessed in its society, in its libraries, its printing presses, etc., for becoming such a centre. But how exactly this centralisation was to be carried out Kármán did not in detail put forth. In any case a whole generation passed before his dream was realised. It was only when a new item in the programme began to be coupled with the idea of making Pesth the headquarters of the movement that it was carried out. This new idea was the foundation of a national Academy in Pesth. The finest intellects of the nation, the most distinguished writers, the best trained scholars, the most expert workers were to unite to organise the movement on educational and scholarly lines, to set the necessary standard in language and literature, to create a national Press, in short to do not only what the Gaelic League has endeavoured to do for Ireland, but to do systematically and methodically what is now left to the efforts of individual writers and scholars.

Strengthened as the men who undertook this work were by the implicit trust of the nation that had committed their task to them, they achieved it triumphantly within the incredibly short period of one generation. The Academy was founded in 1825, but did not set to work properly before 1830. In 1865 its members considered their task done, dissolved and reconstituted themselves into an ordinary Academy of Sciences such as most capitals of Europe possess.

Now, to anyone who studies the various phases of the language revival in Hungary, it will become apparent that the chief reason of its unparalleled success is to be sought in the foundation of this Academy. Indeed the Hungarians themselves regard it as the turning point in the movement. For the results now attained in quick succession surpassed the hopes of the founders themselves. Let me read to you what a cool chronicler of the movement, Mr. Butler of the British Museum, who wrote the article on Hungary in the *Encyclopedia Britannica*, says on this head:

> The establishment of the Hungarian Academy (1830) marks the commencement of a new period, in the first eighteen years of which gigantic exertions were made as regards the literary and intellectual life of the nation. The language, nursed by the Academy, developed rapidly, and showed the capacity for giving expression to almost every form of scientific knowledge. By offering rewards for the best original dramatic productions, the Academy provided that the national theatre should not suffer from a lack of classical dramas. During the earlier part of its existence, the Academy devoted itself mainly to the scientific development of the language and philological research.

It was in the year 1825 that the Academy was founded by the generosity of a patriotic nobleman, Count Széchenyi, who devoted his whole income for one year to the purpose, about £6,000. Very soon, however, the new institution was supported by contributions from all quarters, except the Government, and was thereby enabled to carry out its many-sided and difficult task.

Let me quite briefly enumerate the chief items of the work accomplished by the Academy during the thirty-five years of its existence.

One of the first cares of the Hungarian Academy was to fix the orthography of the language; they set a standard of a uniform literary language by checking on the one hand the encroachments of the dialects and on the other those of foreign idiom and vocabulary, and by developing the inherent powers of the language; they brought out standard dictionaries, grammars, books on the philology and history of the language; they printed the older literature in accurate scholarly editions, and supported the best contemporary writers by every means in their power; they organised and directed the teaching of the language in the schools, and thus brought up a new generation proud to be Hungarians and fully conscious of the possession of a fine and cultivated language and of a noble national literature.

There now followed such an outburst of literature as had not been witnessed before. Masterpieces of prose and poetry appeared which for the first time drew the attention of the world upon Hungarian literature. I refer, e.g., to such writers as Maurus Jokai, the great novelist of Hungary, whose works have been translated into every European language; and to the poet, Alexander Petófi, the Burns of Hungary, best known to English readers by the translations of Sir John Bowring. There can be no doubt that it was, in the first instance, the work achieved by the Academy which rendered such immediate results possible.

From what I have said you will readily understand that I have come here to-night to plead before you, and through you before the Gaelic League throughout the world, for the speedy establishment of a Gaelic National Academy in Dublin on the lines of the old Hungarian Academy at Pesth. I can do no more than throw out this idea, trusting that it will fall on fertile ground, that men and money will be found to carry it out, so that it may become a potent factor in the progress of the Gaelic movement.

If it were said that the existence of the Gaelic League makes such an institution unnecessary, my answer would be that the League is far too large and popular a body to deal efficiently with such work as would fall within the province of an Academy; that indeed it has so much to do already that a partial devolution of its work on to the shoulders of such an institution might be welcome to it. Moreover, much of the work that has to be done and can no longer be delayed is of such a nature that it can only be carried out in academic leisure and by comparatively few men.

It is only the best writers, the best trained scholars in the land who are competent to deal with it. There is no lack of such men and women in Ireland now. Many names will occur at once to everyone. Douglas Hyde, Father P. O'Leary, Dr. O'Hickey, Father Dinneen, John MacNeill, Miss O'Farrelly, and others who have done such splendid work already, might constitute themselves as the first members of an Academy. An appeal to the nation at large would raise the necessary money, or perhaps some Irish or American Széchenyi will be found to set apart funds for such a purpose.

As for the programme of work to be carried out by our Irish Academicians, or under their direction, I think they could not do better than follow point by point the programme of their elder brethren of Hungary. Perhaps you will bear with me a little longer while I sketch in greater detail one or two of the most urgent needs which I think should be committed to the care of an Academy.

In the first place they would have to fix the orthography of Irish, which is now in a more chaotic state than it has probably ever been before. Some people may be inclined to regard spelling reform as a trifle. It is essentially a task that can no longer be safely deferred or left to chance and caprice. I would ask them to remember how much depends on the ease and rapidity with which a child or beginner can learn to read and spell a language. It is one of the great advantages of modern Welsh, and one of the reasons why that language has retained a firmer hold of the people than any other Celtic language, that its spelling is so perfect, so consistent and easy to grasp, so that a child when it has but mastered the forms of the letters can learn to read and write correctly in a short time. A spelling reform, then, a rigorous standard, is urgently needed.

Next comes the even more important question of the dialects and the standard language. This, you will remember, was one of the points not settled in Hungary until the Academy took it in hand. Indeed it cannot be settled by individuals, though naturally the best writers will always exercise a deep and lasting influence upon the literary language. If the problem is left to itself, it will take many generations before a standard national language will develop. Without such a standard, however, the beginner is sadly bewildered. He looks in vain for a pattern upon which to mould his language. It will not do in the 20th century to set up the model of a writer of the 17th, such as Keating. The national language of every country is based upon an adaptation and compromise between the living dialects. It incorporates what is either common to all, or so widespread that it is intelligible, or can easily become so, to the greater part of the people. It avoids all localisms or solecisms.

Another task awaiting our academical dictators is to free the language more and more from a slavish imitation of English idiom which now disfigures so many pages of Irish writing and makes it often impossible for the student to understand some of the Irish now being written without first translating it into English, such phrases I mean as fághail amach, déanamh amach, déanamh suas na meanman, teacht suas le, etc. The best and standard Irish should draw instead upon the racy and unadulterated idiom of the best native speakers and scholars, as well as upon the inexhaustible store of genuine Gaelic preserved in the literature of the past. The reformers should next stem the tide and influx of loan words from English and other sources, reduce it within proper limits and revive and reintroduce many an ancient Gaelic word, so that, e.g., instead of pósaidh or plúr the old word sgoth may be heard once more.

It should not be forgotten that the Irish being the first western nation to cultivate classical learning long ago developed expressive native terms of its own for every scientific term of Greek or Latin. In mathematics and medicine, in astronomy and grammar, they had a perfect native terminology, including words for such terms as *zodiac, superlunar, horoscopist, septentrio,* etc., and in grammar for *denominative, hiatus, patronymic, synaeresis,* etc.

Among the minor points to which the Academy should turn its attention is the restoration of the old native placenames of Ireland. Here, again, Hungary may serve as a model. Every town and village in Hungary has now its old native name restored to it. In Ireland, English pronunciation, the most rigid and unadaptive in the world, has sadly disfigured and vulgarised many fine old Irish names. Such caricatures as Shankhill, Adavoyle, Annalong, and many others, should disappear from Irish topography.

But indeed, it would take me far too long, and would weary you, if I were to go at the same length through all the problems and tasks which await our Academy. Let me therefore conclude by pointing out the great need there is of books, good books and cheap. The workers of the League know how the lack of good Irish libraries hampers their efforts. The older books are all too rare and expensive now; and for lack of support or enterprise Irish publishers still allow much Irish literature to be published abroad. Is it not an anomaly that O'Donnell's Life of St. Columcille should first appear in a German periodical?[2] or that a scholarly edition and translation of the *Midnight Court* should be brought out in the same periodical rather than in Ireland?[3] But indeed the books that are needed are so varied and numerous that one does not know where to begin in enumerating them.

Dictionaries, English-Irish and Irish-English, etymological dictionaries of synonyms and phrases; grammars of the spoken and written language, histories of the language, text-books of all kinds, readers of older and modern prose and poetry, translations of the masterpieces of the older literature into modern Irish, editions of the literature buried in countless manuscripts, collections of folklore, Irish histories compiled from the best sources – these are but some of the most pressing needs of an Irish library. I am, of course, aware that in all these matters a beginning and a good beginning has already been made by the enterprise and energy of private scholars and societies. But they need support and encouragement, and a great deal remains to be done on a much larger scale. We have all welcomed the appearance of Father Dinneen's Dictionary, and too much praise cannot be given to his scholarly and painstaking performance. But what is it but the first attempt to gather the modern Irish vocabulary, briefly and for immediate and practical purposes? How far removed is it from a thesaurus of the living language with all its varieties and idioms, or of the whole Gaelic vocabulary, an Irish dictionary which could take its place worthily by the side of the monumental dictionaries of other languages! Do what you will in the vast domain of Irish language and literature, for a long time to come there is no fear of exhausting it easily, or of interfering or overlapping with the work of others. But there is a well-grounded fear of urgent and necessary work being delayed, of other work being never done at all, of energies and talents being wasted because they are left unsupported or uncultivated, and of the progress of the great cause which we have all at heart being thus retarded.

References

1. The series of articles *The Resurrection of Hungary* by Arthur Griffith ran weekly in the *United Irishman* (Dublin) from 2 January to 2 July 1904.

2. O'Donnell's Life of St. Columcille, *Betha Colaim Chille*, up to Section 232 of the text, first appeared in *Zeitschrift für celtische Philologie* during 1901-1914, the work of Richard Henebry and Andrew O'Kelleher. The complete text was published in 1918 by the University of Illinois.

3. *Cúirt an mheadhóin oidhche* edited by L.C. Stern. *ZCP* Vol. 5, 193-415. Halle 1904.

Appendix III

Meyer the Propagandist

Kuno Meyer, from the beginning of his career, set out to be a militant propagandist on behalf of the Celtic languages, particularly Irish, proclaiming their value and importance from platform and press on every occasion that offered. The following appeal, printed in the *Glasgow Herald* of 23 February 1904, may be given as a typical example of his call for their study and recognition. I thank the National Library of Scotland for kindly supplying the text.

Glasgow University

Proposed Celtic Chair
Appeal by Professor Kuno Meyer

In bringing to a close his course of lectures at Glasgow University on 'The Celtic Church of Britain and Ireland', Professor Meyer yesterday addressed himself to the subject of 'The Irish Missionaries', and detailed the various movements which resulted in the submission of the Celtic Church to Rome. At the conclusion of the lecture he made the following appeal in support of the founding of a Celtic Chair in the University.

The Field for Research

If there is one point more than any other which I hope to have brought out in the course of these lectures, it is this – that the study of everything connected with the Celt, his language, literature and history, in spite of all that has been hitherto achieved, is still, if not actually in its infancy, yet far removed from that certainty which older, more recognised studies can boast of. Indeed, we may say that Celtic Studies are at present in a stage at which Teutonic and Romance Studies were at the beginning of the last century. But while this is so – and I shall presently point out on whom the blame of it falls – there cannot be the smallest doubt that there is here a field of research as important and interesting as any within the reach of human knowledge. On that I need not dwell again. Let me only state what has yet to be done. There are still hundreds of MSS to be searched through, to be edited and translated; the splendid collection of Gaelic MSS at the Advocates' Library, e.g., still remains uncatalogued and unpublished. Documents may be discovered any day that will throw unexpected light on the most vexed problems of mediaeval history and literature; the laws governing the language have to be fixed; its grammar and etymology have to be brought into relation with the kindred Aryan languages; palaeography and archaeology, the handmaids of history, may yet be expected to yield new and important results; while the study of art and literature promises even a richer harvest.

Great Future for Celtic Study

How, then, is it that these studies are not more eagerly and profitably prosecuted in this country, which above all others should be their home and centre? There is only one answer. It is because the Universities have not done their duty in this matter. Too much occupied and too contented with giving instruction in certain recognised subjects only, and with imparting knowledge which is already common property, they have neglected to · encourage and facilitate that increase and advance of knowledge which is the true object of all learning. Now, Celtic can never become a bread-and-butter study. But for anyone who has watched the progress of Celtic scholarship during the last decade or two it is easy to foretell that it has a great future before it; that as soon as the acquisition of the modern and older Celtic languages will have been made easier than it is now by the publication of grammars, dictionaries and other handbooks, there will be a rush of students into this neglected field of research. The great philological, literary, and historical interest attaching to Gaelic and Welsh and Breton, the important part which the Celtic nations have played in the history of the early middle ages, the intrinsic value of their literature, and the influence which it has more than once exerted upon that of Europe – all this is sure to attract students more and more.

Who should do the work?

Now, who is more called upon or more fitted to do the work of which I have here only sketched the outline than he who is born to the knowledge of a Celtic language, who has spoken it from his childhood, and loves it with a far-brought love, a love from out the storied past? And the Celt has another advantage over the foreigner. The fact that he knows two languages side by side, languages so widely different in structure and in organism make him a born comparative philologist. At any rate, he has there not only a mental training of great value, but the best basis for a comparative study of language though, of course, without training, without guidance he will go astray. The field, then, is there, the materials are abundant, there is sure to be no lack of students; but the workshops, the laboratory, as it were, has to be equipped, and that is the business of a University. Is it not an anomaly, to say the least, that there should be in this city large and hardworking classes of young Gaelic scholars at the High School, and in the various branches of the Highland societies, and of the Gaelic League – one of the largest branches of that body anywhere out of Ireland – while no provision is made for them to continue their studies at the University? Is their work to be left unfinished and uncrowned, broken off just when its real interest and importance begins to dawn on them?

Surely, among those hundreds of young men and women there must be some who would, had they but the opportunity, make themselves into good Celtic scholars able to carry out the work which I have sketched above. Indeed, it is from among them that the future philologists and historians of Celtic Scotland should come.

Example of Welsh Colleges

Shall the study of the Celtic past be left as hitherto to a few isolated enthusiasts? Let me tell you what has recently been done elsewhere. In Wales the three University Colleges each have their Celtic Chairs occupied by scholars of great learning, whose classes are attended by hundreds of the most promising students of the Principality. At Cardiff and Aberystwyth national libraries have been founded. In my own University of Liverpool, which is making such rapid strides forward, the founding of a Celtic Chair is only a question of time. In Ireland, under the auspices of the Gaelic League, a School of Irish Learning has been founded, which is attended by 40 students from all parts of Ireland. Even Trinity College, antagonistic as it has long been to the national cause and spirit, has felt the influence of this revival of native scholarship, and is about to do something for Irish studies. On the Continent, Celtic is studied under some of the greatest philologists of our age at Berlin, Leipzig, Freiburg, Greifswald, Christiania, Copenhagen, Upsala, Paris and Rennes, and young scholars fully equipped to deal with the inviting problems of Celtic lore are turned out every year from all these universities.

Duty of Glasgow University

Let me, then, urge the authorities of this University to take up this cause, which may well be called a national one, to enlist the support of the great Gaelic societies of this city and of the country at large, to appeal to all men and women who are proud to have Celtic blood in their veins, to all who care for the advance of native scholarship, for the purpose of establishing here also a Celtic chair, to be occupied by the best scholar of the country, and of thus founding a school of Celtic studies in the capital of the Highlands and Islands that may take its place worthily by the side of Berlin and Leipzig, Paris and Oxford.

Appendix IV

A Note on the Zeuss Family

The following letter from Dr. Hans Hablitzel is of importance in clarifying the religious background of Johann Kaspar Zeuss, which derived from earlier historical circumstances.

Dr. Hablitzel is Honorary Professor for Public Law in the Catholic University of Eichstätt and is the author of *Prof. Dr. Johann Kaspar Zeuss 1806-1856* (Kronach 1987) a valuable source-book for the life and work of Zeuss. His biography of Zeuss is due to be published in 1998 in the *Fränkische Lebensbilder*, edited by the Archive of the University of Erlangen-Nürnberg. An essay on Zeuss from his hand appears in the quarterly *Stimme der Pfalz* No 4, 1997, a Journal of Politics, Culture and Economics, pp. 11-13.

Prof. Dr. iur. Dr. phil. Hans Hablitzel
Ministerialrat

81675 München
Max-Planck-Straße 8
29.11.1994

Dear Mr. Ó Lúing,

With great interest I have read your contribution to the *Zeitschrift für celtische Philologie* entitled 'Celtic Scholars of Germany'. I was very glad that you also mentioned Johann Kaspar Zeuss – the famous scholar who is almost forgotten in Germany and my little book.

But may I bring some remarks on your article?

Page 250 says that Zeuss was son of a mixed Protestant-Catholic marriage – also Shaw stated this. But this cannot be true. In my book on Zeuss (page 313 and footnote 6) I proved that both of the parents of Zeuss must have been Catholic. One must see the peculiarity of Upper Franconia: One village was Catholic, the next Protestant – because of the different reign a village belonged to. Vogtendorf, the native village of Zeuss, was 100% Catholic. Moreover: The genealogy of Zeuss and the inscriptions in the baptism-register in the Protestant village Fischbach (the next village with a distance of perhaps 3 km to Vogtendorf) are unequivocal. But there was another peculiarity: Vogtendorf had no church of its own. The Catholic children were baptized in the Protestant church of Fischbach and the Protestant pastor had to keep the Catholic Baptism-register!

May I make another remark? I think Zeuss was not really poor. His parents were both farmers and building-trades; I think they were not rich but surely also not poor. Naturally Zeuss had to earn his money by himself. The brother of Zeuss was later keeper of the building-trade.

I am enclosing my little book on Zeuss which I hope you will like. Moreover is enclosed fotocopy from a new book in German on Celtic Culture and Religion in which Zeuss is cited.

Yours very sincerely,

(Signed) Hans Hablitzel

Seán Ó Lúing and his brother Pádraig, at University College Galway, 26 June 1995, on his being conferred with an honorary doctorate.

Saothar Gaeilge Sheáin Uí Lúing

Gearóid Ó Lúing

Rugadh Seán Ó Lúing i mBaile an Fheirtéaraigh i nGaeltacht Iarthar Chiarraí sa mbliain 1917. Fuair sé a chuid oideachais i gColáiste Bhreandáin (Cill Áirne) agus sa Choláiste Ollscoile Baile Átha Cliath. Bhain sé amach céim sa Ghaeilge agus sa Laidin, agus iarchéim sa Ghaeilge ar ábhar Laidean-Gaeilge. Chaith sé tamall ag múineadh scoile i gColáiste Darragh i mBaile Átha Cliath agus i Scoil na mBráthar, Cúil an tSúdaire. Fuair sé post i Rannóg Aistriúcháin an Oireachtais i 1943. D'fhoilsigh Seán Ó Lúing roinnt gearrscealta agus aistí nuair a bhí sé ina mhac léinn, ach ní raibh deis aige tabhairt faoi shaothar mór go dtí sin. Chinn sé scríobh ar Art Ó Gríofa, fealsún náisiúnta agus fear stáit a bhí gníomhach i gcuid mhaith de na heachtraí a bhain le gluaiseacht shaoirse na hÉireann sa fiche bliain tosaigh den chéad seo. Bhí an Leabharlann Náisiúnta béal dorais, bhí traidisiún scríbhneoireachta sa Rannóg, agus bhí seanchara le Art Ó Gríofa ag obair ar an gcéad urlár eile; do b'é sin Pádraig Ó Caoimh, a bhí tráth ina Runaí ar Shinn Féin:

> Thug se dhom leabhair agus scríbhinní iomadúla a bhain leis an ngluaiseacht, agus chabhraigh sé liom go fial ó thus go deireadh na hoibre seo…[1]

Mhol Séamas Ó Mórdha do aistí a chur ar aghaidh go dtí *An tUltach,* agus is san tréimhseachán sin a foilsíodh go leor dá thaighde.

Do tharla athbheochan sa Ghaeilge ó 1939 amach tar éis athbhunú an Oireachtais. Bunaíodh na tréimhseachain *Comhar* i 1942 agus *Feasta* i 1948, dhá iris a chuir tathag i scríobh na Ghaeilge. Sa mbliain 1945, bhunaigh Seán Ó hÉigeartaigh Comhlacht Sáirséal agus Dill. Chabhraigh na forbairtí sin go mór le scríbhneoir óg na Gaeilge.

> Scríobh Seán Ó hÉigeartaigh chugam …. Thug sé gach uile mhisneach dom … Chuir sé bail an-bhreá air mar leabhar … tá buíochas na hÉireann ag dul do as an saothar a rinne sé ar son na Gaeilge.[2]

Nuaíocht i scríobh na Gaeilge ab ea *Art Ó Gríofa*. Ghnóthaigh an scríbhinn Duais an Chlub Leabhar i 1952. Mar ba léir ó na léirmheasanna i gcoitinne, fáiltíodh roimhe go fairsing. D'fhoilsigh Liam Ó Briain léirmheas tuisceanach i g*Comhar.*

Tá taighde agus léamh cruaidh na mblianta ann, tá cruinneas iontach ann, tá tuiscint thar na bearta ar chúrsaí poilitíochta gach ré de shaol an Ghríofaigh, tá rud iontach taitneamhach ann, oireasbaidh iomlán searbhais agus foirbhreithe pearsanta, toisc óige an údair nach raibh aon bhaint aige féin, buíochas le Dia, leis na cúrsaí atá sé 'innsint. Tá cumas Gaeilge agus cumas stíle, fearúil, fuinniúil, soiléir, gunta ó thús deiridh aige, firiúlacht agus macántacht an fhíor-staraí, croí Gaelach, lán de thír-ghrá, a bheir lán-combaidh dhó leis an laoch dar thug sé staidéar agus dúthracht a óige go dtí seo...[3]

agus, san *Cork Examiner*, dúirt Uaitéar Mac Craith

I nGaedhilg bhinn so-léighte na Mumhan atá an leabhar scríofa, agus i ngach leathanach de tá an dian-staidéar a dhein an t-úghdar ar bheatha, ar shaothar, agus ar scríbhinní an Ghríofaigh le tabhairt fé ndeara.[4]

Tá cáilíochtaí an údair le feiscint ón gcéad leathanach; stíl soiléir, eolas ar na foinsí, acmhainn taighde, agus breithiúnas cothrom. D'fhoilsigh Seán Ó Lúing aiste ghairid i g*Combar* (Bealtaine 1963) a thugann léargas dúinn ar a dhearcadh:

I ngan fhios dúinn féin, amannta, bíonn baint ag an eolas a fuaireamar ar an saol leis na rudaí ba mhaith linn a scríobh. Bhíodh polaitíocht an lae ina chómhra tinteáin, ceartán, aonaigh agus tábhairne le linn m'óige in Iarthar Chorca Dhuibhne. Ba bhreá liom bheith ag éisteacht leis na daoine ag trácht air, bhí meon polaitíochta chomh haibidh, barúlach, cothrom san acu. Déarfainn go raibh formhór na ndaoine sa dúiche inar tógadh mé i gcoinne an tSaorstáit. Ní rabhas ach im leanbh nuair a troideadh an cogadh síbhialta. Agus níor fhág sé aon rian ar m'aigne.[5]

Is léir gur chabhraigh an comhrá a chuala sé ina thimpeall mar bhuachaill lena thuiscint. Tamall fada tar éis foilsiú an leabhair, dúirt Piaras Béaslaí (fear a raibh an-eolas aige ar an ngluaiseacht náisiúnta)

Seán was too young to have known Griffith, but it was really astonishing to note what a good grasp he had of the period he was describing.[6]

De réir Béaslaí, 'with all respect to my old friend Padraic Colum [údar *Arthur Griffith* (1958)], it is still, taken all round, the best',[7] agus de réir Thomáis Uí Néill, 'The work can well bear comparison with anything written in English on the period and must be judged by the highest standards'.[8] Dúirt Brian Maye, an beathaisnéiseoir is déanaí ar Ó Gríofa, 'his pioneering work remains unsurpassed'.[9]

Ní hé amháin gur beathaisnéis cumasach é; is cuid de stair na nuaGhaeilge é freisin, mar a thuig Breandán Ó Madagáin, nuair a scríobh sé ina chóip fhéin:

> Tá scríobh na Gaeilge tagtha in aois! Is í seo teanga shaibhir na Gaeltachta ag plé go nádúrtha lánéifeachtach le saol casta cathrach na haoise seo. An staraí taighdeach géarchúiseach ag cur síos go máistriúil ar gach cor agus ar gach *nuance* de phearsantacht domhain an duine seo.[10]

Mar a deir J. E. Caerwyn Williams and Patrick K. Ford sa leabhar *The Irish literary tradition:*

> Some of the most outstanding achievements have been in the field of biography, and more especially political biography; Leon Ó Broin's *Parnell* (1937) and Seán Ó Lúing's *Art Ó Gríofa* (1953) are good examples of the latter genre.[11]

Cérbh iad na scríbhneoirí a d'imigh i bhfeidhm air, a bhí mar mhúnlaí aige ? Sa Ghaeilge, leabhar a thaitnigh go mór leis ná *Mo chara Stiofán* (i.e. Stephen MacKenna) le Liam Ó Rinn. Mhol sé freisin *The Big Fellow* (scéal Mhichíl Uí Choileáin) le Frank O'Connor: 'tá sé scríofa go céardúil, tá an fear féin léirithe ann ina bheocht, ina chumas, ina dhaonnúlacht; níl focal iomarcach ann'.[12] Is féidir na cáilíochtaí céanna a fheiscint in *Art Ó Gríofa*. Dúirt sé freisin gur chabhraigh beathaisnéisí Sheáin Uí Fhaoláin leis.

Tar éis *Art Ó Gríofa* a chur de láimh, thosnaigh Seán Ó Lúing ar thaighde a dhéanamh ar stair na bhFíníní in Éirinn agus sna Stáit Aontaithe; tháinig dhá bheathaisnéis as an saothar seo. An chéad leabhar ná *John Devoy*, an chéad cursíos iomlán[13] ar 'the greatest of all Irish-American rebels'[14] nó 'the most bitter and persistent, as well as the most dangerous enemy of this country Ireland has produced since Wolfe Tone', de réir *Times* Londain.[15]

Seo mar a scríobh Niall Ó Dónaill faoi *John Devoy*:

> Is iontach an acmhainn taighde atá ag Seán Ó Lúing. Ní hiontaí ná an dearcadh ciúin atá de shíor aige ar chúrsaí staire a mbíodh ár n-aithreacha agus ár n-aithreacha móra ag dul as a gcorp le fíoch chun a chéile mar gheall orthu. Ligeann sé do gach féinní fiata a

ghloim churadh a chur as, agus ansin fuarú ina chraiceann, sul a dtugann sé breithiúnas ar a ghail nó ar a ghníomh. Tá a bhreith i gcónaí bailí, mar go bhfuil sé saor ó mhailís ... Tá mianach ceart an staraí i Seán Ó Lúing. Ní bhíonn a shaothar ag spréacharnaigh le samhailteacha aon uair. Ach tá an tréith is tairbhí aige, go bhfuil a bhreithiúnas cóir.[16]

Is i *John Devoy*, caibidil 5, atá an chéadinsint ar eachtra an Chatalpa.[17]

Ábhar staire de chineál eile a bhí sa chuntas beatha ar *Ó Donnabháin Rosa* (1831-1915). Canfás forleathan ab ea é, ar shaol a bhí roinnte idir Éirinn i bhfos agus na Stáit Aontaithe thall. Bhain sé le ré na bhFíníní agus deascaí an Ghorta Mhóir. Saol fada a chaith Ó Donnabháin Rosa, lán de thrioblóidí, cruáil príosúin, easaontais diana ins na Stáit idir Ghaeil a bhi chomh hionraic lena chéile má bhíodar ar malairt tuairime féin. Portráid í seo de charraig fir nár ghlac le géilleadh ná cúlú. Tá dhá imleabhar toirtiúla ann (Iml. I: 1969; iml. II: 1979) agus taighde bunúsach. Fuair an t-údar cabhair fial ó chuid de chlann Rosa. Bhain an scríbhinn Duais an Chlub Leabhar i 1965 agus Duais an Irish American Cultural Foundation i 1969.

Scríobh Tadhg Ó Ceallaigh léirmheas tuisceanach ar iml. I:

> Beathaisnéis thábhachtach í seo – ar ollmhéad an tsaothair thaighde atá déanta ag an údar, ar éifeacht a bhua mar scríbhneoir, agus ar dhoimhne a léargas ar phearsantacht thírghráthóra Éireannaigh...[18]

Mhol Anna Heussaff iml. II:

> Tuigeann Seán Ó Lúing céard is ceird na staire ann. Tuigeann sé go gcaithfidh an bheathaisnéis imeachtaí shaol an duine aonair a nascadh le cursaí polaitiúla is sóisialta a linne, agus a tionchar.[19]

Leabhar ar leithligh in *oeuvre* Uí Lúing is ea *In Ardchathair na hEorpa: nótaí fánacha*, cursíos ar shaol agus saothar Rannóg an Aistriúcháin sa mBruiséil i 1971-72, 'tráth a bhí ceithre náisiún breise ag réiteach aontachais leis an gComhphobal Eorpach'.[20] Is insint pearsanta é ar lárphointe i stair na hÉireann nua-aimseartha, agus is leabhar neamhghnáthach é. Bhain sé an-thaitneamh as an tréimhse sa mBruiséil. Chuir sé speis sa bhFraincis, in iarsmaí na nÉireannach sa Bheilg, agus i Lováin, comharthaí den cheangal scolártha idir Éire agus an Eoraip. Leabhar pearsanta é freisin: 'Seo fear a bhfuil grinneas, géarchúis agus greann ag roinnt leis, fear a bhfuil an daonnacht féin go smior ann'.[21] Tá an oiread sin taithí againn anois ar thaisteal don Eoraip, agus seal oibre nó saoire a chaitheamh ann, go ndéanaimid dearmad go mba neamhchoitianta ar fad an rud é suas go dtí na seachtóidí. Tá cursíos sa leabhar ar thuras an fhoireann Aistriúcháin ar chathair ina mbíodh láithreacht ag na Gaeil tráth:

> Is léir óna chuntas ar Lováin agus ón dan a chum sé – *Cois Uaighe Mhichíl Uí Chléirigh* – gur bhraith Seán Ó Lúing go raibh saibhreas éigin ansin sa chlapsholas stairiúil, agus go bhfuil baint níos doimhne ag an saibhreas sin leis an meon Éireannach ná mar atá ag téacsanna an Chomhargaidh. B'fhéidir gur aimsigh sé croí an scéil ar an láthair sin.[22]

Cuireann sé i gcuimhne dúinn freisin gur chaith Seán Ó Lúing an formhór dá shaol gairmiúil ag plé leis an nGaeilge, i Rannóg an Aistriúcháin, ag aistriú doiciméidí oifigiúla, díospóireachtaí Parlaiminte, Achtanna an Oireachtais, ionstraimí reachtúla agus ábhar eile den saghas céanna. Bhí sé tamall ina eagarthóir cúnta don *English-Irish Dictionary* curtha in eagar ag Tomás de Bháldraithe, a foilsíodh i 1959.

Mar gheall ar an gcor míthaitneamhach a tháinig ar chúrsaí poiblí, d'iompaigh a spéis ón stair pholaitíochta go stair na scoláireachta Gaeilge, ar an ábhar go príomha go bhfacthas dó an teanga Ghaeilge agus a saothrú a bheith ar an ngné ba bhunúsaí agus ba luachmhaire d'oighreacht na tíre.

> Tuigtear dom gurb í an Ghaeilge an eiliminit is bunúsaí i stair na hÉireann. Is í an Ghaeilge go bunúsach 'identity' no céannacht na hÉireann agus sin é an chúis gur chuireas spéis i scoláireacht na Gaeilge, go h-áirithe na saoithe Eorpacha a chuir bun ar scoláireacht na Gaeilge ó lár an chéid seo caite.[23]

Toradh na spéise sin *Saoir Theangan*, léargas ar chúigear scoláire a shaothraigh chun foirgneamh Gaeilge teann daingean a thógáil ar mhaithe le sibhialtacht na tíre.

> An cúigear atá faoi chaibidil is beag ná go bhféadfá a rá gurbh iad a leag fothaí an léinn Ghaelaigh dúinn síos san aois seo. Tugann Seán Ó Lúing suas do Khuno Meyer gurb é a leacht onóra ó cheart Scoil an Léinn Cheiltigh den Institiúid Ard-Léinn; b'é Richard Irvine Best a chuir an saothar bibliografaíochta ba luachmhaire i gcomhair teanga agus litríocht na Gaeilge le chéile lena linn fara a chuid oibre éachtaí mar leabharlannaí; fuair Seoirse Mac Tomáis inspioráid ar an Oileán Tiar a d'fhuascail 'An Cheist Hóiméireach' agus dhíol sé an comhar le hÉirinn lena

chuid aistriúchán ón nGréigis agus lena chuid obair ollscoile; is cuma nó stair litríocht na Gaeilge ann féin saothar Robin Flower ar lámhscríbhinní Mhusaem na Breataine; agus chuir Dúghlas de hÍde – an 'Duine Uasal thiar i Ros Comáin' – réabhlóid litríochta ar bun nach bhfuil deireadh a n-iarmhairte chugainn fós.[24]

An chéad leabhar eile leis na *Kuno Meyer* (i mBéarla); ach tá i bhfad níos mó sa leabhar sin ná insint ar shaol Meyer;

> toisc go raibh baint chomh mór sin ag Kuno Meyer le bunú an árd-léinn cheiltigh ar an Mór-Roinn agus go háirithe sa tír seo ag tús an chéid, is geall le beo-stair é an leabhar seo ar thús an Léinn Cheiltigh.[25]

Is saghas prologomena don leabhar sin *Saoir theangan*, agus cuireann sé rud eile in iúl dúinn; tá na téamaí agus na spéiseanna céanna le fáil ina shaothar Gaeilge agus atá sna leabhair scríofa i mBéarla.

Tá an-mheas aige ar Sheoirse Mac Tomáis, scoláire ar léann na sean-Ghréige, Marxach, comh-aistritheoir *Fiche blian ag fás* agus duine uasal. Bhí cáirdeas agus comhfhreagras eatarthu, agus bhí dúil acu sna rudaí céanna; na clasaicí, an Ghaeilge, iarthar Chiarraí. Ba mhór an onóir do Sheán Ó Lúing scríbhinní Gaeilge Mhic Thomáis a bhailiú i bhfoirm leabhair: *Gach orlach de mo chroí*.

Scríobh sé leabhráin bheatha freisin ar Mhuintir Chaomhánach, clann cheannasach Dhún Chaoin.

Seachas prós tá trí leabhrán filíochta foilsithe ag Seán Ó Lúing, ar théamaí áitiúla a ghlac sampla ó Patrick Kavanagh agus, i réimse níos leithne, aistriúcháin ón Laidin agus ón bhFraincis, go háirithe as Catullus agus Baudelaire. Baineann formhór an chéad cnuasach *Bánta Dhún Urlann* lena cheantar dúchais. Fuair Gabriel Rosenstock locht air mar gheall ar a 'pharóisteachas'; 'an é gur scríobhadh an leabhar seo go príomha do mhuintir Chorca Dhuibhne?'[26] Más fíor do, cén dochar ? 'Gods make their own importance' mar a dúirt Kavanagh, agus mar a thuig Alan Titley:

> Tá sé sásta a pharóiste féin, a chré féin, a phaiste dúchais féin a cheiliúradh le díograis agus le meanma, agus sásta freisin go n-aireofaí a leabhar féin mar chloch eile ar phaidrín fada litríochta úd Dhún Chaoin. Más gaire mar sin é d'iarfhile an phobail sin, Micheál Ó Gaoithín, agus d'fhilí an Duanaire Duibhneach is mar sin is córa é a mheas, óir tá a bhreith féin tugtha anseo aige i roghnú na n-ábhar do, ar cad is filíocht ann agus ar conas ar cheart di friotháilt ar an duine.[27]

Tar éis a thréimhse sa mBruiséil, rinne Seán Ó Lúing staidéar ar an Fhraincis, go h-áirithe ar fhilíocht an 19ú céad. Tá na torthaí le feiscint san dara cnuasach *Déithe teaghlaigh*, ina bhfuil aistriúcháin ar dhánta le Charles Baudelaire, Paul Verlaine, Marceline Desbordes-Valmore, Gérard de Nerval agus Tristan Corbière.

Ag déanamh taighde do ar na scoláirí Ceilteacha, chuaigh Seán Ó Lúing i dtaithí ar an nGearmáinis, agus sa tríú cnuasach *Dúnmharú Chat Alexandreia*, tá aistriú ar dhán le Hermann Hesse, i measc aistriú ar Jacques Prévèrt, Paul Éluard, Raymond Queneau (leagan iontach de 'Le porc') agus, arís, Catullus.

'Eclectic' is the word that first sprang to mind after a reading of Seán Ó Lúing's *Dúnmharú Chat Alexandreia* ... To say that it leaves the reader gasping for breath is an understatement. If poetry is about engaging the imagination then this certainly fulfils its function. Nevertheless, I have a suspicion that there are three incomplete collections between these covers.[28]

'Eclectic' an *mot juste*, gan amhras!

Tá saothar suntasach, idir Gaeilge agus Béarla, déanta ag Seán Ó Lúing. Scríobhann sé an dá theanga go héasca. In imeachtaí litríochta na haimsire seo in Éirinn tá gá leis an scríbhneoir dátheangach mar bíonn riachtanas air freastal ar dhá phobal léitheoireachta. Tá a chosáin phearsanta féin gafa ag Seán Ó Lúing ina shaothar liteartha agus tá ábhar nua, bunúsach, curtha ar fáil aige ina chuid scríbhinní, cibé teanga a roghnaíonn sé mar mheán scríbhneoireachta.

Tagairtí

1. 'Cead cainte: Agallamh le Seán Ó Lúing': Clár le Seán Ó Tuairisg a craoladh ar Theilifís na Gaeilge, 17 Nollaig 1997.
2. *Ibid.* Tá an dá imleabhar de *Ó Donnabháin Rosa* toirbheartha do Sheán Ó hÉigeartaigh.
3. Liam Ó Briain, 'Art Ó Gríofa' [léirmheas], *Comhar*, Feabhra 1954, lgh. 5-7.
4. [Uaitéar Mac Craith], 'Chuir se an síol ach ní fhaca na torthaí', *Cork Examiner* 31 December 1953, lch. 6.
5. Seán Ó Lúing, 'Ar thóir na fírinne: saothar an staraí', *Comhar*, Bealtaine 1963, lgh. 18-20.
6. Piaras Béaslaí, 'Greatest of all Irish-American "rebels"' (Moods and memories), *Irish Independent*, 31 January 1962, lch. 6.
7. *Ibid.*
8. Thomas P. O'Neill, 'Arthur Griffith as man and politician', *Irish Press*, 2 Márta 1954, lch. 4. (Tá an dara cuid den léirmheas le fáil san *Irish Press*, 3 Márta 1954, lch. 5).
9. Brian Maye, *Arthur Griffith*, Dublin 1997, lch. iii.

10. Breandán Ó Madagáin, in oráid a thug sé tráth ar bronnadh céim dochtúra onórach ar Sheán Ó Lúing, i gColáiste na hOllscoile, Gaillimh, 26 Meitheamh 1995.

11. J. E. Caerwyn Williams and Patrick K. Ford: *The Irish literary tradition*. Revised English-language edition. Cardiff: University of Wales Press, 1992, lch. 324.

12. Seán Ó Lúing, 'Ar thóir na fírinne: saothar an staraí' *Combar*, Bealtaine 1963, lgh. 18-20.

13. Ag trácht dó san 'Irishman's diary', *Irish Times* (10 Samhain 1998, lch. 17), ar bheathaisnéis ar John Devoy le Terry Golway (*Irish rebel: John Devoy and America's fight for Ireland's freedom*. New York: St. Martin's Press, 1998), cuireann Frank Mac Gabhann in iúl nach é sin an chéad chuntas beatha, mar a deirtear ar an seaicéad dusta, mar gur scríobh Seán Ó Lúing 'an excellent biography of Devoy in Irish which was published in 1961.'

14. Béaslai, *op.cit.*

15. *Times* (London) 1 Deireadh Fómhair 1928; *John Devoy*, lch. 226.

16. Niall Ó Dónaill, 'Ardseiftiúnach coinspioráide', *Feasta*, Feabhra 1962, lgh. 18-19.

17. Féach *Fremantle Mission* ina bhfuil cur síos iomlán ar an eachtra iontach sin.

18. Tadhg Ó Ceallaigh, 'Ó Donnabháin Rosa I' [léirmheas]. *Studia Hibernica* 12 (1977), lgh. 172-173.

19. Anna Heussaff, 'Ó Donnabháin Rosa II' [léirmheas]. *Combar*, Márta 1981, lch. 32.

20. Seán Ó Lúing, *In Ardchathair na hEorpa*, nóta taobh istigh den chlúdach.

21. P.D., 'In ardchathair na hEorpa' [léirmheas], *Combar*, Samhain 1976, lch. 19.

22. Rita E. Kelly, 'La puissance commerciale', *Feasta*, Márta 1977, lgh. 17-18.

23. 'Cead cainte'. Tá an-mheas aige ar leabhar Rudolf Pfeiffer: *A History of classical scholarship from 1300 to 1850* (Oxford: Clarendon Press, 1976).

24. Alan Titley, 'Léirstintí léannta', *Books Ireland*, Feabhra 1990, lgh. 10-11.

25. Ó Madagáin, *op.cit.*

26. Gabriel Rosenstock, 'Do Chiarraígh', *Feasta*, Lúnasa 1975, lch. 17.

27. Alan Titley, 'Bánta Dhún Urlann: léirmheas', *Combar*, Eanáir 1976, lch. 6.

28. Pól Ó Muirí, 'Poetry that speaks in many tongues', *Irish Times* (Weekend supplement) 27 Feabhra 1999, lch. 11.

Bibliography

This bibliography includes all of Seán Ó Lúing's books, and all major articles. It does not include details of poems (including translations) published in periodicals, as nearly all of these have been collected in book form. The selection of **Reviews** does not include brief notices.

Books

Art Ó Gríofa. Baile Átha Cliath, Sáirséal agus Dill,1953
– Biography of Arthur Griffith

John Devoy. Baile Átha Cliath, Cló Morainn,1961
– Biography of John Devoy

Fremantle mission. Tralee, Anvil Books, 1965
Republished as
The Catalpa rescue. Dublin, Anvil Books, [1984]
– Relating the rescue of Fenian prisoners from Australia in 1876

Ó Donnabháin Rosa. Vol. I. Baile Átha Cliath, Sáirséal agus Dill, 1969

Ó Donnabháin Rosa. Vol. II. Baile Átha Cliath, Sáirséal agus Dill, 1979
– Biography of Jeremiah O'Donovan Rossa

I die in a good cause: a study of Thomas Ashe, idealist and revolutionary. Tralee, Anvil Books, 1970

Bánta Dhún Urlann. Baile Átha Cliath, Clódhanna Teo., 1975
– Poetry

In Ardchathair na hEorpa: nótaí fánacha. Baile Átha Cliath, Sáirséal agus Dill, 1976
– The experiences of the Translation Section of Dáil Éireann in Brussels during Ireland's accession to the European Economic Community

Déithe Teaghlaigh. Baile Átha Cliath, Coiscéim, 1984
– Poetry, including translations from Catullus, Horace, Charles Baudelaire, Paul Verlaine, Marceline Desbordes-Valmore, Stephane Mallarmé, Paul Valéry, Charles le Goffic, Gérard de Nerval and Tristan Corbière

Seán an Chóta. Baile Átha Cliath, Coiscéim, 1985
– Biographical sketch of Seán Óg Ó Caomhánaigh, brother of Kruger Kavanagh

Kruger. Baile Átha Cliath, Coiscéim, 1986
– Biographical sketch of Kruger Kavanagh

Saoir theangan. Baile Átha Cliath, Coiscéim, 1989
– Essays on Celtic scholars (Kuno Meyer, Richard Irvine Best, George Thomson, Robin Flower, Douglas Hyde)

Kuno Meyer. Dublin, Geography Publications, 1991

In the footsteps of Kuno Meyer. Bonn, Deutsch-Irische Gesellschaft, 1995
(*Hibernia jenseits des meeres*)
– Account of visits to Germany

Dúnmharú Chat Alexandreia. Baile Átha Cliath, Coiscéim, 1997
– Poetry, including translations from Jacques Prévert, Paul Valéry, Raymond Queneau, Francesco Petrarca, Frédéric Mistral, Paul Éluard, Julius Caesar Scaliger, Hermann Hesse, Hélène Vacaresco,Catullus

Celtic studies in Europe and other essays. Dublin, Geography Publications, 2000

Editor
Seoirse Mac Tomáis [George Thomson]: *Gach órlach de mo chroí : dréachta*. Baile Átha Cliath, Coiscéim, 1988
– Irish language writings of George Thomson, Greek scholar, Marxist, and joint translator of *Fiche blian ag fás (Twenty Years A-Growing)*. Réamhrá leis an eagarthóir lgh. 1-9

Articles
'Muinntir na cathrach', *Hibernia* v.1 no. 6 (June 1937) p. 11
Incorrectly attributed to Seán M. Ó Fiathcháin

'Art Ó Gríobhtha: an fear agus a dhúngaois', *An tUltach* iml. 25 uimh. 6 (Bealtaine 1948) lgh. 1-3, 6

'Tithe, Cluan Dolcáin' [pictiúr], *An tUltach* iml. 25 uimh. 8 (Iúl 1948) lch. 1

'Cois Dothra' [pictiúr], *An tUltach* iml.25 uimh. 8 (Lúnasa 1948) lch. 1

'Cumann na nGael, 1900-1905', *An tUltach* iml. 25 uimh. 8 (Lúnasa 1948) lgh. 5, 10

'Carraig Dhún na Más' [pictiúr], *An tUltach* iml. 25 uimh. 9 (Meán Fómhair 1948) lch. 5

'Cumann na nGael, 1900-1905' (ar lean), *An tUltach* iml. 25 [*recte* 26] uimh. 1 (Eanar 1949) lgh. 1, 4

'Art Ó Gríobhtha san Afraic Theas', *An tUltach* iml. 25 [*recte* 26] uimh. 11 (Mí na Samhna 1949) lgh. 6-7

'An tÉireannach Aontaithe 4 Márta, 1899-14 Aibreán, 1906', *An tUltach* iml. 26 [*recte* 27] uimh. 7 [*recte* 8] (Lúnasa 1950) lgh. 6, 10

'An tÉireannach Aontaithe' (ar lean), *An tUltach* iml. 26 [*recte* 27] uimh. 10 (Deire Fómhair, 1950) lgh. 9-10

'Art Ó Gríobhtha agus lucht oibre: an colún léirmheasa', *Comhar* iml. 10 uimh. 10 (Deireadh Fomhair 1951) lgh. 7-8, 25-26

'An Choróin Labhrais', *Feasta* iml. vi uimh. 1 Aibreán 1953 lgh. 9-10

'Seán Ó Mathúna, saighdiúir agus scoláire', *Feasta* iml. vii uimh. 3 (Meitheamh 1954) lgh. 5-6

'Darrell Figgis', *Feasta* iml. viii uimh. 5 (Lúnasa 1955) lgh. 2-4

'Loch Garman: tréithe agus pearsanacht sean-chathrach', *Feasta* iml. viii uimh. 9 (Nollaig 1955) lgh. 12-16

'Sinn Féin and the Volunteers', *Irish Press* 25 April 1957 p. 8

'Patrick Ford', *Feasta* iml. x uimh. 3 (Meitheamh 1957) lgh. 13-14

'An I.R.B.: cuimhneachán céad bliain a bhunaithe', *Comhar* iml. 17 uimh. 4 (Aibreán 1958) lgh. 5-10

'An ciste chatha', *Comhar* iml. 18 uimh. 4 (Aibreán 1959) lgh. 10-13

'Roscománach do b'eadh Ned Duffy – laoch Connachtach', *Roscommon Herald centenary supplement* (December 1959) p. 15

'Alexander Sullivan (I)', *Combar* iml. 18 uimh. 12 (Nollaig) 1959 lgh. 12-18

'Alexander Sullivan (2)', *Combar* iml. 19 uimh. 3 (Márta 1960) lgh. 8-15, 24-25

'George Freeman Fitzgerald', *Combar* iml. 19 uimh. 12 (Nollaig 1960) lgh. 7-9

'The dilemna of Eoin MacNeill', *Irish Times* 24 April 1961 p. 7

'The dilemna of Eoin MacNeill: 2', *Irish Times* 25 April 1961 p. 7

'Tomás Ághas (cuid 1)', [all published] *Feasta* iml. xiv uimh. 6 (Meán Fómhair 1961) lgh. 5-7, 25

'Jim Larkin agus John Devoy', *Combar* iml. 20 uimh. 12 (Nollaig 1961) lgh. 14-16

'An Breitheamh Domhnall Ó Cathalláin', *Combar* iml. 21 uimh. 1 (Eanáir 1962) lgh. 15-17

'Ar thóir na firinne: saothar an staraí' *Combar* iml. 22 uimh. 5 (Bealtaine 1963) lgh. 18-20

'Ó Donnabháin Rosa agus an Ghaeilge' *Feasta* iml. xix uimh. 2 (Bealtaine 1966) lgh. 5-9

'Seán Mac Diarmada (portráid a craoladh ó Radio Éireann)' *Combar* iml. 25 uimh. 6 (Meitheamh 1966) lgh. 5-7

'Éamonn Ceannt (caint a craoladh ó Radio Éireann)' *Combar* iml. 25 uimh. 7 (Iúil 1966) lgh. 9-11

'Mícheál Ó Coileáin', *Irish Independent: Michael Collins Memorial Foundation Supplement* (20 August 1966) p. 8

'Laoch na bhFíníní i gConnachta: Ned Duffy', *Feasta* iml. xx uimh. 1 (Aibreán 1967) lgh. 19-21

'Dúthaigh Uí Dhonnabháin Rosa: (sliocht as an leabhar – Ó Donnabháin Rosa)' *Combar* iml. 26 uimh. 10 (Deireadh Fómhair 1967) lgh. 10-14

'Léacht chuimhneacháin: Tomás Ághas', *Feasta* iml. xx uimh. 8 (Samhain 1967) lgh. 9-15

'Thomas Ashe', *Capuchin Annual* 1967 pp 386-393

'The "German plot" 1918', *Capuchin Annual* 1968 pp 377-381

'A contribution to a study of Fenianism in Breifne', *Breifne* v. iii no. 10 (1967) pp 155-174

'Some travellers in Kerry', *Journal of the Kerry Archaeological and Historical Society* no. 1 (1968) pp 56-72

'The Phoenix Society in Kerry', *Journal of the Kerry Archaeological and Historical Society* no 2 (1969) pp 5-26

'Seanán Ó Muíneacháin (1900-1970)', *Feasta* iml. xxiii uimh. 6 (Meán Fómhair 1970) lch. 8

'Máirtín Ó Cadhain', *Inniu* 23 Deireadh Fómhair 1970 lch. 3

'Aspects of the Fenian Rising in Kerry, 1867; I: The rising and its background', *Journal of the Kerry Archaeological and Historical Society* no. 3 (1970) pp 131-153

'Aspects of the Fenian Rising in Kerry, 1867; II: Aftermath', *Journal of the Kerry Archaeological and Historical Society* no. 4 (1971) pp 139-164

'Éamon de Valera agus a ré', *Studies* v. lx, no. 237 (Spring 1971) pp 1-11

'Arthur Griffith, 1871-1922: thoughts on a centenary', *Studies* v. lx no. 238 (Summer 1971) pp 127-138

'Aspects of the Fenian Rising in Kerry, 1867; III: Prelude to the trials', *Journal of the Kerry Archaeological and Historical Society* no. 5 (1972) pp 103-132

'Ioldánacht Uí Gríofa', *Combar* iml. 31 uimh. 11 (Samhain 1972) lgh. 10-12, 42

'Douglas Hyde and the Gaelic League', *Studies* v. lxii no. 246 (Summer 1973) pp 123-138

'Aspects of the Fenian Rising in Kerry, 1867; IV: Kerry Summer Assizes, 1867', *Journal of the Kerry Archaeological and Historical Society* no. 6 (1973) pp 172-194

'Aspects of the Fenian Rising in Kerry, 1867; V: Personalities and problems', *Journal of the Kerry Archaeological and Historical Society* no. 7 (1974) pp 107-133

'Richard Griffith and the roads of Kerry; I', *Journal of the Kerry Archaeological and Historical Society* no. 8 (1975) pp 89-113

'Beartas an Chraoibhín i gConradh na Gaeilge', *Feasta* iml. xxviii uimh. 6 (Meán Fómhair 1975) lgh. 5-10

A longer version of this appears in *Saoir theangan*, also in *Feasta* iml. xxxxvi uimh. 1 (Eanáir 1993) lgh. 17-16, 22-29

'Richard Griffith and the roads of Kerry; II', *Journal of the Kerry Archaeological and Historical Society* no. 9 (1976) pp 92-124

'Robin Flower, oileánach agus máistir léinn', *Journal of the Kerry Archaeological and Historical Society* no. 10 (1977) pp 111-142

'Seán Óg Ó Caomhanaigh', *Journal of the Kerry Archaeological and Historical Society* no. 11 (1978) pp 56-84

'Local government in Dingle, Ardfert and Tralee in 1833', *Journal of the Kerry Archaeological and Historical Society* no. 12 (1979) pp 119-158

'Seoirse Mac Tomáis – George Derwent Thomson', *Journal of the Kerry Archaeological and Historical Society* no. 13 (1980) pp 149-172

'W. T. Cosgrave', *The Word* June 1980 pp 11-14

'"To be a German' – Oidhreacht Khuno Meyer', *Scríobh* 5 (1981) lgh. 258-281

'Robin Flower (1881-1946)', *Studies* v. lxx no. 228-229 (Summer/Autumn 1981) pp 121-134

'Kuno Meyer by Augustus John: a brief history of a famous portrait', *Studies* v. lxxi no. 284 (Winter 1982) pp 325-343

'The scholars' path to Kerry's west', *Cork Holly Bough* 1982 pp 6, 17, 32

'Muiris Caomhánach i Meirice', *Journal of the Kerry Archaeological and Historical Society* no. 15-16 (1982-3) pp 157-189

'An Seabhac' [Padraig Ó Siochfhradha], *Feasta* iml. xxxvi uimh. 3 (Marta 1983) lgh. 24-25

'Kruger agus a ré', *Journal of the Kerry Archaeological and Historical Society* no. 17 (1984) pp 127-152

'An ceol san anam: léargas ar Thomás Ághas', *An Aisling: irisleabhar taighde agus forbartha de chuid Chomhaltas Ceoltóirí Éireann, Baile Uí Thaidhg* iml. 1 (1984) lgh. 187-191

'Carl Marstrander (1883-1965)', *Journal of the Cork Historical and Archaeological Society* v. lxxix (1984) pp 108-124

'Richard Irvine Best', *Scríobh* 6 (1984) lgh. 134-146

'Irish and English: conflict and marriage', *Lebende Sprachen* Heft 3 (1984) pp 105-108

'Thomas Ashe', *Irish philatelic bulletin = Nuachtlitir stampshanais na hÉireann* 5/85 (20 June 1985) p. [3]

'William Maunsell Hennessy, Celtic scholar, 1829-89', *Journal of the Kerry Archaeological and Historical Society* no. 19 (1986) pp 80-120

'Marie-Louise Sjoestedt, Celtic scholar, 1900-1940', *Journal of the Kerry Archaeological and Historical Society* no. 20 (1987) pp 79-93

'Caoimhín Ó Nualláin: billeog cuimhne', *Irish Times* 21 January 1988 p. 9

'Celtic scholars of Germany: a brief survey' *Zeitschrift für celtische Philologie* Band 46 (1994)
pp 249-271

'Donn Sigerson Piatt: Laighneach ó Linn Life', *Féile Zozimus* v. 3 (1994) lgh. 47-68

'The present position of the Irish language' *Lebende Sprachen* Heft 1 (1995) pp 8-12

'George Thomson' *Classics Ireland* v. 3 (1996) pp 141-162

'Richard Irvine Best: librarian and Celtic scholar' *Zeitschrift für celtische Philologie* Band 49-50 (1997) pp 682-697

Gearrscéalta
'Páidín agus an spideóg', *An Iodh Morainn: bliainiris Choláiste na h-Ollscoile Áth Cliath* iml. 1 uimh. 3 (1942) lgh. 26-29

'Gal toitín', *Feasta* iml.iii uimh.i (Aibreán 1950) lgh. 4-5

'An cheist mhatamaitice', *Comhar* iml.9 uimh.8 (Lúnasa 1950) lgh. 25-27

Contributions, prefaces, introductions to books, etc.
'Ó Donnabháin Rosa agus a theaghlach' in *Ó Donnabháin Rosa 1831-1915.* Dublin, published by the O'Donovan Rossa Memorial Committee, 1954, pp 16-17

'Arthur Griffith and Sinn Féin' in F.X. Martin (ed.), *Leaders and men of the Easter Rising: Dublin 1916.* London, Methuen, 1967, pp 55-66

Joseph Denieffe: *A personal narrative of the Irish Revolutionary Brotherhood.* Shannon, Irish University Press, 1969
Facsimile reprint, with new introduction, of book first published New York, Gael Publishing Co., 1906
Introduction pp v-xiii

Michael Davitt: *The fall of feudalism in Ireland.* Shannon, Irish University Press, 1970
Facsimile reprint, with new introduction, of book first published London and New York, Harper and Brothers Publishers, 1904.
Introduction pp v-x

John Devoy: *Recollections of an Irish rebel.* Shannon, Irish University Press, 1969
Facsimile reprint, with new introduction, of book first published New York, 1929
Introduction pp v-viii

'An ghluaiseacht náisiúnta i gCorca Dhuibhne' in Mícheál Ó Ciosain (ed.) *Céad bliain 1871-1971,* Baile an Fheirtéaraigh, Muintir Phiarais, 1973, lgh. 90-101

Jeremiah O'Donovan Rossa: *Rossa's recollections*. Shannon, Irish University Press, 1973
Facsimile reprint, with new introduction, of book first published New York, 1898
Introduction and select bibliography pp v-xvi

Richard Davis: *Arthur Griffith and non-violent Sinn Féin*. Dublin, Anvil Books, 1974
Foreword pp ix-x

'Seán Óg MacMurrough Kavanagh' in Denis P. Kelleher (ed.), *Kerrymen 1881-1981*. New York, Kerrymens' Patriotic and Benevolent Association of New York, 1981, pp 93-98

Donn Piatt: *Cois Life fadó agus ábhair eile*. Baile Átha Cliath, Foilseacháin Náisiúnta Teoranta, 1985
Brollach lgh. 9-13

Patrick Henchy: *The National Library of Ireland, 1941-1976: a look back*. Dublin, National Library of Ireland Society, 1986
Réamhrá pp 3-6

An tSr. Bosco Costigan i gcomhar le Seán Ó Curraoin: *De ghlaschloich an oileáin: beatha agus saothar Mháirtín Uí Chadhain*. Béal an Daingin (Conamara), Cló Iar-Chonnachta, 1987
[Píosa gairid ar Ó Cadhain, lch. 81]

'William Smith O'Brien and the Irish language: a note' in Richard Davis, *William Smith O'Brien: Ireland – 1848 – Tasmania*. Dublin, Geography Publications,1989, pp 66-68

'Lucht léinn ón iasacht' in Aogán Ó Muircheartaigh (ed.): *Oidhreacht an Bhlascaoid*. Baile Átha Cliath, Coiscéim, 1989, lgh. 143-154

F. S. Keane, 'Brother Denis Aelred Long (1891-1979), in *Christian Brothers' Educational Record* (1990), pp 120-132
Memoir pp 120-121

Pádraig Ó Lúing: *Memories of St. Brendan's Seminary, Killarney*. Tralee, the author, 1994
Prologue, pp 3-4

Robert Welch (ed.), *Oxford companion to Irish literature*. Oxford, Oxford University Press, 1996

Entries on: Kuno Meyer, p. 364, Johann Kaspar Zeuss p. 614, Heinrich Zimmer p. 614

Brian Maye: *Arthur Griffith.* Dublin, Griffith College Publications, 1997
Foreword pp v-x

Léachtaí Cholm Cille XXVII: Scoláirí Gaeilge in eagar ag Ruairí Ó hUiginn. Maigh Nuad, An Sagart, 1997
Réamhrá lgh. 7-10

Selected reviews
'Leabhar nua i dtaobh na nÉireannach ins na Stáit' (Léirmheas ar *The Irish in America* le Carl Wittke), *Feasta* iml. ix uimh. 8 (Samhain 1956) lgh. 14-16

'An Seabhac siúlach' (léirmheas ar *The Fenian chief* [James Stephens] le Desmond Ryan), *Feasta* iml. xxi uimh. 2 (Bealtaine 1968) lgh. 28-30

'*Fiche blian ag fás* le Muiris Ó Súilleabháin [eagrán nua, curtha in eagar ag Seoirse Mac Tomáis]: léirmheas', *Irish Press* 28 April 1976 p. 9

'*Revolutionary underground: the story of the Irish Republican Brotherhood 1858-1924* by Leon Ó Broin' [review], *Studies,* v. lxvi no. 262 (Summer/Autumn 1977) pp 233-237

'*Patrick Pearse: the triumph of failure* by Ruth Dudley Edwards' [review], *Studies,* v. lxvi no. 262 (Summer/Autumn 1977) pp 237-238

'*In great haste: the letters of Michael Collins and Kitty Kiernan*, edited by Leon O Broin' [review], *Studies,* v. lxxxiii no. 290 (Summer 1984), pp 233-237

'*A political odyssey: Thomas O'Donnell*, by J. Anthony Gaughan' [review], *Studia Hibernica*, no. 24 (1984), pp 190-193

'Éacht aistriúcháin' (léirmheas ar *An Odaisé*, aistrithe ag an Monsignor Pádraig de Brún), *Anois* iml. 6 uimh. 49 (4-5 Lúnasa 1990) lch. 13

'Rogha scoláire' [Breandán Ó Doibhlín] (léirmheas ar *Féilscríbhinn an Doibhlinigh,* eag. Tadhg Ó Dúshláine), *Comhar* iml. 56 uimh. 7 (Iúil 1997) lch. 25

Index

316